C000212530

BROOKLANDS

THE OFFICIAL *Centenary* HISTORY

Other books by this author include

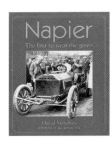

*Napier: The First to
Wear the Green*

*Bugatti:
A Racing History*

BROOKLANDS

THE OFFICIAL *Centenary* HISTORY

DAVID VENABLES
Foreword by Bill Boddy MBE

Haynes Publishing

To TGV

© David Venables 2007

All rights reserved. No part of this publication may be reproduced, stored in a retrieval system or transmitted, in any form or by any means, electronic, mechanical, photocopying, recording or otherwise, without prior permission in writing from the publisher.

First published in May 2007

A catalogue record for this book is available from the British Library

ISBN 978 184425 329 6

Library of Congress control no 2007921998

Published by Haynes Publishing, Sparkford, Yeovil, Somerset BA22 7JJ, UK
Tel: 01963 442030 Fax: 01963 440001
Int. tel: +44 1963 442030 Int. fax: +44 1963 440001
E-mail: sales@haynes.co.uk
Website: www.haynes.co.uk

Haynes North America Inc.,
861 Lawrence Drive, Newbury Park, California 91320, USA

Page layout by G&M Designs Limited, Raunds, Northamptonshire
Printed and bound in Britain by J. H. Haynes & Co. Ltd, Sparkford

Jacket illustrations:

FRONT, UPPER *The Napier-Railton, holder of the all-time lap record, on the Members' Banking. (LAT)*

FRONT, LOWER *Concorde 'Delta Golf' taking off. (PRM Aviation Collection)*

FRONT FLAP *The Viscount production line in 1955. (BAE Systems per Brooklands Museum)*

REAR, UPPER *Start of a match race in 1908 between Edge (Napier) and Stocks (De Dion). (LAT)*

REAR, LOWER LEFT *Start of the Senior motor cycle handicap at the 1922 Royal Meeting. (Brooklands Society)*

REAR, LOWER RIGHT *The Martinsyde 'Raymor' about to fail in its attempt to make the first Atlantic flight in 1919. (Brooklands Museum)*

CONTENTS

— BROOKLANDS —

Foreword by Bill Boddy MBE	6
Preface	7
Concept to reality	8
Edwardian overture	14
1907	15
1908	24
1909	29
1910	33
1911	36
1912	40
1913	43
1914	48
Fledgling flying	52
1914–1918 War	64
Euphoria of peace	70
1920	71
1921	76
1922	83
1923	89
1924	93
1925	99
Era of the sports car	104
1926	105
1927	113
1928	120
1929	126
1930	133
The flying twenties	140
Carefree racing	152
1931	153
1932	161
1933	171
1934	178
Clouds gather	188
1935	189
1936	199
1937	205
1938	212
1939	218
Aviation matures	226
1939–1945 War	240
Post-war prosperity	246
Site still evolving	258
Oddball sidelights	264
Bookies	265
Filming at the track	266
Bicycles	266
The oddball, unusual and eerie	268
Topography: then and now	269
Appendix 1 Outer Circuit lap records	271
Appendix 2 Winners of long-distance races	272
Appendix 3 Aircraft built at Brooklands	275
Appendix 4 Maps	278
Bibliography	282
Index	283

FOREWORD

BY BILL BODDY MBE

Founder of the Brooklands Society

It was an unexpected honour to be asked to write the Foreword for this Official Centenary History of Brooklands, by David Venables. Brooklands, completed in 1907, was such a famous and wonderful place to which to go, until war closed it as a race track in 1939. There have been a number of books about different aspects of Brooklands, but David's one is unique in encompassing the entire history.

The first book about the circuit was *Wheels Take Wings* (Foulis, 1933), by Michael Burn and A. Percy Bradley. This was, I think, based on the press cuttings book kept by the Brooklands (later British) Automobile Racing Club (BARC), with reports not only in the leading newspapers but from the most humble of local papers too. It was perhaps intended as a means of telling the public what Brooklands was all about.

I would not have been so audacious as to follow that with my own history, had John Morgan not given me the BARC race cards containing the official lap-speeds of the cars raced there, when Brooklands ARC became the British ARC after the war had ended. It took me three years to assemble the facts and figures that these race cards disclosed. They were published in three separate small volumes with an extra one on the JCC 200-mile light car races. I felt that, although I should have left the task to others, this provided an incentive to describe the full car history (Grenville, 1957/1979) which was brought out in a de-luxe edition by Motor Racing Publications in 2001.

MRP listed my book as *The Complete History of Brooklands*, but in fact it is only about the car events and records. So was I disgruntled when I heard about David's colossal – and surely daunting but rewarding – task of writing another book on this enthralling subject? No, I was not. Indeed, I was gruntled (I cannot find this word in my dictionary but surely if disgruntled implies vexed, then gruntled must express the opposite).

I am delighted about this centenary recognition of Locke King's enormous undertaking in having constructed the motor track at Weybridge, because this is the entire story, about the motorcycle races and aviation as well as the BARC's regular race meetings. The BMCRC bike events were well-covered by Peter Hartley in his two books (Argos, 1980) which described separately each 'Bemsee' race up to 1929. In 1956, to mark the anniversary which Vickers-Armstrongs organised in 1950, Charles Gardner had an account written of the history of flying at Brooklands, asking me to compile the two brief chapters about the car and motorcycle side. Lord Montagu of Beaulieu followed (Dalton Watson, 1978) with pictorial coverage, as listed in David's bibliography, and I am delighted with the excellence of paper and pictures in my recent book for Haynes, *Brooklands Giants*, now combined in one volume with *Aero-Engined Racing Cars at Brooklands*.

But it is thanks to David Venables, who is the Assistant Editor of the never-to-be-missed *VSCC Bulletin*, that we now have a truly complete account of all these important and exciting happenings at the ever-fascinating institution in the Surrey countryside, which I enjoyed so much from 1927 onwards, and almost daily from 1933 to around 1934 when I was the unpaid motoring writer of Capt. O.V. Holmes' *Brooklands – Track and Air* magazine, which previously had been the *Brooklands Aero Club Journal*.

To follow all this and a few individual accounts in other books so very efficiently, interestingly and accurately is an enormous tribute to David Venables to whom I, and everyone else with memories of the old track, will be extremely grateful. It probably will be the heaviest book I shall ever review, and I look forward to doing that as a proper welcome to a very necessary task so ably done. The book is much enhanced by the splendid number of excellent and large pictures from LAT and *Motor Sport* etc and the in-set panels of biographies of famous drivers. Altogether this is an unbelievably complete account of an important aspect of motor racing history.

PREFACE

I agreed to write this book with considerable reluctance. I felt that a true history of Brooklands deserved a multi-volume work and furthermore, others, who knew much more about the subject than I did, had already produced some magnificent books. Bill Boddy's history of the motor racing at the track is one of the all-time greats and Peter Hartley's two books on motor cycle racing are immensely detailed and comprehensive. However, as I studied the subject, I began to realise that there was more to the story than the racing; the aviation and the developments after World War Two were equally important and no one had tried to draw all these threads of the story of the first 100 years into one book.

I have attempted to give an outline of the story and to mention all the major aspects. I realise that certain parts will seem sparse to the enthusiast, but hope the book will go some way towards recording the development and activities of a major and vital site in the history of Britain in the 20th century. It is probably true to say that without Brooklands, this country – and perhaps even the world – would be a very different place today. I hope that what I have written will help to preserve the memory, and also the physical remains of a remarkable place, and will encourage the reader to support the preservation of the track and also perhaps to find out more about such a fascinating place. I realise there will be mistakes and omissions in the text and for these I seek the forbearance of the reader. The book could have been five times as long and still have left out important points, but the length has essentially been dictated by commercial considerations.

In its preparation I have received much help and advice. Foremost among those who have kindly given their time and effort is Tony Hutchings, the Archivist of the Brooklands Society. He provided me with much material and has painstakingly sought out the answers to countless questions. I am also most grateful to Kathy Ager of LAT Photographic; Annice Collett of the Vintage Motor Cycle Club; David Comber; Trevor Dunmore, the Librarian of the Royal Automobile Club; Bob French of the Veteran Cycle Club; Bryan Goodman; Malcolm Jeal; Dick Lewis; John Maitland; Bryan Reynolds; Graham Skillen; David Thirlby; and John Warburton. I have been greatly helped by Allan Winn, the Director of the Brooklands Museum, John Pulford, the Museum's Head of Collections and Interpretation, and Julian Temple, the General Manager, Museum Operations. They have given me full access to the Museum's archives and reference library and have also studied the text and made many valuable comments and amendments. I hope those who have been inadvertently omitted from this list will accept my apologies and my thanks.

David Venables
Spring 2007

CHAPTER ONE

CONCEPT
TO REALITY

Brooklands, the cradle of motor racing and the birthplace of aviation in Great Britain, was a concept of the imagination, foresight and ambition of one man, Hugh Fortescue Locke King. Locke King was born on 7 October 1848. His father, Peter Locke King, had inherited substantial agricultural estates in the Weybridge district of Surrey, from his own father, the seventh Lord King. Peter had added to his inheritance by buying more land, and among his purchases were Hollick Farm and Wintersells Farm, both south-west of Weybridge, and the future site of Brooklands. When Peter died in 1885 his estate was valued at £500,000 – probably in excess of £30 million in the values of the 21st century. This passed to Hugh.

Hugh had been called to the Bar in 1873, but he probably did not practise as a barrister. He joined the Inns of Court Volunteers, one of the predecessors of the Territorial Army, and became an enthusiastic member of the National Rifle Association. In December 1884 he married Ethel Gore Browne, younger daughter of Sir Thomas Gore Browne, the Governor of Tasmania and subsequently the Governor of New Zealand. After the death of his father the couple lived at Brooklands House, a mansion built by Peter in 1862.

While Peter had endeavoured to increase the size of his estates by prudent land purchases, it seems that Hugh regarded his inheritance as a foundation for an extravagant lifestyle. During the years following their marriage, Hugh and Ethel

Construction work in progress during the winter of 1906/7. (Brooklands Society)

lived well and spent money freely. The winters were spent in a warm climate and there were several visits to Egypt, where they bought Mena House – a mansion in Cairo – in 1887. After a short while this was converted into a luxurious hotel, but it was a poor investment and the Locke Kings lost money. Hugh also began to develop parts of his land, and an early project was the Portmore Estate, which lay between the growing village of Weybridge and the River Thames. Although he was spending money, and parts of his estate were mortgaged to provide funds, Hugh was also a substantial local benefactor. The fire station and Weybridge Cottage Hospital were among the amenities he provided for the community.

The motor car appeared in England in the last few years of the 19th century and Hugh became an enthusiastic early motorist. He made extended European tours, and in September 1905 he visited Italy, driving a 70hp Itala, to be a spectator at the Coppa Florio, held on a 100-mile circuit at Brescia. His interest was heightened when the race was won by an Itala driven by Raggio. Many of the major European manufacturers had entered cars, and Hugh asked the competitors why no British

cars were taking part. He was told the British were unable to build suitable cars, as there was no place in England where cars could be raced, or tested at speed. The European practice of closing public roads for racing was illegal in England, so Hugh concluded that there was an urgent need for a suitable track to be built.

Early in 1906 he had a meeting with Lord Northcliffe, the proprietor of the *Daily Mail*, at Sutton Place near Guildford, and Northcliffe expressed his support for the building of a track. Shortly after this meeting, Julian Orde, the secretary of the Automobile Club of Great Britain and Ireland (soon to be the Royal Automobile Club), also stated that the building of a circular track in England was essential. Consequently, in September 1906, Hugh held a meeting to canvass the views of important sporting motorists, including the two leading British racing drivers, S.F. Edge, who had won the 1902 Gordon Bennett race driving a Napier, and Charles Jarrott, who had competed in many of the European open-road races. To help him with the project, Hugh also enlisted the aid of Ernst, Baron de Rodakowski, an Austrian who had settled in England after his marriage to Hugh's distant relative Lady Dora Carnegie, and had already been involved in the management of the Mena House Hotel.

Hugh proposed that he should build a four-mile road course around his estate, which would enable manufacturers to test and improve cars and where races could also be held. The course would be 20ft wide, with long sweeping curves. Jarrott, however, said a wide track was needed to enable high speeds to be maintained in safety, and Edge added that it should be visible to spectators throughout its length and, with the possibility of ten or twelve cars running abreast, the width should be 100ft. Hugh accepted this expert advice and suggested that the track should be built on the site of Wintersells and Hollick farms. The site was then inspected and everyone agreed that it was ideal. As the meeting ended, Edge said that if the track was built, he wanted to book it as soon as it was completed so that he could attempt to drive a car on it for 24 hours at an average speed of 60mph.

Locke King described his feelings in later years: 'Poor old England – the cradle of sport as she used to be called, and now she is nowhere. The time has surely come when England should no longer lag behind the rest of the world but take her place in the very forefront, if possible, and reassert herself as the arbiter of sport.

'This feeling revived when a few months later I heard the suggestion made that a circular track was what was needed in this country, where cars could

BELOW *An informal study of Hugh Locke King, the creator of Brooklands. (Brooklands Society)*

be watched over the whole course. The site was not far to seek. When a few who were consulted saw the place, they owned that nature seemed to have formed it for the purpose.'

Having established the type of track that was needed, Hugh Locke King enlisted the help of Colonel Henry Capel Loftt Holden of the Royal Engineers to draw up the design and specification. Holden, who was Superintendent of the Royal Gun Factories at Woolwich and an ex-Chairman of the Automobile Club of Great Britain and Ireland, immediately pointed out that for cars to negotiate the track at the speeds anticipated, it was essential for the curves to be banked. Holden drew up plans for a 2¾-mile oval track which used the maximum available area. It would require a huge excavation at the northern end, where the banking would be built into a cutting and would be elevated in some sections to avoid flooding from the River Wey, which would also need diverting. There was a slight, but unavoidable, flaw in Holden's design: Locke King did not own all the land needed on the eastern boundary of the proposed track – shortly before he decided to build it, he had sold a piece of land to the Itala company as the site of a small factory and depot for the English off-shoot of the Italian car manufacturer, of which he was a keen customer. To accommodate this, the eastern leg of the track had a slight unbanked reverse kink, which would later cause exciting problems for the drivers of faster cars.

Holden considered three materials for the construction. Tarmacadam, then a new and relatively untried material and laid on an aggregate foundation, was ruled out as it would be impossible to roll it out on the higher banking sections. Asphalt had the same problem and had to be laid on a concrete foundation, which would be expensive. Concrete was therefore decided upon. This too was a relatively new material, not previously used for roadbuilding, so the new track would be pioneering in terms of construction as well as concept. It was felt that concrete would be simple to use as it could be laid in small sections, retained by shuttering to prevent the mix pouring down the slope before setting; but it would have to be laid almost dry. Concrete had an additional advantage – the gravel could be obtained from local gravel beds, and some may even have been extracted from within the confines of the track.

In October 1906 Holden engaged Alexander Donaldson, a leading railway engineer, to survey the site and lay out the track. Realising that the bridging of the River Wey was a problem, as the banking was steep at the point of the crossing, they consulted L.G. Mouchel & Partners, who had the

LEFT *Dame Ethel Locke King, who shared her husband's enthusiasm for the track.* (Brooklands Society)

British agency for the Hennebique method of construction, developed in Belgium, which used concrete reinforced with steel. The proposed bridge was to be curved in plan and elevation, 180ft long, 100ft wide, and supported by concrete piles, some of them sunk into the riverbed. This, too, was a pioneering venture.

The clearing of the woodland and the preparation of the site began in the summer of 1906. Initially, Hugh used his own farm labourers supplemented by workers engaged locally, but Donaldson realised that the magnitude of the task required a proper contractor. He therefore approached a building and civil engineering firm, Price & Reeves, who signed a contract for the work in January 1907. The introduction of Price & Reeves raised several problems. It seems that Hugh had originally budgeted for the expenditure of £22,000 (£1.32 million at current values) from his available resources, believing that the track would be a level road, but Donaldson prepared an estimate for the building of the banked track which was double that figure – and worse was to come. Price & Reeves estimated that the expenditure would be £60,750 (£3.7 million). They wanted to surface the track with 'Tarfaalt', a proprietary form of asphalt, but this would have been even more expensive and difficult to lay, so it was agreed that the

ABOVE *Colonel (later Sir Henry) Loftt Holden, the designer of the track. (Flight)*

construction should be of concrete as planned, laid in a 6in layer directly onto the sand subsoil.

Work continued at a great pace, but Hugh was by now in serious financial difficulties and Ethel had to lend him some of her own capital. Price & Reeves, who were evidently concerned about getting their money, demanded that they should be paid every month for the work done and took a charge on a Sussex farm belonging to Hugh. Subsequently they were given a charge on all the Locke King properties as security. When the July 1907 monthly account was not settled Price & Reeves exercised their right to sell the mortgaged farm.

Even while the financial problems dragged on, the woods and farmland were transformed at an astonishing speed. Initially about 500 men were engaged in clearing the site and cutting through the hill at the northern end, but the workforce increased to about 2,000 when Price & Reeves took over, many of the labourers coming from Ireland. Some lived in local lodgings but the majority stayed on site in rough shelters. They were paid 6d an hour. Much of the work was done by hand, but there were two light locomotives, 68 side-tip wagons, ten end-tip wagons, ten steam grabs and countless horses. Eight miles of railway was laid within the track confines – linked to the London & South Western Railway line, which ran

past the site – to carry the building materials, which arrived continuously.

Holden's plan provided for a course 2 miles 1,350 yards in length, measured at the mid-point of the 100ft track. It was intended that the cars should lap the track in an anti-clockwise direction and it would provide for cars travelling at speeds up to 120mph. The northern banking, called the Home or Members' Banking, was struck at a mean radius of 1,000ft and had a maximum height of 28ft 8ins. The southern banking, called the Byfleet, was struck at a mean radius of 1,550ft and had a maximum height of 21ft 10in. The northern end of the site was higher than the southern end, so on the approach from the Byfleet to the Members' Banking the track rose at a gradient of 1:30, and after it crossed the Hennebique bridge near the end of the Members' Banking the fall was 1:25. The Railway Straight – which ran beside the L&SWR line and was linked to the Members' and Byfleet bankings – was level.

As previously mentioned, there was a slight reverse curve between the Byfleet and Members' Bankings and at this point, on the north-eastern corner of the track, the Finishing Straight ran off on the left-hand side and joined the Members' Banking at a point about two-thirds along its length. The Finishing Straight rose at its top end, with a gradient of 1:12. Cars would pull into the Finishing Straight where the finish line would be situated, and the slight rise at the end was expected to help them to slow and stop after a race.

A contract was signed with a separate contractor, Foster & Disksee, to build a clubhouse and offices beside the Finishing Straight, with an adjoining paddock containing 75 stalls for competitors' cars. During the construction, 30 acres of woodland was felled, 350,000 cubic yards of earth were moved, and 200,000 tons of concrete were laid. In recent years it has been suggested that Locke King may have been cheated by the contractors, as calculations indicate that to lay the track area with concrete to an average depth of 6in would have only required 52,000 tons – a puzzle which will never be solved.

Much of the organisation and preparation for the running of the race meetings was deputed to Rodakowski. He was appointed Clerk of the Course and played an important part in the formation of the Brooklands Automobile Racing Club, or BARC. This came into being in December 1906 as the organising club, with an office at Carlton House in Regent Street, London. It was expected that the racing would be run on similar lines to horse racing, and the committee of the new club included many notable horse racing owners, among them the Duke of Beaufort and the Duke of Westminster, while the president was Lord Lonsdale. In anticipation of the horse racing links Rodakowski sought the advice of Joseph Davis, the managing director of nearby Hurst Park race course, on many aspects of the club's organisation. There was even a tentative plan that a horse racing course might be laid out in the centre of the track, but nothing came of it.

It was hoped that up to 30,000 spectators would attend a race meeting. The main public enclosure was laid out on the hill between the Members' Banking and the Finishing Straight. This provided seating for 5,000, with tiers of seats, covered grandstands and elevated terraces. Spectators who came by train would walk along a path from Weybridge station and enter the hill enclosure via a tunnel under the track. BARC members arriving on foot would have a separate enclosure on the hill, entered by the Members' Bridge across the Members' Banking adjacent to the Finishing Straight, where they would find a restaurant and other facilities. The public coming by car parked outside the Members' Banking and joined the pedestrians in the tunnel under the track, while BARC members arriving by car drove through a tunnel under the Members' Banking and parked beside the paddock. Admission to the public enclosure was 2s 6d, while the rail fare from Waterloo to Weybridge was 3s 0d. For the less well-off it could therefore be an expensive day out, when a clerk in a London office was earning only about £1 10s a week.

Although Hugh Locke King had many problems to resolve during the design and building of the track, he was spared the modern burden of Local Authority planning permission or even compliance with building regulations. If planning permission had been needed Brooklands would probably not have been built. A battle with the planning committee, local objections, a rejected application, appeals, adjudication by the Minister and judicial reviews would perhaps have set the project back by three or four years and Locke King might well have lost heart by then. The Local Government Board did express concern at the living conditions of the workers building the track but it had no authority to intervene.

There was strong local opposition, though. *The Surrey Herald* said in September 1906: 'The people of Weybridge will view the construction of a race course in their midst with horror and aversion, and no good can possibly accrue from such an institution tacked on to a track upon which the fiendish motor car can indulge its wicked lust for speed to the utmost … Here the merry motorist may pursue his career of destruction unchecked.'

The aim was to have the track ready for racing and a formal opening in June 1907. Though Price & Reeves forecast that it would not be ready until October, a surge of sustained effort saw the track completed by the appointed date. The whole task, from first ground clearance to final details, had taken about ten months. By today's accepted standards this was an astonishing achievement – unlike modern projects, there was no 'slippage' or 'over-run'!

It is not known who first completed a lap of the course. It seems likely that it was Ethel Locke King, driving either an Itala or her Rochet-Schneider, but there is a possibility that a local 11-year-old boy, Dougal Marchant, had preceded her, riding his mother's tricycle. Marchant was subsequently to become a successful motor cycle racer at Brooklands.

BELOW *The Hennebique Bridge nearing completion. (Brooklands Society)*

CHAPTER TWO

EDWARDIAN OVERTURE

1907

As soon as it was formed in December 1906, the BARC received from the Automobile Club of Great Britain and Ireland a licence to hold races, and immediately issued a prospectus for its first race meeting. This was to take place on 6 July 1907. The entry fees ranged from £15 to £50, with reductions for entries made before 15 January. These fees were high, but the value of the race prizes was commensurate, ranging from £250 to £1,400. The winner of each race would also take home a cup valued at £200. In true horse racing tradition, the winnings were declared in sovereigns, many of the races were called 'Plates', and the distances were given in furlongs. In addition, cars would not carry racing numbers but their drivers would instead wear smocks in the registered colours of the entrants.

The track was formally opened by the Earl of Lonsdale on Monday 17 June. A lunch was held in the BARC Pavilion for notables and the press; it was a relatively informal occasion and Hugh Locke King made a very short speech. After thanking those concerned in its construction, he said that the future of the track – and whether it succeeded or failed – rested with the automobile world: there was no need to say more, as the track spoke for itself. The assembled company then moved to the paddock, and from there drove out onto the

The start of the team race at the 1909 Whit Monday meeting. E. Hobson (Nagant-Hobson) of the winning No 3 team gets away, while his team-mate Sir George Abercromby (Napier) looks on. (LAT)

Finishing Straight. Drawing up in two lines, led by a 40hp Itala driven by Ethel Locke King with Hugh as a passenger, the procession moved out onto the Members' Banking with the strict injunction that there was to be no overtaking. However, this stipulation was optimistic, and almost immediately the faster cars speeded up and began to explore the possibilities of the banked track.

Those who took part were most enthusiastic and Colonel Holden received considerable praise for the design of the banking and the apparently inherent safety of the track. The only slight criticism was directed at the Finishing Straight, which, it was considered, might be too short for the fastest cars to stop safely; a prescient opinion.

Brooklands had meanwhile attracted considerable international interest and, on the opening day, it was announced in Berlin that Kaiser Wilhelm II had directed that a permanent motor course should be built in Germany. The outcome of this directive was the Avus track, on the western outskirts of Berlin.

S.F. (Selwyn) Edge's intention to attempt a 24-hour record as soon as the Brooklands track was opened was no idle boast. Edge was the guiding force behind Napier, then perhaps the leading British

manufacturer and already eminent in the motor racing field. His plan was to run three production 60hp T21 models for 24 hours at an average speed of 60mph. If this succeeded, not only would it gain valuable publicity for Napier, but it would also secure the world 24-hour record for the company. For Brooklands, a record feat of such magnitude would also be splendid publicity in advance of the first race meeting. The record run was fixed for Friday 28 June, but the team of three cars were at the track for several days beforehand and the fastest car lapped at its maximum speed, 89mph. The drivers found that their acetylene headlights were useless at night, so the track was marked with red lanterns placed on the 50ft line (the centre of the track) and spaced at 10yd intervals; 352 of these were obtained from road mending firms in the London area. The top of the banking was illuminated by flares. The record run began at 6pm on the 28th and the trio lapped steadily throughout the night and into the following day with few problems.

The public had been admitted to watch and were charged 10s 0d on the Friday but only 2s 6d at 2:30pm on the Saturday. As news of the run spread a big crowd gathered, and the Napier team was loudly applauded when the 1,440-mile target was

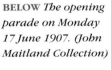

BELOW *The opening parade on Monday 17 June 1907. (John Maitland Collection)*

passed by Edge, who was leading the team, at 3:40pm and the 60mph average was achieved. This was not achieved without incident. Because the cars were running continuously on the 50ft line, the newly-laid concrete began to break up, and workmen had to dash onto the track to repair the largest holes with gravel. Then, towards the end of the run, one of the cars stopped to replace a broken rear spring. Shortly after this the windscreen of Edge's car shattered.

Edge had driven single-handed without relief, and to prepare himself for this he had adopted a training regime established by Sandow, a well-known body-builder and fitness trainer. During the 24-hour run he actually drove 1,581 miles 1,310 yards at an average of 65.09mph. The other cars covered a slightly shorter distance, but achieved the 60mph goal easily.

Both Edge and Brooklands gained the desired publicity, though when the damage to the track surface was assessed one wag suggested that Brooklands should be renamed 'Edge-wear Road'. Though Edge's run was blamed for Brooklands's poor track surface for the rest of its racing history this was probably an unfair criticism. It seems more likely that the new concrete had not fully cured and that the sand foundations were already settling.

After Edge's record success prospects seemed excellent for the first meeting on Saturday 6 July,

but unfortunately the meeting turned out to be what was described as 'a ghastly failure'. Though some 13,500 people attended – there were over 500 visitors' cars – this figure was well short of the 30,000 anticipated by Rodakowski. In addition, while the handful of faster cars in the programme were impressive on the banking, the slower and more mundane machines looked sluggish against

ABOVE *The timekeeper's box on the Finishing Straight. (Brooklands Society)*

BELOW *The first timing gear. (Brooklands Society)*

ABOVE *S.F. Edge and his team of Napiers line up for the start of the 24-hour record run on 28 June 1907. (LAT)*

RIGHT *The crowds queue at the entrance for the first meeting on 6 July 1907. (LAT)*

ABOVE *The paddock at the opening meeting. (LAT)*

the huge concrete backdrop, and spectators felt disappointed. The drivers could not be identified in their coloured smocks, the catering was inadequate, and there were frustratingly long delays getting in and out of the track.

The inaugural race, the first heat of the Marcel Renault Memorial Trophy, was won by Henry Tryon, one of the 24-hour run drivers, in a T20 Napier entered by Edge. The racing was not especially close, but the public were later compensated by the 10.3-mile Byfleet Plate, in which there was a dead heat between Charles Jarrott in a 60hp de Dietrich and Frank Newton, another 24-hour run driver, in a 45hp T23 Napier, also entered by Edge. Newton speeded up as the cars entered the Finishing Straight and caught Jarrott on the line. Jarrott considered he had won, but his appeal was rejected and the pair split the prize money.

The meeting had attracted foreign interest too. Louis Wagner of France was in a Fiat which had won the French Grand Prix at Dieppe only four days earlier, driven by his team-mate Felice Nazzaro. At Brooklands, however, Wagner was unable to match the speed of Jarrott and Newton. Another foreign driver, the Italian Dario Resta, had a comfortable lead in his 1906 GP Mercedes as he approached the Finishing Straight in the major race of the day, the First Montagu Cup, but said he was waved on to do another lap by an official, so did not take the flag. His appeal was rejected and he did not get the £1,400 prize to which he must have felt entitled. This went to

RIGHT *Frank Newton (Napier) and Charles Jarrott (Lorraine-Dietrich) dead-heat in the Byfleet Plate at the opening meeting. Newton may be crouching down to turn on the disputed oxygen cylinder. (LAT)*

another Mercedes driver, J.E. Hutton, who was also in a 14-litre 1906 GP car.

After the meeting, Charles Jarrott said that Newton had gained an unfair advantage in their dead-heat as the Napier had carried an oxygen cylinder, concealed under the floor. Newton, he claimed, opened and discharged this into the Napier's carburettor towards the end of the race, thus gaining the extra speed which enabled him to catch Jarrott on the line. Since many journalists had been unable to get passes, the problems were reported in the press with malicious glee.

Huntley Walker, while avoiding a collision with the winning Napier, spun his Darracq and went over the top of the banking at the end of the Finishing Straight. Amazingly, the driver and mechanic were unhurt and the car was almost undamaged.

The oxygen controversy caused many tensions among the competitors, so to resolve the matter the BARC drew up a rule which took immediate effect: 'No fuel other than petroleum spirit shall be used in internal combustion engines, except where specially provided in the race proposition, and the use of any other ingredient shall be deemed a corrupt practice and dealt with accordingly'.

The oxygen ban was in force for the August Bank Holiday meeting, by which time it was evident that other lessons had also been learned. More press passes were issued and the admission charges for the public enclosures were reduced to 2s 6d and 1s 0d. The drivers' coloured smocks were retained for the time being, but the cars were now also numbered. The BARC committee was only reluctantly persuaded that this change was necessary. A guiding force in the decision was A.V. Ebblewhite, the official timekeeper and starter who, away from the track, ran a musical instrument shop in Aldgate High Street in London's East End. 'Ebby', as he became affectionately known to successive generations of Brooklands drivers, was a constant and reassuring figure at the track from the first race meeting until the last.

The oxygen ban seemed to have little effect on the performance of Edge's team of Napiers, which gained several successes including a victory in the Selling Plate, another carry-over from horse racing. The winning T20 Napier was sold for £215, of which £100 went to Edge. The main race was the

A second meeting was held on 20 July. It was realised that in order to improve the quality of racing for the spectators a system of handicapping was needed. The horse racing system of adding weight was therefore adopted, but this was ineffective, as was a calculation based on the price of the cars.

While S.F. Edge had been cagey about the use of oxygen in the opening meeting, at the second meeting the Napiers used it openly, and Henry Tryon won a race easily after 'putting on a fine oxygen sprint in the last half mile'. This meeting also saw Brooklands's first spectacular accident when

BELOW *The formidable Ernst de Rodakowski, the Clerk of the Course from 1907 until 1909, gives instructions to a driver. (Brooklands Society)*

ABOVE *Tyres are changed on Frank Newton's T23 Napier before the September 1907 meeting. (LAT)*

BELOW *14 September 1907, Henry Tryon's Napier (No 3) beats Hinds-Howell's Iris off the mark at the start of the One-lap Sprint. (LAT)*

15¾-mile Prix de France for cars complying with the 1907 GP de l'ACF (French GP) regulations. The result was a Mercedes 1–2, with Resta leading Hutton home, but it was Hutton who provided the drama, as his car lost its bonnet, sprayed its water away, broke its accelerator pedal and burst a tyre as it crossed the line!

The BARC committee realised that to keep the spectators' interest, and therefore to maintain the gate attendance, it was necessary to have close racing. The weight handicapping system had not worked so a new method was tried for the meeting on 14 September. Carefully measured starting lines were drawn around the track and the cars, grouped by Ebblewhite according to their expected performance, were started from these points: the limit car had a start of 1,750 yards from the scratch car. It was a slow process, taking over 30 minutes to

assemble the cars and it was difficult for the drivers to see the firing of a rocket which signalled the start, but it worked after a fashion. This event, forerunner of a multitude of such races, was the First Five Mile Handicap and was won by Frank Newton in a T21 Napier.

Unfortunately, this meeting was marred by Brooklands's first fatal accident. In the First 60hp race, Sydney Smith, the winner, driving Edge's 24-hour run car, lost a tyre and drove the last part of the race on the rim. He slowed at the top of the Finishing Straight and turned onto the banking to return to the paddock, but as soon as he had turned he stopped. Coming up fast behind was Vincent Herman driving a Minerva entered by John Moore-Brabazon (later Lord Brabazon of Tara). Herman swerved as he saw the Napier and went up to the top of the banking where the car slid and overturned, rolling down to the bottom. Herman and the mechanic were thrown out and the unfortunate driver died a few hours later from his injuries. There was a fight between BARC officials and photographers trying to record the scene. The BARC itself was stunned by the accident because it had believed that the track was completely safe. The inquest on Herman absolved Smith from any blame and recorded that the accident had been caused by Herman's inexperience.

The racing season closed with a meeting on Saturday 12 October, which only drew a small crowd. Napier had been the most successful marque in terms of wins, but Mercedes was on top in terms of prize money, collecting £2,800 compared to Napier's £2,000.

Hugh Locke King's intention that the track should be used by the motor industry for testing and development was soon realised. Dust was a constant problem for early motorists and in July

1907 the RAC held some trials which included cars brought by manufacturers, some belonging to enthusiasts, and some specially modified to prevent them raising dust. The trials lasted for two days, with the cars being driven over a specially prepared section of track coated with fine limestone dust. Then in August, S.F. Edge produced a specially prepared Napier fitted with a device to give a measured increase of the frontal area, and trials to establish the effect of wind resistance were conducted in collaboration with the BARC.

Meanwhile, following Edge's 24-hour run the BARC had established six class categories, based on RAC horsepower ratings, and announced that it would recognise class records set in each of these categories. By the end of the season it seemed that these records would be a Napier preserve, as 37 were set under Edge's aegis. But in December a 60hp Thames, driven by Clifford Earp, set World records for 50 and 150 miles and for one and two hours. The hour record was established at 76.26mph. Then in October Sir Algernon Guinness Bt, who owned the 22½-litre 200hp Darracq which had set the World Land Speed record in 1905, drove the car at a timed 115.4mph during a demonstration while endeavouring to sell it to an American buyer. Despite this speed, the highest then recorded at Brooklands, the sale fell through!

In November 1907 Kaiser Wilhelm II paid a state visit to England and it was reported that he would be going to Brooklands to watch a motor racing demonstration on the track. However, nothing came of it.

Hugh Locke King's financial anxieties were relieved at the end of 1907 when Ethel's family rallied around, paid off the outstanding debt to Price & Reeves, and made further loans to Hugh, taking mortgages and charges on the Locke King

S.F. Edge

S.F. Edge was the first great personality to emerge at Brooklands. He was born in New South Wales, Australia, in 1868 but came to England in 1871. He was a keen bicycle racer, and then in the late 1890s, raced a motor tricycle. He befriended Montagu Napier and, with his flair for publicity and salesmanship, was the moving force behind the emergence and development of the Napier car. Driving a Napier, Edge won the 1902 Gordon Bennett race and was a regular competitor with Napiers until 1904. When Brooklands opened in 1907, Edge made his legendary 24-hour record run with a team of three Napiers and was a regular entrant of Napiers in 1907 and 1908. At that time his team was the most successful at the track. Napier withdrew from racing at the end of 1908 and Edge subsequently split with Montagu Napier and agreed to leave the motor industry. This agreement expired in 1921 and Edge then obtained a controlling interest in the AC company and became a regular entrant of ACs at Brooklands and supervised many record attempts. In 1922 he drove a Spyker in a successful attempt to break his own 1908 record figures, driving in two 12-hour sessions and establishing new British and Class G records. He also made record attempts in a Lanchester. Edge lost his personal fortune when AC failed in 1929, and died in straitened circumstances in 1940. A man of great courage and energy, his commercial flair placed Edge in some respects a century ahead of his time.

estates in return. The total amount loaned to him in the relevant Declaration of Trust was £24,850.

The first indications of a problem that was to bedevil Brooklands came in the autumn of 1907, when the owners of several large houses nearby sought an injunction in the High Court to restrain the noise from the track and to prevent the nuisance caused by the crowds using the private road past their properties as an entrance to the track. Hugh undertook to reduce the engine noise, the private road was gated, and a new entrance road was built.

BELOW The first fatal accident. Herman's Minerva after his crash on 14 September 1907. (LAT)

1908

In the first decade of the 20th century the motor car was the preserve of the well-to-do, whereas for those of lesser means and the young, the motor cycle provided an exciting mode of transport. Keen motor cyclists therefore looked hopefully to Brooklands when it opened, seeing it as a centre for competition and speed much as sporting motorist did. There was no motor cycle event at Brooklands in 1907, but on 25 February 1908 two Oxford undergraduates from Magdalen College, Gordon McMinnies and Oscar Bickford, took their motor cycles to Brooklands by train, for a match race. McMinnies had a 3½hp 476cc TT Triumph and Bickford had a 5hp 670cc TT Vindec Special, both belt-driven. The race was over one lap and McMinnies was the winner. Ernst de Rodakowski, watching the two duellists, was impressed, and decided that a motor cycle race should be on the card for the two-day Easter meeting which opened the 1908 season.

During the winter the track surface had been improved and repaired and a new grandstand was erected on the Members' Hill. The circuit had by now become recognised as a centre for motoring activities as well as a racing track, and in February it became the scene of a remarkable demonstration. Fred Bennett, the Cadillac agent in England, brought along three new single-cylinder Cadillac runabouts and they were driven round the track for ten laps and then, under RAC supervision, stripped down completely into a pile of 2,163 components each. The components were jumbled into a heap, and two mechanics reassembled three cars from the piled parts. The cars were then driven around the track again. For this feat, the RAC awarded the Dewar Trophy to the Anglo-American Motor Car Co for the most meritorious observed trial of the year.

Both days of the Easter meeting were cold and there were snow showers on the Monday. However, the meeting had royal patronage as it was attended by George, Prince of Wales, later to become King George V.

S.F. Edge had intended to enter his protégé, Dorothy Levitt, who was establishing a considerable reputation as a competition driver in sprints and hill climbs, but the BARC decreed that lady drivers were banned. Saturday was devoted to short races, but there was a more important race on the Monday, the Third 90mph race. Newton was driving a Napier with a 17.2-litre engine known as 'Samson', which had held the Land Speed Record for a short time in 1905. This was matched against a Mercedes driven by Resta. The pair fought for the lead and, on the last lap, Newton passed Resta on the Byfleet Banking and the Napier slid down the banking and their wheels touched. The Mercedes lost two hub caps and several rim securing bolts, while the Napier lost about half the spokes from its front and back wheels. Both drivers recovered but it was Newton who won. Resta lodged a protest which was dismissed by the stewards.

The first motor cycle race was held on the Monday. It was from scratch over two laps and limited to machines with a capacity not exceeding 492cc per cylinder. Twenty-one riders came to the line and Will Cook, riding an NLG-Peugeot, romped away, winning by over half a mile from Kirkham on a Leader-Peugeot and Collier on a Matchless-JAP.

BELOW *Felice Nazzaro in the 90hp Fiat which beat Newton's Napier in the celebrated match race at the 1908 Whitsun meeting and set the much disputed lap record of 121.64mph. (LAT)*

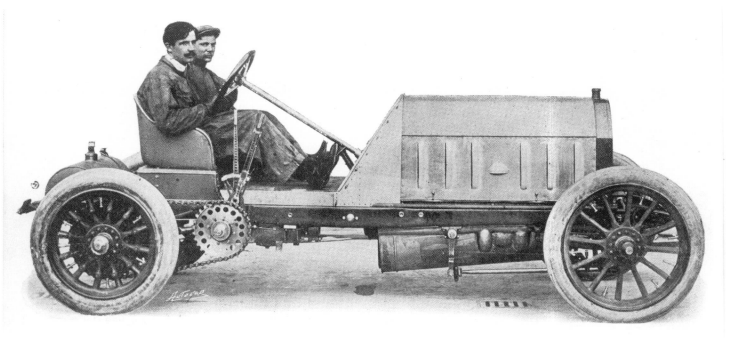

Cook averaged 63mph and received a prize of 20 sovereigns (£20). Unlike the car drivers, who needed the banking when racing, the motor cyclists held to the inside of the track, keeping as close to the verge as possible, and until speeds rose in later years 'grass-cutting' remained the accepted mode of racing. The day finished with a novelty race in which the competitors had to stop to change a wheel and tyre and, as an added refinement, the tyre had to be inflated by the driver.

The meeting's motor cycle competitors expressed the view that to provide more interesting racing for the public there should be handicapping, so at the next meeting, on 9 May, their race became the Motor Cycle Handicap Plate for machines with a capacity not exceeding 532cc per cylinder; the first prize was 25 sovereigns. The handicap was based on the times recorded at the Easter meeting. Thirty-one riders started and the winner was H. Shanks (Chater Lea). However, there were further complaints about noise levels following this meeting and the motor cycles were held to be the prime culprits. Following the meeting, motor cycles were banned from using the track and the BARC decided to hold no more motor cycle races.

The basing of handicaps on times was suggested by 'Ebby', who persuaded the BARC that handicapping by distance was unworkable. He had been keeping recorded times since the first meeting, employing a sophisticated method devised by Colonel Holden, working with K. Elphinstone of Elliott Bros. This used pneumatic rubber strips separating a duplicated system of copper contacts and stretched across the track

surface. When a wheel passed over the strips, a circuit was completed and the recording mechanism was actuated. A feeder-led tape, running at a rate of one foot per minute, went past three recording pens which produced three ink-line traces. The middle trace recorded two-second blips from a pendulum-controlled electrical timer and acted as a time base. The top trace recorded a blip when a wheel passed over the pneumatic strip, and the lower trace was a back-up in the event of the first trace failing.

After the combined car and motor cycle meeting on 9 May, the next big attraction came with the two-day Whitsun meeting on 6 and 8 June. For this event the BARC had agreed – at the request of car importer and entrant Colin Defries – that, for an additional entry fee, cars could be entered under individual 'pet' names. This may have amused the entrants but it has confused posterity, as apart from the marque the programme provided no other

ABOVE *Frank Newton in the Napier 'Samson' which retired from the match race with Nazzaro. (Author's collection)*

BELOW *Two Aries and a Rolls-Royce in the 200-mile high speed trial which concluded the RAC 2,000-Mile Trial in June 1908. The Rolls-Royce, driven by Percy Northey, was a class winner. (LAT)*

RIGHT *The first woman to win at Brooklands. Muriel Thompson, who won the Ladies' Bracelet race on 4 July 1908 in her 25/30hp Austin 'Pobble'. (Author's collection)*

details for the participating cars. Not even the engine sizes were given.

Edge guarded the reputation of Napier with a savage jealousy and earlier in the year had issued challenges to rival marques to take part in match races with 26, 40 and 90hp cars for a stake of £500. His 90hp challenge was taken up by D'Arcy Baker, the Fiat importer, who agreed to enter a 15.2-litre 90hp Fiat called 'Mephistopheles', similar to the car which had won the 1907 Grand Prix de l'ACF in a nine-lap 27.25-mile match race against the Napier 'Samson'. 'Samson', which had a new engine of 20.1 litres, was driven by Newton and the winner of the 1907 GP, Felice Nazzaro, drove the Fiat. Bookmakers attending the meeting had the Fiat at odds-on and the Napier at evens.

Newton led from the start and pulled out an eight-second lead, but as the cars went behind the Members' Hill at the end of the third lap the Napier slowed and stopped, its crankshaft broken. Nazzaro went on to win despite being hit in the face by a bird. This was a bitter blow for Edge, as it was the first time a Napier had retired from a Brooklands race with mechanical failure. But the real sensation came afterwards. The race had been timed with the electrical timing gear and 'Ebby' announced that on its second circuit the Fiat had lapped at 121.64mph. The validity of this time has been a matter of discussion ever since. The dispute was exacerbated by the fact that hand-timing indicated the Fiat's fastest lap to be 107.98mph. The matter has never been resolved, but the Fiat's electrically recorded speed was duly noted as an outright lap record by the BARC and stood until 1922.

In June 1908 the RAC held the 2,000-Mile Trial, which was a severe test for production cars. It started in London, ran to Scotland with various tests and hill climbs en route, and ended at Brooklands with a 200-mile event which would now be called a high-speed trial. At a minor meeting in July, which faced the competing attraction of the Olympic Games being held in London, the ban on lady drivers was relaxed to the extent that they were allowed to drive in a race of their own for a prize, 'The Ladies' Bracelet'. The winner was Miss Muriel Thompson, driving a modified 25/30hp Austin known as 'Pobble' which was entered by her brother and was subsequently raced successfully at Brooklands by him and other drivers for several years.

BELOW *The last race of the day on 4 July 1908, a four-lap match race between S.F. Edge's Napier and J.W. Stocks's De Dion. Stocks was the victor. (LAT)*

ABOVE *The competitors about to leave the paddock for the Motor Cycle Handicap on 3 October 1908. (Brooklands Society)*

BELOW *Charlie Collier is congratulated by his father after setting a new World one-hour record on his 964cc Matchless-JAP on 8 October 1908. A bowler-hatted Ernst de Rodakowski is on the right of the group. (Brooklands Society)*

The two-day August Bank Holiday meeting drew a crowd of over 7,000 on the Monday and was attended by the chairman of the RAC, Prince Francis of Teck, the brother of the Princess of Wales (later Queen Mary). The main race was on the Monday and was to be the longest yet held in England, over 37 laps – 100 miles – for the First O'Gorman Trophy. It was a formule libre race with no restrictions apart from the requirement that the cars should have two seats. Pits were erected next to the Fork, as cars were expected to stop for tyres and fuel.

The race had seven starters and a 1908 GP Mercedes driven by Charles Lane took the lead at the start, followed by a 1908 GP Napier driven by Reynolds. Lane set a fast pace and after 15 laps had lapped the field. Then he stopped at the pits to cure a misfire. Once he got going again he

regained the lead from Reynolds, but made another stop on lap 25. Reynolds, meanwhile, had a puncture as he passed the top of the Finishing Straight, and when he pulled down the banking a wheel went over the bottom edge and the Napier overturned. Reynolds and his mechanic escaped with bruises. This left Newton with another Napier in the lead, but Lane, who was too far behind to win, was still lapping at unabated speed. As he approached the Hennebique Bridge the car spun and slid down the banking, hitting the bridge parapet. It crashed over the top, breaking up as it landed on the riverbank, and caught fire. Lane, seriously injured, was thrown into the River Wey, while Burke, his mechanic, hit the bank and died within a few minutes. Newton went on to take the flag and pulled into a silent and stunned paddock. After some delay it was decided to abandon the rest of the meeting.

Burke's death had considerable repercussions. *The Times*, in a leading article, fiercely attacked motor racing, and it was realised that a ban on the sport in Great Britain was a distinct possibility. At Brooklands there was an immediate effect, as S.F. Edge announced that Napier would be withdrawing from the sport as 'there is now an immense volume of feeling against dangerous motor racing'. Napier had been the pre-eminent and most successful marque for the track's first two seasons, but there were no Napiers in the entry lists published for the autumn meeting on 3 October. The BARC lifted its ban on motor cycles for this meeting and there was a two-lap handicap race which was won by Gordon Gibson's Triumph.

Record breaking had continued at the track throughout 1908. In January, Henry Tryon was uninjured when he overturned his T21 Napier after a tyre burst while attempting to take the one-hour record. He attributed his escape to divine intervention and thereafter became an evangelical Christian. Frank Newton was more successful and took the hour record on 6 February at 85.55mph as well as other records. The 60hp and 90hp half-mile records changed hands several times, being contested between Resta, driving two Mercedes, and Newton with the Napiers. At the end of the season Resta held the 60hp record with 103.15mph but Newton had the 90hp honours with 119.34mph in 'Samson', driving through the measured distance on the Railway Straight in a clockwise direction and coming off the Byfleet Banking. Newton estimated that he was doing 130mph on the banking. The first motor cycle record came on 8 October when Charlie Collier, riding a 964cc TT Matchless-JAP, established a World motor cycle hour record at 70.05mph.

1909

There were a number of changes and developments at Brooklands in 1909. Ernst de Rodakowski, who had done so much to establish the track, was replaced as Clerk of the Course by Major Frederick Lindsay Lloyd. Rodakowski was a loud, extrovert, flamboyant man whose enthusiasm and energy were essential to launch Brooklands, but once the track was established there was a need for a quieter, more methodical approach.

Lindsay Lloyd, who was 42, had retired from the Royal Engineers, where he had been secretary of the Mechanical Transport Committee, while away from his Army duties he had been a member of the RAC committee. One of his first tasks at Brooklands was to supervise the construction of the Test Hill. This ran from the Finishing Straight

BELOW *The Test Hill is opened on 25 March 1909. (LAT)*

up to the crest of the Members' Hill. It was a concrete strip 352ft in length and had an average gradient of 1:5, with a maximum gradient of 1:4. The Test Hill linked up to the Members' Bridge and was intended to offer a steep gradient for testing and, in the reverse direction, for braking. It was formally opened on 25 March and the first car certified to have climbed it was a 20hp Vauxhall, driven by Percy Kidner, in 15.04sec. The first successful motor cycle was a Matchless-JAP ridden by George Reynolds, who took 6.17sec, aided by a 30yd run-in. Despite the temporary noise ban, the BARC had now decided to accept motor cycles and, at a meeting at the Carlton House headquarters of the BARC, the British Motor Cycle Racing Club (BMCRC) was formed, with Lindsay Lloyd and 'Ebby' on its committee.

The Easter meeting was held over two days. The Saturday was fine but the Monday was cold and showery, though this did not deter a good-sized crowd. There were two motor cycle races on each day and among the 41 starters in the Spring Handicap was a young rider, Walter Owen Bentley,

on a Rex: in the future the name Bentley would become synonymous with Brooklands. The meeting was successful for Bobby Tate who won a race on each day with his 60hp Mercedes, lapping at 95mph. A one-make Sizaire-Naudin race ended in a dead heat.

The newly-formed BMCRC held its first meeting on Thursday 22 April, and the opening race – a two-lap 1,000cc scratch event – was won by Martin Geiger on an NSU. Understandably, as a midweek event it only attracted a handful of spectators. As well as the track races there was a hill climb handicap on the Test Hill, but heavy rain brought the meeting to an early finish and the last race was abandoned.

The BARC Whitsun meeting attracted a small crowd, which was attributed to poor publicity, but there was an innovation with a two-car team relay race. The big draw at the midweek Summer meeting on Wednesday 30 June was the reappearance of Felice Nazzaro, entered by D'Arcy Baker in a 12-litre Fiat. It was announced that he would attempt to break the World one-mile and

LEFT *The riders line up in the paddock before the 1909 Easter Plate. (Brooklands Society)*

BELOW LEFT *Willie Cook, the winner of the May Motor Cycle Handicap and the Championship Motor Cycle Plate with his 984cc NLG-Peugeot on 29 May 1909. Cook won the first motor cycle race on the track at Easter 1908. (Brooklands Society)*

BELOW *The start of a relay race at the 1909 August Bank Holiday meeting. (LAT)*

kilometre records, and so set a new World Land Speed Record. He would also attempt to establish a new lap record, perhaps hoping to settle the controversy surrounding the 1908 speed. It was a disappointing failure, as the mile and kilometre speeds were less than 100mph and the lap speed was a mere 102.01mph. The Montagu Cup for the powerful racers of 35hp and over was a win for the 41.9hp Bianchi of Sydney Harbutt, who was chased home by a GP Napier driven by Astley. After the race Harbutt's entrant, H.P. Eggleston, was suspended for the rest of the season, as Harbutt had broken the rules by turning round in the Finishing Straight to return to the paddock.

At the August Bank Holiday meeting, run over two days, the main race was the O'Gorman Trophy, limited to cars of less than 21hp. It was a successful race for Vauxhall, as the 3,053cc 20hp cars prepared by the factory took first and second places, A.J. (Jock) Hancock leading home Percy Kidner, the proprietor of Vauxhall. A relay race had six two-car teams and was won by the pairing of Oscar Thompson in the Austin 'Pobble' and Kidner in his 20hp Vauxhall. There were six motor cycle races of which Guy Lee Evans, riding a 638cc Indian, won four, including a car/motor cycle winners' handicap, where he headed two Napiers.

The BMCRC continued with monthly midweek meetings throughout the season, these taking place on Wednesdays, which was found to be a more popular day as many retail businesses closed on Wednesday afternoons. The May meeting had a more ambitious event, a one-hour race, won by Harry Bashall on a 1,000cc BAT-JAP. On 6 June, Will Cook brought a bizarre machine to the track. This was an NLG with a 120mm x 120mm V-twin engine

and a capacity of 2.7 litres. His aim was to take the world record, held by French rider Henri Cissac. Cook recorded 84.25mph for the flying mile, which did not reach Cissac's figures but was the fastest speed yet set by a motor cycle at Brooklands. Cook brought the NLG-JAP back for another record attempt in November, but although he was hand-timed at over 90mph the timing gear failed, and on a second attempt the camshaft drive broke.

At the BMCRC meeting on 13 September a new name appeared in the winners' list when D.R. ('Dan') O'Donovan took first place riding a 500cc Norton in a one-lap sprint. It was to be the first of continuous wins at the track for the marque for which O'Donovan would become an ace tuner. The club was even more ambitious at the closing meeting on 9 October, with a two-hour race which had 14 starters. The winner was Bert Colver (964cc Matchless-JAP), who covered 118 miles.

Just before the track closed for the season, Victor Hemery arrived on 8 November with the famous 21-litre 'Blitzen' Benz, with the aim of taking the flying mile and kilometre records to establish a new World Record. His target was 121.57mph, set by a Stanley Steamer in 1906. He recorded 127.87mph over the half mile, 125.94mph over the kilometre, and 115.92mph over the mile, and achieved these speeds running clockwise round the track, which was considered to be the slower direction. Hemery did not make runs in the other direction, but as the AIACR accepted one-way runs as records at that time, the kilometre record was acknowledged as a new World Land Speed Record, which gave Brooklands a new and unique distinction.

BELOW *The 'Blitzen' Benz in which Victor Hemery set the World Land Speed Record of 125.94mph at the track on 9 November 1909. (Daimler-Benz AG)*

1910

The BARC received stern criticism from *The Autocar* when reporting the 1910 Easter meeting: 'The advertised racing at 100mph did not materialise owing to the absence of the crack high-powered cars.' Despite this, the crowds were entertained by a new 20hp Vauxhall, called the 'KN' (nicknamed 'Hot Stuff'), which had a remarkable slim, streamlined body, setting a new trend. With it, Hancock had an easy win and there was extra excitement when a Berliet and a Mercedes collided in the Finishing Straight after the end of a race and the rear wheel of the Mercedes collapsed. Among the winners was a stripped touring 2,412cc 12/16hp Sunbeam driven by the company's chief engineer, Louis Coatalen, who also drove a 4,257cc single-seater 'Nautilus', with a polished conical front cowling – the first appearance of this marque at the track. The BARC Whitsun meeting was postponed as a mark of respect after the death of King Edward VII on 6 May, but was run on Saturday 28 May and saw the fastest lap of the season set by Sir George Abercromby in his Tipo S61 10-litre Fiat at 106.38mph.

The speed of the Vauxhalls may have scared off the opposition, as at the August Bank Holiday

meeting the marque produced the only three runners for the O'Gorman Trophy. Hancock had a new 20hp car with an even slimmer body than 'KN' and ran away with the race, followed by Kidner and Rudolph Selz. In the August Sprint handicap, Lord Vernon in a 1908 GP Mercedes just caught Oscar Thompson in the Austin 'Pobble' on the line. Vernon would be killed in action in 1915.

ABOVE Louis Coatalen in the 4.2-litre Sunbeam 'Nautilus'. This was the first appearance of a Sunbeam at the track at the 1910 Easter meeting and a first tentative step into the field of aerodynamics. (John Maitland Collection)

LEFT Harry Collier on his 770cc Matchless-JAP at the MCC meeting on 4 June 1910. (Brooklands Society)

The BMCRC received royal patronage for the 16 March meeting when Prince Francis of Teck attended. He was entertained by a one-hour race for TT specification machines which was won by Charlie Bennett on a 638cc Indian, with W.O. Bentley coming second on a similar machine. A new regulation came into effect at this meeting, as riders were allowed the help of a pusher at the start.

The BMCRC had an imaginative approach to its events and on Wednesday 22 June it held the longest motor cycle race yet, over 60 laps (163 miles). The aim of the race was to encourage the development of multi-cylinder motor cycles, and 18 'multis' were entered as well as 20 500cc 'singles'. The race was dominated in the early stages by the BAT-JAPs, but their pace took its toll and gradually they fell out or their riders fell off, and the race went to a 639cc Indian ridden by Arthur Moorhouse, who averaged 56.72mph. A Trump-JAP 500 ridden by Arthur McNab was second and it was generally agreed that the race was a great success.

At the ACU meeting on 24 September there was a novelty race when McNab on his Trump-JAP was matched over four laps against the French pilot Blondeau in a Farman biplane. Blondeau had to fly round the track keeping outside pylons, but was 36sec behind at the finish. This meeting ran late and the last race, a one-hour scratch event, finished in the dark, so a red lantern was waved at the riders to indicate the end of the hour.

The last BMCRC meeting on 8 October had a 100-mile reliability trial, and the 500cc sidecar class was won by Miss Beatrice Langston with a Triumph, the first time a lady rider had taken part in a Brooklands motor cycle event. Riding in the wickerwork sidecar was the owner, and Miss Langston's fiancé, the Reverend P.W. Bishcoff.

BELOW Another study in aerodynamics. Jock Hancock's 3,053cc Vauxhall 'KN' which was a winner at the 1910 Easter meeting. (Brooklands Society)

ABOVE *Bashall's 20hp Vauxhall leads Thompson's Austin 'Pobble' at the rolling start of the Invitation Race at the meeting on 28 May 1910. The Vauxhall retired with a broken fuel line and 'Pobble' won. The Sizaire pace car is pulling off amid the smoke. (LAT)*

LEFT *Sam Wright makes a refuelling stop on his 499cc Humber during the 60-lap TT race while his team-mate Bert Yates, who retired in the opening laps, looks on. (Brooklands Society)*

1911

The BARC recognised that members might want to enjoy activities other than motoring, so in 1911 four hard tennis courts were laid down behind the paddock on the site now occupied by the Jackson shed which houses the Grand Prix display. The club's racing events continued at full pace and eight meetings were held during the season. The usual track repairs were finished at the beginning of February and the ACU held lamp trials to assess the quality of lighting equipment fitted to standard motor cycles.

The BMCRC opened the competition season with a meeting on Saturday 18 March. The opening BARC meeting was held on 25 March, a cold wintry day with snow showers. Its star was Ligurd G. Hornsted, usually known as 'Cupid', driving a 5.7-litre Benz. This had come from the German factory the previous year and been modified for Brooklands by Hornsted, who was the company's competition representative in England. The modifications were effective and he won two races.

A competitor who would play a big part in future events attended the Easter Meeting. This was Malcolm Campbell, a 26-year-old insurance broker, who had first appeared in 1908 driving a 1903 Renault. This time he ran a 1908 TT Darracq and won the 60mph Handicap. There was

additional excitement for the spectators when Lacon's 12.9-litre Mercedes collided with Wilkinson's 5.7-litre Benz after the finish of a race and the Benz went over the top of the Members Banking; Wilkinson escaped but was seriously injured. Coatalen had a new Sunbeam, a 3.2-litre single-seater called 'Toodles II' ('Toodles' being his pet name for his wife), in which he competed in a two-lap match race against an 11½-litre T21/24 Napier driven by Christopher Bird. It was an indication how far racing car design had progressed that the Sunbeam won by over half a mile. This was the last appearance of a Napier at Brooklands before the war. 'Toodles II' was a lively performer and gained two further wins at the BARC May meeting.

The first true long-distance race to be held in England was run at the track on Tuesday 13 June. Organised by the RAC, it was a 100-lap, 277-mile race for four-cylinder standard production cars not exceeding an RAC rating of 15.9hp, so the cylinder bore could not exceed 80mm. No alterations were permitted to the chassis or engine but there were no bodywork restrictions. Twenty-three entries were received, and on race morning the cars were weighed and carefully scrutineered before the event began at 10:30am. A Thames driven by C.M. Smith led for the opening laps, but when it retired

BELOW *The start of the RAC Standard Car race.* (LAT)

FAR LEFT *Oliver Godfrey vaults onto his 944cc Indian as he starts from scratch in the 70mph Handicap at the BARC Opening meeting in 1911. His athleticism was rewarded with victory. (Brooklands Society)*

LEFT *C.M. Smith pads himself with a cushion against the rigours of the RAC Standard Car race on 16 June 1911 before climbing into his Thames, which has very evident non-standard bodywork. (LAT)*

with broken valve stems Cathie's Star went to the front. Cathie and Cecil Bianchi (Crossley) then exchanged the lead until a magneto strap broke on the Crossley after 37 laps and Bianchi made a long stop to repair it. This left Cathie in front, followed by his team-mate Lisle driving a second Star. Cathie was averaging 55–56mph. Further back a Singer

RIGHT *A tired-looking Cathie sits in his equally tired-looking Star after winning the RAC Standard Car race. (LAT)*

BELOW *Oliver Godfrey (497cc Indian) and Jack Haswell (499cc Triumph) battle for the lead in the One Hour race at the BMCRC meeting on 26 August 1911. 'Wizard' Stanley (499cc Singer) keeps out of the way. (Brooklands Society)*

driven by Tysoe had made a slow start but was gradually catching the two Stars, and at the 80-lap mark caught Lisle and moved into second place. However, Tysoe was too far back to make an impression on Cathie, who came home to win after 4hr 55min 9.25sec at an average of 56.24mph. His margin over Tysoe was 2min 14sec. Lisle was third,

a Gladiator driven by Usmar was fourth, and Hornsted, who had forsaken Benz for an Armstrong-Whitworth, was fifth. Twelve cars finished the course.

Back in his Benz, Hornsted had an exotic royal audience in the form of the Sultans of Perak and Kedah (among many visiting dignitaries attending

the coronation of King George V) when he won two races at the Summer meeting. Match racing was popular and at the August meeting Lord Vernon in a 1908 GP Mercedes was matched against Eric Loder in a Renault owned by the Maharajah of Tikali, which was said to be 'a GP type', for a stake of £100. Vernon won. He was also victorious in a 100mph Short Handicap, but was bested by Hornsted's Benz in a Sprint Handicap.

Coatalen had by now produced a bigger Sunbeam, 'Toodles IV', which had a 6.1-litre six-cylinder engine, and he gained an exciting win in this at the October meeting, when he beat Percy Lambert's much-modified 2.8-litre Austin 15, called 'Pearley III', by just a length in a 100mph Long Handicap. 'Toodles IV' had already achieved much more, as on 1 September Coatalen and his co-driver T.H. Richards had taken World records from 400 to 900 miles and from four hours to 12 hours. The 12-hour average was 75.66mph.

The track was also being used continuously by manufacturers for testing, and although Rolls-Royce had eschewed racing it was content to test a 'London–Edinburgh' Silver Ghost with a racing body. Driven by Ernest Hives, later Lord Hives and chairman of Rolls-Royce, the car covered a half mile at 101.8mph. Motor cycles were also tested, and a standard 300cc New Hudson was the first motor cycle under 350cc to climb the Test Hill.

The classes for the Isle of Man TT races had meanwhile been changed to Junior (up to 300cc) and Senior (500cc singles and 585cc twins), so the BMCRC decided that the one-hour races held at the monthly meetings would comply with this. The first Senior race on 26 April was won by Charlie Collier on a 580cc Matchless-JAP. The target of 60 miles in the hour on a 500cc machine was sought by many and on 25 May, after two failures, Victor Surridge achieved it on a Rudge, covering 60 miles 783 yards. He was honoured the following week by a dinner given at the Savoy Hotel in London by the Rudge-Whitworth company. Sadly, a month later Surridge was killed on the Isle of Man while practising for the TT.

Early in 1911 the American rider Jake de Rosier was reported to have covered 84 miles in the hour on a 998cc Indian. This feat was doubted by some British riders, so there was great excitement when de Rosier came to Brooklands in July. He agreed to attempt the World flying mile and kilometre records at the MCC meeting on 8 July, and came out at the end of the day for his runs, watched by a big crowd. He set a flying mile at 85.32mph and a flying kilometre at 87.38mph on his 994cc Indian and gained new World motor cycle records. It was also agreed that he would compete in three match

ABOVE *Jake de Rosier (994cc Indian) prepares for the start of his match race with Charlie Collier on 15 July 1911. (Brooklands Society)*

races against Charlie Collier, then regarded as the leading British rider, at the BMCRC meeting on the following Saturday, 15 July. Collier rode his 998cc Matchless-JAP and in the first race over two laps led from a rolling start, but de Rosier was slipstreaming the Matchless and pulled out to cross the line and win by about a length. In the second race, over five laps, Collier led again, but de Rosier then dropped out as he had lost a front tyre. The prize purse of £130 therefore hung on the outcome of the third race, over ten laps. The lead changed hands twice in the first three laps. Then Collier went ahead and began to pull away, but the ignition switch on the Matchless was turned off by the vibration from the track and by the time he realised this, de Rosier was too far ahead to be caught.

Early in the morning on Friday 4 August de Rosier was back at Brooklands, breaking his own records by doing 88.77mph over the kilometre and 88.23mph for the mile. That evening he was the guest of honour at a dinner held by H.H. Collier, the proprietor of Matchless, at Frascati's restaurant in London, and the following morning he sailed for the United States.

For Charlie Collier, surpassing the de Rosier triumphs was a matter of prestige for him, for Matchless, and for Britain, and on the evening of Friday 11 August he took his Matchless-JAP back to Brooklands and covered a kilometre at 89.49mph. Then, tightening the driving belt, he set a new mile record at 91.31mph. Both were World records, and the mile result was the first time that a motor cycle had exceeded 90mph. Personal, marque and national honour were satisfied.

1912

The War Office had realised that any future war would be highly mechanised and appreciated that messages would need to be carried by motor cycles. Manufacturers were therefore invited to submit their standard machines for supervised tests at Brooklands. These trials were held on 29 January, as soon as the winter track repairs had been finished, and the main test was for 500cc machines to do a flying lap at 45mph and for 350s to lap at 40mph. There were also Test Hill runs. None of the 500s could reach the target, though a Douglas did manage the 350 lap.

The BMCRC opened its 1912 racing season on Wednesday 27 March, when its programme included the first cyclecar race to be held on the track. A three-lap event, it was an easy win for the Morgan-JAP of Harry Martin, which ran away from the Sabella-JAPs that came second and third.

The BARC Easter meeting was attended by Hornsted with a new works-supported 15-litre Benz. Lapping at 103.33mph he won the 100mph Long Handicap, and followed this with a second win in the Easter Sprint. Heavy rain caused the May meeting to be abandoned after two races, but the Summer meeting on 15 June continued despite rain and wind. *The Autocar* commented that the 'Half Crown Hill' was well filled with spectators. Malcolm Campbell, who had ridden a 500cc Triumph to third place at the Easter meeting, had

BELOW *Harry Martin (Morgan-Martin-JAP) waits on the start line for the first-ever cyclecar race at the track, at the BMCRC meeting on 27 March 1912. Martin was an easy winner. (Brooklands Society)*

bought a second Darracq, a 1906 10½-litre Vanderbilt Cup car which he called 'Blue Bird', the first of his many cars to carry this name, and this gave him wins in the 100mph Short Handicap and the Winners Handicap. A team of three 3-litre Sunbeams had swept the board in the Coupe de L'Auto at Dieppe in June and the three cars were invited to compete in a special sprint race at the July meeting, Dario Resta leading the trio home in a virtual demonstration run.

Encouraged by the success of the 1911 Production Car race, the RAC repeated it on Tuesday 16 July, but the rules were changed so that four-cylinder cars with a 90mm bore and therefore an RAC rating of 20.1hp were eligible. It attracted 14 entries but there were six non-starters, including two Sunbeams which were withdrawn as a non-standard higher axle ratio was not permitted, and the two successful Stars of 1911, which were disqualified as being too sporting. The Stars were only rejected by the scrutineers on the morning of the race, so there was no time to make the necessary changes to ensure eligibility. Consequently only eight cars took part in the 100-lap, 278-mile race. At the start, a French SCAR took the lead driven by Sidney Cummings, the English agent, and was clearly the fastest car competing, but after a few laps it dropped back with lubrication problems. The team of three Singers then led, pursued by another French entry, the Gladiator driven by Gordon Usmar. By lap 20 Usmar had been lapped by the Singer trio led by Haywood, but the Singers all stopped for water, which let Usmar regain the lost lap and take second place behind Haywood. The Gladiator only made one stop for oil and retained second place, while the Singers of Rollason and Geach dropped out with broken timing chains. The SCAR recovered sufficiently to record the fastest lap at 68.25mph before retiring with a broken propshaft.

Just when it seemed that Haywood could not be caught he had to stop, as the Singer's exhaust pipe had broken and was trailing on the ground. This let Usmar into the lead. Once going again the Singer closed the gap and took back the lead, only to make another stop for more exhaust repairs. With eight laps to go Usmar had a lead of 56sec, but Haywood was lapping seven seconds faster. At the start of the last lap the Gladiator was still in front, but Haywood took the lead on the Members' Banking. Still Usmar did not give up and he retook the lead on the Byfleet Banking, but as the cars ran to the line at the Fork Haywood eased ahead and won by 0.8sec. The Singer had averaged 57.49mph. There was only one other finisher, a

Turcat-Méry, which was one-and-a-half hours behind. The winner received £100, £40 was awarded for second place and the third place prize was £10. The race was adjudged a success but was not held again.

Although not in the RAC race the Sunbeams were on form, as Coatalen brought out 'Toodles IV' at the August Bank Holiday meeting and won the 100mph Long Handicap, while Bird, who had forsaken Napier for a Coupe de L'Auto Sunbeam, won the Private Competitors Handicap. There were two marque races for single-cylinder Le Zebres and for Model T Fords. The Model T race was won by Arthur George in a single-seater with a burnished copper body, and among the spectators was Henry Ford himself.

The BARC seemed reluctant to run long races and the O'Gorman Trophy at the October meeting,

run on 28 September, was the longest of the season. This was a scratch race over 10 laps limited to 3-litre cars. It attracted seven starters and was won by Percy Lambert in the Vauxhall which had been developed from 'KN', with an even slimmer body. In the only motor cycle race on the card, E.M. Remington crossed the line first on his Matchless-JAP then had a front brake failure and went up the banking and over the top. He was unhurt but the stewards disqualified him for not stopping in the prescribed distance! Among the motor cyclists it was considered that the accident pointed once more to the dangers of completing races in the Finishing Straight.

The BMCRC continued its monthly meetings in 1912, but at the second, on Saturday 20 April, there was a fatal accident, the first on a motor cycle at Brooklands. In the one-hour race, Arthur

ABOVE The 3-litre Coupe de l'Auto Sunbeam, driven by Dario Resta and Crossman, rejoins the track after a stop during the successful World 12-Hour Record run on 21 September 1912. (John Maitland Collection)

BELOW Alan Mander won the Sprint Handicap at the BARC meeting on 15 June 1912 in his 1908 GP Mercedes, fitted with a 13½-litre engine. (LAT)

Moorhouse on a 994cc Indian had made a bad start before coming through the field to take the lead. Then, coming off the Members Banking on lap seven the spindle nuts holding his back wheel loosened and the wheel canted. The machine came down the banking and hit a telegraph pole on the inside of the track. Moorhouse was killed instantly. It is said his friends buried the Indian on the site of the accident.

At the 1 June meeting there were three unusual races in which motor cycles – the winners of eliminating trials at the previous meeting – were matched against cars over three laps from a rolling start. The cars won all three races, a 3,047cc Cameron, a 2,694cc Bedford and a 9,237cc

BELOW *The Australian rider Les Bailey on his Douglas after taking the 350cc class flying start kilometre record on 17 December 1912. (Brooklands Society)*

Mercedes beating a 499cc Singer and 741cc and 998cc Matchless-JAPs respectively.

The longest motor cycle races of the season, the 150-mile Junior and Senior TT events, were held on 14 August. Only a handful of machines finished the Junior race and the stragglers were so slow that the Senior race was started while they were still on the course. The Senior race was a much more serious business and saw a battle between Charlie Collier on his Matchless-JAP and Jack Emerson riding a Norton. Emerson had not ridden at Brooklands before, but despite his lack of experience came home the winner.

The Open Championship meeting on 12 October had a one-hour cyclecar race which was won by J.T. Wood (GWK) who headed a Bedelia and a Sabella. At the final BMCRC meeting on 9 November there was a much grander sounding event for cyclecars and sidecars, the Olympic Passenger Machine Races. This was run for one hour and saw a runaway win for a Morgan-JAP driven by its constructor H.F.S. Morgan, who covered over 55 miles and finished over eight miles ahead of a Sabella. There were problems in the one-hour Senior race as Oliver Godfrey (Indian) and Sydney Garrett (Regal-Green) were battling wheel to wheel and it would be difficult to ascertain who was in front at the end of the 60 minutes. 'Ebby' solved the problem by sending his assistant to the top of the tower at the Fork with a synchronised stopwatch and binoculars. At the appointed time he noted Oliver was in front and he was declared the winner. By the time the machines had reached the Fork the order had changed and Garrett made a protest, but it was overruled and 'Ebby's' methods were upheld.

There was much record-breaking activity at the track during 1912, in which Sunbeams were most prominent. A Coupe de L'Auto 3-litre car was at the track on 17 September and as well as setting class records established World records for 400 miles, four hours and five hours. The highest speed was 79.78mph for the four hours. The run ended when the car ran a big-end after 412 miles, but it was out again four days later and took more class records and the World records for 900 miles, 1,000 miles, 12 hours and 13 hours. The 12-hour record was gained at 75.92mph. 'Toodles IV' came out on 15 October driven by Resta and took the World hour record at 92.45mph. But the coveted '100 in the hour' remained the ultimate target and Victor Hemery attempted it at the end of November in the 15-litre Lorraine-Dietrich which had run in the French GP the previous July. He set several class records and raised the hour figure to 97.57mph.

1913

Percy Lambert had joined Talbot and had taken class records at Brooklands in the autumn of 1912 with a 4,531cc 25hp Talbot fitted with a slim, single-seater body. As soon as the track reopened in February 1913 the Talbot arrived to attempt the hour record. Lambert made a run on Saturday 8 February, but a tyre burst and he stopped after taking the World 50-mile record. A week later he made another attempt. It was a misty day and the track was damp, but he started soon after 12:30 and the Talbot lapped steadily at 103/104mph. Lambert reeled off the laps and at the end of the 60 minutes had covered 103 miles 1,470 yards. The run had attracted many spectators, who warmly applauded Lambert and his landmark record. During the run he also established new World 50-mile and 100-mile records.

The BARC season began with the Easter meeting on 24 March, where the star turn was Jules Goux with a 7,603cc 1912 GP Peugeot, who won the 100mph Short handicap from Tate's 9,570cc 37/90 Mercedes and Crossman in 'Toodles IV'. The last race on the card was a sidecar and cyclecar handicap which was won by Wood (GWK) who just caught Barnes (Zenith Gradua-JAP sidecar) on the line to win by a mere yard.

Goux and his team stayed on at Brooklands and brought the Peugeot out for a record attempt. After an initial abortive run he came out again on

BELOW *Percy Lambert is acclaimed by his team and supporters on 16 February 1913 after becoming the first driver to cover 100 miles in the hour, and taking the World Hour Record at 103.84mph in his 4½-litre Talbot. His supporters seem to have been slightly optimistic. (Brooklands Society)*

ABOVE *Construction of the new tennis courts is almost finished in the spring of 1913. (LAT)*

RIGHT *Lambert's record did not stand for long, as Jules Goux in a 1912 GP Peugeot set a new figure of 106.22mph on 13 April 1913. (Brooklands Society)*

Wednesday 13 April and, in a spectacular run during which he dislodged bits of concrete from the banking rim, he set new World 50- and 100-mile records and, more importantly, took the 'Hour' at 106.22mph. This spurred the Clement-Talbot company and Lambert into action and the 25hp Talbot was back at the track a week before the Whitsun meeting. But the car was not running well, and after several practice runs which interrupted official practice for the Whitsun meeting it was taken away on a lorry. Rain forced the Whitsun meeting itself to be abandoned and the Benzole Handicap, intended to encourage the use of the new fuel, was held over until 21 June. J.H. Toop, driving a works Coupe de L'Auto Sunbeam with a short-stroke engine, was the winner from Hancock in a new Vauxhall 'KN2' based on a Prince Henry touring car.

Before the Whitsun meeting, the Argyll company brought a modified 2,614cc 15/30hp model to Brooklands with the intention of demonstrating that their sleeve-valve designs were reliable. With Hornsted and W.G. Scott as drivers, the car ran all day on 19 May and set a new World record for 14 hours, beating Edge's 1907 figure.

The team were so encouraged that the car was brought out again on 27 May and broke the World 12-hour record at 76.20mph and also took the World 1,000 mile record.

The popularity of Brooklands was shown when the August Bank Holiday meeting had 219 entries. The main event, the 100mph Handicap, was run in two heats and a final, in which Lambert in the 'Hour' Talbot, lapping at 112.68mph, beat Hancock's 'KN2' into second place. In the 75mph Short Handicap, W.O. Bentley, who had graduated to cars, was the winner in a DFP, for which he had become the English agent.

The 12-hour record set by Argyll in May was a tempting target and on 30 August, Hancock brought out 'KN2'. Starting the run in thick mist, which seemed to have little effect on his speed – he was lapping at nearly 90mph – he was running well despite minor problems when a front spring shackle casting broke and he was forced to stop. During the run he had taken the World 700-mile record at 87.74mph. Sunbeam also had an eye on the Argyll record, and on 2 October introduced a new car to Brooklands, the 4,254cc model which

ABOVE *The start of the second beat of the Public Schools' Handicap at the BMCRC meeting on 26 April 1913. (Brooklands Society)*

had run in the French GP in July. Fitted with a single-seater body, it broke World records from two hours to 12 hours, from 200 miles to 1,000 miles, and from 250km to 1,700km. During a hard day's drive Jean Chassagne, Dario Resta and Kenelm Lee Guinness broke 36 World records. But Louis Coatalen had devised a much more potent machine, 'Toodles V'. This was a 9,048cc V12, the first V12 car to be built in Europe. It made its debut

at the BARC October meeting when it won a 100mph Handicap lapping at 117.46mph. Then on 10 October Chassagne took another clutch of World records with it, from 50 miles to 200km, including the Hour at 107.95mph.

Keen to regain the Hour record the Clement Talbot company enlarged the engine of its 25hp Talbot to 4,754cc and Lambert did tests and took the World 50-mile and 50km records. Then on

RIGHT *The start of a relay race at the RAC Associated Clubs meeting on 31 May 1913. (Brooklands Society)*

Friday 31 October he made another attempt on the Hour. The Talbot was lapping steadily at 110mph when, on the 21st lap, a tyre burst on the Members' Banking. The car swerved and overturned and Lambert was killed instantly. He was 31 years old and had promised his fiancée that after the run he would give up high speed motoring. His Hour record at the start of the year had made him a Brooklands hero, so the motoring world was deeply saddened by his death.

The BMCRC continued to be ambitious in 1913 and on 16 July it ran the longest race yet to be held at the track, a six-hour event for motor cycles, sidecars and cyclecars. There were strict rules that repairs could only be made at the pits, which were set up at the Fork. The 50 starters were divided into capacity classes, but soon after the 11:38am start Jack Haswell took his 500cc Triumph into the overall lead. He was slowed by a flat tyre and the first to complete 50 laps was Cyril Pullin (500cc Rudge-Multi), but at the three-hour mark Haswell led from Pullin and Hugh Mason (350cc NUT-JAP). Haswell still held the lead when he and Mason both made stops at the beginning of the last hour. Mason was away first but made another stop to replace a valve cotter, and Haswell then stayed in front to the finish, having averaged 58.62mph. Pullin was second home, and Mason was third, winning the 350cc class by a big margin. G.W. Hands (Calthorpe) won the cyclecar class, his average of 51.78mph making an interesting comparison with the speed of the winning Singer in the previous year's RAC Standard Car race.

There was a one-hour cyclecar race at the BMCRC championship meeting on 18 October. Hands took an immediate lead and pulled away from the field until his Calthorpe's differential broke after 16 laps, leaving the race to Hayward's 1,096cc Singer, which averaged 62.31mph. But Hands had the last word, as on 23 October, despite thick fog, he took class records from four to six hours and from 250 to 400 miles with the repaired Calthorpe.

ABOVE The start of the longest race yet held at Brooklands, the BMCRC Six-Hour Race on 16 July 1913. (Brooklands Society)

LEFT During October 1913 there were several record attempts, so the fuel companies set up temporary stations on the paddock entrance road. Here, Jean Chassagne is filling-up before his successful 'Hour' run in the 9,048cc V-12 Sunbeam on 10 October. (Brooklands Society)

1914

By 1914 motoring had grown from being a pastime for the well-to-do. Motor cars were becoming a means of transport for the more prosperous middle classes and an accepted fact of life for most of the population. It was recognised that many medical practitioners would visit their patients by car, and in London the motor bus and the taxi cab had replaced horse-drawn vehicles. Brooklands was no longer a novelty and was attracting a substantial nucleus of enthusiasts as well as being a social milieu. The world was prosperous and social conditions for the less fortunate, although still

hard, were improving and the glass seemed to be set at fair for the foreseeable future. The Balkans was a scene of continuing unrest and there had been threats of war, but despite an arms race led by Britain and Germany few believed that a major conflict was likely, or even possible. Political unrest in Ireland seemed of much greater significance.

Before the racing season began there was an early flurry of record-breaking. On Tuesday 13 January, Jack Emerson, riding a 500cc horizontal-twin ABC, broke the international class flying-start mile and kilometre records at 78.26mph and 80.47mph respectively, the first time a 500cc motor cycle had officially exceeded 80mph. To enter the measured distance on the Railway Straight at maximum speed Emerson rode high on the Members' Banking and dived off it. Hornsted was on the track at the time, testing the 200hp Benz, and had to brake sharply to avoid a collision with him. The 21½-litre Benz, which was to become a legendary car, had been sent to England by the Benz factory in October 1913. As early as 22 December Hornsted had set World half-mile and kilometre records with it and on 14 January he brought it out and took a clutch of records for the World two-, five- and ten-mile and kilometre distances at speeds from 116.08mph to 122.05mph, and set a new local Class J record for the mile at 123.54mph.

The racing season opened with a BMCRC meeting on 28 March where the main event was a 100-mile high-speed reliability trial for cyclecars, supported by a series of three-lap motor cycle races. The prize money for the motor cycles was always better at the BARC meetings, so the Easter Monday meeting had full entries for the two motor cycle handicaps. Prize money for cars had also been increased and the winner of a Lightning Long Handicap now received £60, while the winner of a Short Handicap took home £50.

The Easter meeting attracted two interesting entries, a 1913 8,325cc GP Itala which had a rotary valve engine and won a Long Handicap at over 100mph, and, even more exciting, an Opel which was intended for the 1914 French GP and had been sent from Germany for a preliminary outing. Driven by Carl Joerns it started from scratch in a 100mph Long Handicap and finished third, lapping at 99.41mph. Brooklands was still the only venue where a car could be given an extended full throttle run and such a test gave the Opel team much valuable information.

The BMCRC's meeting on 2 May saw a new record during the time trials which began the event. Sidney George recorded 93.48mph for the flying start kilometre on his 994cc eight-valve Indian,

BELOW *The Prince Henry Vauxhall of Lyndhurst Bruce battles with the DFP of W.O. Bentley at the 1914 Easter meeting. (LAT)*

breaking Charlie Collier's record and setting the fastest speed yet for a motor cycle at the track.

'Cupid' Hornsted's aim was the World Hour record and he made several attempts at it in the spring of 1914 but was defeated by tyre failure on each occasion. The BARC Whitsun meeting drew a big crowd and saw the abolition of the rule that drivers should wear coloured smocks, the cars being identified in the programme by their colour scheme as well as a racing number. The BARC ran meetings which it felt would entertain the public, so short races were the usual fare, but the BMCRC was more adventurous. Its meetings only attracted small crowds comprised of keen motor cycling enthusiasts, so it laid on events which would appeal to such aficionados as well as to the competitors. It ran an ambitious meeting on 13 June. There were only two races on the programme, each of 56 laps (152 miles). These were the Junior and Senior Brooklands TT races for 350cc and 500cc machines of the type which had competed in the Isle of Man TT. Each race had two classes, for riders who had ridden in the TT and for those who had not. The Junior race, run in the morning, attracted 13 starters and was won by Cyril Williams on an AJS, who averaged 53.99mph and finished ahead of Keyte on a Royal Enfield. The Senior race, run after lunch, had 25 starters and victory went to Charles Collier on a V-twin MAG-engined Matchless after a battle with a Norton ridden by W.T. McKenna (the son of Reginald McKenna MP, the Home Secretary). After the Norton dropped out with a burst cylinder Collier went on to win from the ABC of Jack Emerson, having averaged 60.84mph.

A week later Brooklands was the scene of a great mock drama, a Field Day in aid of the Chertsey Division of the British Red Cross, where army detachments held the track against attacking forces with the support of aircraft from the Royal Flying Corps. The centre of the track became a casualty clearing station and members of the newly-formed Voluntary Aid Detachment practised their nursing skills on the 'casualties'. All this happened with a Royal presence, as Queen Alexandra came to watch accompanied by her sister the Dowager Czarina Marie Fedorovna of Russia. Also present was Field Marshal Lord Roberts. It all seemed great and relatively innocent fun, but was an unwitting foretaste of what was soon to come. It was reported that Queen Alexandra wanted to see racing cars in action but was disappointed.

Four days later, on Wednesday 24 June, Hornsted made another attempt on the Hour record with the dark blue 200hp Benz but had to stop when a tyre tread was thrown, hitting him on

the elbow. Slightly bruised but undaunted, after a lunch break he brought the Benz out again to attempt the flying mile record and thus take the World Land Speed Record. The AIACR had altered the rules in 1911 and decreed that for a record to be recognised there had to be two runs in opposite directions. On his first run he entered the measured distance on the Railway Straight from the Byfleet Banking and covered it at 120.28mph. He then made the second run in the usual direction of the track and his speed was 128.16mph, taking the World Land Speed record at an average of 124.10mph. However his record was not recognised everywhere, as single runs were still accepted in the USA and Bob Burman had apparently gone faster there in a Benz, but in Europe it was accepted as the fastest and Burman subsequently admitted that his 'mile' may have been slightly short. This feat, together with Hemery's earlier record, must have made Hugh Locke King feel that all the tribulations of building the track were justified.

On Sunday 28 June the Archduke Ferdinand of Austria and his wife were assassinated while visiting Sarajevo in Serbia. To the few elements of the British public who took note of, or even heard of, the shooting it was yet another minor Balkan incident and there was no likelihood of it impinging on their settled way of life. On the

ABOVE *G.H. Fry's passenger looks relaxed after his victory with his 499cc Rudge-Multi in the Sidecar Sprint Handicap at the BMCRC meeting on 2 May 1914. (Brooklands Society)*

following Tuesday, 30 June, the Oxford and Cambridge Clubs held the Inter-Varsity meeting which had been postponed since 21 March. It was a combined car/motor cycle meeting and E.H. Lees won two races on a 500cc ABC, while amongst the successful car drivers were two who would become prominent at a later date. The two-lap cyclecar race was won by a Singer driven by Lionel Martin, later to be the instigator of Aston Martin; and an Isotta-Fraschini was also a winner, driven by Humphrey Cook, later to be a co-founder of ERA.

The BMCRC meeting on 25 July had some close racing and there was a fierce battle in the ten-mile 500cc solo race when O'Donovan (Norton) just pipped Stanley (Triumph). Afterwards Stanley said he had let O'Donovan through thinking it was his Triumph team-mate Jimmy Cocker, who was in third place. In the ten-mile cyclecar race Lionel Martin (Singer) won again, just heading E.B. Ware (Morgan). By now the rumblings of an impending conflict were all too apparent, but few could have realised that this would be the last BMCRC meeting for six years.

Bank Holiday Monday, 3 August, saw big crowds flocking into Brooklands. The previous day Germany had demanded that Belgium should give the German army free access across its territory to attack France, and that afternoon

BELOW *A tented encampment is pitched at the foot of the Members' Hill for the British Red Cross Field Day on 20 June 1914. (LAT)*

Germany issued a formal declaration of war against France. British involvement seemed inevitable and everyone at Brooklands realised that the time for wishful optimism was over and the meeting was likely to be the last for some time. Even while it was on troop trains could be seen proceeding along the L&SWR line. Two GP Opels were among the cars that had been entered that day, but although they were still in the paddock their driver, Carl Joerns, had departed rapidly for Germany.

The day began with sunshine, but in keeping with the general mood dark clouds steadily built up. There were two motor cycle races and in the second, the Short Handicap over two laps, there were 44 starters and Eddie Kirkham on a Douglas was the winner. The fastest race of the day, the Lightning Long Handicap, was won by Dario Resta in the V12 Sunbeam at 106.88mph; he lapped at 113.97mph, the fastest lap of the season. The meeting ended with a sprint handicap in which Nicholson's Alfonso model Hispano-Suiza was the winner from Sandford's Bedford-Buick, while Malcolm Campbell was third in a Gregoire. It would be six years before cars raced on the track again and many who had been there on that memorable Monday would not see a motor race again.

BELOW 'Cupid' Hornsted's 'Blitzen' Benz is swung into action for his Land Speed Record run on 24 June 1914. (Brooklands Society)

BOTTOM 'Cupid' Hornsted's passenger looks bashful as the pair pose for the camera in the Land Speed Record 'Blitzen' Benz. (Brooklands Society)

FLEDGLING FLYING

Brooklands can claim to be the birthplace of British aviation, and the first tentative flying enterprise occurred before the track was even completed. A bizarre Frenchman, Bellamy, appeared at the track site in December 1906 with a biplane, mostly constructed of bamboo with a 35hp Panhard pusher engine, and told Locke King that he had already been a successful aviator in France and wanted to be the first to fly in England. Locke King loaned him £100 to meet his expenses and a piece of ground parallel to the L&SWR line was rolled flat as a runway. The machine was kept under the Seven Arch Bridge which carried the railway line over the River Wey and a huge tent was erected to house it. But the Bellamy machine never flew. Initially it was mounted on a pair of punts and was taxied on a lake in the grounds of Brooklands House, but the punts hit an underwater obstruction and the whole contraption sank. Bellamy then reconstructed the machine with wheels and proposed to fly it from within the track, but subsequently disappeared and set up a new camp near Richmond, leaving a string of debts in the Weybridge area.

The suggestion, possibly stimulated by the Bellamy fiasco, that the centre of the track should be a flying ground was already being discussed while the construction of the track was being completed. Soon after its formation the BARC had offered a prize of £2,500 to the first aviator to fly a

A Sopwith Tabloid in 1914, one of the first Sopwith designs flown at Brooklands. (BAE Systems per Brooklands Museum)

ABOVE *The first Brooklands flying venture in December 1906. Bellamy stands on top of his ineffective machine. (Getty Images)*

complete circuit of the track before the end of 1907. Cynics said that the club realised its money was safe, but it was excellent publicity. Attracted by the possible prize, Alliott Verdon Roe asked if he could build a shed to house an aircraft which he had constructed in a garage at Putney. He had a meeting with Rodakowski (who he described as 'a belligerent character, who was entirely sceptical of the possibility of flight'), who agreed reluctantly that Roe could build a shed at his own expense beside the Finishing Straight. The shed was 40ft long and 20ft wide and the aircraft, called the 'Avroplane', could only be pushed into it sideways.

Roe having prepared his machine, in September 1907 it was pulled to the top of the Members' Banking. With its borrowed 9hp JAP engine at full throttle, it rolled down the banking onto the Finishing Straight but was capable of no more than propelling itself forwards. For a while John Moore-Brabazon established himself in a shed beside Roe, on the Finishing Straight, and the pair eyed each other suspiciously, knowing that they were rivals for the prize, but Moore-Brabazon's aircraft – a glider built by the Short brothers and fitted with a

Buchet engine – was too flimsy even to taxi on the track surface and he left to continue his experiments elsewhere. Roe, meanwhile, was having problems with Rodakowski, who appears to have considered that he was giving Brooklands the wrong kind of image, possibly because Roe was living in his shed and subsisting on the most meagre rations. Though he was ordered to move the shed to the other side of the paddock he continued his experiments, greatly aided by the loan of a 24hp eight-cylinder Antoinette engine, until on 8 June 1908 he found that he had taken to the air while taxiing. He reputedly flew for about 150ft, but the aircraft was subsequently wrecked when it was dropped by his helpers while being lifted over the railings onto the track.

Although his accomplishment has never been officially recognised it is now accepted by many that Roe may have been the first man to design, build and fly a powered aircraft in this country. To replace his wrecked machine he next built a triplane, but this crashed in the centre of the track during testing, so Rodakowski stepped in and gave him three weeks' notice to leave. Roe departed, selling his shed for £15.

On Sunday 5 July 1909 Louis Blériot flew across the English Channel and there was a national awakening to the fact that aviation was a reality. With this stimulus the BARC embraced flying with enthusiasm, perhaps encouraged by Major Lindsay Lloyd, the new Clerk of the Course, who appreciated that aviation went hand-in-hand with motoring at Brooklands. But the real stimulus came from George Holt Thomas, the proprietor of *The Graphic* newspaper, who had seen the enthusiasm for flying in France and appreciated its possibilities. He was the British agent for the French Farman biplane and arranged for one to attend the Blackpool Aviation Meeting on 18 October 1909. He suggested to Locke King that the Farman should be flown at Brooklands, so the ground inside the track at the Byfleet end was cleared and a shed was erected to house the aircraft.

A meeting was organised at Brooklands on 28, 29 and 30 October, at which the Farman pusher 'La Gypaète' would be flown by its French pilot, Louis Paulhan. An expensive 20-page programme was produced, with a light blue cover showing a photograph of 'the celebrated aviator Paulhan'. In his first flights, in front of a crowd estimated at 20,000, Paulhan reached a height of 720ft. He flew the Farman again on 1 November and then made a flight of 96 miles which broke the British distance record. It was hoped that the venture would be profitable, but despite the big attendance Holt Thomas's ten per cent share of the gate money was only £18. While Paulhan was at Brooklands he took Ethel Locke King for a flight as his passenger.

Encouraged by the Farman flight, the levelling of the Byfleet end was completed in the autumn and rows of sheds were built to house aircraft. In November leases were offered to tenants at rents of £100 per annum or £10 per month, and by May 1910 seventeen sheds had been built and were occupied by 22 aircraft. By the end of 1910 at least 30 sheds had been built and let. The tenants were allowed unlimited use of the flying ground and among the first to return was Roe, who flew his new triplane 'Mercury' on 17 April – and crashed again.

BELOW A.V. Roe stands inside his shed on the Finishing Straight in 1907, with his first aircraft, perhaps waiting for a visit from de Rodakowski. (Brooklands Society)

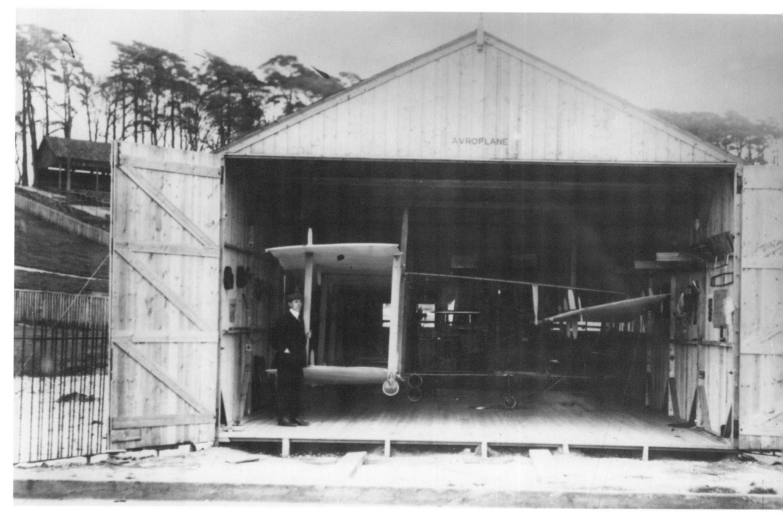

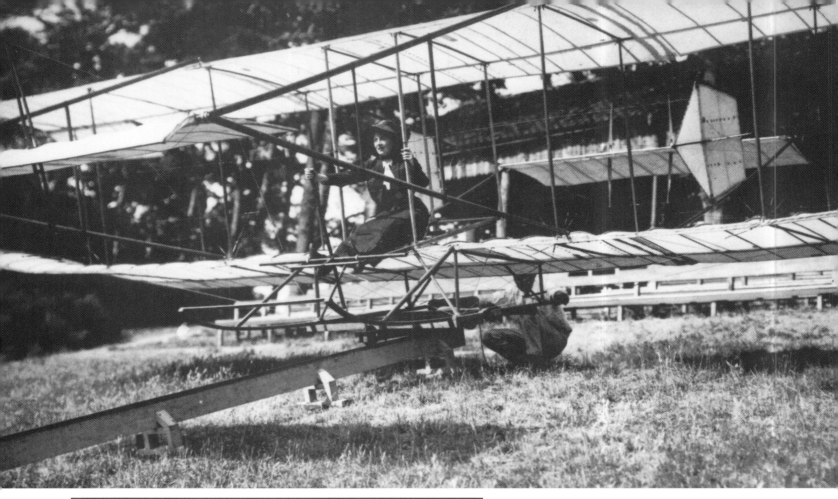

Sir Thomas Sopwith

Thomas Sopwith was born in 1888 and studied engineering at Lee-on-Solent. He came to Brooklands in 1910 and after having a flight with Gustav Blondeau he bought a Howard Wright biplane and taught himself to fly it, gaining his RAeC certificate in November 1910. In December that year he won the Baron de Forest prize of £4,000 for making the longest flight from a point in England to anywhere in Europe when he flew from Dover to the far side of Belgium. In 1912 he established the Sopwith Flying School at Brooklands, and then founded Sopwith Aviation in 1913, which was based at Kingston-upon-Thames, though all the aircraft built by the company were flown at Brooklands.

An immediate success was gained when the Sopwith Tabloid won the 1914 Schneider Trophy, and the company became a leading manufacturer during World War One, first with the 1½-Strutter, then the Pup, Camel, Snipe and Dolphin. Tax demands forced Sopwith Aviation into liquidation in 1920, and Tommy Sopwith then formed H.G. Hawker Engineering, based at Kingston but with sheds and hangars at Brooklands. Hawker prospered during the 1920s and 1930s and grew into the Hawker-Siddeley Group in 1935, with Sopwith as Chairman. Hawker-Siddeley remained at Brooklands until 1942.

Away from aviation, Sopwith was a keen yachtsman and made two unsuccessful challenges for the America's Cup in 1934 and 1937. He was knighted in 1953 and died in 1989 aged 101. Although he was not personally active at Brooklands after 1914 he was frequently at the track, and attended the first flight of the Hurricane in 1935. In addition his companies remained a centre of aviation activity there for 30 years.

Flying was quickly accepted as a pastime and at the 1910 Easter Monday meeting the BARC offered a prize for the best flight of more than 50 yards. The winner was Lionel Mander, who flew 500 yards in a Blériot, though his success was slightly marred when he hit a badly parked roller while landing. Reliability and duration improved rapidly and at the Whit Monday meeting there was a 12-mile handicap race around the circumference of the track. It was run in two heats and a final and the winner was Fred Raynham in an Avro biplane, followed by Collyns Pizey in a Bristol biplane.

Growing enthusiasm for flying brought forward eager pupils, and by the end of 1910 eight small flying schools had been established at Brooklands where aspiring pilots could qualify for a Royal Aero Club pilot's certificate: by the beginning of 1911 some 50 had qualified. Alongside the flying field, inside the track, was a sewage farm which had been there when the track construction began. This seemed to have a fatal and magnetic attraction for the pioneer pilots and it was said that a pilot was not fully qualified until he had crashed into the sewage farm and subsequently been decontaminated. One of Roe's later triplanes which was used for tuition at the A.V. Roe Flying School was said to have spent more time in the sewage farm than in the air.

One of the schools was opened by a French pilot, Gustav Blondeau, in partnership with Hilda Hewlett, the first qualified British woman pilot, who received her licence in August 1911. But the first woman to 'fly' at Brooklands was a Mrs Gavin, who in July 1910 piloted a glider from a gliding school run by Charles Lane on the Members' Hill. As well as lessons, Hewlett & Blondeau offered short flights for £5, and in the summer of 1910 one of their customers was a 21-year-old yachting enthusiast Tommy Sopwith, who was instantly captivated. He bought a Blériot-type Avis monoplane which was being marketed at £630, and it was delivered to him at Brooklands on 21 October. He immediately made several short 'hops', then crashed. But Sopwith was undaunted. The Avis was repaired and flown again, and another crash followed. Sopwith then bought a Howard Wright Farman-Type pusher and this arrived at Brooklands on 21 November. He flew it immediately without instruction and this time there were no mishaps and he qualified for his pilot's certificate.

During the autumn of 1910, there was keen competition to win the British Empire Michelin Cup and a prize of £500 for the greatest distance covered by a British pilot and aircraft over a closed circuit before the end of the year. Sopwith confidently believed he was the winner when he covered 150.14 miles in 4hr 7min at Brooklands on 31 December, but his distance was exceeded by Samuel Franklin Cody, flying at Farnborough later the same day.

There was some dispute abut the price of passenger flights until Keith Prowse, the London ticket agents, opened an office at Brooklands in 1911 and charged a fixed rate for tickets. A short flight of about five minutes was two guineas (£2 2s), three circuits of the airfield was four guineas, and a short cross-country flight was ten guineas.

Though the BARC provided the clubhouse for its members there was no comparable facility for flyers, so the venue where news and gossip was exchanged and business was often done was the 'Blue Bird' café. Converted from the shed erected to house Paulhan's Farman during its 1909 demonstration, this was run by Mrs Eardley Billing and her husband. As well as food and drink the café could provide sleeping accommodation for up to ten. The Billings had two glamorous daughters who helped in the café and were an added attraction of the premises. Both girls were frequently taken for short flights.

Brooklands did not have a monopoly of flying, as in 1909 the Royal Aero Club had taken a lease on a field at Eastchurch in Kent and there was friendly rivalry between the pilots. The possibility of watching aeroplanes in flight became an

LEFT *Mrs Gavin, the first woman to 'fly' at Brooklands, about to take off in a glider from the Members' Hill in July 1910. (Getty Images)*

BELOW *The first flying sheds in 1911. (Brooklands Society)*

attraction for spectators, even if no sporting event had been arranged, and there was an immediate guide to flying activity. If a black flag was raised on the aerodrome office conditions were unsuitable for flying; a white flag indicated that flying might take place; and a red flag showed that there would be flying.

In 1910 several embryo aircraft manufacturers were working in the sheds in what became know as 'The Flying Village' and they made much use of the engineering facilities in the Itala factory, where the manager F.W. Thorpe was always willing to help the aviators. Humber, the car manufacturer, had a shed, and others were let to companies and individuals with names which would soon achieve household fame, including Thomas Sopwith, the British & Colonial Aeroplane Co (Bristol), Martin & Handasyde, and Vickers, which would subsequently play a crucial part in the Brooklands story.

Vickers had begun aircraft manufacture in 1911, at a small factory at Erith in Kent, and initially made the French REP under licence. The first Vickers aircraft, known as 'No. 1', was a modified and greatly improved REP. This was finished in the summer of 1911 and was taken to Brooklands for its first flight. Its designer, Major Archibald Lowe, intended to be the pilot, but Herbert Wood, who was in charge of the project, entrusted the machine to another pilot who crashed the aircraft on take-off, fortunately without injury. The damaged 'No. 1' was repaired in the Vickers shed and Lowe subsequently resigned. Wood, who had previously worked for Bristol, began to recruit Bristol design staff to work in the Vickers shed at Brooklands and one of these, Geoffrey Challenger, was given the task of redesigning the Bristol Boxkite as a trainer for use in the Vickers flying school. Not only had Bristol lost its staff, but it had seen its design lifted too!

At the beginning of 1911 the BARC and the owners of Hendon aerodrome put up £50 jointly, consisting of a £30 first prize and £20 second prize, for the pilots flying from Brooklands to Hendon and back, or vice versa, in the shortest time on the same day. The trial was held on four Saturdays in February and March and the winner of the first prize was Gustav Hamel in a Blériot XI.

On 6 May 1911 the first Brooklands to Brighton race was held, after three postponements owing to stormy weather. It was a handicap with a prize of £80 and there were four starters. The winner was Hamel in his Blériot, who took 57min 10sec for the flight, circling the balloon on Brighton Palace Pier which marked the finish and landing at Shoreham. The following day, to the acclamation of a large crowd, Hamel received the £80 prize from the Mayoress of Brighton.

Air racing received a big boost when the *Daily Mail* announced that it was to sponsor a Round Britain Air Race which was to start from Brooklands on Saturday 22 July 1911, with a prize of £10,000 going to the winner. This race attracted 30 entries and 21 pilots took part. *Flight* commented: 'A few years ago, crowds used to assemble to see a motor car, and the generation that introduced the automobile is now assembled in honour of the aeroplane. Brooklands itself was built for the car, yet it is the aeroplane that attracts most people to its grounds. How soon and to what extent will the aeroplane invade the territory of the car as a useful and everyday sort of vehicle, must have been a question in the minds of many of those who looked on at the start of the Circuit of Britain on Saturday.'

The course went via Hendon to Edinburgh with intermediate stops at Harrogate and Newcastle-upon-Tyne, and then returned via Bristol with stops at Stirling, Glasgow, Carlisle and Manchester. The last leg was from Bristol to Shoreham and thence to Brooklands. It was reported that a crowd of 50,000 watched the start at Brooklands, including

LEFT *A Bristol Boxkite is pulled out of the Bristol School.* (Brooklands Museum)

LEFT *The Vickers Flying School in 1912.* (Brooklands Museum)

Fledgling flying **59**

ABOVE *The Blue Bird Restaurant in 1913. The Keith Prowse Flight Ticket Office is on the right. (Brooklands Museum)*

Prince Henry of Prussia, the Kaiser's brother, who was accompanied by General von Neiber of the German Army general staff. Two aircraft crashed on take-off and Roe's entry had already crashed on a test flight on the morning of the race, but 17 aircraft took off on the first leg to Hendon. The race was closely contested all the way by two French pilots, Jules Védrines in a Morane-Borel and André Beaumont in a Blériot. The pair landed in the dark at Bristol and on the last day, Wednesday 26 July, Beaumont left Bristol at 4:50am and Védrines was two minutes behind him. Védrines led at Salisbury, but on the last leg from Shoreham Beaumont went to the front and arrived at Brooklands at 2:07pm, seven minutes ahead of his rival. Beaumont was feted when he landed and the following day was presented to King George V at Buckingham Palace. The first British pilot to finish was James Valentine in a Deperdussin.

The first fatal flying accident at Brooklands occurred in August 1911, when Gerald Napier in a Bristol Biplane stalled when turning sharply at about 50ft. He was killed instantly. The plane was a single-seater but Napier had rigged up a temporary seat for a passenger, who escaped with minor injuries. There were seven meetings at the track in 1911 and a total of £803 prize money was distributed. Awards were given for flights of over 15

minutes and prizes for the three best aggregate flights of the season. A standard of reliability had been reached where regular handicap races were organised throughout the spring and summer of 1912. The first was on Saturday 13 April over a six-mile course to Chertsey Bridge and back. The winner was Collyns Pizey in a Bristol Boxkite, who finished in front of the scratch pilot, Tommy Sopwith in a Blériot, while Fisher (Flanders) was third. The next day another race was held over a nine-mile course and this was won by Sopwith. The 1912 competition season continued at Brooklands until Sunday 24 November, ending with the two-lap Speed Handicap. The winner was John Alcock flying a Henry Farman in his first race. Seven years later he would achieve immortality as the first man to fly the Atlantic Ocean.

Aviation in Britain received a tremendous boost in April 1912 when the Royal Flying Corps was formed. This had an immediate effect at Brooklands as it was arranged that military and naval pilots would receive their basic training at a civilian flying school and obtain their RAeC certificate before going on to the newly formed Central Flying School. One of the early pupils at the Sopwith School, who obtained his brevet on 31 July, was Major Hugh Trenchard, subsequently to become 'the father of the RAF'. A growing appreciation throughout the world of the military applications of flying brought a steady flow of foreign pupils to the Brooklands schools. With the formation of the RFC came the establishment of the Royal Aircraft Factory at Farnborough that became the centre of technical development in Britain, although Brooklands was still the principal centre for testing and for sporting flying.

In the autumn of 1912, Tommy Sopwith, encouraged by his chief engineer Fred Sigrist and perhaps hoping for RFC contracts, began to ponder on the possibility of becoming a manufacturer. The Burgess-Wright which was used at the Sopwith School was modified in the Sopwith shed by Sigrist, with an ABC engine. With Harry Hawker as the pilot, on 24 October it won the British Empire Michelin Cup for endurance, with a flight lasting 8hr 23min.

A.V. Roe received orders for nine of his own new design, the Type 500 biplane with a Gnome engine. With the need for space in the shed, the four aircraft of the Avro flying school were moved to Shoreham. Roe was not resting on his laurels, and work at his Manchester factory continued on a successor to the 500. This was brought to Brooklands for its first flight in July 1913. This aircraft, the 504, was to become one of the all-time flying legends, and with development was to serve the RFC and RAF for more than 20 years, as well as being flown by countless civilian pilots.

There was no space at Brooklands for Sopwith to manufacture aircraft, so he started work in an old skating rink at Kingston-upon-Thames, but all his aircraft were taken to Brooklands to be erected and flown. The new company soon made its mark when, on 31 May 1913, Hawker in a three-seater Sopwith Olympia, approaching the height limit without oxygen, set a new British altitude record at 11,450ft.

The first major Sopwith design was the Tabloid. This aircraft, notably small, first flew at Brooklands in November the same year, and with quick development at the track, and fitted with floats, was taken to Monte Carlo in April 1914 for the Schneider Trophy, recognised as a key demonstration of national superiority in aircraft design. Flown by Howard Pixton, the Tabloid was the winner.

Racing continued at Brooklands in 1913 and John Alcock was winner of the 50 guinea prize

ABOVE The Ticket Office, in front of the Blue Bird Restaurant, with a Boxkite flying overhead. (Brooklands Society)

BELOW A view of the airfield in 1913. (Brooklands Society)

given by British Petroleum for the Easter Aeroplane handicap on 24 March. On Whit Monday, Hawker won the 12-mile Cross-Country handicap in a Sopwith Three-seater, though wind and rain reduced the field to three starters.

A major feat of early pilots was to perform a loop. This was first done by Adolph Pégoud in France, flying a Blériot, early in 1913, and it was subsequently announced that he would come to Brooklands to give a demonstration. Pégoud and his aircraft arrived during the summer, but several weeks of testing followed before, with Louis Blériot in attendance, the feat was finally performed on Saturday 25 September, to huge acclaim from a crowd said to be the biggest yet seen at the track. A few weeks earlier Pégoud had achieved another feat in France when he used a parachute for the first time and successfully made a descent from an aircraft.

Noel Pemberton-Billing, the brother of the proprietor of the 'Blue Bird' café, was an entrepreneur who arrived in aviation in 1909 when he bought 3,000 acres of marshland at Fambridge in Essex, hoping it could be used as an airfield. It was said of him that he had wealth which 'he acquired by buying luxury yachts with money he had not got and selling them for cash to people who did not

want them'. He attempted to interest a youthful Frederick Handley Page in the Fambridge ground without success and the scheme faded away. Years later, in 1914, Handley Page extolled the virtues of the stability of his 'Yellow Peril' monoplane to Pemberton-Billing and said that with such a machine anyone could learn to fly in 24 hours. But Pemberton-Billing said stability was immaterial: 'Any man who had enough sense to come in out of the wet could learn to fly a known flying machine in one summer's day.' A wager was struck for £500 and soon after dawn the following morning Pemberton-Billing knocked up Warren Merriam, the chief instructor of the Bristol flying school at Brooklands, and explained his requirement. Merriam refused to take responsibility for the request and referred him to the Vickers school; but Bertie Wood, in charge of the school, was also unwilling to take on the task. Immediately Pemberton-Billing bought the oldest Farman at Brooklands and persuaded Harold Barnwell, one of the Vickers instructors, to accompany him on a first flight. After 25 minutes Barnwell let him go solo. Rain then intervened but when it stopped, Barnwell gave some additional dual instruction on the art of turning, then sent for the RAeC observer. Meanwhile Pemberton-Billing

BELOW *Hubert Latham's Antoinette undershoots into a shed roof in January 1911. (Brooklands Society)*

ABOVE *Tommy Sopwith.*
(Brooklands Society)

had narrowly avoided a crash, but when the observer appeared he carried out the requisite tests and received his certificate. Handley Page paid up, and spurred by his success Pemberton-Billing found premises at Southampton and opened his own manufacturing company, Supermarine. Unhappily not all the pupils had the good fortune of Pemberton-Billing, and C. Lindsay Campbell was killed on 3 August 1912 when he crashed a Bristol monoplane.

By 1914 the RFC was expanding rapidly, as it was realised that if war came in Europe aeroplanes would have a vital role to play. The earlier generation had consisted of sporting machines which could be adapted for military purposes, but this was changing. Now manufacturers were looking at designs intended for purely military use. Vickers, produced the EFB3, which became known as the 'Gunbus', and this was tested by Harold Barnwell at Brooklands. It was also realised that the Army and the Royal Navy had different aviation needs, so in May 1914 the Royal Flying Corps became a wholly army unit and the Royal Naval Air Service (RNAS) was formed. All airships were transferred to the RNAS. No 1 Squadron RFC had been an airship unit, so as a temporary measure it was restyled 'Airship Detachment RFC' and transferred from Farnborough to Brooklands as a cadre unit, with two officers and 13 other ranks, to await reforming with aircraft.

There were fewer air races at the track in 1914, but the Whitsun meeting gave an opportunity for manufacturers to test and display their military aircraft. In the Whitsun Aeroplane Handicap, the Tabloid flown by Sopwith himself and the Bristol Scout flown by Lord Carbery both competed. In the June Aeroplane Handicap, Barnwell flew the 'Gunbus'.

While the prospect of RFC and RNAS orders was attracting most manufacturers, for some there was another allurement: the *Daily Mail* had offered a £10,000 for the first successful flight across the Atlantic. Taking up the challenge, Scottish financier MacKay Edgar approached the public's favourite glamorous flying hero, Gustav Hamel, and suggested that he should pilot an aircraft which Edgar would sponsor. This would be manufactured by Martin & Handasyde, who had been one of the first tenants in the 'Village' – making aircraft under the 'Martinsyde' name – and had a reputation for high quality workmanship. Edgar's order was for a 65ft wingspan monoplane powered by a 12-cylinder 215hp Sunbeam engine. It was the largest aeroplane yet designed in Britain and construction had already begun when Hamel disappeared on 23 May during a flight from France to England in a new Morane-Saulnier monoplane, which he was to fly in the Hendon Aerial Derby. With his death the project came to a halt.

CHAPTER FOUR

1914–1918 WAR

I mmediately the First World War began Hugh
Locke King offered Brooklands to the War
Office, and the RFC took possession of the
track and flying ground on 5 August. The remaining
BARC and BMCRC fixtures were cancelled and
Major Lindsay Lloyd was recalled to his regiment.
The RFC had a mere 63 aircraft at the outbreak of
war and the RNAS had 50, with six airships, so
expansion was imperative. No 1 Squadron RFC was
embodied on 14 August and was equipped with
Farman 'Shorthorns' and Bristol and Vickers
Boxkites commandeered from the flying schools.
The 'Blue Bird' café became the officers' mess, but
was unfortunately destroyed by fire in March 1917.

In the years before the war, more pupils had
qualified to fly at Brooklands than anywhere else in
Britain, so it was not unexpected when the Bristol,
Sopwith and Vickers Schools were taken over on 21
August to become an initial flying training school.
This was soon re-equipped with Farman
'Shorthorns' and Avro 504s as standard equipment.
A pupil with no experience was expected to reach
the standard to become a qualified RFC pilot in six
weeks, and was told to maintain a height of 300ft
over the Members' Bridge when landing or the
sewage farm would beckon. Of the 664 pupils who
had obtained their certificates before the war
nearly half had been trained at the Bristol school,
so its reputation was high.

There was some motor cycle activity on the
track for the first few weeks after the war began,

*A completed SE5a. (BAE Systems per Brooklands
Museum)*

but from 30 September on all members of the general public were barred from entering. Thereafter Brooklands was guarded by a detachment of the Royal West Surrey Regiment.

The Sopwith Aviation Co had begun to produce Tabloids in limited numbers for an RFC contract when war began, and these were built in the Kingston-upon-Thames factory and taken to Brooklands for erection and test flying. Stimulated by the Tabloid's success Martin & Handasyde had designed a 'scout' (fighter) of their own, the S1, and received an order to put it into production in their hangars at the track. The first S1s were delivered to the RFC at the end of 1914 and about 60 were built in all.

The Royal Aircraft Factory had designed a two-seater biplane, the BE2, which first flew in 1911 and was developed into the BE2c, a reconnaissance aircraft. 'Factory' was actually a misleading title for this organisation, as the establishment at Farnborough was devoted to research design and testing. Production facilities were minimal. Manufacture of the BE2c was therefore subcontracted and Martin & Handasyde received an order to build 12 for the RNAS.

Blériot Aeronautics had been founded at the track in 1914 as an English off-shoot of the French

concern, and they now received a contract to construct Avro 504s in five hangars converted into an erecting shop.

Vickers had built up a strong connection at Brooklands before the start of the war, with its flying school and the use of the airfield for testing, but the company was building its aircraft in a factory at Erith in Kent, where there was also a flying ground. The company now received orders for the FB5 Gunbus and its development, the FB9, as well as subcontracts for the BE2c and FE8 (another Royal Aircraft Factory design), but the facilities at Erith were limited. Early in 1915, therefore, Vickers took over the Itala factory adjoining the Fork.

War having made trading conditions impossible, Itala Automobiles Ltd had gone into voluntary liquidation in August 1914 and the buildings were empty. A collection of wooden buildings that were now erected around the Itala premises became known as the 'First Extension'. When more space was needed in 1916 a 'Second Extension', of permanent construction, was added, while the erecting shops which flanked the track at the Fork – producing the facade which became a famous feature of Brooklands for the next 20 years – became the 'Third Extension', constructed in 1918.

BELOW A BE2c, No 1760, the first production aircraft built by Vickers at Weybridge in 1915. (BAE Systems per Brooklands Museum)

Although work had begun in March, the purchase of the Itala factory by Vickers, for £4,750, was not completed until November 1915. Later, in June 1917, Hugh Locke King sold them Pinewood House and two other pieces of land adjoining the Itala factory for £1,600.

The BMCRC had optimistically published a provisional list of dates for seven race meetings at the track in 1915, but it was soon realised that the track would not be fit for racing using the whole Outer Circuit, as the passage of heavy RFC Leyland and Thornycroft lorries with solid tyres was breaking up the surface. By May 1915 the damage had become so severe that the lorries were banned from using the track and repairs were put in hand. This enabled Dan O'Donovan, who was still producing tuned Norton engines in his workshop, to use the Railway Straight on 14 June to break the local flying start 500cc mile and kilometre records on a Norton, setting figures of 78.95mph for the mile and 82.85mph for the kilometre.

A sprint race meeting for service personnel, intended to boost morale, was arranged for 31 July 1915 but had to be postponed until Saturday 7 August so that the track repairs could be completed. An entry of 172 riders was received from all the services, and since all competed in uniform it was known as the 'All-Khaki Meeting'. As a concession, the public was admitted. There were five half-mile scratch sprint races on the Railway Straight, three hill climb classes on the Test Hill, and some gymkhana events in the paddock. Fastest time in the sprints was set by Lieutenant A. Lindsay with a 500cc Norton, while in the Test Hill climbs there was a tie between Private G. Kendall (Norton), Second Lieutenant G. Barnard (500cc Sunbeam) and Private H.F. Edwards (994cc Zenith-Gradua). Fifteen years later, Edwards would be secretary of the British Racing Drivers Club.

Another meeting was held on 4 September, for which 195 entries were received. The half-mile sprints were moved to the Finishing Straight so that the Test Hill climbs could be expedited. Private Kendall set the best time in the sprints on his 500cc Norton, but Sergeant A. Milner scored a double, winning the 350cc class in the sprints and on the Test Hill with his Diamond. On 22 September O'Donovan came out again and was able to use the whole repaired track to set a local five-mile flying start 500cc sidecar record at 58.78mph.

Spurred by the success of the Combined Service meetings, a final meeting was held on Saturday

BELOW *A Sopwith Camel, one of many test-flown at the track.* (BAE Systems per Brooklands Museum)

23 October for the benefit of the workers at the Royal Aircraft Factory at Farnborough, and presumably also for the production workers in the various factories and workshops at Brooklands. There were 245 entries and a big crowd arrived to watch. The Finishing Straight was used again and the sprints were all handicaps, as were the Test Hill climbs. The best time on outright speed was set by P. Davey on a 965cc Matchless. The day was cold and grey and ended with rain. This was the last wartime meeting, as the public mood was changing. The war had become a grim business and there had been severe casualties at the Battle of Loos in September. Many of these had been among the 'Kitchener' volunteers who had joined up so enthusiastically when the war began. Frivolities such as motor cycle racing could not be tolerated in a country which was now committed to 'total war'.

Throughout 1915 and 1916 the RFC struggled on in the skies over the Western Front with inferior aircraft and suffered appalling losses at the hands of German pilots flying much better machines. The situation was slightly redressed when the Sopwith Pup appeared in 1916. This was first test flown by Harry Hawker at the track in February 1916 and 1,770 were subsequently ordered, at first for the RNAS and subsequently for the RFC. The size of the order was too big for the Kingston factory so some production was subcontracted, but many were

erected and test flown at Brooklands. Hawker had a habit of enlivening his testing by flying the Pups under the footbridge over the Byfleet Banking! On 26 April 1916 he set a new British altitude record, achieving 24,408ft in a Sopwith 1½-Strutter flown from Brooklands.

By 1917 the British aviation industry was producing designs which were equal to and sometimes superior to their German rivals. From Sopwith came the Triplane and then the Camel. Like the Pup, many were built at Kingston, but the demands of the RFC meant that a substantial number were subcontracted. The Kingston production, at least 500 aircraft, was taken to Brooklands by road, where they were erected and test flown. The Royal Aircraft Factory, meanwhile, had designed the SE5a, probably the best British fighter of the war. A few were built at Farnborough, but the majority were produced at Brooklands. In all, 2,165 came from Vickers, 500 from Martinsyde (the renamed Martin & Handasyde company) and 336 from the Air Navigation & Engineering Co, the reformed Blériot company (this had moved to a factory at Addlestone, about a mile from Brooklands, though its aircraft were erected and flown from the track).

In addition Martinsyde were producing their own G100/G102, which although intended to be a fighter saw service as a light bomber, and of these 271 were built. In 1918 Martinsyde designed the

BELOW *An early production Sopwith Snipe stands on the airfield in March 1918. The test flying of rebuilt Snipes upset local residents after the end of World War One. (BAE Systems per Brooklands Museum)*

Buzzard, an advanced fighter, and an order was placed for 1,450 for delivery in 1919. However, the end of the war killed the venture and only 338 were built, of which only 57 reached the RAF.

The need for more factory space had resulted in a big expansion at Vickers. Before commencing SE5a production the company had built 100 of its own scout, the FB14 biplane pusher, and it subsequently built 53 of the FB19, a more advanced design.

In 1917 No 10 Air Acceptance Park was established at the track by the RFC to handle the newly-produced aircraft, and many of the old sheds and hangars in the 'Village' were pulled down. In their place three Belfast truss-type hangars were built. Two of these measured 170ft by 160ft and the third 170ft by 240ft. The track had also been a base for working up new squadrons at the beginning of the war and Nos 1, 8, 9, 10 and 46 had passed through. The first commanding officer of No 9 was Major Hugh Dowding who would subsequently be the AOC-in-C of Fighter Command during the Battle of Britain. In 1916 the Wireless & Observer School was established at Brooklands and was the centre of training in radio communications.

Apart from production aircraft many prototypes were flown at Brooklands during the war. The RFC and RNAS were seeking an effective heavy bomber and among the types tested were the Sopwith B1

and Cuckoo. In 1917 W.G. Tarrant, a woodwork manufacturer at Byfleet which supplied many sub-components to the firms at the track, produced a design for a four-engined biplane bomber which was then reworked to become a six-engined triplane, the Tarrant Tabor. With a span of 131ft and a height of 37ft this bizarre machine was too large to erect in the Brooklands hangars, so was taken to an airship shed at Farnborough. The venture ended in disaster when it overturned on its first take-off, killing both pilots.

By the end of World War One in November 1918, 4,344 aircraft had been built at Brooklands, and many more had been flight tested there. It had become the largest single centre of aircraft manufacture in Great Britain.

From the earliest days of the conflict Ethel Locke King had been active as the Vice-president of the North Surrey and Kingston division of the Red Cross. The many casualties in France and Belgium resulted in a pressing need for military hospitals and by the end of the war she had been responsible for the establishment and organisation of 15 in her area, several in properties owned by Hugh. She also raised nearly £5,000 in donations, which was used to pay for supplies for the hospitals and to send ambulances to France. In January 1918 she was appointed a Dame of the Order of the British Empire in recognition of her services.

ABOVE *A production line of SE5as under construction in the Vickers works in 1918. (BAE Systems per Brooklands Museum)*

CHAPTER FIVE

EUPHORIA OF PEACE

1920

When the war ended there were high hopes that racing would be able to start again in 1919, but the RAF were slow to leave the track, and the War Department, which had agreed to carry out the required repairs, was also tardy, and repair work did not start until September 1919. The track surface was in a very poor state. The traffic of Leyland and Thornycroft lorries had resumed in 1916 and three years' unrelenting wear by their solid tyres had broken up the relatively thin concrete surface. Colonel Lindsay Lloyd returned as Clerk of the Course and supervised the recommissioning of the track. The only section still usable was the Railway Straight, which was utilised for testing by the Norton tuner O'Donovan and other motor cyclists towards the end of 1919. The repairs were finished in March 1920 and the whole track was reopened for testing on 1 April. Drivers of faster cars found that the Vickers erecting sheds flanking the Fork – which during 1920 were painted with the famous 'Vickers Brooklands' sign – caused crosswinds which could make handling tricky.

A combined BARC/BMCRC meeting was fixed for Easter Monday, 5 April, but heavy rain forced a postponement until the following Saturday. The weather cleared later in the day and about 500 vehicles then took to the track to celebrate the reopening; the first out was S.T.B. Cripps riding a

The start of the Senior Handicap at the 1922 Royal meeting. (Brooklands Society)

Harley-Davidson. A big crowd had come, so as compensation for the disappointment of the postponement Malcolm Campbell, driving the Lorraine-Dietrich 'Vieux Charles Trois' which had run in the 1912 French GP and is now in the Brooklands Museum, had a match race against Jack Woodhouse riding a 994cc Matchless-MAG. Campbell won, and then matched his 2.6-litre 15/20 Talbot against George Bedford's 1,496cc Hillman, winning again.

At the postponed meeting, Campbell, driving the Lorraine-Dietrich, won the first heat of the Short Essex Easter Handicap, and so was Brooklands's first official post-war winner. Beadle's Waverley won the final. Then Campbell brought out the Talbot and had a second success in the final of the Long Essex Easter Handicap. Jack Emerson, who had been testing his 398cc ABC the previous autumn, won the first post-war motor cycle race, the three-lap Victory

Handicap, and had a second win in the 500cc Solo Sprint.

At the Whitsun meeting on 24 May one of the GP Opels abandoned in the paddock in August 1914 appeared, driven by Captain Henry Segrave, who had recently been demobilised from the RAF. Segrave lost a tyre in his first race, but won the Whitsun Sprint Handicap, beating two other drivers who were just starting illustrious careers, Henry Birkin driving a DFP and Woolf Barnato in a Calthorpe. Harry Hawker, exchanging an aircraft cockpit for a steering wheel, drove a new 4.9-litre Sunbeam which had been intended for the 1919 Indianapolis 500 but had not been allowed to race, as the engine was over-sized. A failure at 'Indy' was mildly compensated by wins in the Short and Long Lightning Handicaps.

The BMCRC reverted to its pre-war policy of longer races and there were two one-hour events at the 29 May meeting. The Senior event saw Emerson's ABC win again. The BARC had a change of policy and decided that its own meetings would only be for cars, so there were no motor cycles at the Summer meeting on 19 June.

An exciting new machine appeared at this meeting which was soon to make history at Brooklands: an 18.3-litre V12 Sunbeam. Unfortunately it did not start as a tyre burst while Harry Hawker was practising on race morning and the car went through the corrugated iron fence lining the Railway Straight and was too badly damaged to race. Among the winners was Archie Frazer-Nash, in his racing GN 'Kim', probably the fastest cyclecar of all at the time. He was less fortunate at the August Bank Holiday

ABOVE *Malcolm Campbell with the 1912 GP Lorraine-Dietrich 'Vieux Charles III' at the 1920 Easter meeting. With this car, Campbell won the first post-war races at the track, both unofficial and official. The car is now in the Brooklands Museum. (LAT)*

ABOVE LEFT *Wartime neglect is evident when the Byfleet Banking is inspected in January 1920. (LAT)*

LEFT *The start of the 75mph Short Handicap at the 1920 Whitsun meeting. The winner, Dario Resta in a 1912 Coupe de l'Auto Sunbeam, is flanked by No 2, the Hillman of George Bedford. No 7 is the Shelsley Crossley of Alastair Miller and No 8 is the Eric Campbell of Noel Macklin. (LAT)*

meeting when he had a serious crash in 'Kim' and was lucky to escape. He said that the crash made the car faster after it was rebuilt, as the accident 'had relieved the stresses'. A star that was to dazzle for all too brief a time also attended this meeting – Count Louis Zborowski, Anglo-American heir to part of the Astor fortune. Driving a 1914 GP Mercedes alleged to have won the legendary race at Lyon in July 1914, he came second in the Private Competitors' Handicap. Zborowski was a flamboyant character and his team was easily recognisable in the paddock, wearing loud check 'Moplah' caps, allegedly imported from Palm Beach.

The fastest lap of the season came in the BARC Autumn meeting when Jean Chassagne lapped at 112.17mph in a 1919 Indianapolis 4.8-litre Ballot which had the correct-sized engine.

The BMCRC were hardly affected by the BARC's attitude towards motor cycles and continued to hold monthly events. The meeting on 26 June saw two 100-mile races for Junior and Senior machines. The Senior race saw a win for Woodhouse (Matchless) ahead of Emerson's ABC, which was slowed by a puncture. At the meeting on 17 July, the last race of the day – a three-lap All Comers' Handicap – was won by Violet Longden riding a 349cc Douglas, the first victory for a woman rider at the track.

While the BARC spurned motor cycles, other clubs were happy to have combined meetings. The track was used by several clubs for minor meetings

during the 1920 season, the Junior Car Club (JCC) holding two meetings, the Motor Cycle Club (MCC) holding a combined meeting, and the Essex Motor Club holding two combined meetings with the BMCRC. At the first of the joint Essex Motor Club/BMCRC meetings on 14 August Zborowski scored his first victory, driving a 1908 12.9-litre Mercedes owned by Jack Hartshorne-Cooper.

On Saturday 11 September the BMCRC had its sixth meeting of the season, and in the 500cc Solo One-Hour race Victor Horsman set a new local one-hour record on his Norton at 71.68mph. There was drama at the meeting co-promoted with the Essex MC on 2 October when Reuben Harveyson (997cc Indian) could not slow his engine after crossing the line in the Finishing Straight and rode up and over the top of the Members' Banking. Everyone expected the worst, but Harveyson appeared among the bushes at the top of the banking and slid down it on his seat having suffered only a dislocated shoulder and torn muscles.

Record-breaking among the cars was mostly restricted to short distances, but at the end of the season an Anzani-engined AC took 11 1,500cc records up to 400 miles and George Bedford brought out his Hillman and took the 1,500cc Hour record at 78.72mph. The motor cyclists were more adventurous, and Stanley Gill on a 350cc two-stroke Alecto took international records for all classes up to 750cc and over distances and times up to 12 hours, while on outright speed Bert Le

Vack rode his 994cc Indian over the flying start mile at 95.24mph to break the 1,000cc solo record. The motor cycles were pressing hard to reach the magic 100mph, while the grit and endurance to do 12 hours solo over the Brooklands bumps on a primitive motor cycle would be hard to appreciate in the 21st century.

ABOVE *The 2.4-litre Waverley of McVicar leads Whale's Calthorpe and Marshall's Mathis on the Byfleet Banking during the 1920 Whitsun meeting. (LAT)*

FAR LEFT *Jack Emerson looks tired after taking twelve 500cc class records from one hour to 350 miles, with his ABC on 9 September 1920. (Brooklands Society)*

LEFT *Kaye Don with the AJS on which he won the 350cc Solo Championship at the BMCRC meeting on 9 October 1920. (Brooklands Society)*

1921

The BARC began its 1921 racing season with the Easter Monday meeting on 28 March. After a slightly low-key beginning in 1920, racing was now entering a golden era. Zborowski entered the first 'Chitty-Bang-Bang', a Mercedes with a 23-litre Maybach engine, and was matched against other giants, the V12 Sunbeam and a 1908 10-litre Tipo S61 Fiat. 'Chitty' won the first race, while in a later race driving the 1914 GP Mercedes, Zborowski beat the V12 Sunbeam, which had made a slow start. This was driven by Kenelm Lee Guinness, who had the consolation of a lap at 120.01mph – probably the first time the two-miles-a-minute barrier was crossed at Brooklands, bearing in mind the doubts over the Nazzaro figure of 1908. Segrave's successes in 1920 had gained him a Sunbeam works drive and he was a winner in the 3-litre Scratch race, with the prototype of the 1921 Sunbeam GP car.

The BMCRC changed a rule for its first meeting on 16 April, deciding that the pushers allowed to get machines started would only be permitted for the first 30 yards. Beyond that the rider had to do it alone. This was no handicap to Douglas Davidson, who ran away with the 1,000cc Solo on his Harley-Davidson and during the course of the race set a new local 1,000cc five-mile record.

A lure for motor cyclists at the time was the chance of winning the Godfrey Cup by being the first rider to exceed 100mph. Duncan Watson, the British agent for Harley-Davidson, had imported two board-track Harleys to this end and these were brought out on the evening of Wednesday 27 April for Douglas Davidson and Claude Temple to attempt the national 1,000cc flying start kilometre record. Bert Le Vack joined the party with his 994cc Indian but no one could reach the magic '100'. They therefore adjourned until the following afternoon when Davidson, diving into the measured kilometre off the Members' Banking, achieved 100.76mph and won the Cup. Le Vack, who had been troubled by stretching valves, returned to the track next day, and while he could no longer win the Cup he had the satisfaction of covering the kilometre at 106.5mph. Perhaps spurred by Le Vack's efforts, on 4 May Tony Vandervell – subsequently the founder of the Vanwall Grand Prix team – set a new motor cycle record of 8.57sec for the Test Hill on a 500cc Norton.

There was tragedy before the BARC Whitsun meeting when Jack Hartsthorne-Cooper crashed his 1908 Mercedes, now fitted with a 19-litre Cooper-Clerget aero engine, near the Vickers sheds during practice and died of head injuries soon afterwards. The meeting itself had a most significant entry, the second prototype 3-litre

BELOW *W.O. Bentley brings the prototype 3-litre Bentley 'EXP3' down the Test Hill in January 1921. His passenger is Sammy Davis, the sports editor of The Autocar. (LAT)*

ABOVE *Henry Segrave won the 3-litre Scratch race in the prototype GP Sunbeam at the 1921 Easter meeting. (LAT)*

LEFT *Count Louis Zborowski in the legendary 'Chitty-Bang-Bang I' at the 1921 Easter meeting. (LAT)*

Euphoria of peace **77**

ABOVE *The view from the Members' Hill at the 1921 Easter meeting. (LAT)*

BELOW *John Duff in the 10-litre S61 Fiat which he raced during the 1921 season. John Cobb later began racing with this car. (Brooklands Society)*

Bentley, entered for Frank Clement. It had been entered for an earlier Essex MC meeting on 7 May and had been withdrawn with oiled plugs, but it now scored a first win for the marque in the Junior Sprint Handicap. Zborowski was also a winner, taking the Lightning Short Handicap in 'Chitty'.

'Cupid' Hornsted reappeared for the Mid-summer BARC meeting on 25 June, driving a 200hp Benz which was said to be his 1914 record-breaking car. John Duff brought an equally famous car, the Fiat 'Mephistopheles'. Racing against a new generation of Brooklands monsters including

'Chitty', neither the Benz nor the Fiat were placed, possibly being out-handicapped by their pre-war reputations and performance. A rare entry was Sanderson's Rolls-Royce Silver Ghost, which won a Short Handicap – probably incurring the severe displeasure of the Rolls-Royce company, which did not countenance such frivolities!

The BMCRC extended its ambitions still further on Saturday 2 July when it ran a 500-mile race. The 200-guinea gold Miller Cup was to go to the winner with class and team awards. This revolutionary event attracted 64 runners. The mass start, at the Fork, was at 7:00am, with the Members' Hill still shrouded in mist. The riders lined up in coloured jackets to denote their class: in the front row the 250s wore white and the 350s wore blue, the 500s in row two were in yellow, the 750s behind had green, and the 1,000cc machines at the rear sported red. Among the riders were Kaye Don, who would become a dominant figure at the track at the end of the decade, and Tony Vandervell, while a 350cc Douglas was entered by HRH the Duke of York (later King George VI) and ridden by his chauffeur S.E. Wood.

At the 37-lap, 100-mile mark Bert Le Vack (Indian) led at an average of 80.77mph, but after 45 laps he came to a stop on the Railway Straight with a puncture and had to push his machine to the pits at the Fork. This gave a six-lap lead to Douglas Davidson (Harley-Davidson), but he was passed by Freddie Dixon on another Harley. Davidson fought back and was in front again at the 300-mile mark, while Dixon had a frightening skid almost the length of the Railway Straight and was thrown off when a front tyre burst. He remounted and rode

back to the pits, where the wheel was changed, and then he carried on. Harry Read (Dot-JAP) was thrown off at the Vickers sheds when a tyre burst at 80mph, but picked himself up, received medical attention, and then rejoined the race.

Meanwhile Le Vack had been riding on relentlessly and retook the lead when Davidson stopped with a broken valve. Davidson pushed his machine back to the pits but was hampered by a war wound and received outside help, so was disqualified. Once in front Le Vack eased off, but with three laps to go he stopped on the Byfleet Banking as a plug had oiled up. He made a quick change and rode on to win after 7hr 5min 59.6sec

Bert Le Vack

Bert (Herbert) Le Vack first raced at Brooklands in 1912 at the MCC meeting, riding a Motosacoche. At that time there was a rule that the minimum age for competitors was 18. His age was queried and it seems that he was probably only 17. There was always slight uncertainty about his age, though he was probably born in 1895. He remained faithful to Motosacoche until the start of the war and his first win was at the July 1914 MCC meeting in a three-lap handicap.

Although he had no formal engineering training Le Vack had a natural talent, and after the war he became involved with the development of the unsuccessful Duzmo machine. He was then signed as the 'works' rider for Indian in 1920, winning his first post-war race at the 1920 BMCRC August meeting. Other successes soon followed and early in 1921 he joined in a needle match with Douglas Davidson to compete for the Godfrey Cup (for the first rider to exceed 100mph in England). Davidson won the duel, but two days later Le Vack was timed at 106.5mph, a British record. Later in 1921 he gained a legendary win in the only 500-mile motor cycle race to be held at the track.

In 1922 he joined J.A. Prestwich as a development engineer, working on JAP engines which he raced in Zenith and New Imperial frames. He gained a number of wins and achieved the first 100mph lap of the track riding a Zenith.

At the BMCRC solo 200-miles races in 1923 Le Vack showed he was an iron man by winning the 350cc event on a New Imperial, before transferring to a Brough for the 1,000cc race, which he also won. Later in the season he fitted a sidecar to the Brough and won the 200-mile sidecar race. Many records also fell to him during the year. The successes continued in 1924 and there was a win in the 350cc 200-mile solo race. He took the Zenith-JAP to Arpajon in France twice to raise the World Motor Cycle Record to 113.61mph and later to 119.05mph. In 1925 the JAP engines were fitted to Coventry Eagle and HRD. At the BMCRC Champions Day, Le Vack scored a hat trick with wins in the 250cc and 350cc solo races on a Coventry Eagle and on an HRD in the 500cc solo race. He won the Buckley Cup for the first 100mph race lap on a 500cc machine.

When J.A. Prestwich gave up racing at the end of 1925 Le Vack moved on to New Hudson but did little racing during 1926. In 1927 he achieved wins in the 200-mile 600cc sidecar race and the Champions' 500cc solo race on New Hudsons. He was still at the top of his form in 1928 and had two wins at the BMCRC opening meeting, winning the 500cc solo race; then, winning a handicap race riding a 655cc New Hudson, he set a new 750cc lap record en route. Later in the year there was a win in the 200-mile 500cc solo race. His last Brooklands race was the 1929 250cc 200-mile solo event, when his New Imperial retired. In August 1929 he took the Brough Superior-JAP to Arpajon, where he set a new World Motor Cycle Record at 129.07mph. When the BMCRC Gold Star for 100mph laps was instituted, Le Vack was the first to receive the award in recognition of his 1922 lap.

Le Vack had several rides in the IoM TT races and his best result was second place in the 1923 Lightweight race on a New Imperial. In 1929 he went to Switzerland to work in the competition department of Motosacoche, where he developed a new ohc racing engine. He was killed in a road accident in Switzerland on 17 September 1931 riding a sidecar combination. His ashes were interred in Byfleet Cemetery, near the grave of Parry Thomas. Writing about Le Vack in *Motor Cycling* in 1958, Dennis May said: 'The greatest of them all? Well if you don't think so, name me a greater.'

ABOVE *The riders line up in the morning mist for the start of the BMCRC 500-Mile race on 2 July 1921.* (Brooklands Society)

Imperial-JAP, took just under ten hours to complete the event. Last of the 32 finishers, as light was beginning to fade, was Reg Weatherell on a 350cc RW Scout, who took 11hr 6min, though some stragglers were still valiantly battling on when the flag came out at 7:00pm. The other class winners were Norris (350cc Ivy), Horsman (500cc Norton) and Parham (750cc Coventry-Victor), while the team prize went to the three Martinsydes, the aircraft company having gone into motor cycle manufacture after the war. Though deemed a success the race was never repeated. It was considered too gruelling and, more crucially, it had attracted many local complaints about the 12 hours of noise.

At the end of the season, after the Autumn BARC meeting, there was another long-distance race. This was for 1,500cc cars, over 200 miles of the Outer Circuit, and was organised by the Junior Car Club. It was the first long-distance car race to be held in England since the war and the first for small capacity cars. There were two classes, 1,100cc and 1,500cc, and the outright winner would receive the T.P. André Gold Cup. The JCC received 58 entries for the race, which was held on Saturday 22 October, and 38 came to the line. It was an opportunity for many small manufacturers to get publicity and, possibly, to gain glory.

of racing, having averaged 70.42mph. Dixon came home in second place, some ten minutes behind, and Reuben Harveyson (Indian) was third.

Although the larger machines had finished, the race was still on for the smaller classes, and the winner of the 250cc class, Bert Kershaw on a New

Among the entrants were three Type 56 Talbot-Darracqs, to be driven by Segrave, Malcolm Campbell and Guinness. Clement Talbot had amalgamated with Darracq in 1919, followed by a merger with Sunbeam in 1920 to form the Sunbeam-Talbot-Darracq combine, an Anglo-French operation with cars being built on both sides of the Channel. The Sunbeam part of the business entered major events such as the French GP, while the Talbot-Darracq section, based in Paris, built and entered cars for voiturette, or 1,500cc, races. The Type 56 had already shown that it was virtually invincible in this class, so the outcome of the JCC 200 was almost certain as soon as the entry list was published, and practice showed the gap in performance between the Talbot-Darracqs and the rest of the field.

A crowd of over 6,000 came to watch and the cars were lined up at the Fork in four rows, with the 1,100cc cyclecars in the front row. The cars were flagged away at noon and the three Talbot-Darracqs immediately went to the front. The only cars able to give any kind of chase were the two Type 13 Bugattis sent from the Molsheim factory, and even these fell back. Thereafter Segrave led Campbell and Guinness, though Campbell lost his place when a tyre burst as he crossed the Fork on lap 36 and he had to stop for a wheel change. The

ABOVE *H.J. Line pushes his 250cc Martin off after a pit stop in the 500-Mile race, while Captain Alastair Miller turns away from his 994cc Martin-MAG. Miller presented the cup for the winner of the race. (Brooklands Society)*

LEFT *The start of the 500-Mile race. No 51 is Reg Weatherell (250cc RW Scout). (Brooklands Society)*

ABOVE *King Smith (249cc Morris-Warne) is followed round the Byfleet Banking by Miller during the 500-Mile race. (Brooklands Society)*

BELOW *Bert Le Vack with his 1912 994cc Indian 'The Camel' after taking the 1,000cc flying start kilometre record at 107.55mph on 17 November 1921. (Brooklands Society)*

race ran out with Segrave the winner, having averaged 88.82mph. Guinness was 5.8sec behind while Campbell finished four minutes later. Such was the Talbot-Darracq pace that Pierre de Vizcaya in his fourth-placed Bugatti was ten minutes behind Segrave.

The cyclecar class was more closely fought. Ware led initially in a Morgan but his clutch broke and he was out after 20 laps. This left Frazer-Nash (GN) and the French driver André Lombard (Salmson) contesting the lead, but Lombard braked too hard when stopping for fuel and hit the concrete kerb in front of the pit, damaging two wheels. By the time these were changed he was too far behind, and the GN won by nine minutes.

Before the race there had been gloomy forecasts of gory accidents, but there was little carnage and the only serious mishap occurred when a tyre burst on Munday's AC and it overturned into the Byfleet Banking ditch, fracturing the driver's femur. It was commented after the race that 'several prominent members of the automobile world expressed their joy at having seen a real race on Brooklands instead of exhibitions of the handicapper's prowess, good as is that latter.'

Throughout the summer and into the autumn the AC firm was active at the track, attempting and breaking 1,500cc class records. AC wanted to have the distinction of being the first 1,500cc car to exceed 100mph. On 3 June, Harry Hawker brought out a specially prepared single-seater with a very slim and elongated body, built at the Hawker factory at Kingston. With this he covered a flying half-mile at 105.14mph, so the target was achieved – although over the shortest possible distance. This was Hawker's last appearance at the track, as he was killed when he crashed near Hendon on 12 July during a test flight before the Aerial Derby.

The most ambitious venture was an attempt to set a faster speed for 24 hours than S.F. Edge had done in 1907. It was not permitted to run a car at Brooklands during the night, so the RAC agreed that the AC could do a 12-hour stint and then be locked away, to come out the following day for another 12-hour run. The run started on 27 September and at the end of the day 31 class records had been taken up to 12 hours, at speeds from 70 to 72mph. Next morning the car came out again, but after seven hours a piston seized and the run was over.

1922

This was a year which saw some remarkable and historic records set at Brooklands. Record-breaking was a useful and profitable exercise. For a manufacturer it was a means of demonstrating the performance and reliability of his products and gaining the greatest publicity, while for a private owner it could be most profitable, as the fuel, oil and tyre companies, as well as the manufacturers of the accessories involved, would pay generous bonuses for successful attempts.

1922 also saw the first appearance of another driver whose name would always be linked with the track, J.G. Parry Thomas. Thomas, who was the chief engineer and designer of the Leyland company, had produced a remarkable machine, the Leyland Eight, which had a 7.2-litre straight-eight engine and was intended to be a superb luxury car. It was marketed at £2,500 as a chassis, so it was the most expensive car on the British market. With great reluctance the Leyland directors agreed that Thomas could race a Leyland at Brooklands, provided it was a production 'Speed Model' in full touring trim. Thomas entered the car for the Easter Monday meeting on 17 April, but it was an unhappy debut as the clutch slipped badly and the car failed to finish.

Kaye Don had taken over Hawker's single-seater AC and with this he won the Light Car Scratch race. Then in a subsequent handicap he lapped at 100.61mph, the first time a 1,500cc car had broken the '100 lap' barrier. The last race of the day, the 100mph Long Handicap, saw Zborowski win in the 200hp Benz.

At the BARC May meeting Kenelm Lee Guinness won the Lightning Short Handicap in the V12 Sunbeam at 111.42mph, but this was only a foretaste of his feats on the following Wednesday, 17 May. Running over the measured mile and kilometre on the Railway Straight, and covering the course in both directions, he set a new flying-start kilometre record at a mean speed of 133.75mph, which constituted a new World Land Speed Record. The mile speed was slightly slower at 129.17mph. Guinness also took the half-mile record, and on one run in the clockwise direction, aided by the downhill run from the Members' Banking, the Sunbeam clocked 140.51mph. During these runs the Sunbeam completed several laps of the track, the fastest of which was 123.39mph, so at last there was an indisputable new lap record and Nazzaro's speed with the Fiat 'Mephistopheles' had been beaten.

In the motor cycle world a small milestone had been reached in March. Both Rex Judd (Norton) and Cyril Pullin (Douglas) had been trying to be the first in Britain to achieve 100mph on a 500cc machine. Judd was just short of the target on 22 March and the following morning Pullin came out and recorded 100.06mph over the half-mile distance.

The BMCRC ran its regular monthly meetings throughout the season, but there was a combined meeting with the Essex MC on 20 May which was attended by HRH the Duke of York and was fittingly called the Brooklands Royal Meeting. The Duke was greeted by the Earl of Athlone and a Persian carpet was laid out on the track when he arrived. The

LEFT *Tony Vandervell, who built and sponsored the GP Vanwall team in the 1950s, in a Ford Model T racer at the 1922 Easter meeting. (Brooklands Society)*

ABOVE *Kenelm Lee Guinness in the 350hp Sunbeam when he set a World Land Speed Record of 133.75mph for the kilometre on 17 May 1922. (Brooklands Society)*

Duke had entered his chauffeur S.E. Wood on a 350cc Douglas and a 988cc Trump-Anzani, and before one race he was introduced to the riders. Wood, who wore the Duke's colours (a scarlet jersey with blue stripes and sleeves), was unplaced in his races. In the car races Parry Thomas brought out the Leyland and gained his first Brooklands place, coming third in the Earl of Athlone Handicap. The Essex club having a more enlightened attitude than the BARC, women drivers were also permitted to race in front of the Duke, and Ivy Cummings won the Duke of York Long Handicap in a 1912 Coupe de l'Auto Sunbeam.

On 17 June the Ealing & District MCC ran an unusual event, a 200-mile sidecar race with the 350cc, 600cc and 1,000cc classes running concurrently. The 350s started at noon, the 500s at 1:00pm and the 1,000s at 2:10pm. Pullin

(Douglas) and Bridgman (Indian) had runaway wins in the two lesser classes, but among the big machines there was a hard fight between Davidson (Indian) and Le Vack (Zenith-JAP), who finished in that order.

At the BARC Whit Monday meeting on 6 June, Parry Thomas won his first Brooklands race, averaging 103.11mph with the Leyland in the 100mph Short Handicap, his car impressing spectators by its smooth running and silence. Perhaps it was an acknowledgment of the new Sunbeam lap record, but 'Mephistopheles', being driven by John Duff, stopped abruptly on the Byfleet Banking when the cylinder block lifted and the engine literally exploded into countless fragments. In the last race of the day Zborowski scored again, this time in the 1914 GP Mercedes. The August Bank Holiday meeting was marred by a fatal crash when D.J. Gibson pulled his 1914 GP Vauxhall off the Byfleet Banking too early and overturned at the Fork.

Noise continued to be a problem at the track and the local residents threatened to seek an injunction: the 500-mile motor cycle race in 1921 had been most unpopular, and the recent sidecar races had exacerbated the problem. Competitors attending the BMCRC meeting on 15 July were told to reduce their noise immediately, and a similar warning was given to competitors in the second JCC 200-Mile race on 19 August. This was divided into two parts, the cyclecars starting at 8:30am and the bigger cars at 2:00pm.

There were 15 starters in the 1,100cc race. The French Salmson team had entered three cars, and one of these, driven by Robert Benoist, led from the start, followed by Frazer-Nash (GN). When Benoist burst a tyre the GN took the lead, but then stopped with a broken piston which it took Frazer-Nash 35 minutes to change. This left the Salmson in command and Benoist won from his team-mate Desvaux at an average of 81.88mph, while the three GNs of Godfrey, Hawkins and Frazer-Nash were the only other cars to finish.

The Talbot-Darracqs were expected to have an easy win in the second race, but Kensington-Moir (Aston Martin) led for the first five laps until his magneto failed. This left Segrave in front, but his car began to misfire. Meanwhile Chassagne in the second Talbot-Darracq had a burst tyre and the car went over the top of the Byfleet Banking. He and his mechanic were thrown out but were unhurt. Guinness now took the lead with the third Talbot-Darracq and went on to win, followed by Stead (Aston Martin) who had driven steadily and profited from the various Talbot-Darracq problems. Segrave finished third.

When the BMCRC 500-Mile race planned for 23 September was cancelled the motor cycling community felt it was being made a scapegoat for the noise problem, but the BARC also cancelled a proposed 500-mile race for 2-litre cars for the same reason.

There was drama at the BARC autumn meeting when Duff, driving the 200hp Benz, was unable to pull up in time in the Finishing Straight and went

ABOVE *HRH the Duke of York (later King George VI) talks to his chauffeur, S.E. Wood, who was riding a 998cc Trump-Anzani entered by the Duke at the Royal meeting. (Brooklands Society)*

FAR LEFT *The riders prepare for the Junior Handicap at the Royal meeting on 20 May 1922. (Brooklands Society)*

LEFT *S.F. Edge and Gwenda Janson after their record runs on 19 and 20 July 1922. (Brooklands Society)*

FAR LEFT *The 1,100cc class on its way from the paddock to the start of the JCC 200-Mile race on 19 August 1922. Nos 3, 2 and 1 are the GNs of Archie Frazer-Nash, Ron Godfrey and Hawkins, No 8 is the Eric-Longden driven by its constructor, and No 6 is the Salmson of Lucien Desvaux. (John Maitland Collection)*

LEFT *Segrave makes a stop to cure a misfire on his Talbot Darracq in the 1922 JCC 200-Mile race. (LAT)*

BELOW *Gordon England's Austin 7 passes L.F. Peaty's Eric-Longden on the Byfleet Banking during the 1923 200-Mile race. (LAT)*

over the top of the Members' Banking. Fortunately he was unhurt, but it emphasised an increasing problem. During practice for the meeting Zborowski had burst a tyre in 'Chitty 1' on the Members' Banking and the car had slid down and hit the timing box at the beginning of the Railway Straight, tearing off the front axle and slightly injuring an official, though Zborowski was unhurt. Bentleys were beginning to appear regularly in the programme and Clement, driving a car entered by 'WO', had two wins at this meeting.

The Land Speed Record was only one of several impressive records at the track in 1922. An Aston Martin driven by Kensington-Moir had taken the Test Hill record in March, but the small company had a much larger ambition. On 24 and 25 May an Aston Martin came out to tackle the 1,500cc Double 12-hour record, and AC brought a car to the track for the same purpose at the same time. The Aston Martin began at 4:30am and ran for 19 hours, taking not only class records but also many of the World records set by Edge in 1907. It did not come out the next day, but the AC forged on and ran for almost 12 hour before the crankshaft broke, by which time it had taken the light car and British Double-12 records.

On 19 and 20 July S.F. Edge himself appeared with a Dutch Spyker fitted with a 5.7-litre Maybach engine, with the aim of going further than he had in 1907 in two 12-hour stints. He suggested to *The Motor* that he should receive a copper medal if he beat his 1907 figures, and if he failed he would give £100 to the Motor Trades Benevolent Fund. He was successful, setting a new British Class G Double-12 record, and was presented by *The Motor* with a gold medal in recognition of his efforts. He was not alone on the track, as circulating at the same time was a 250cc Trump-JAP ridden by Gwenda Janson, who was after the Double-12 motor cycle record which had not been attempted before. In a riposte to the BARC and those who would patronise 'the little woman', she achieved her aim at an average of 44.65mph for the 24 hours.

Even more was to come from the motor cycles, as Bert Le Vack, while taking the 1,000cc five-mile record on his Zenith-JAP on 2 October, lapped the track at 100.27mph, thus breaking the 'magic 100' barrier. After his record-breaking run Le Vack protested to the BARC that the correct speed for his lap should have been 102.69mph, as he had been riding above the 50ft line and all motor cycle records were calculated on a line 10ft from the inner edge of the track, so he had covered a greater distance. His protests were fruitful and from the beginning of 1923 all motor cycle records were calculated from the 50ft line.

At the end of an amazing season, just as the track was about to close for the winter, John Joyce came out with the single-seater AC and took the 1,500cc Hour record at 100.39mph.

BELOW *Ivy Cummings in her 1912 3-litre Sunbeam after winning the Essex Junior Long Handicap at the Essex MC meeting on 30 September 1922. The minor clubs had more progressive views than the BARC concerning women drivers. (Brooklands Society)*

1923

The year 1922 had emphasised that the war, although not forgotten, was now in the past. The fact that a new era had begun had been demonstrated by the thrills and dramas at Brooklands, so 1923 was perhaps a slight anti-climax.

The track was closed for three months during the winter and there were extensive repairs to its surface. New sections were laid on the Members' Banking and it was reported that 400 tons of concrete were laid in an attempt to smooth out the bump on the Members' Banking. The Byfleet Banking was also patched. The repairs were delayed when parts of the track and some of the car parks were flooded in February, but it was reopened for testing on 5 March.

The BARC held its regular calendar of meetings, as did the BMCRC. Zborowski only appeared at the end of the season as he was preoccupied in taking a team of Bugattis to Indianapolis and racing a Miller in the French GP, but Parry Thomas was becoming the track's new hero. He had left Leyland and set up as an engineering consultant, moving into a bungalow in the 'Village' which was known as 'The Hermitage'. Here he worked on his own Leyland and tuned two others for customers. He was also working on engine and chassis designs intended for production. During the season he gained eight victories at BARC meetings and

meetings organised by other clubs, driving the Leyland Eight, which now had a racing body. At the BARC Mid-summer meeting on 23 June he won the Lightning Long Handicap at 115.25mph, setting a new record average speed for a Brooklands race. The Leyland was also used for record breaking, and in June, as well as taking class records, established World records for five and ten miles. While setting these records Thomas lapped the track at 124.12mph, but this was not recognised as a new lap record.

On 11 July Thomas set out to attempt the British Double-12 record, sharing the driving with Captain Alastair Miller. The run began at 6:00am and was initially hampered by thick mist, but a much more serious problem soon emerged. It became a very hot day and the Leyland was devouring tyres. Miller was even hit on the head and arm by a thrown tread which knocked him out momentarily. By noon ten tyres had collapsed and the reserve stock was running low. Worse still the Leyland had run round the track on a bare rim twice and this caused damage to the transmission, bringing the run to an end after nine hours.

The wrecked Fiat 'Mephistopheles' was sold to Ernest Eldridge during the winter of 1922, allegedly for £25, and Eldridge did a major reconstruction. The chassis was lengthened using sections from a dismantled London bus and the burst engine was replaced by a 21.7-litre Fiat A12 aero engine. When

BELOW *Parry Thomas's Leyland-Thomas in its original form in 1923. (John Maitland Collection)*

ABOVE *Maurice Harvey in the modified 12/50 Alvis with which he won the 1923 JCC 200-Mile race. He is wearing earphones, as unsuccessful attempts were made to use pit/car radio communications before the race. (Brooklands Society)*

the rebuilt car was raced during the 1923 season Eldridge was not notably successful, but on 28 June, while Thomas was making record runs with the Leyland, Eldridge took the Fiat out and did a lap at 124.33mph, which was officially recognised as a new lap record.

Establishing a motor racing name that would later become a legend, Alfred Moss, the father of Sir Stirling Moss, won a handicap at the Easter meeting in an Anzani-Crouch and repeated this win at the Autumn meeting. Zborowski also ran at the

Autumn meeting, driving a Leyland belonging to Captain Howey, which was prepared by Thomas. He and Thomas started from the scratch mark in the Lightning Long Handicap, but Thomas left him behind, taking second place.

During the season pulling up in the Finishing Straight became a pressing problem. Kaye Don in the Viper, a Napier with a Wolseley-Hispano aero engine, was only able to stop by running the car into the earth bank at the side of the track, and even a 1,500cc Crouch found it hard to stop after a race.

A motor cycle milestone was passed at the BMCRC meeting on 26 May. There was a fierce struggle in the three-lap 1,000cc race between Claude Temple (British Anzani), Bert Le Vack (Zenith-Jap), Freddie Dixon (Harley-Davidson) and Oliver Baldwin (Matchless-MAG). Temple led all the way, with Le Vack chasing until he dropped out, leaving Dixon and Baldwin to take the places, but during the race Temple lapped at 101.23mph, the first 100mph race lap.

On Saturday 21 July the BMCRC held the 200-Mile solo race meeting. There were two 200-mile races, with the 250s and 350s running together in the morning while the 500s, 750s and 1,000s had a race after lunch. Bert Le Vack showed his determination riding a 350 New Imperial-JAP in the 350 race. Stopped by a burst rear tyre after seven laps, he lost nearly four laps getting it changed but pressed on and by half-distance was in front again. With 20 laps to go he stopped again, with a defective plug, and lost a lap to George Tottey (New Imperial). Once again Le Vack gave chase and retook the lead, coming home to win from Tottey.

The big class race began at 2:00pm and Le Vack was out again, riding a Brough Superior-JAP. Dixon (Harley-Davidson) led initially, then Le Vack went to the front and Dixon fell back with various problems, but once these were resolved he set off

in pursuit. Le Vack, however, was too quick and Dixon had to settle for second place.

Dan O'Donovan, the Norton tuner and entrant, had lost his No 1 rider, Rex Judd, to Douglas. One day in May 1923, while in Weybridge, he was almost knocked over by a butcher's delivery boy riding a motor cycle. O'Donovan was impressed by the rider's skill and asked him to come to Brooklands. The rider, Bert Denly, was a natural racer and although he had never been to the track he took to it immediately, as he showed by winning the 500cc class of the 200-Mile race. Denly was small in stature and riders had to weigh more than 132lb, so O'Donovan screwed lead weights to the soles of Denly's boots and sewed sheet lead into a cushion wrapped round his waist. Two weeks later Denly took the Norton out and gained the coveted 500cc Hour record at 82.66mph.

BELOW LEFT *J.A. Joyce's AC clears the top of the Test Hill when setting a new record of 8.28sec in November 1923. (John Maitland Collection)*

BELOW *The exhausted rider is lifted from his 998cc Rudge at the end of the successful attempts on sidecar 1,000cc 500 miles and five- to eight-hour records by Bert Mathers and Bob Dicker on 8 June 1923. (Brooklands Society)*

The JCC ran the 200-Mile race again on 13 13 laps Salamano was in the pits with oil and

October, and as in 1922 it was divided into separate smoke pouring from the engine, and two laps later

races. There were 13 starters in the 1,100cc event Campbell's car met the same fate. This left George

and Frazer-Nash (GN) led initially, but the Salmson Eyston leading with an Aston Martin, but at half-

team was soon in front before it ran into problems. distance he stopped to change plugs, allowing

Benoist had to make frequent stops for water and Maurice Harvey in a mildly-modified 12/50 sports

Wilson-Jones had a holed fuel tank, caused when a Alvis take the lead. Harvey carried on to win from

nut flew out of the clutch. However, the third car, the Bugatti of Leon Cushman, while Joyce (AC) was

driven by Bueno, had no bothers and went on to third. It was a popular win, as a British car had seen

win, while Eric Gordon England in a very quick off the European competition.

Austin Seven, which he had modified extensively, Eyston's plug change possibly cost Aston Martin

took second place from Benoist. the 200-Mile race, but an Aston Martin driven by

The 1,500cc race had been anticipated as Major Frank Halford – who was later to design the

another walk-over for the Talbot-Darracqs, but a DH aero engines, the first DH jet engine, and the

new rival, the Tipo 803 Fiat, had appeared in Napier Sabre aero engine – set a Test Hill record of

voiturette races and when it was known that two 9.14sec in June. This was broken by Cushman in

Fiats would be at Brooklands the Talbot-Darracq his 200-Mile Race Bugatti on 17 October, the new

team found a pressing engagement elsewhere. At figure being 8.4sec, but in November Joyce

the start the two Fiats, driven by Malcolm Campbell lowered the record again in an AC, leaving it at

and Carlo Salamano, roared into the lead, but after 8.28 sec.

1924

Complaints about the noise of the track intensified in 1924. Ten local residents commenced proceedings in the High Court, seeking to have the track closed on the grounds that the testing and racing was a nuisance, destroyed the peace of a rural neighbourhood and was causing a decline in the value of local property. The case was not heard in 1924, but the BARC realised that it was essential that tougher silencing regulations should be imposed. Consequently in May 1924 the famous and perhaps notorious Brooklands silencer regulations were published and were enforced immediately. It was also decreed that at BMCRC meetings, machines should be taken from the paddock to the start line with engines stopped and could not be started before the fall of the flag.

The BMCRC members felt they were being 'got at' and matters came to a head when Dougal Marchant was refused admission to the track when it was decided that his Zenith-Blackburne was too noisy. A protest was made to Colonel Lindsay Lloyd, who said that as undertakings about noise had been given to local residents the BARC had no alternative. He would attend the BMCRC meeting on 10 May and would exclude any machine which he considered to be too noisy. The riders therefore held a poll and by 23 votes to 3 decided to abstain from riding at the meeting. As it was a wet day there would probably have been no racing anyway,

but the outcome was the publication of the new regulations on 12 May which established what type of silencer was acceptable to the BARC, removing the previous uncertainty.

There has to be sympathy for the riders, who appreciated the problem but felt that they were being victimised, as the matter was handled in a very haphazard and autocratic manner by the BARC, without warning or consultation. The BARC had little alternative though, and had to act quickly as the whole future of the track could have been in jeopardy. When the permanent silencer regulations were established there was probably little effect on the noise levels, but the residents had been mollified, and as the years went by they gradually became accustomed to higher noise levels in an increasingly mechanical age.

The problems of the Finishing Straight were acknowledged and at the Easter meeting the faster handicaps started at the beginning of the Railway Straight and finished halfway down it. This was a solution which seemed to have been given little thought, as the spectators in the paddock and the Hill enclosures could have little idea of the race results and could not see any close finishes, but it was an indication of the inherent problems of the track design, as the siting of the sewage farm made it impossible to have a spectators' enclosure beside the Railway Straight finishing line.

A rise in the price of petrol to 2s 0d a gallon had not affected the size of the Brooklands crowds,

BELOW *Alfred Ellison in the Lorraine-Dietrich 'Vieux Charles III' leads Dario Resta's 3-litre Sunbeam in the 37th 100mph Long Handicap at the 1924 Easter Meeting. (Brooklands Society)*

RIGHT *Parry Thomas in his 1½-litre Thomas Special after winning the first Essex Senior Short Handicap on 23 July 1924. (Brooklands Society)*

BELOW *Parry Thomas in the Leyland-Thomas sweeps past Dr J.D. Benjafield's 3-litre Bentley on the Byfleet Banking during the 100mph Long Handicap at the 1924 Autumn meeting. (Brooklands Society)*

although it had been predicted that it would discourage pleasure motoring. At the Easter meeting, Zborowski was a winner in the Indianapolis Type 30 Bugatti. The fastest race of the day was the Founders' Gold Cup, which was truly a race of the giants. Zborowski drove his latest creation, the Higham Special, which had a 27-litre V12 Liberty engine in a specially built chassis made by Rubery Owen; it was the largest-engined car to race at Brooklands. Matched against him was Eldridge in 'Mephistopheles', Le Champion in the 20-litre Isotta-Maybach, a car built by Eldridge in 1923, and Captain Howey in a Leyland prepared by Thomas. Against these monsters, a 5-litre Sunbeam and Ballot seemed positively dainty. Le Champion won the race, but in chasing through to second place Eldridge lapped at 122.37mph. Zborowski was third.

At the Whitsun meeting there was a fatal accident when Captain J.H. Toop swerved inexplicably on the Byfleet Banking while driving the Peugeot which had won the 1913 French GP.

The car went over the top of the banking and 41-year-old Toop, an experienced driver who had been racing since 1913 and had prepared Hornsted's Benz for the 1914 record runs, was killed instantly when the car hit a tree. The meeting was abandoned after the accident.

Parry Thomas had rebuilt the Leyland during the winter of 1923. With its body lowered and its engine modified to give much more power it was now known as the Leyland-Thomas. Thomas was in top form at the BARC Summer meeting. Running in the Lightning Long Handicap he seemed to have little chance of catching Zborowski in 'Chitty III', a 28/95 sports Mercedes fitted with a 14.7-litre Mercedes aero engine, but by dint of a new lap record at 125.14mph he took Zborowski on the line to win by about two yards.

The 100 Short Handicap at the August meeting saw a clash which would have delighted latter-day vintage enthusiasts when Dr Dudley Benjafield's 3-litre Bentley just beat Major Leonard Ropner's 30-98 Vauxhall by a few yards, both cars lapping at 98mph.

BELOW *The Talbot-Darracq team have a conference near the aircraft sheds on the Byfleet Banking before the 1924 200-Mile Race. Left to right: a mechanic, Kenelm Lee Guinness, George Duller (back to camera), Henry Segrave (in car), a mechanic, Parry Thomas (in Fair Isle jersey), and Captain Irving (team manager). (John Maitland Collection)*

At this meeting, although defeated by his handicap, Thomas did another amazing lap in the Leyland-Thomas, setting a new lap record at 128.36mph. It was a reflection on the regime that had become firmly established at Brooklands that even a record lap could not ensure victory for a driver.

At the Autumn meeting Thomas won the Lightning Long Handicap by yards from Humphrey Cook's TT Vauxhall at the highest race speed yet seen, 120.15mph, and was the acknowledged king of the track. On 26 June he had attempted several records successfully in the Leyland-Thomas, and during the day had covered a flying mile in both directions at a mean average of 129.73mph, so was technically the holder of the World Land Speed Record. Malcolm Campbell had gone faster at Fanøe in Denmark with the V12 Sunbeam, but the timing of his run was not accepted by the AIACR, the international governing body. The glamour which would soon attach to this record was yet to come.

New records were also being set at the BMCRC meetings. On 7 June Claude Temple, riding the 996cc Montgomery-British Anzani, won the five-lap 1,000cc solo race at 105.32mph (a new race record) and lapped at 109.94mph, while Le Vack, riding

New Imperial, Zenith and Brough-Superior machines, won five races. The imposition of silencers seemed to have little effect on speeds, which were rising continuously, and the restrictions did not deter the spectators, who came in large numbers for the BMCRC 200-Mile solo races on Saturday 6 September. Bert Le Vack (New Imperial-JAP) ran away with the 350cc race, which had the biggest field of the day, and the 500cc race was won by Lieutenant Terry Grogan, a naval officer, riding a Norton. Sadly Grogan lost his life when HMS *Hood* was sunk in 1941. The BMCRC season finished with the club championships on 7 October, but these were spoiled by heavy rain.

The JCC 200-Mile race, held on 20 September, was now a regular fixture and was still the only long-distance car race being held at Brooklands. The Talbot-Darracq team returned; the supercharger had become an almost universal fitting in grand prix racing, and the team's voiturettes had this now-essential adjunct to high performance. The result was not in doubt, the Talbot-Darracqs finishing at the front of the 38-strong field in a convincing 1–2–3 led by Guinness, with jockey-turned-racing driver George Duller in the second car and Segrave, the team's grand prix

BELOW *The start of the JCC 200-Mile race on 20 September 1924. Harvey's Alvis leads Kenelm Lee Guinness's Talbot-Darracq. (LAT)*

LEFT *J.A. Joyce in the AC which set a 1,500cc Hour record at 104.19mph on 17 November 1924. (John Maitland Collection)*

BELOW *Bob Spikins on his 348cc Zenith-Blackburne after winning the 1,000cc Three Wheel Handicap at the Ealing DMCC meeting on 24 May 1924. The Swallow sidecar was the venture of William Lyons which led to the Jaguar car. (LAT)*

RIGHT *J.T. Boyd-Henry (No 4, 348cc Douglas), W.H. Julian (No 34, 247cc Levis) and D. Prentice (No 57, 1,045cc Morgan-Anzani) at the pits during the High Speed Trial at the MCC meeting on 26 July 1924. Heavy rain later forced the meeting to be abandoned. (Brooklands Society)*

Parry Thomas

Parry Thomas was the first great racing hero of Brooklands and regarded by many, including Percy Bradley, as the greatest of them all, winning 37 races at the track, more than any other driver. The son of a clergyman, he was born at Wrexham in 1885. He studied electrical engineering and in 1907 established a company to develop an electro-mechanical transmission which he had designed. This brought him into contact with Leyland Motors Ltd, and in 1917 he was appointed chief engineer of Leyland. He designed a luxury car, the Leyland Eight, which had many advanced features, and began his racing career in an Eight at Brooklands in 1922.

When Leyland decided not to go into production with the Eight, Thomas left the company and moved to Brooklands, where he became a consulting engineer, living in the 'Village' and working closely with Ken Thomson, with whom he had been a student and who had founded Thomson & Taylor as tuners and engineers at the track. Thomas began to develop a Leyland as a track car and this became the Leyland-Thomas, with which he won many races and established many World and international class records, including the coveted Hour. He broke the Brooklands lap record several times between 1923 and 1925, finally setting it at 129.36mph. With the Leyland-Thomas he also set a new Land Speed Record at the track in June 1924 at 129.73mph, which, while not the fastest speed recorded, was officially accepted as the record.

In 1925 he bought the Higham Special which had previously been owned by Count Zborowski, calling it 'Babs'. He developed this as a track car and a Land Speed Record contender. He broke the Land Speed Record with 'Babs' at Pendine Sands in April 1926 at 171.09mph, but was killed in a further record attempt at Pendine in March 1927. A shy, modest man, Thomas was deeply mourned. It was discovered after his death that he had maintained a cot at Great Ormond Street Hospital and this was permanently endowed as a memorial to him.

hero, in the third. The winner's average was 102.55mph.

The 1,100cc class, where the cars were rapidly becoming small racing cars and shaking off their spidery cyclecar image, was won by the Salmson of Owen Wilson-Jones. Like the Talbot-Darracqs, the Salmson had been dominant, as the Austin of Gordon England in second place, was 19 minutes behind. There was a spectacular accident when the chain of Ware's Morgan became entangled with the rear wheel and the car hit the fence adjoining the Vickers sheds at the Fork. Ware and his mechanic were both seriously injured.

The Talbot-Darracq win in the '200' was perhaps a slight consolation for the team, as Dario Resta driving a 2-litre GP Sunbeam, acknowledged as the fastest grand prix car during the 1924 season, had been killed on 3 September while attempting the International Class 'E' (2-litre) record for ten miles, when a tyre came off the rim on the Railway Straight and the car crashed through the boundary fence. Parry Thomas was luckier when a tyre burst during a World Hour Record attempt on 11 November and the Leyland-Thomas almost went over the top of the Members' Banking. Undaunted, he brought the car out again six days later and this time the Rapson tyres withstood the strain and he took the Hour at 109.09mph.

An air of sadness hung over Brooklands in the autumn, as Louis Zborowski, who had brought a new aura of glamour and excitement to the track, had been killed driving a 2-litre Mercedes in the Italian GP at Monza on 19 October.

1925

The application to restrain the noise at Brooklands was heard in the High Court on 2 July 1925, when it was agreed that the matter should be stayed, on an undertaking given by the BARC and Hugh Locke King that the track would comply with the terms agreed between the parties and set out in the Court's Order. The number of events was to be limited and the track was to be closed from 8:00pm until 8:00am. Motor cycles were barred from the track on Mondays and Thursdays and no motor cycle speed trial or race was to last for more than three hours, though this would not apply for four days in each month when record runs of up to 12 hours were permitted. On four days in the year motor cycle races of up to four hours were permitted. Smaller clubs were barred from the track.

The effect of this was to cause the cancellation of seven events. It can be seen that motor cycles were regarded as the major problem, though the 12-hour rules applied to cars too. The BARC imposed an additional silencing regulation in March 1925 which required all cars and motor cycles to have a fishtail fitted to the end of the exhaust pipe. Brooklands assumed an additional importance in March when the RAC imposed an immediate ban on all speed events on public roads following an accident involving a spectator at Kop Hill Climb in Essex. This left Brooklands and the Shelsley Walsh hill climb as the only permanent speed venues in England, Wales and Scotland, although sprint events on private land were not affected.

For the benefit of the spectators the 75mph (or slower) handicap finishes were returned to the Finishing Straight, but the faster races were cancelled at the Easter meeting as drizzle made the Outer Circuit unsafe. The Finishing Straight was the site of the finish for an Austin Seven race at the Whitsun meeting when, in the 100mph Short Handicap, Parry Thomas put a wheel of the Leyland-Thomas over the top edge of the Byfleet Banking, removing a shrub, but pressed on regardless, lapping at 125.77mph. There had already been drama in the race when Coe overturned his 30-98 Vauxhall when he pulled off the Members' Banking too sharply; fortunately he escaped with minor injuries. Thomas then won the Founders' Gold Cup race, postponed from Easter, and rounded off the meeting with a win in the Lightning Long Handicap, setting a new lap record on the way at 129.36mph.

The JCC held a new event on 2 May, a High Speed Trial where competitors had to cover a specified distance during an hour to win an award. This used a novel circuit with the Byfleet Banking and Railway Straight, from which the drivers turned onto the paddock return road, then on to the paddock entrance road, through the tunnel under the track, and thence round to the Members' Bridge and down the Test Hill to the Finishing

BELOW Jack Barclay won the First Long Handicap at the Surbiton MC meeting on 25 April 1925 in his 3-litre TT Vauxhall. He is on the Finishing Straight and behind him are the Fork grandstands. (LAT)

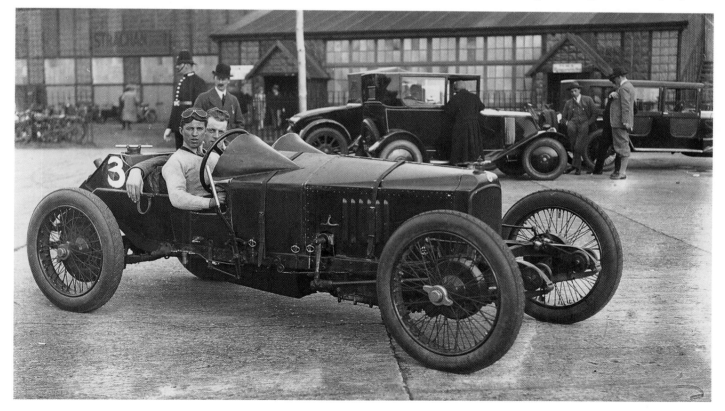

RIGHT *The start of the 100mph Short Handicap at the Summer 1925 meeting. Lanfranchi's 22/90 Alfa Romeo is nearest the camera and at the end of the row is the Leyland Thomas on scratch. (LAT)*

BELOW *The start of the legendary match race between Parry Thomas and Eldridge at the West Kent MC meeting on 11 July 1925. (Brooklands Society)*

Straight. Drivers had to obey a strict speed limit on the Test Hill. The entry was limited to 50 cars and was over-subscribed. It was a success and drew a big crowd, though Morgan owners were aggrieved at being excluded, perhaps as a consequence of Ware's accident in the 1924 '200'.

Saturday 11 July saw perhaps the most heroic race ever run at Brooklands. The restrictions on smaller clubs had forced West Kent MC to cut the motor cycle races from its programme on 11 July, but these were replaced by a momentous event, a match race over three laps between Parry Thomas with the Leyland-Thomas and Ernest Eldridge in the Fiat 'Mephistopheles'. It was reported that each driver put up a stake of £500. Only 2,000 spectators came to watch, though the weather was superb.

LEFT *Raymond Mays runs round his AC in the pits during the JCC 200 on 29 September 1925. Newman's Salmson is in front of the AC. Both retired from the race. (LAT)*

The start was in the Railway Straight. Thomas rode alone, but Eldridge had a passenger, Dudley Froy, who worked for Thomas and would later be a most active driver at the track. Thomas led away but the red Fiat was in front on the Byfleet Banking and crossed the Fork in a series of skids. The Fiat began to pull away slightly, but Thomas closed up again and on the second lap tried to pass on the Members' Banking, but the white and blue Leyland-Thomas slid down and he had to ease off. Eldridge slid sideways on the Byfleet Banking and again at the Fork. Going onto the Members' Banking on the third lap, Eldridge left room for Thomas to pass if he had the speed and the Leyland-Thomas went ahead. On the banking, to the horror of the spectators, Eldridge lost a rear tyre tread and Thomas lost a front tread, but neither lifted off and Thomas came home to win, having averaged 123.23mph and set a new lap record at 129.70mph, though it was not recognised, as 'Ebby' was not the timekeeper. After the race *The Autocar* commented 'a more horrid spectacle to sit and watch has probably never been seen in motor racing'. But when the horrified spectators recovered they realised that they had seen a superb demonstration of skill and courteous sportsmanship. This meeting was also historic in witnessing the debut of John Cobb, who would gain as big a reputation as Thomas in the next decade. On this occasion he won a handicap in a 1911 10-litre S61 Fiat.

Thomas was unstoppable. At the BARC August Bank Holiday meeting he entered the Leyland-Thomas and also the Thomas Special. This was a small single-seater with a narrow body and long tail. The chassis was made up of specialised components and the engine was a 1,847cc four-cylinder unit which had many features of the Leyland Eight. He won the 75mph Long Handicap with the Special, then won the 100mph Long Handicap in a 6-litre Lanchester entered by Rapson, the tyre manufacturer, and finished the day with a win in the 100-mile *News of the World* Handicap in

BELOW *Alf Depper's Austin 7 leads an Austin group around the artificial corner in the Finishing Straight during the 1925 JCC 200. Depper came third in the 750cc class. (LAT)*

RIGHT *H.M. Walters, sitting on the edge of the cockpit, gained 16 class records with the tiny 346cc Jappic during 1925. (Brooklands Society)*

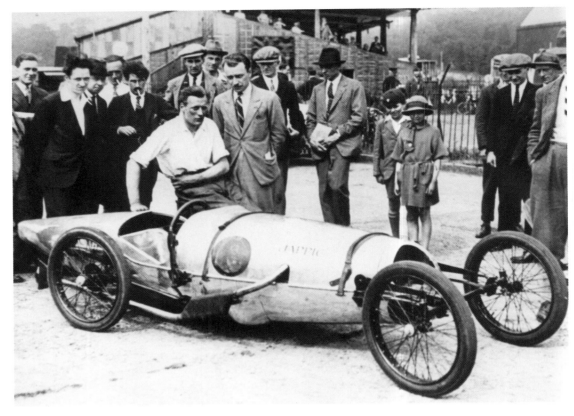

BELOW *A group, including a Morgan, on the Byfleet Banking during the MCC High Speed Trial on 17 October 1925. (Brooklands Society)*

the Special. While Thomas was busy on the track the local fire brigade was busy extinguishing a small fire in the Clubhouse.

As well as his racing pre-eminence, Thomas had also been breaking records, and among those he took during the season was the World Hour, in which he raised his previous speed to 110.64mph.

The JCC broke new ground with the 200-Mile race on 26 September. Instead of a flat-out run on the Outer Circuit, the cars ran off the Byfleet Banking into the Finishing Straight, where they rounded a barrel by making a hairpin turn, then ran back to the Fork and back on to the Outer Circuit again. There were 25 starters and both classes ran together. The Talbot-Darracq team had returned and Segrave ran away with the race, leading from start to finish. An Alvis driven by Harvey ran second for a while but then dropped back, and second place was held at the end by the Talbot-Darracq of Count Giulio Masetti. The quickest 1,100cc was the Salmson of Pierre Goutte, which finished third.

Despite the silencing restrictions motor cycle racing continued, and on 16 May the BMCRC initiated a new event, the 'Hutchinson 100', a 100-mile handicap which was to become an annual fixture. It was a difficult race for the spectators to follow as the limit 250cc P&P had a 28-minute start over the scratch 996cc McEvoy-Temple. One of the back markers, Longman on a 996cc Harley-Davidson, came through to win from the 350cc Zenith-JAP of Walters.

The BMCRC 'Cup' day on 18 July produced a big crowd in fine weather, and in the three-lap 1,000cc solo race Joe Wright was the winner on a 980cc Zenith-JAP at an average of 103.76mph, the second-fastest race speed yet. More importantly, on his second lap he went round the track at 110.43mph, a new motor cycle lap record. New class records were being set too, and on 19 August Harold Beart brought out a 1,098cc Morgan-Blackburne and recorded 104.37mph for a flying kilometre, the first time a three-wheeler had exceeded the '100'.

For many riders, however, the 500cc Hour record was the ultimate prize, and on 13 November Wal Handley did an amazing run on a 350cc Rex-Acme-Blackburne to record 89.39mph, taking the 500cc record despite the 150cc handicap. But he did not hold the record for long, as the very next day Vic Horsman did an hour at 90.79mph on a works 500cc Triumph. Horsman was the agent for Triumph in Liverpool, and mindful of the duration of the publicity he set the record on the last day the track was open, knowing that it could not be beaten until the following spring.

Records were being made off the track too, as there had been hot competition on the Test Hill during the season. The record passed several times between Joyce in an AC and Frazer-Nash in one of his own cars, with Frazer-Nash having the last word on 12 November with a time of 7.69sec – though this was only the car record, as Russell Coes had climbed the slope in 7.30sec with a Brough Superior SS 100.

Brooklands now had a rival as a record-breaking venue, as the Montlhéry track had opened outside Paris the previous year. The French course enjoyed many advantages over Brooklands: 24-hour running was permitted, there were no silencing regulations, and the surface was much superior. For the faster drivers and riders it was also safer, a pure banked oval with no unbanked reverse Vickers curve, which was an appreciable hazard for the faster runners. The poor surface at Brooklands was by now a serious problem. It was punishing on car suspensions and broken chassis frames were not uncommon, while motor cycles with minimal front springing and no rear springing at all suffered even more. The pounding on rider and machine was relentless and mechanical failures were common, with broken frames and even handlebar fractures.

BELOW J.W. Wheeler won the 350/1,000cc Solo Handicap at the Essex MC meeting on 9 May 1925 riding his 500cc Douglas. (LAT)

CHAPTER SIX

ERA OF THE SPORTS CAR

1926

Hugh Locke King died at Brooklands House on 28 January 1926 aged 77, and was buried in Weybridge Cemetery after a short service in the cemetery chapel. His estate was valued at £53,782 (about £2 million by present-day standards), and the sole beneficiary of his will was his wife Ethel. In August 1922 they had jointly formed the Brooklands Estate Co and were the sole shareholders. The track, flying ground and some other properties had been transferred to the company at a price of £100,000, and Hugh had been paid a salary of £2,500 as governing director. Hugh's shares in the company now passed to Ethel and she became in effect the sole proprietor and governing director of both track and airfield.

The track had been damaged when the River Wey flooded in February 1926 after 18 days of continuous rain, but the repairs had been completed by the time it opened on 8 March. At the suggestion of Parry Thomas a dotted black line was painted 10ft from the top of the Members' Banking and competitors were required to drive sufficiently far below this line to enable another competitor to overtake. The line was not to be crossed unless there was no possibility of obstructing another driver.

It was to be a landmark year for Brooklands with the staging of the track's first major international

Robert Benoist in his Delage, on the way to victory in the 1927 British Grand Prix and to securing the 1927 World Championship, follows George Eyston's Type 39A Bugatti onto the Members' Banking. (LAT)

the amateur riders, for whom racing at the track had already become a way of life, little changed except that the fields were smaller and there was less competition from the manufacturers. A decision of much greater importance to Brooklands riders was the announcement by J.A. Prestwich & Co, the makers of JAP engines, that it was closing its racing department, a decision forced upon it by the growing national economic depression. This closure forced Bert Le Vack to seek a new employer, and he joined New Hudson.

Foreign competitors at the BARC meetings were unusual. Most expressed the view that they preferred scratch races where the result was in their own hands and not reliant on the stopwatches of 'Ebby', but at the Easter Monday meeting on 5 April, Pierre Goutte – who had risen through the ranks as a fitter in the Salmson workshops – came from France and ran his 1,100cc Salmson. Despite lurid skids, he gained a first and a second, and set a 1,100cc lap record of 114.49mph which was to stand for many years.

The BMCRC meeting the following Saturday was notable for the high speeds attained and in the 1,000cc solo race there was a fierce fight between Joe Wright (Zenith-JAP), George Patchett (McEvoy-JAP) and Knight (Zenith-JAP). Wright won and the pace was so fast that he set a new motor cycle lap record of 113.45mph, which was equalled later in the meeting by Oliver Baldwin (Zenith-JAP).

ABOVE *An official gazes thoughtfully at the engine of H.J. Aldington's Frazer Nash which retired from the JCC Production Car Race on 17 July 1926. The grandstands overlooking the pits burned down in September 1926. (LAT)*

motor race. Motor cycle racing, however, would be affected by a decision of the Autocycle Union (ACU) that machines competing in the Isle of Man TT races should be restricted to pump fuel; alcohol-based fuels were banned. This rule was also adopted by continental European clubs, so the attractions of racing at the track were considerably reduced for manufacturers, who were not inclined to have a separate range of alcohol engines for Brooklands, where success attracted much less publicity than that gained in the Isle of Man. For

ABOVE *Malcolm Campbell's Type 39A Bugatti leads a Talbot through the Finishing Straight chicanes. The new bridge with somewhat hazardous supports can be seen in the distance. Campbell finished the Grand Prix in second place. (LAT)*

LEFT *The field lines up at the top of the Finishing Straight for the start of the first British GP on 7 August 1926. (LAT)*

ABOVE *The winning Delage slides wide at one of the sandbank chicanes in the Finishing Straight while being chased by Divo's Talbot in the later stages of the Grand Prix. (LAT)*

BELOW *The victorious Robert Senechal and Louis Wagner, perhaps nursing their burned feet, at the end of the British GP. (LAT)*

Parry Thomas had bought the Higham Special from Zborowski's executors and this was rebuilt and extensively modified during 1925. Renamed 'Babs', it appeared on the track during April 1926 while Thomas tested it in preparation for an attempt on the World Land Speed record at Pendine in Wales. Thomas was successful and set a new record of 171.09mph on 28 April, so there was great excitement when 'Babs' was entered for the BARC Whitsun meeting. The crowd was not disappointed and Thomas gained a second place, though 'Babs' never lapped Brooklands as fast as the faithful Leyland-Thomas.

At the beginning of May the country was paralysed by the General Strike and many of the Brooklands drivers and riders, including Segrave,

signed up with the hastily formed Organisation for the Maintenance of Supplies to assist in keeping essential services running.

The 200-Mile sidecar races on 26 June almost deteriorated into farce. The 350cc race, won by E.S. Prestwich on a Coventry Eagle-JAP, had only two finishers – the rest were limping around or had retired – and there was only one finisher in the 600cc race, Vic Horsman (Triumph), who just made the finish by coasting in with a dead engine. Worse still, in the 1,000cc race there were no finishers at all; the whole field fell out with mechanical problems. There was a better spectacle in the 'Hutchinson 100' on 28 August, though the handicapping was too harsh for the faster machines and the 1,000cc scratch man was expected to lap at a speed faster than the 1,000cc 100-mile international class record. Not surprisingly, the winner – Cecil Barrow on a 246cc Royal Enfield – came from the earlier starters.

The JCC was much more enterprising than the BARC and on 17 July it organised a three-hour race for production cars up to 1,500cc over a course similar to that used for the 1925 '200'. The cars ran in three classes, up to 750cc, 1,100cc and 1,500cc, each class being a separate race. Harvey's 12/50 Alvis led in the opening laps, then dropped out with run big ends, and at the end of the three hours Hazlehurst's Salmson had covered the greatest distance, winning the 1,100cc class. Bagshawe's Frazer Nash was the 1,500cc class winner.

There was a fatal accident during practice for the August Bank Holiday meeting when the Napier-

Sunbeam, a Napier chassis with a Sunbeam aero engine, overturned on the Byfleet Banking after a front axle U-bolt broke. Its driver, Bone, escaped, but his fiancée, who was the passenger, was killed. This was the second fatality of 1926, as G.L. Parkes was killed on 20 July when testing a Brough Superior-JAP which went over the top of the Members' Banking. He was the second motor cyclist to die at Brooklands.

Thomas scored two wins with the Leyland-Thomas at the August meeting, while the big race of the day, the *Evening News* 100-mile handicap, was won by Captain Douglas in a Type 37 Bugatti. Bugattis were appearing in ever-increasing numbers at the track and there was a Bugatti-only handicap at the Summer meeting.

Although grand prix racing to the established international formula was regarded as the pinnacle of the sport, Britain had never yet staged a GP. The 2-litre GP formula which was in force from 1922 until 1925 had attracted large fields on the Continent, with cars from many manufacturers, and a successful 2-litre formula race might have had a beneficial effect on the development of motor racing in Britain. When the new 1,500cc formula came into effect in 1926 the manufacturers' support disappeared and only three French companies – Delage, Bugatti and Talbot, the French arm of the Sunbeam-Talbot-Darracq combine – built new cars. It was therefore an inauspicious time for the RAC to enter the grand prix field, but the first RAC British Grand Prix was nevertheless held on 7 August. This

BELOW *Albert Divo (Talbot) leads Frank Halford (Halford Special) on to the Members' Banking, and Jules Moriceau attempts to dig his Talbot out of the sandbank, during the JCC 200-Mile race on 25 September 1926. (John Maitland Collection)*

was run over 110 laps (287 miles) of a course which used the Railway Straight, the Byfleet Banking and the Finishing Straight, where two chicanes were made of sandbags. A bridge was built across the Finishing Straight, with supports in the middle of the track protected by sandbags, so that spectators could walk across from the Members' Hill to the paddock.

The race attracted 14 entries, but only nine of these arrived to race. Bugatti, which had won the two previous GPs of the year, did not come, and the star attractions were the teams from Delage and Talbot. The Delages were fast but had found problems on their debut in Spain, while the Talbot team was racing the new Type 700 for the first time. The three British entries were a Type 39 Bugatti which Malcolm Campbell had persuaded the factory to release, the Halford Special, and an elderly Aston Martin driven by George Eyston. One of the Talbots fell out with a broken front axle on the opening lap, but Segrave and Divo in the other cars held the lead in the early stages.

When Divo's engine misfired and Segrave stopped for tyres Robert Benoist took the lead in a Delage. He then had problems with the exhaust, which ran too close to the driver's feet and was burning him. The third Delage had dropped out, so the drivers of the remaining pair took turns at the wheel while their feet recovered. Divo, whose

car was going well again, began to catch up, but just when it seemed he might take the lead the Talbot retired with a seized supercharger. This left the Delage shared by Robert Senechal and Louis Wagner in front, but it had further problems as the exhaust had broken and there were signs of an incipient fire under the bonnet. The pair nevertheless nursed the car home to take the flag, followed by Campbell's Bugatti which had run steadily throughout. Third place was taken by the second Delage of Benoist, who was sharing it with André Dubonnet, the aperitif heir. There were no other finishers. Benoist would be captured in France during World War Two whilst serving as an MI5 agent and would later be executed in Buchenwald concentration camp.

After the excitement of the Grand Prix it was back to the normal calendar, and the Essex MC ran an unusual race at its meeting a week later with a three-lap match handicap race between Thomas in the Leyland-Thomas, Campbell in a Type 35 Bugatti, the 350cc Grindlay Peerless-JAP of Bill Lacey, and Knight's 980cc Zenith-JAP. Campbell caught Lacey, but Thomas almost collided with Knight crossing the Fork and had to ease off, so he finished fourth. After the race Thomas commented tersely to Knight: 'You're fortunate to be alive.'

The BARC Autumn meeting saw two more wins for Parry Thomas in the Leyland-Thomas. These

LEFT *Victor Horsman (599cc Triumph sidecar combination) and Freddie Dixon (500cc Douglas) at the BMCRC opening meeting on 20 March 1926. The seating position of the passenger was not unusual. (Brooklands Society)*

BELOW *E.S. Prestwich is congratulated after winning the 350cc class with his Coventry Eagle at the 200-Mile Sidecar meeting on 26 June 1926. (Brooklands Society)*

ABOVE *Dougal Marchant gained the BMCRC 350cc Sidecar Championship on his Chater Lea, with the aid of a very young passenger, on 18 September 1926. (Brooklands Society)*

were to be his last at BARC meetings. The JCC 200 on 25 September complied with the new GP formula and attracted a much larger field than the British GP. There were 44 entries and 23 of these were 1,500cc cars. The Talbot team headed the list together with Campbell's Bugatti, but there were interesting entries which had not been ready for the Grand Prix. The Alvis company had produced two front-wheel-drive straight-eight cars which were revolutionary in design, and Parry Thomas had designed and built two Thomas Specials for the new GP formula which had a straight-eight engine in a notably low chassis. These were consequently nicknamed the 'Thomas Flat-Irons'.

The race was over a course which used the Finishing Straight, Railway Straight and Byfleet Banking. The cars ran past the Fork then rounded a hairpin and returned to the Finishing Straight, where there was a sandbank chicane at the top end. The lap distance was 2.76 miles. Shortly before the race the grandstand facing the Vickers sheds at the Fork burned down. The race itself, over 73 laps, was an easy win for the Talbot team. Divo led at the start from Moriceau and Segrave, but Moriceau then slid into the chicane sandbank and took some time to free his car, so Segrave went past Divo and on to win. Divo was second and Harold Purdy in a Type 37 Bugatti was third, just keeping in front of the fastest 1,100cc car, the 6C Amilcar of Martin. Both Alvises retired, but Thomas finished eighth in his 'Flat-Iron'.

The Brooklands motor racing season closed on 2 October with another meeting organised by the

active Essex MC, which received royal patronage with the presence of King Faisal of Iraq. The King watched Thomas win a handicap with the Leyland-Thomas, then gain a second victory driving the new Thomas Special in the main event of the day, a 50-mile handicap. The Brooklands crowd would not see Thomas race again.

To coincide with the last day of the Motor Cycle Show at Olympia, the BMCRC held an innovative meeting for the Grand Prix Motor Cycle Races. This used what would become known as the Mountain Circuit. The riders started by the Clubhouse in the Finishing Straight, then negotiated a sandbank bend before going onto the Members' Banking in a clockwise direction and running down to the sharp hairpin at the Fork. In the Finishing Straight, a fast bend was marked out before the riders reached the start-finish line. The crowd could see most of the action and it was a most successful meeting, with close and exciting racing. Each class raced over 43 laps and in the 250cc race victory went to newcomer Eric Fernihough on a Zenith-JAP. He would become a major figure in motor cycle racing at the track.

Seven World and 18 International car class records were broken at Brooklands during 1926. At the top of the tree, Thomas pushed the World Hour record up to 121.74mph in the Leyland-Thomas on 21 October, while at the other end of the scale Kaye Don brought out the minute Avon-Jappic with a 500cc engine and in several separate runs during the season took the class hour at 62.2mph and the three-hour class record at 61.96mph.

As already mentioned, record-breaking was a profitable business, though it needed endurance, skill and good preparation. A driver or rider who took a record could expect to receive good financial bonuses from the fuel, oil and tyre companies and also from other companies whose products were associated with the record. For a short distance record, a mile or kilometre, Castrol would pay a bonus of £5, which was a reasonable payment when the average weekly wage in the 1920s was £2. Enterprising competitors would break a record by only a small margin, then come out again for another attempt and continue to break the record by small margins, cashing in each time. This practice became so widespread that the AIACR and FICM, the governing bodies for car and motor cycle racing, stepped in and ruled that for a record to receive a bonus it had to stand for 29 days. There were reports that some of the more active record-breakers 'leaned' on the lesser lights who wanted to make attempts, pointing out that if a record was broken it would be regained within the 29-day period, leaving the newcomer empty-handed.

1927

The motor racing world was shattered by the news that Parry Thomas had been killed on 3 March while attempting to break the World Land Speed record at Pendine Sands in Carmarthenshire, driving 'Babs'. For those closely connected with Brooklands the news was more poignant, as Thomas lived at the track, which, with his cars, was his whole life. At 41, a bachelor whose homely appearance in a Fair Isle sweater and grubby flannels was the very antithesis of a motor racing hero, Thomas was nonetheless a true champion, especially to those who watched his incredible drives at the track. The statistics tell the story, as he won more races there than any other driver.

Severe weather delayed repairs to the track, which were extensive during the winter of 1926/7. Much of the surface was relaid on the Members' Banking under the Members' Bridge, at the Fork, and from the end of the Railway Straight to halfway round the Byfleet Banking. The pedestrian bridge across the Finishing Straight was rebuilt with a single span and a new building was erected at the Fork, which had a bar, tea room, press office and a club room for the BMCRC. On top there was a grandstand with 20 seats and standing room for 500. This replaced the old grandstand, which had burnt down the previous September.

Delays to the repairs caused the cancellation of the opening BARC meeting on 19 March, so the Easter meeting opened the season. Kaye Don had a successful day, driving the 4.9-litre Sunbeam built in 1924 to attempt the 24-hour record. He won the Founders' Gold Cup and the 100mph Long Handicap, and was second in the Lightning Long Handicap behind Malcolm Campbell's Type 35B Bugatti. The Bugatti made the fastest lap of the day at 119.15mph.

The JCC was innovative again at its own meeting on 30 April, holding the Junior Grand Prix for 1,500cc cars on the Mountain Circuit, with two chicanes in the Finishing Straight. The race was won by Purdy's Type 37 Bugatti.

The early and mid-1920s saw the rapid evolution of the sports car. Before World War One, a driver with sporting inclinations had the alternative of a racing car or a fast touring car, both only affordable by the rich. But the arrival of the sports car in the early 1920s catered for many pockets, providing a variety of models ranging from the expensive high-performance car, typified by the Bentley, to small sports car which had developed from the cyclecar, such as the Amilcar and sports Austin Seven. At Brooklands, the club meetings provided events for these cars, while in the international world the Le Mans 24-Hour race, which had begun in 1923, had in four years become the pinnacle for both drivers and manufacturers. It was felt that there should be

BELOW *Hayward's Excelsior follows a Salmson and Jackson's Sunbeam in the Essex MC 6-Hour Race on 7 May 1927.* **The cars ran in the early laps with hoods erected. The bridge supports had been removed during the previous winter.** *(LAT)*

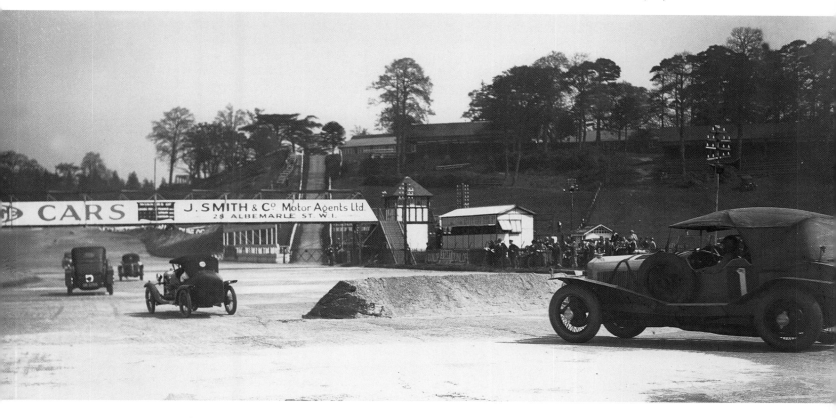

ABOVE *Sammy Davis,*
the winner on handicap
of the 1927 6-Hour race,
takes his 12/50 Alvis
through the chicane
ahead of Durlacher's
Diatto. (LAT)

BELOW *Kaye Don in the*
2-litre GP Sunbeam
after winning the Gold
Star Handicap at the
1927 Whitsun meeting.
(Brooklands Society)

a similar type of race in England: 24 hours at
Brooklands was impossible, but 12 hours was
feasible. A race was considered by several clubs and
the Essex MC accepted the challenge and
organised a six-hour event for mildly-modified
unsupercharged production sports cars on 7 May,
which would be the longest car race yet held on
the British mainland.

The 2.6 mile course used the Finishing Straight
with two chicanes, the Railway Straight, and the
Byfleet Banking. Forty-six cars were entered and 29
of these, ranging from a 30-98 Vauxhall, 3-litre
Bentleys and Sunbeams down to two Austin
Sevens, started the race. It began with a 'Le Mans'

start where the drivers and mechanics ran across
the track to their car, erected the hoods, and set
off, having to do ten laps before the hoods could
be lowered. In the early stages the 3-litre Bentleys
of Clement and Benjafield led the 3-litre Sunbeams
of Segrave and Duller. The Bentleys, however, had
new duralumin rockers which broke up, and two
retired, while Segrave's Sunbeam ran out of fuel.
This was to be Segrave's last motor race: he had
lost interest in the sport and was drawn by the
attractions of motor boat racing and by record-
breaking on land and water.

Duller's Sunbeam continued to lead. He was
followed by the Bentley shared by Henry (Tim)
Birkin and his brother Charles, but this had
gearbox problems and a broken spare wheel
mounting and fell back, to be passed by a 12/50
Alvis driven by S.C.H. (Sammy) Davis, the sports
editor of *The Autocar*. Duller won, having covered
386 miles at an average of 64.3mph. Davis was
second, 14 miles behind, and the Bentley limped
into third place. Duller received the Barnato Cup
while *The Autocar* Cup for the best performance
on handicap was won by Davis, who received
much gentle ribbing about his connection with
the journal. Eighteen cars finished the race, while
two more were still running at the end but were
not classified.

The principal race at the BARC Whitsun meeting
was for the Gold Star, and the presentation after
the race was to be made by Edgar Wallace, the
detective novelist, but the meeting was spoiled by
heavy rain and was abandoned after four races. The
World Land Speed Record had been broken at

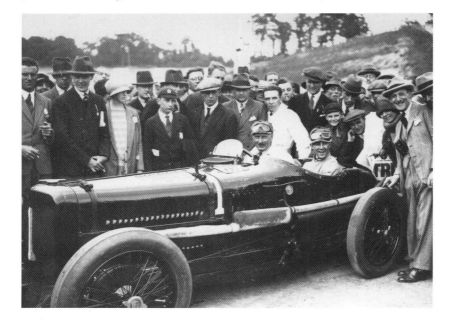

Daytona Beach in Florida in March, by Henry Segrave, driving a twin-engined 1,000hp Sunbeam at 207mph. Despite the rain he demonstrated the car at the Whitsun meeting, though he could only run at a touring speed.

The postponed Gold Star race, over 25 miles, was run on 8 June and Kaye Don was the winner in a 1924 2-litre GP Sunbeam at 118.58mph, lapping at 124.51mph. The days of the big monsters were ending and small-capacity cars were lapping at the same speeds. Three days later there was an Alvis Day sponsored by the London dealer and distributor, Henlys. There was a full programme of short races in which Alvises were prominent.

It was a poor summer. Rain forced the cancellation of the August Bank Holiday meeting and it rained again for the JCC Four-Hour Sporting car race on 13 August. This was for cars up to 1½-litre capacity. The race was another success for Alvis, with the 12/50s of Harvey and Green taking first and second places. Harvey led at the start but made a long pit stop for new plugs which left Peacock (Lea Francis) in the lead, and then Green went to the front. Meanwhile Harvey was climbing through the field, coping with the appalling weather conditions, and by the beginning of the

third hour he was back in the lead where he stayed for the rest of the race.

Sports car races were becoming popular, and the Surbiton Motor Club organised a 150-mile event at the track with a handicap based on fuel consumption. It was won by an Austin Seven, with a Type 43 Bugatti driven by Campbell in second place.

The September BARC meeting had good weather and saw the debut of the prototype Brooklands Riley Nine, a car developed for Riley by Parry Thomas and raced by Reid Railton, who had been Thomas's assistant. Railton had an easy win in the 90mph Short Handicap, the first of many for this model in the years to come. The main event was the 50-Mile Handicap, which saw another Alvis win, Hallam's 12/50 coming in first followed by John Cobb in a 1922 TT Vauxhall.

The 1,500cc Grand Prix formula, meanwhile, had not been a success and the fields were small. It was recognised that the formula would change at the end of the 1927 season and would be replaced by a de facto formule libre. The season had been dominated by the Delage team, and Robert Benoist, its No 1 driver, had won all three previous grande epreuves, so when he came to Brooklands on 1 October for the 2nd RAC British Grand Prix he

ABOVE *Raymond Mays looks strained, as his 2-litre eight-cylinder Mercedes gave him a difficult ride when taking second place in the Second 100mph Long Handicap at the 1927 Autumn meeting. (John Maitland Collection)*

was seeking a fourth victory as a triumphal conclusion to his season. The race attracted a thin field. The Talbot team had withdrawn from racing and the Type 39A Bugattis were no match for the Delages, so on a cold day the three Delages were faced by just three works Bugattis, three private Bugattis, and the two Thomas Specials. The course was the same as the previous year, but the race was longer, over 125 laps (327 miles).

When the field was flagged away from the start line at the end of the Members' Banking, Emilio Materassi held the lead for the first lap in his works Bugatti. But the three Delages then swept past and they were not challenged again, simply swapping places to relieve the monotony. The three Bugattis faded away behind, while the Thomas Specials only lasted for a few laps and the other private entrants dropped out. A light drizzle fell before the end of the race but it did not deter Benoist, who won at an average of 85.59mph, having taken 3hr 49min 14.6sec for his drive. He was followed by his team-mates Bourlier and Divo, while Louis Chiron, the 'new boy' in the Bugatti team, was the only other driver to complete the distance, being 28min behind Benoist at the finish. The other two Bugattis were flagged off. It had been a dull, grey day and for the spectators the race was equally dull. It would be 21 years before the RAC ran another British GP, in a very different setting at Silverstone.

Despite the anticlimax of the Grand Prix, the JCC ran the 200-Mile race again two weeks later, on

LEFT *The Type 39A Bugattis of Emilio Materassi (No 11), Louis Chiron (No 12) and Malcolm Campbell (No 5) lead the field at the start of the British GP on 1 October 1927. (LAT)*

BELOW LEFT *Chiron's Bugatti leads Divo's Delage through the chicane in front of the pits during the Grand Prix. (LAT)*

BELOW *Harold Purdy's Thomas Special leads at the start of the JCC 200 on 15 October 1927. The cars missed the chicanes on the first lap, though Urquhart-Dykes's 12/50 Alvis seems to have different tactics. (LAT)*

RIGHT *Broken and retired cars lined up at the trackside during the JCC 200. The Bugattis of Eyston and Scott are prominent. (LAT)*

TOP RIGHT *Bill Lacey with his 498cc Grindlay-Peerless-JAP after winning the 90mph Handicap at the BMCRC meeting on 20 April 1927. During the race he lapped at 100.41mph. Lacey was renowned for the superb finish of his machines. (Brooklands Society)*

MIDDLE RIGHT *Wal Phillips grins happily after winning the Private Owners' Handicap on his 344cc Cotton-JAP at the BMCRC meeting on 25 June 1927. Phillips was Bert Le Vack's nephew. (Brooklands Society)*

BOTTOM RIGHT *A group of riders on the Byfleet Banking during the 'Hutchinson 100' on 3 September 1927. (Brooklands Society)*

15 October, which seems to have been an unfortunate example of calendar planning. With the inclusion of 1,100cc and 750cc classes, a big field took part and there were 28 starters. The front-wheel-drive GP Alvis which had not been ready for the Grand Prix led in the early laps, followed by the Type 39A Bugattis of George Eyston and Campbell. Eyston led at ten laps, then Campbell took the lead and stayed there. Eyston dropped out and Campbell was then pursued by the very fast C6 Amilcar of André Morel, which was dominating the 1,100cc class. Campbell nevertheless won, and was followed home by Morel and two more Amilcars, whilst a Thomas driven by Purdy was fifth.

The shortcomings of Brooklands as a record-breaking venue for cars became obvious in 1927. Although many class records were broken during the season there were no World records. Montlhéry had become the centre for these attempts. The motor cyclists still sought records, though, and the first notable achievement came on 2 April when Bert Denly on a 588cc Norton covered 5km at 105.91mph, the highest speed yet

achieved with a single-cylinder machine. The Norton was tuned by Nigel Spring, who had taken over the works Nortons at the track when Dan O'Donovan retired at the end of 1926. Denly was out with the Norton again on 20 April for the second BMCRC meeting. It was a glorious, sunny day, and perhaps encouraged by this he beat Bert Le Vack (496cc New Hudson) in the 500cc race and became the first rider to win a Brooklands race on a 500 at over 100mph.

The BMCRC 200-Mile solo race meeting on 9 July was a typical 1927 day with heavy rain which partially flooded the track. Indeed, the rainfall that year hit record levels, being 80 per cent greater than the average. At the meeting J.S. (Woolly) Worters, who had established a considerable reputation as a tuner at the track, led all the way to win the 250cc race on an Excelsior-JAP. Then Chris Staniland, an RAF pilot, rode a Worters-tuned Excelsior-JAP to win the 350cc race after A.P. (Ginger) Hamilton, who had led until halfway, stopped to repair a loose tank on his Velocette and subsequently came in second.

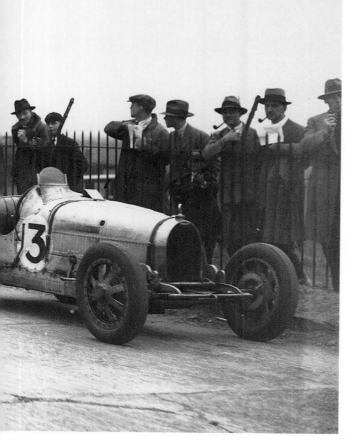

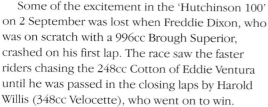

Some of the excitement in the 'Hutchinson 100' on 2 September was lost when Freddie Dixon, who was on scratch with a 996cc Brough Superior, crashed on his first lap. The race saw the faster riders chasing the 248cc Cotton of Eddie Ventura until he was passed in the closing laps by Harold Willis (348cc Velocette), who went on to win.

An unusual record run took place on 18 and 19 October. Six standard roadgoing ES2 Nortons were taken off the production line and delivered to Brooklands where one was selected by ACU officials. This was ridden by Spring, Staniland, Emerson and Denly to take the Double-12 record. The run was completed in the dusk by means of the headlights of a following Lagonda. The result was a record run of 1,494.69 miles.

In November the FICM prohibited the use of Brooklands for flying-start mile and kilometre records, as the measured distance was approached from the Members' Banking where the gradient gave an additional advantage. At the end of the year the BMCRC announced that a Gold Star would be awarded to any rider who officially lapped Brooklands at over 100mph.

1928

The winter of 1927/8 was severe. In March blizzards swept Britain, and rain and poor visibility caused the cancellation of the first BMCRC meeting. Fortunately there was much better weather for the BARC Easter meeting. For spectators coming to Brooklands by train, the Southern Railway service had been improved by the electrification of the line from Waterloo at the beginning of the year. The main attraction of the meeting itself was a demonstration by Malcolm Campbell driving the Napier-engined 'Blue Bird' with which he had broken the Land Speed Record at Daytona in February at 206.95mph. Campbell drove the car around the 'Mountain' at quite a rapid pace. The racing provided wins in the 100mph and 90mph Short Handicaps for Chris Staniland in a Type 37A Bugatti.

Two weeks later there was a midweek charity meeting in aid of the Royal Westminster Ophthalmic Hospital and this was followed by the JCC Spring meeting, where the Mountain course was used for the 20-lap Junior Grand Prix. With the end of the 1½-litre GP formula the Delage company had withdrawn from racing and Campbell had bought one of their all-conquering 1½-litre cars. This dominated the field much as it had done in the British GP the previous autumn,

and the Bugattis of Eyston and Benjafield pursued it in vain.

The Essex MC repeated its Six-Hour Endurance race on 12 May, running it on the same course as in 1927. The principal award would go to the car with the best result on handicap, with a lesser award to the car covering the greatest distance. Forty-six entries were received, including factory teams from Bentley and Alfa Romeo, and 39 cars started, covering the first ten laps with hoods erected. The Type 43 Bugattis of Lord Curzon and Campbell led initially, but both soon dropped back with tyre and ignition bothers. A 4½-litre Bentley driven by Woolf Barnato then took the lead on the road, though the race was being led on handicap by Giulio Ramponi's 6C-1500 Alfa Romeo. Frank Clement, who had taken over the leading Bentley, had problems with stretched brake rods and Tim Birkin in the team's second car took the lead on the road and maintained the pursuit of Ramponi on handicap.

There was drama when a Lea Francis caught fire on the Railway Straight and a darkening sky threatened rain. On the road, the Bentley team continued to dominate the race, but on handicap Ramponi was uncatchable, while an Austin Seven driven by Dingle was also coming into the handicap reckoning. The rain held off and at the end of the

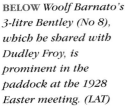

BELOW *Woolf Barnato's 3-litre Bentley (No 8), which he shared with Dudley Froy, is prominent in the paddock at the 1928 Easter meeting. (LAT)*

LEFT *Malcolm Campbell's World Land Speed Record Napier-Campbell 'Blue Bird' being readied for a demonstration at the 1928 Easter meeting. (LAT)*

BELOW *Campbell's GP Delage leads Eyston's Bugatti onto the Members' Banking during the Junior Grand Prix at the JCC meeting on 28 April 1928. There was no room for an adult passenger in the Delage, so Campbell carried a schoolboy, Alec Rivers-Fletcher. (LAT)*

ABOVE *A variety of Lagondas in the paddock at the Lagonda Fête on 5 July 1928. (LAT)*

RIGHT *A.V. Ebblewhite 'Ebby', the legendary Brooklands timekeeper. (Brooklands Society)*

FAR RIGHT *Perhaps the most versatile of all competitors at Brooklands. Chris Staniland – outstanding as a driver, rider and pilot – works on his Type 37A Bugatti. He did a remarkable lap of 121.47mph in this at the 1928 September meeting. (Brooklands Society)*

six hours the Bentley of Birkin had covered the greatest distance followed by the cars shared by Benjafield and Rubin and by Barnato and Clement. Ramponi took the Essex Cup for the handicap win, with Dingle in second place.

Sunbeam had cut back on racing, and with Segrave's retirement Kaye Don had become the principal works driver. As well as the 1924 2-litre GP Sunbeam he drove the 4-litre V12 Sunbeam with which Segrave had broken the Land Speed Record on Southport Sands at 152.33mph in March 1926. Sunbeam had built two 4-litre V12 cars designed with the dual purpose of racing and record-breaking. 'Babs' was the last Land Speed car with this flexibility and by the beginning of 1927 Land Speed Record cars had become a specialised breed.

Kaye Don had taken class records up to 100km with the 4-litre car, named 'Tiger', during the week before the BARC Whitsun meeting, and he raced it for the first time on 28 May. Running in the Gold Star Handicap, Don came through from scratch to win at 128.36mph, the fastest race average yet at the track. More significantly, during the race he set a new lap record at 131.76mph. There was additional excitement for the spectators when Turnbull's Type 35 Bugatti spun on the Members' Banking and collided with R.F. Oats's OM. A wheel was torn off the Bugatti but neither driver was hurt.

The Surbiton MC repeated its 150-mile sports car fuel consumption handicap on 9 June. Taylor's 19/100 Austro-Daimler was the winner, followed home by Lord Curzon's Type 43 Bugatti. To celebrate midsummer, the BARC held an evening meeting on 21 June. One of the races was a ladies' handicap, which was won by Miss Maconochie in a Salmson, beating five other lady drivers. Miss Maconochie and her Salmson were successful again at the Middlesex MC meeting on 1 July, where Mrs Jill Scott won a three-lap handicap in a C6 Amilcar, then, promoted to a works drive, went on to win the main race of the day, the 18-lap 50-mile Middlesex Handicap. Driving the 2-litre GP Sunbeam she came through the field from scratch, passing her husband W.B. ('Bummer') Scott in an Amilcar en route. Her average of 110.43mph was the fastest recorded speed achieved by a woman at the track up to that time. 'Bummer' Scott had himself achieved a sporting distinction, being a Cambridge rugby blue.

The JCC returned to Brooklands for the 200-Mile race on 21 July. Run over 73 laps on the same course as the previous years it drew 30 entries, of which 26 started. The dominant car was Campbell's Delage, which led from start to finish. On the opening lap Basil Eyston, driving his brother George's Type 39A Bugatti, had a minor collision with the Thomas Special being driven by Purdy. The Thomas retired with a bent frame, but the Bugatti carried on and, shared by George, finished second, albeit 22min behind the Delage. Kaye Don, continuing his successful season, was third in a Lea Francis; a month later he would win the first Ulster Tourist Trophy in a similar car. In fourth place, winning the 1,100cc class, was Vernon Balls in a C6 Amilcar. The race drew a thin crowd despite such other attractions as watching the end of the King's Cup Air Race at the aerodrome. Tastes were changing and a race of this type no longer had a strong public appeal, so the JCC dropped it and did not revive it again until 1936.

At the August Bank Holiday meeting a match race was run between Don in the 2-litre Sunbeam and Jack Dunfee in a 3-litre GP Ballot. This was a rerun for second place in a handicap at the Whitsun meeting, where Dunfee, who was a leading London theatrical agent, had jumped the start in error. Don was the winner by 0.02sec. The principal race of the day, the President's Gold Plate, also went to Don in a Lea Francis.

The New Cyclecar Club held a meeting on 25 August. The main event was a 20-lap Cyclecar Grand Prix held over the same course as the British GP. Three wheels were quicker than four, as the race was won by Clive Lones (Morgan-JAP) from a Riley and an Amilcar.

The BARC Autumn meeting saw George Eyston and Don winning two races each. Eyston, driving a 1½-litre GP OM, a car which had been unsuccessful

Kaye Don

Kaye Don was one of the stars of Brooklands between 1928 and 1931. He was born in Dublin in 1892 and after serving in the RFC in World War One he joined the Avon tyre company and became the sales manager and company representative at Brooklands. He began racing motor cycles, riding an AJS and Zenith-JAP, then graduated to cars in 1922 with the Hispano-engined Wolseley Viper.

Although he drove many other makes he was principally connected with Sunbeam as a works driver, starting with the 4.9-litre Indianapolis car then moving on to the 2-litre GP cars and the 4-litre V12 cars 'Tiger' and 'Tigress'. He broke the lap record three times with the 4-litre cars, finally establishing it at 137.58mph in 1930. Away from Brooklands he won the 1928 Ulster TT in a Lea Francis. In 1930 he made an unsuccessful attempt on the World Land Speed Record at Daytona with the Sunbeam 'Silver Bullet', but was more successful on water, taking the Water Speed Record in 1931 and 1932, becoming the first man to exceed 120mph on water.

He returned to racing at Brooklands in 1933 with a Type 54 Bugatti, but his career virtually came to an end in 1934 when he was imprisoned for manslaughter after an accident while testing an MG before the Mannin Beg race on the Isle of Man in which his mechanic was killed. Subsequently, immediately before World War Two, Don was the British importer of Pontiac cars, and after the war he became the founder and manufacturer of Ambassador motor cycles. He died in 1981.

in grands prix, won the 90mph Short and Long Handicaps, and Don scored in the Lightning Short and Long Handicaps driving the 2-litre Sunbeam. In the Short race he battled with Staniland's Bugatti and while passing this and Dunfee's Ballot he skidded down the Members' Banking, but recovered without mishap.

Although Parliament had given full voting rights to women in May 1928 the BARC was still unwilling to let ladies race on equal terms. Instead it offered a ladies handicap which was won by Jill Scott in the 2-litre Sunbeam. She was in very good form, as she drove the Sunbeam at the Essex MC meeting on 29 September and won a ten-lap handicap at an average of 114.23mph, and, even more impressively, during the race did a lap at 120.88mph – the fastest done by a lady driver at that time, by a considerable margin.

Despite the diminished attraction of Brooklands as a venue for world records there was still regular activity in search of international class records. Don was active with both Sunbeams and the Scotts used their Amilcar, while records were also taken by Salmson, Bentley, Bugatti, Lea Francis and Riley among others. Perhaps the most unusual record-breaker was a 903cc Jowett. The Bradford company had been building utilitarian cars for many years, but in 1928 fitted a sports body to an otherwise unremarkable car and took it to Brooklands in August. It was driven by Jimmy Hall, who had made

a reputation – and an appreciable income – breaking records on small capacity motor cycles. He shared the car with Horace Grimley, the company's development engineer, and the pair set a Class G (1,100cc) record for 12 hours at 54.89mph. Encouraged by this, Jowett produced a limited number of sporting-bodied cars.

On motor cycles, Chris Staniland had an excellent season. Riding Excelsior-JAPs tuned by Worters, he scored at the opening BMCRC meeting on 11 April, then later in the month took 175cc class records. The BMCRC 200-Mile solo races in June saw him take the 250cc event in front of another Excelsior ridden by Eric Fernihough. In the 350cc race, Ernie Thomas stopped at the foot of the Byfleet Banking to seek out a problem and his Rex-Acme was hit by the Chater-Lea of A.G. Walker. Walker was thrown off and broke his arm, but despite this rode on to the pits before he retired from the race. The 500cc Solo race was a win by the veteran Bert Le Vack on a New Hudson.

The Grand Prix meeting, run around the Mountain on 28 July, gave riders and spectators a change from the usual flat-out Outer Circuit events. Here too Staniland had a win, taking the 250cc race on his Excelsior before coming second in the 350cc race. The following Wednesday, 1 August, a landmark was passed as Bill Lacey on a Grindlay Peerless-JAP won *The Motor Cycle Cup* for being the first rider to exceed 100 miles in the hour with

a 500cc machine on a British track. Lacey had a reputation for immaculate preparation and his motor cycles were always superbly presented.

Staniland did not have all the honours at the BMCRC Championship meeting on 8 September: he won the 250cc race with his Excelsior, but Freddie Hicks beat him in the 350c event on a Velocette, then brought the Velocette out again and beat all the 500s in the bigger capacity race. To round off his day, Hicks bolted on a sidecar and took the 350cc sidecar race too.

The Essex MC meeting on 29 September had a three-lap ladies' handicap. The BMCRC was unwilling to encourage lady riders, probably following the BARC line, and it was the lesser clubs who advanced the cause of women. The Essex club's race had ten competitors, members of the London Ladies Motor Club, who must have been heartened by the additional blow struck for women racing drivers and riders by Jill Scott's record lap in the Sunbeam during the meeting. The winner was Miss May Ruffell, riding Lacey's 350cc Grindlay Peerless-JAP.

Staniland and Lacey were the heroes of the day at the BMCRC 'Cup' meeting on 6 October. Staniland won three of the seven races and also took a second place, while Lacey won two. Lacey had a notable ride in the final of the 'Sir Charles Wakefield' Cup, a 1,000cc Solo handicap, when he lapped his 500cc Grindlay Peerless at 109.94mph, a new 500cc lap record. The following week he was the guest of honour at a BMCRC lunch at the Royal Automobile Club in recognition of his 500cc hour record.

LEFT *The 350cc sidecars go onto the Members' Banking at the Grand Prix meeting on 28 July 1928. Staniland (Excelsior) leads Fred Hicks (Velocette) and Pat Driscoll (Norton). (Brooklands Society)*

BELOW LEFT *Matt Wright looks concerned as he pauses from work on his 250cc New Imperial. The work paid off, as he set class records from 9 to 12 hours and for 1,000km on 25 September 1928. (Brooklands Society)*

BELOW *The lady riders get a push-start for their race at the Essex MC meeting on 29 September 1928. The winner was May Ruffell on Lacey's 350cc Grindlay-Peerless-JAP. (Brooklands Society)*

1929

Attendances had been down at the BARC meeting in 1928. With such ventures as the evening meetings, the club had held 15 in all, and it was realised that this prodigality had had a detrimental effect on spectator attendance, so the calendar was reduced to eight meetings for 1929. The usual winter repairs had taken longer than expected and there were still drying areas of concrete when the BMCRC held its first meeting on 24 March.

As soon as the track was ready the enthusiastic Don came out with the V12 Sunbeam to take class records and prepare for the BARC Easter meeting. He had a rival for ultimate speed, as John Cobb had acquired the 10½-litre V12 Delage which had broken the World Land Speed Record at Arpajon in France in 1924. There was a gale-force wind and occasional rain when the Delage and Sunbeam came out for the Founders' Gold Cup. Both were on scratch, but Don made a bad start, and the handicapper expected too much of Cobb, so neither was placed. Between races Don made an attempt to break his lap record, but the wind was too strong and the best he could do was 129.36mph. By the time he came out in the V12 Sunbeam again for the Lightning Long Handicap the conditions had perhaps eased, as he lapped at 130.04mph, not far short of the record.

Having seen the success of the Essex MC Six-Hour race the JCC decided to attempt a much bigger project. Their ambition was to run a 24-hour race, a rival to Le Mans, but the local restrictions made this impossible, so they came up with the next best thing: a 24-hour race for mildly improved production cars, run over two days. This would take place on Friday 10 and Saturday 11 May, with 12 hours' racing each day and the cars impounded overnight. This handicap race, which became known as the 'Double-12', would be run over the 2.6-mile Finishing Straight–Railway Straight–Byfleet Banking course, and the winner would receive £1,000 donated by the *Daily Telegraph* and a gold cup presented by the SMMT. Fifty-seven entries were received and 52 cars came to the line for a Le Mans start at 8:00am. To keep the spectators amused if the racing was dull an RAF band attended and there was dancing and an amusement park in the public enclosure, with dodgems.

When the race began the drivers ran to their cars, put up the hood and drove the first ten laps with the hood erected. It quickly became apparent that in terms of outright speed there were no rivals to the four Bentleys – a Speed Six and three 4½-litres – entered by the works, backed by the Scotts in another 4½-litre; on handicap, however, the likely winners appeared to be one of the three 6C-1500 Alfa Romeos which had come from the

BELOW *Drivers and mechanics dash for the cars at the start of the Double-12 Hour race on 10 May 1929. Heading the line-up is the 5½-litre Studebaker of Holledge and Laird. (LAT)*

Italian factory. After three hours the Bentleys led on the road and on handicap but the Alfas were close behind, and the race became a battle in the pits, as the Alfa Romeos were only taking a minute for their stops while the Bentleys, with wheel changes and big tanks to fill, were stationary for three minutes.

The Speed Six Bentley, leading the race at 4:00pm, made a long stop to repair a broken dynamo coupling, and when it rejoined the race without the dynamo connected it was disqualified. This let Ramponi's Alfa take the lead on handicap; he had decided to drive single-handed and his co-driver, Count 'Johnny' Lurani, sat frustrated in the pits throughout the whole race. Ramponi was followed by the 4½-litre Bentley of Sammy Davis and Sir Roland Gunter. At 6:30pm the Bentley team had another misfortune when Birkin's car caught fire at a pit stop and the mechanic was badly burned. At the end of the first day Ramponi led, but the Davis/Gunter Bentley was tied in second place with another Alfa Romeo, driven by Ivanowski, while the Birkin Bentley was third.

The cars were lined up in front of the pits overnight, and when the starting signal was given at 8:00am the next morning the race began again – not with engines bursting into life, but with frenzied activity on the cars. Once they were away Ramponi led again, but the second car in the Alfa Romeo team, driven by Don and Jack Dunfee, retired with stripped timing gears. A Salmson driven by Casse and Clarke had moved into second place, but the Davis/Gunter Bentley speeded up, despite a rain shower, and moved into the lead when Ramponi stopped to repair a broken battery

ABOVE The 2-litre Lagonda of Frank King and Howard Wolfe is worked on during the Double-12. It finished in 18th place. (LAT)

behind Cobb and came third in the red Sunbeam, and he also lapped in 132.11mph, so the lap record was shared.

Sadly the Essex MC had gone into liquidation so it was surprising when the BARC decided to run the Six-Hour race again on 29 June. A long-distance race seemed alien to the club's policy and it was run only seven weeks after the Double-12. Using the same course as the Double-12, but with sandbank chicanes in the Finishing Straight, it was a handicap for modified production cars. Each was given credit laps according to engine size, and although the event was deemed to be of six hours' duration the fastest cars had to complete 175 laps of the 2.6-mile circuit. For the spectators it was therefore an easier race to follow than the Double-12.

There were 38 starters, and the Bentley team – which came to the race having completed a hat-trick of Le Mans victories two weeks earlier – was again prominent. The factory entered two cars, the Le Mans-winning Speed Six backed by a 4½-litre, while Tim Birkin made a private entry of the prototype supercharged 4½-litre, a car which would soon become a Brooklands legend. The race began at 11:00am and the Speed Six Bentley, shared by Barnato and Jack Dunfee, took an immediate lead on the road, though on handicap the leader was the Austin Seven of the Barnes brothers, which continued to hold the lead as the faster cars pulled back the credit laps.

The chicanes proved hard on brakes and several cars made contact, including a Lea Francis which ended perched on top of the sandbank. At the

LEFT *The 4½-litre Bentley of Sammy Davis and Sir Roland Gunter leads Ivanowski's 6C-1500 Alfa Romeo on the Byfleet Banking in the Double-12. The Bentley finished in second place. Recent repairs to the banking are evident. (LAT)*

BELOW LEFT *The V-12 Sunbeams 'Tiger' and 'Tigress' in the pits during the 1929 BRDC 500. No 28 driven by Don and Froy retired with a broken rear spring. No 29 driven by Cobb and Cyril Paul was third despite a broken chassis frame. (John Maitland Collection)*

BELOW *The Speed Six Bentley of Sammy Davis and Clive Dunfee makes a stop during the 1929 BRDC 500 to change a shredded tyre. They finished in second place. (LAT)*

bracket. The Bentley was slowed by an extra stop after a tyre burst on the Byfleet Banking and then stopped again to secure a bonnet fastener. During the last hour Ramponi tried to slipstream the Bentley, but Davis shook him off. Nevertheless, when the flag was waved at 8:00pm Ramponi had won from the Bentley by 0.0003 on the handicap formula, an incredibly close margin. The Salmson was third and Ivanowski's Alfa Romeo was fourth. Twenty-six cars finished the race.

The BARC Whitsun meeting saw a resumption of the friendly Don/Cobb rivalry. Don scored first, taking the Lightning Short Handicap in the V12 Sunbeam, then switched to the 2-litre Sunbeam for the Gold Vase race. In a tight finish, he won by a length from Jack Dunfee in a second 2-litre Sunbeam, while Cobb in the V12 Delage was only a length behind Dunfee. The duel the crowd expected came in the Lightning Long Handicap when Cobb came home to win in the blue and silver Delage, setting a new lap record at 132.11mph. Don had started from scratch 10sec

ABOVE *Frank Clement and Jack Barclay enjoy the plaudits after their win in the 1929 BRDC 500. (LAT)*

BELOW *Clive Lones (Morgan-JAP) and Ted Baragwanath (Brough Superior-JAP) battle it out in the three-lap 1,100cc Passenger Handicap at the BMCRC meeting on 23 March 1929. (Brooklands Society)*

four-hour mark the Austin led from Whitcroft's 1,100cc Brooklands Riley, while the Speed Six was third and closing up. At 4:00pm, with an hour to go, the Bentley took the lead and the race was effectively over. Barnato and Dunfee were the winners, a 6C-1500 Alfa Romeo driven by Leonard Headlam was second, and a private entry 4½-litre Bentley shared by Humphrey Cook and Leslie Callingham was third. The Birkin 'Blower' 4½-litre Bentley retired with lubrication problems.

Although the FICM was unwilling to recognise short-distance motor cycle records at the track the AIACR had a more relaxed attitude about car records, and on 1 July Don brought out the V12 Sunbeam and broke the World Standing Start Mile Record at 100.77mph, then went on to take

International Class C (5,000cc) records for the mile and kilometre, including a flying kilometre at 140.95mph, the highest speed yet timed at Brooklands. During July and August a remarkable record run was made in a 4½-litre Invicta by Violette Cordery, the sister-in-law of Invicta manufacturer Noel Macklin. Under RAC supervision, and sharing the driving with her sister Evelyn, she drove 30,000 miles in 30,000 minutes. There could be no running at night, so the car was impounded at the end of each day's run, and there were delays while race meetings were held. The run took 48 days. Five hours was spent in routine servicing during the run and the average speed was 61.57mph. For this feat Miss Cordery was awarded the Dewar Trophy by the RAC.

A renewal of the Cobb/Don duel was eagerly anticipated at the August Bank Holiday BARC meeting. Cobb began well, winning the 100mph Short Handicap and lapping only slightly slower than the lap record. Then, despite a frightening slide which nearly took him over the Byfleet Banking, he came second in the Lightning Short Handicap in front of Don in the 2-litre Sunbeam. Don took a second place in the Lightning Long Handicap, from which the Delage dropped out, racing no more that day. His last race was the nine-lap Gold Star Handicap, in which he started from scratch but came through to second at the end, behind the GP OM of Wilkinson. During the race he lapped at 134.24mph and regained the lap record, despite a broken oil pipe which sprayed the

cockpit and filled it with smoke. In all these record-breaking races Don was accompanied by a brave passenger, H.E. Plaister.

The BARC Autumn meeting had a small crowd, visitors possibly being discouraged by the gloomy weather. Don was not there, but the 2-litre Sunbeam was driven by Jack Dunfee, who came through to win the Lightning Long Handicap, staving off Cobb's Delage which was slightly off-colour with a misfire. Cobb had consolation in the Lightning Short when he caught the GP Ballot driven by Clive Dunfee, Jack's brother, on the line. The following Monday, 23 September, Don brought out the V12 Sunbeam and as well as setting Class C records up to 200 miles he established a new World 200km record at 120.1mph.

The British Racing Drivers' Club (BRDC) had been founded in March 1928, having originated in a series of dinners given by Dr Benjafield in 1927. Its purpose was to provide a social club for recognised racing drivers and to act as a mild 'trade union' to look after their interests. To expand its interests and influence the club decided to promote a 500-mile race which was held at Brooklands on 12 October, the first of a series which ran for some years. It was a class handicap and was a 'flat-out blind' on the Outer Circuit. It was concluded that this was a good way to end the season, as cars suffering expensive damage could be repaired during the winter.

Unfortunately, there was a slight difference of opinion with 'Ebby' so Colonel Lindsay Lloyd formulated the handicaps. The field had to cover the whole distance of 181 laps and was divided into classes: those up to 1,100cc were flagged away at 10:00am, the 1,500s were released at 10:30, the 3-litres at 10:51, those up to 5-litres at 11:03, and the unlimited cars were away at 11:08am. Both V12 Sunbeams, now painted white, were entered in the 5-litre class, one driven by Don and Froy, the other by Cobb and Cyril Paul. Facing these were three works 4½-litre Bentleys, while in the unlimited class the Speed Six Bentley driven by Sammy Davis and Clive Dunfee was matched by the ex-Zborowski 16.2-litre Mercedes-engined 'Chitty III'.

As the first group departed, Vernon Balls in a 6C Amilcar took an immediate and commanding lead from the Austin Sevens. By the time the 3-litre class started, led by the 2-litre Sunbeam with George Eyston at the wheel, Balls had covered 25 laps. With the release of the 5-litre class the crowd saw the duel it expected as Don in the V12 Sunbeam battled with Birkin in the 'Blower' Bentley. The pair swapped places, but the Bentley was leaking oil; then its exhaust broke and it fell back. Balls led for

ABOVE *The BMCRC paddock at the Fork during the meeting on 20 April 1929. (Brooklands Society)*

95 laps then retired with a broken valve and the lead passed to Eyston in the 2-litre Sunbeam. When this retired with a broken spring Don went to the front in the big Sunbeam, and when he retired with a broken rear spring the second V12 Sunbeam took the lead.

The harsh pounding of the track continued to take its toll and the second Sunbeam had to slow, its chassis frame having cracked. Birkin was trying to make up lost ground, but flames from the broken exhaust set fire to the body and the car was out of the race. From the rear of the field, Davis in the Speed Six Bentley was the fastest car on the track and he now began to come into the reckoning. But the major excitement came from Jack Barclay, who spun the 4½-litre Bentley twice on the Members' Banking and put a wheel over the top on the second excursion. Both times he stopped to change a wheel, and Frank Clement took over, but despite this the Bentley led the race. Although the Speed Six was gaining ground, making the fastest lap of the race at 126.09mph, it had to make stops for tyres, and the race ran out with Barclay and Clement as winners and Davis and Dunfee in second place, followed by the V12 Sunbeam nursed to the finish by Cobb and Paul. Nine cars were classified as finishers and three more were flagged off. It established the event as

ABOVE *Joe Wright, who set a motor cycle lap record on his Zenith-JAP five times between 1925 and 1929, leaving it at 118.86mph on 1 June 1929. (Brooklands Society)*

Fred Hicks (Velocette) and Chris Staniland (Excelsior-JAP) fought all the way in the 350cc race, with Hicks winning by a length at the finish.

There were mutterings about the handicapping at the BMCRC meeting on 1 June. Joe Wright was riding the Zenith in the 350/1,000cc three-lap handicap and could only manage a second place, despite yet another lap record at 118.86mph. It was felt that the riders of the faster machines were expected to take considerable risks without any gain.

The Grand Prix meeting around the Mountain on 22 June was held in the rain, but was a Staniland triumph, as on the Worters-tuned Excelsior-JAPs he won the 250cc and 350cc solo races, and then the 350cc sidecar race as well. Staniland and Worters were a formidable partnership and the Excelsior-JAP marked up another win in the 250cc 200-Mile solo race on 27 July. Staniland won by a few lengths from Joe Hewitt on another Worters Excelsior. A decade later the partnership would be as effective on four wheels.

On 7 September, a very hot day, an alternative attraction was offered by the Schneider Trophy at Calshot on Southampton Water, but those who went to Brooklands saw Maurice McCudden win the 350cc sidecar race on an Excelsior-JAP. McCudden was the brother of Major James McCudden VC, the fighter ace, who had gained many of his victories in an SE5a perhaps built at the track. Following the same policy as the BRDC, the BMCRC season finished on 19 October with a 'flat-out blind' in the 'Hutchinson 100', where victory went to R. Gibson (346cc Sunbeam).

It was noticeable that as a new decade was about to begin, the face of motor cycle racing at Brooklands was changing. The Wall Street stock market had crashed on 24 October and the Great Depression had begun. Economic hardships were affecting both manufacturers and trade suppliers. Several companies – including Sunbeam and AJS – were pulling out of the sport, and others were attracted more to the world of road racing and grands prix. The trade and accessory manufacturers were no longer willing or able to pay bonuses and retainers at the level which had been maintained throughout the 1920s. Motor cycle racing at the track would continue with the same level of enthusiasm, but it would be in a more amateur form with less outside money coming into it.

The pinch affected motor racing too and Bentley would soon become a prominent victim, but although the level of manufacturers' and trade support diminished it did not drop away as sharply as it had done in the motor cycle world.

the fastest 500-mile race at that time, outstripping the 'Indy' 500.

The 1,000cc solo race at the opening BMCRC meeting on 23 March had both interest and excitement. Bert Denly was racing a new AJS which had a single-cylinder 743cc engine, the biggest single ever raced at Brooklands. He was up against Joe Wright on his 996cc Zenith-JAP, and although the AJS was fast it was no match for the Zenith, which not only won but set a new outright lap record at 113.71mph. Wright was on form, as at the next meeting on 20 April, he scored a double while winning the 1,000cc solo race, achieving the highest race average yet at 111.52mph and pushing the lap record even higher, to 117.19mph.

Many of the motor cycle races were unexciting processions, but the crowd had its money's worth at the 200-Mile sidecar meeting on 4 May when

1930

There was a major change at Brooklands in 1930. Colonel Lindsay Lloyd retired and was replaced as Clerk of the Course by A. Percy Bradley. Bradley had grown up in the motor sporting world. He had been a founder of the Cyclecar Club and had then become secretary of the Junior Car Club, so he had expertise founded on the organisation of the 200-Mile race and the Double-12, as well as many lesser events. Unlike Lindsay Lloyd he did not have the underlying ethos of the horse racing world.

The BARC was honoured by the Prince of Wales consenting to become its Patron, and the club's London office was closed and the secretary and staff were accommodated in the Clubhouse. A new members' bar and lounge were added to the latter and a bar and restaurant were provided for the BMCRC members, though to emphasise their perceived social differences this had a separate entrance! A new enclosure was also opened on the Railway Straight so that spectators could have a better view of race finishes.

The separate entrance for BMCRC members emphasised a shortcoming at Brooklands which lasted until the track closed in 1939: there was a strong inherent snobbery in the BARC, which regarded motor cyclists as socially inferior. In his book *Brooklands and Beyond* Charles Mortimer recalled that BMCRC members, even if they rented paddock sheds, were not permitted to be paddock spectators at a BARC meeting. The club's slogan, 'The Right Crowd and No Crowding', was also regarded by many as socially divisive.

Possibly influenced by the success of the BMCRC Grand Prix meetings and by the Junior Grand Prix which he had organised for the JCC, Bradley introduced Mountain handicaps at the BARC opening meeting. These Mountain events were to become the most popular form of Brooklands racing throughout the 1930s.

The star attraction at the opening meeting on 22 March was Birkin's rebuilt 'Blower' Bentley. This now had a slim off-set single-seater body and was painted blue. W.O. Bentley did not approve of the supercharged car and Birkin was developing it independently at his small workshops at Welwyn Garden City. He was sponsored by the Hon Dorothy Paget, the daughter of Lord Queensborough, a very rich woman who owned a string of race horses. It has been suggested that her motor racing enthusiasm sprang from watching Birkin in the 1929 BRDC 500, as a result of which she bought the Birkin team of supercharged cars early in 1930.

The race Birkin ran in was the Kent Short Handicap, the BARC having abandoned its previous

BELOW *The Speed Six Bentley in which Sammy Davis and Clive Dunfee finished second in the 1930 Double-12, coming out of the Finishing Straight and onto the Members' Banking. (LAT)*

ABOVE *One of the ill-fated Talbot team; the car of Rabagliati and Wolfe makes a pit stop in the Double-12. (LAT)*

BELOW *Quite humble cars ran at the club meetings. A Morris Minor heads a line of Austins and MGs waiting for the start of the High Speed Trial at the MCC meeting on 27 September 1930. (LAT)*

nomenclature for the handicaps which were henceforth named after places. He just failed to catch Staniland's Type 37A Bugatti, despite a cracked supercharger casing patched with plasticine. In the Essex Long Handicap he caught Thomas's Type 35 Bugatti on the line to win by a second. The very first Mountain handicap over 10 laps and for modified production sports cars was won by Lord Howe's Type 43 Bugatti from Frank Ashby's Brooklands Riley, while Hendy's Hyper Lea Francis was third.

A crowd estimated at between 15,000 and 20,000 came to the Easter meeting. Kaye Don was absent in the United States making an abortive attempt on the World Land Speed Record with the Sunbeam 'Silver Bullet' and Cobb, who was ill, was a non-starter with the V12 Delage, so once again Birkin was the main attraction. He did not disappoint. After winning the Bedford Short Handicap he was billed to have a match race with Jack Dunfee in the GP Sunbeam, but this had broken a con rod in an earlier race so Birkin came out alone for an attempt on the lap record. He was successful and the new speed was 135.33mph. Birkin also drove an unsupercharged 4½-litre car in a Mountain race with Dorothy Paget as his passenger. After the meeting he flew to Le Touquet to claim a dinner which Woolf Barnato had promised him if he broke Don's lap record.

The JCC ran the Double-12 again on 9 and 10 May. The course and regulations were the same as in 1929, except that the hoods did not have to be raised at the start. There were 59 starters and the field was dominated by the two works Speed Six Bentleys, with the Paget/Birkin team of three 'Blower' 4½-litre cars running independently. Also competing was a team of three Talbot 90s. Birkin led the field from the 8:00am start and the Speed Sixes could not match his pace, but by 11:00am the Birkin cars were flagging and the Speed Sixes were dominating the race, while the speed and silence of the Talbots running in team formation made a big impression. By late afternoon the two Bentleys led on the road and on handicap. Bertelli's 1½-litre Aston Martin was third followed

by the Talbot of the Hon Max Aitken. Then at 6:10pm there was tragedy.

The Talbots of Rabagliati and Hebeler had been battling with the 6C-1750 Alfa Romeo of George Eyston. As the three cars ran up the Finishing Straight the Talbots touched and Rabagliati's car hit the railings lining the track. Rabagliati's mechanic Ted Allery and a spectator, a Mr Hurworth, were killed and another 12 spectators were injured. Hebeler's car overturned, but driver and mechanic both escaped with minor injuries. The race continued and the first day ended at 8:00pm to universal relief, with the two Bentleys leading followed by Whitcroft's Riley and the Bertelli Aston Martin.

There was an immediate discussion between the JCC, the BARC and the track owners about the desirability of continuing the race the next day, but it was decided that it should go on. By then 19 cars had dropped out including the surviving Talbot, which had been withdrawn, and a subdued field set off for the second day's racing. For a while Marinoni's 1750-6C Alfa Romeo led on handicap, as the Bentleys took some time to get into their stride, but Marinoni made a long stop to repair a broken camshaft drive and the Bentleys took command of the race again. Bertelli had held third place but was caught by Whitcroft after two hours. Rain fell heavily in the afternoon but there were no more serious incidents and Barnato and Clement

were flagged off as the winners at 8:00pm, having covered 2,080 miles at an average of 85.68mph. Sammy Davis and Clive Dunfee were second in their Speed Six and Whitcroft and Hamilton took third place in a Brooklands Riley, ahead of Bertelli and Holder's Aston Martin. Twenty-eight cars were classified as finishers.

An inquest on the race victims, held in Weybridge Parish Hall on the Tuesday following the race, absolved the drivers and organisers of any responsibility for the accident, but the jury added a rider that the rules of racing at the track should be tightened. The BARC took immediate note and it was decreed that inexperienced drivers could not take part in long-distance races; competitors should be medically examined; inexperienced drivers should be observed before racing; and new safety barriers were erected. The BARC also introduced a rule that effectively prevented most cars more than ten years old from competing in the club's races. This excluded many of the older large-engined cars. One of the injured spectators subsequently brought an unsuccessful action against the BARC as lessees of the track, and the case – Hall v BARC – established important legal guidelines concerning the safety of spectators at motor racing meetings. The warning 'Motor Racing is Dangerous', which appears on all motor racing admission tickets and programmes, was an outcome of the case.

BELOW The second day of the Double-12 was wet. Kehoe's Brooklands Riley splashes through a puddle in the Finishing Straight. (LAT)

ABOVE *Sammy Davis and Lord March with their Ulster Austin after their 1930 BRDC 500 victory. (John Maitland Collection)*

RIGHT *The coupon which brought the uncontrollable crowds to the Motor Cycle 21st Anniversary meeting on 5 April 1930.*

British Motor Cycle Racing Club

BROOKLANDS, WEYBRIDGE, SURREY

21st ANNIVERSARY MEETING.

THE **MOTOR CYCLE** DAY APRIL 5th, 1930.

Admit bearer to the track on production of this coupon at re=duced price of 1s. 3d., including motor cycle.

The meeting begins at 2 p.m.

On 24 May the BARC held the Stanley Cup meeting to encourage new drivers, although many of the recognised aces had entered. Birkin ran the 'Blower' Bentley, but it was off-form and retired in a cloud of smoke. The Stanley Cup itself, an inter-club team competition, was won by the MCC team of the Aldington brothers and Kehoe, driving Frazer Nashes.

Birkin was absent from the BARC Whitsun meeting: the 'Blower' car may have been unready or he may have been fully occupied preparing the team for Le Mans. A recovered Cobb raced the V12 Delage and won the Devon Lightning Short Handicap. Kaye Don was on scratch with the V12 Sunbeam and was not placed, but he equalled Birkin's lap record. In the Mountain Speed Handicap, adjudged by the press to be the most exciting race of the day, Malcolm Campbell came through to win in his 38/250 Mercedes-Benz, pursued throughout by H.J. Aldington's Frazer Nash. There was nostalgia for the crowd when Dudley Froy won the Devon Senior Short Handicap in the Leyland-Thomas, despite a fierce skid on the Byfleet Banking, but he retired in a subsequent race with a cracked cylinder block. There was more nostalgia in the Devon Lightning Long Handicap when Cyril Paul ran the 1913 21½-litre Benz alleged to have been the staff car of Field Marshal Hindenburg in the war, which had eluded the ten-year rule. Paul came through to win, but in second place from scratch was Don in the V12 Sunbeam. He had covered his second lap at 137.58mph and shattered Birkin's record by 2.25mph.

There were several minor meetings at the track during the season and the Lagonda company sponsored an all-Lagonda 'fete' on 19 July with some light-hearted short races and gymkhana contests. Sadly, at the Brighton & Hove MC meeting on 6 September there was another fatal accident when A.E.S. Walther overturned his MG Midget.

Birkin was back at the BARC August Bank Holiday meeting. This was called 'the half-crown day', as the public was admitted for 2s 6d, which brought in a big crowd described as 'almost a record'. Birkin's aim was to regain the lap record in the absence of Don, who was without the V12 Sunbeams as the company had decided to withdraw from racing and had put the two V12s up for sale. The principal race was the Gold Star Handicap, from which Birkin retired with a split fuel tank. The race became a battle between the 1½-litre GP Delages of Campbell and Scott. Scott came home first but was disqualified for crossing a newly instituted painted line at the Fork intended to keep the slower cars out of the way of faster competitors. Birkin, who appeared in an unusual car, a borrowed Type 35B Bugatti, had crossed the line first in the earlier Cornwall Short Handicap and had been disqualified for the same reason. Scott appealed and the decision was reversed so he was awarded the race, but Birkin's appeal was dismissed and he resigned from the BARC panel of judges in protest at what he considered to be an unfair decision.

The meeting finished with an innovation, a two-lap Mountain Handicap for veteran cars built before 1905. There were 39 entries and the result went to the car with the best improvement on handicap. The lower-powered cars found the pull up the hill at the top of the Finishing Straight was a problem, but victory went to an 1899 Progress driven by Maurice Davenport, who also raced an Excelsior-JAP with the BMCRC.

The BARC closing meeting on 20 September was badly affected by strong winds so there was no possibility of high speeds on the Outer Circuit. The emphasis was on the Mountain events and the main race was the ten-lap Mountain Racing Handicap. It was won by Clifton Penn-Hughes in a Type 35C Bugatti, who came very close to the top of the banking when leaving the Finishing Straight but avoided disaster. Behind him Malcolm Campbell, on scratch in the 1½-litre GP Delage, came storming through the field to second place, setting a new lap record for the Mountain Circuit at 73.11mph.

Encouraged by its success in 1929 the BRDC ran the 500-Mile race again on Saturday 4 October. It was run in continuous rain which was an additional handicap for the faster cars. Bentley Motors, in serious financial trouble, had announced a withdrawal from racing in the late summer, so the only Bentley representation and the fastest in the field was the Paget team of supercharged cars, led by Birkin in the single-seater. When the 750cc class was released at 10:30am it was seen that the works Ulster Austin of Sammy Davis and the Earl of March would be hard to catch, and the little orange car lapped steadily at 83mph. The 2-litre Sunbeam driven by the Dunfee brothers moved up to second place at 200 miles and seemed a possible winner, but it lost a rear wheel which just missed the leading Austin. Birkin's Bentley was off-form and misfiring, so the main Bentley challenge came from the 'Blower' car of Benjafield and Eddie Hall, which was averaging 112mph, with a best lap at 122.97mph despite the conditions. Davis responded and speeded up, raising the Austin's average to 87mph. The Austin could not be caught and came home the winner at 83.41mph. The Bentley was seven minutes behind and as Hall crossed the line a rear tyre threw a tread with a loud bang. The second 2-litre Sunbeam of Cushman and Purdy was third and a Talbot 90 driven by Lord Howe and Brian Lewis was fourth. Nine cars were classified as finishers. The popular press made much of two peers being placed in the

race with such headlines as 'Two Earls and thirty three Misters race at Brooklands'!

As 1930 was the 21st anniversary of the founding of the BMCRC, the club, in collaboration with the weekly magazine *The Motor Cycle*, promoted a celebratory event to open the season on 5 April. Spectators could gain admission to the track for 1s 3d by presenting a coupon cut from the magazine. The result was probably the biggest crowd ever – estimated at 25,000 – to attend Brooklands for a race meeting. Many had come for a day out and it was a very different crowd from the usual gathering of enthusiasts for a BMCRC meeting. The enclosures became so full of spectators that they even lined the top of the

BELOW *The crowds line the top of the Members' Banking at the Motor Cycle Anniversary meeting. (Brooklands Society)*

Members' Banking and sometimes slid down it with little appreciation of the dangers. All the roads leading to the track were jammed with cars and motor cycles and the path from Weybridge Station was choked with pedestrians.

Fortunately the day passed off without any serious incident and the crowds saw good racing. The opening race, a 250cc one-lap sprint, was won by Chris Staniland on a Rex-Acme-Blackburne, so he had the distinction of winning both the opening car and opening motor cycle races of the Brooklands season. Taking second place on a Cotton-Blackburne in the 500cc sprint was Leslie Hawthorn, whose son Michael, then aged only 12 months, would grow up to become the first British motor racing F1 World Champion in 1958. It was a good day for Staniland as he was also a member of the winning team in a relay race and won the three-lap invitation race. During the meeting Joe Wright brought out what was said to be an OEC but was evidently a Zenith-Jap and made an ineffective attempt to set a new lap record. Before the end of the season he would set a new 137.32mph World Speed Record for motor cycles at Arpajon riding the Zenith-JAP.

BELOW *Chris Staniland (Rex Acme) leads Paddy Johnston (OK Supreme) and Ben Bickell (Chater Lea) through the Finishing Straight chicane in the 250cc race at the BMCRC Grand Prix meeting on 16 August 1930. (Brooklands Society)*

The Sidecar meeting on 4 May was run in heavy rain and was described by *Motor Cycling* as 'a flop: complete and positive'. The economic climate was making it hard to promote long-distance motor cycle races and this was to be the last of the 200-Mile Sidecar meetings. In the 500cc event Bernard Hieatt on the Worters Excelsior-JAP was holding a two-lap lead approaching the end of the race when he stopped for fuel and carried on without goggles, saying these hampered his visibility. He lost control coming off the Byfleet Banking, hit the bridge over the River Wey and was killed instantly. Hieatt, and Moorhouse in 1912, were the only men to be killed riding in motor cycle races at the track, which was an indication of the inherent safety of Brooklands, despite the problems of the bumpy surface for riders. There was an accepted procedure among the riders that if an accident was likely the rider would slide off the machine over the rear wheel and take his chance on the track, protected by his leathers and helmet, while leaving the motor cycle to its fate.

The BMCRC Grand Prix meeting over the Mountain Circuit on 1 June attracted small fields. The 250cc race was a battle between Staniland on

his Worters-prepared Rex-Acme and Fernihough riding an Excelsior. Staniland had an easy win after Fernihough fell off when hitting a sandbank chicane. George Rowley had a good day, winning the 350cc and 500cc races on an AJS. In later years Worters said that although he appeared to be entering various makes of machine, the frames were the same and the identity was changed by fitting a different fuel tank!

Another grand prix-type meeting was held in August which pulled in a good crowd and better fields, but the racing was disappointing and Freddie Hicks had easy wins on his AJS in the 350cc and 500cc races. The BMCRC was aware that the crowds were getting smaller – probably an indication of the growing economic problems in the wider world – so, hoping to attract greater interest, it introduced a new class for 175cc machines at the 200-Mile solo meeting on 13 September. There was heavy rain on the day, which forced a postponement of the 600cc and 1,000cc races and a mere five riders ran in the new class, which saw a win for Tommy Meeten on a Francis Barnett at 54.36mph. Staniland was once again on top form, dominating the 250cc race on his Rex-Acme and winning by almost 12 minutes at

78.02mph. In the 350cc class the weather caused so many retirements that Baker (AJS) was the only finisher.

The sun shone at the 'Hutchinson 100' meeting, the last of the season, but there was a bitter wind and the attendance was meagre. The '100' was led for a long time by G.E. Horsman's 172cc Zenith-Villiers as he had a 41-minute start, but the faster machines came into the picture in the closing laps and on the penultimate lap, Hurst Mitchell (350cc Velocette) caught Horsman and went on to win at 94.68mph. Horsman held onto second place ahead of Fernihough (Excelsior-JAP).

Despite the astonishing attendance at the '21st' meeting the crowds at motor cycle meetings had been poor throughout 1930 and the racing had often not lived up to expectations. Then at the end of the year a severe blow hit both the car and motor cycle racing communities at Brooklands when the oil companies and accessory manufacturers announced that retainers and bonuses would be severely cut back in 1931 – another indication of the national economic gloom. One of the victims was the 200-Mile solo race meeting, which was not held again.

BELOW *The track is repaired in December 1930. (Brooklands Society)*

CHAPTER SEVEN

THE FLYING TWENTIES

W hen the Armistice was signed in November 1918 the flying field and the 'Village' were soon relinquished by the RFC. The three major aircraft manufacturers associated with Brooklands faced an uncertain future. The contract held by Vickers to build SE5as was terminated immediately. The company had a new aircraft, the Vimy, designed by Rex Pierson. It was a twin-engined bomber, intended to raid Berlin from East Anglia or Northern France, and production had just started when the war ended. The company received a contract to build 150 at the Crayford works and an additional 200 at Brooklands. Six had been built at the track when the war ended and the contract was drastically reduced. Limited production continued and eventually 99 Vimys were built at the track for the RAF.

Sopwith had been phasing out the Camel, which was replaced in production at the Kingston factory by the Dolphin and the Snipe. In all, 1,400 of the 2,074 Dolphins manufactured were built at Kingston, but few were erected at Brooklands as delays in the delivery of the Wolseley-Hispano engines resulted in the majority being scrapped before they were flown. The prototype Snipe had first flown at Brooklands in November 1917 and the RAF had decided that the Snipe would be the standard fighter aircraft for the drastically reduced

The Commercial Vimy No 41 'City of London' in the Instone Air Line livery (it was later owned by Imperial Airways). It stands on the Byfleet Banking and the engines are running, although the tail is jacked up. (BAE Systems per Brooklands Museum)

post-war service, but those already delivered were deemed to be sufficient and the majority of the remainder were also scrapped.

Martinsyde's contract to build SE5as was terminated immediately hostilities ceased and the limited orders for the company's own G100 and G102 were also cancelled.

As soon as the war ended the *Daily Mail* again offered a prize of £10,000 for the first successful non-stop transatlantic flight. While in 1914 it had seemed a daunting task, the huge leaps in aircraft design and performance during the war now made it more feasible. Wartime inflation had reduced the value of the prize but it was still an alluring target for aircraft manufacturers, and Martinsyde, Sopwith and Vickers all set to work to build suitable contenders. Perhaps impressed by the company's abandoned project of a contender for Hamel in 1914, Martinsyde was commissioned by Fred Raynham, their test pilot, and Captain C.W.F. Morgan, an RAF pilot, to build a suitable machine. The company had designed a single-engined light bomber, the F6, which had not gone into production though one had been completed with a Rolls-Royce Eagle engine. This was modified for the attempt, fitted with extra fuel tanks, called the Type A, and named the 'Raymor' by its pilots.

BELOW *A line of Vimys in the erecting shop at the track early in 1919. (BAE Systems per Brooklands Museum)*

The Sopwith contender was to be flown by Harry Hawker and Lieutenant-Commander K. Mackenzie-Grieve. It was an extensively-modified Sopwith B1, a single-engined torpedo bomber designed to have an extended range and duration

over water but not adopted by the RNAS and RAF. This too was fitted with an Eagle engine and larger fuel tanks, and was named the 'Atlantic'.

The third contender was a Vickers Vimy, also fitted with Rolls-Royce Eagle engines, and was the 13th aircraft off the Brooklands production line. Its preparation and modification was supervised by works manager Percy Maxwell-Muller in the erecting sheds beside the track. All the military equipment was removed and the tankage was increased from 516 gallons to 865. The crew would be Captain John Alcock, the pilot, and Lieutenant Arthur Whitten Brown, the navigator. Both had served in the RFC and RAF and had been seconded to Vickers for testing in the latter days of the war. Alcock had raced a 350cc Douglas in the Services meeting at the track in 1915, and the ground staff team was headed by Bob Dicker, who had raced a Chater Lea before the war and would be a successful rider of Rudge and Norton motor cycles in the 1920s.

The three aircraft were shipped to Newfoundland in the spring of 1919, but there was a delay until the weather was suitable for an attempt. Hawker was the first to go and took off from St Johns's at 3:42am local time on Tuesday 18 May. The flight was beset with problems, as the engine overheated, and with a lack of power Hawker was unable to climb above storm clouds. He found it was impossible to cool the engine and realised he would have to ditch, so he flew south towards the shipping lanes, made a forced landing,

and was picked up by a passing ship. He had flown 1,400 miles, so it was a most honourable failure. It was suggested later that the overheating was caused by a malfunction of the radiator shutters.

The red and yellow Martinsyde took off an hour after the Sopwith, but, overloaded, it was caught by a crosswind as it lifted off, stalled, and crashed.

Alcock and Brown waited nearly a month for the optimum conditions and took off at 3:11am local time on Saturday 14 June. Their flight became legend and they landed in an Irish bog 16 hours 28 minutes later, and were feted on their return to England. They made a triumphal return to Brooklands, where they were acclaimed by the Vickers workers and given a civic reception in the Weybridge District Council offices. Two days later they went to Windsor Castle and were knighted by King George V. The Vimy was recovered from the bog and after being repaired and rebuilt at Brooklands became a permanent exhibit at the Science Museum in London.

The fate of the three transatlantic contenders mirrored that of the companies which constructed them. Martinsyde attempted to continue making aircraft but there were insufficient orders to keep the company alive, although some aircraft were sold to the embryo Irish Air Corps and the Royal Canadian Air Force. A Martinsyde Semiquaver flown by Fred Raynham also won the Aerial Derby on 24 July 1920 – the race, over two laps of a 100-mile

ABOVE *The Martinsyde A 'Raymor' being run-up before the take-off accident in Newfoundland. (Brooklands Museum)*

BELOW *A production Vimy stands on the track on the approach before the Members' Banking, probably awaiting a first test flight. (BAE Systems per Brooklands Museum)*

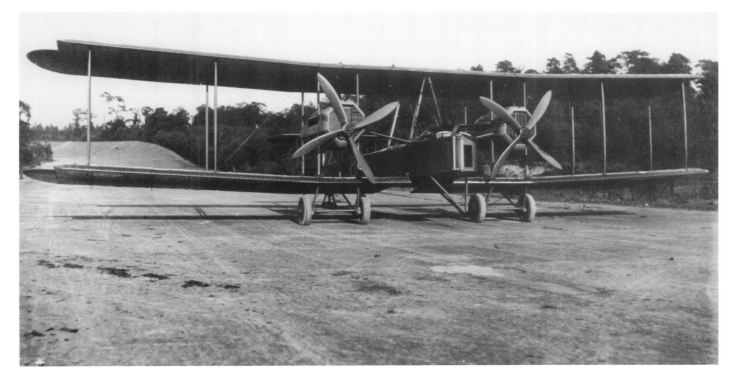

ABOVE *Three early production Vickers Viking amphibians. (BAE Systems per Brooklands Museum)*

BELOW *The Vickers Wibault Scout Type 121 stands on the airfield in 1925. (BAE Systems per Brooklands Museum)*

course, ran from Hendon, and Brooklands was a turning point. Though Martinsyde diversified into motor cycle manufacture at the end of 1919 and gained a considerable reputation for the quality of its machines it was not enough to keep the company alive, and it went into liquidation in 1923. Their small works adjoining the 'Village' became the depot for T.B. André, the shock absorber and accessory manufacturer.

Sopwith realised there would be an expansion of commercial aviation and struggled to keep going in anticipation of it by making car and sidecar bodies. In 1920 the Inland Revenue lodged an enormous claim against the company for Excess War Profits Duty. It was not possible to pay this immediately, so to protect the claims of the creditors the company was put into receivership. A new company was formed in 1920, H.G. Hawker Engineering Ltd, which took over the assets of the Sopwith company, including the hangars and erecting shops at Brooklands. The RAF had meanwhile found that too many Snipes had been

scrapped and it was necessary to renovate the survivors. This profitable work went to the new company, which stripped each aircraft down and rebuilt it at Kingston. Each was then taken to Brooklands for erection and test flying, which brought forth some complaints from Weybridge residents. Sadly, as previously recounted, Harry Hawker collapsed at the controls of a Nieuport Goshawk which he was testing for the Aerial Derby and crashed fatally at Hendon on 12 July 1921. The problems of Martinsyde benefited the new Hawker

company, as the services of Fred Raynham were acquired as a test pilot and a promising draughtsman. Sydney Camm also joined from Martinsyde.

Vickers had a limited but essential order for RAF Vimys, and also began development of a commercial version. At the end of 1918 Rex Pierson, the chief designer, had completed the design of an amphibian flying boat, the Viking, and the prototype was built at Brooklands. It was believed that an amphibian would overcome the shortage of landing grounds in many parts of the world and would be a big commercial success. Though these hopes were not fully realised 34 were built and sold. On 18 December 1919 Sir John Alcock, by then Vickers's chief test pilot, flew the Viking from Brooklands to the Paris Aero Show. Sadly he crashed in fog near Rouen and was killed.

The Australian Government had put up a prize of £10,000 (Australian) for the first flight by Australians to Australia from Britain. The flight had to be completed within 30 days and before the end of 1919. Percy Maxwell-Muller prepared a standard military Vimy for the challenge and this was flown by Ross and Keith Smith of the Royal Australian Air Force. They achieved the goal, reaching Darwin in just under 28 days on 10 December 1919. The route had been flown before as far as Calcutta, but from there to Darwin it was a pioneering flight. Like Alcock and Brown, the Smith brothers were knighted for their achievement and the Vimy was permanently preserved in Adelaide.

BELOW *A view from the rear gunner's position of a Virginia approaching Brooklands in the 1920s. (Brooklands Society)*

RIGHT *A Hawker Horsley which was specially prepared for long-distance records, at the track awaiting delivery to RAF Cranwell. It broke the World Long-Distance Record in May 1927, but held this for only a few hours as it was captured by Lindbergh on his famous transatlantic flight. (BAE Systems per Brooklands Museum)*

BELOW *The Vickers Vireo Type 125, fitted with floats, being pushed out onto the Fork in 1928. It was a long way to the nearest suitable stretch of water, but the Vireo was unsuccessful and was never flown in this form. (BAE Systems per Brooklands Museum)*

The third great pioneering flight was from England to South Africa. A standard military Vimy left Brooklands and on 4 February 1920, flown by Lieutenant-Colonel Pierre van Ryneveld and Major Quintin Brand of the South African Air Force. They crashed between Cairo and Khartoum but continued the flight in a Vimy loaned by the RAF in Egypt. This too had troubles at Bulawayo in Southern Rhodesia (Zimbabwe) and the final leg to Cape Town was completed in a borrowed DH9. The pair duly received their knighthoods from King George V.

The final great flight was to have been a round-the-world venture and a Viking was prepared for this at Brooklands. It was to be flown by the Smith brothers, but on 13 April 1922 Sir Ross Smith made a test flight and stalled over the airfield. The Viking spun in, hitting the outside of the Byfleet Banking by the River Wey, and Smith and the flight mechanic, James Bennett, were killed.

The anticipated boom in private flying was not as great as the aircraft manufacturers had expected. Hawkers survived, though, as limited orders were received from the RAF. An army co-operation

OPPOSITE *Captain Duncan Davis (on the right), the owner of the Brooklands School of Flying from 1928 until the track's closure in 1939. He is with Sir Sefton Branckner, the Director of Civil Aviation who was killed in the R101 airship crash in 1930. The aircraft is a Renault-engined Avro 504, one of the School's first trainers. (Brooklands Museum)*

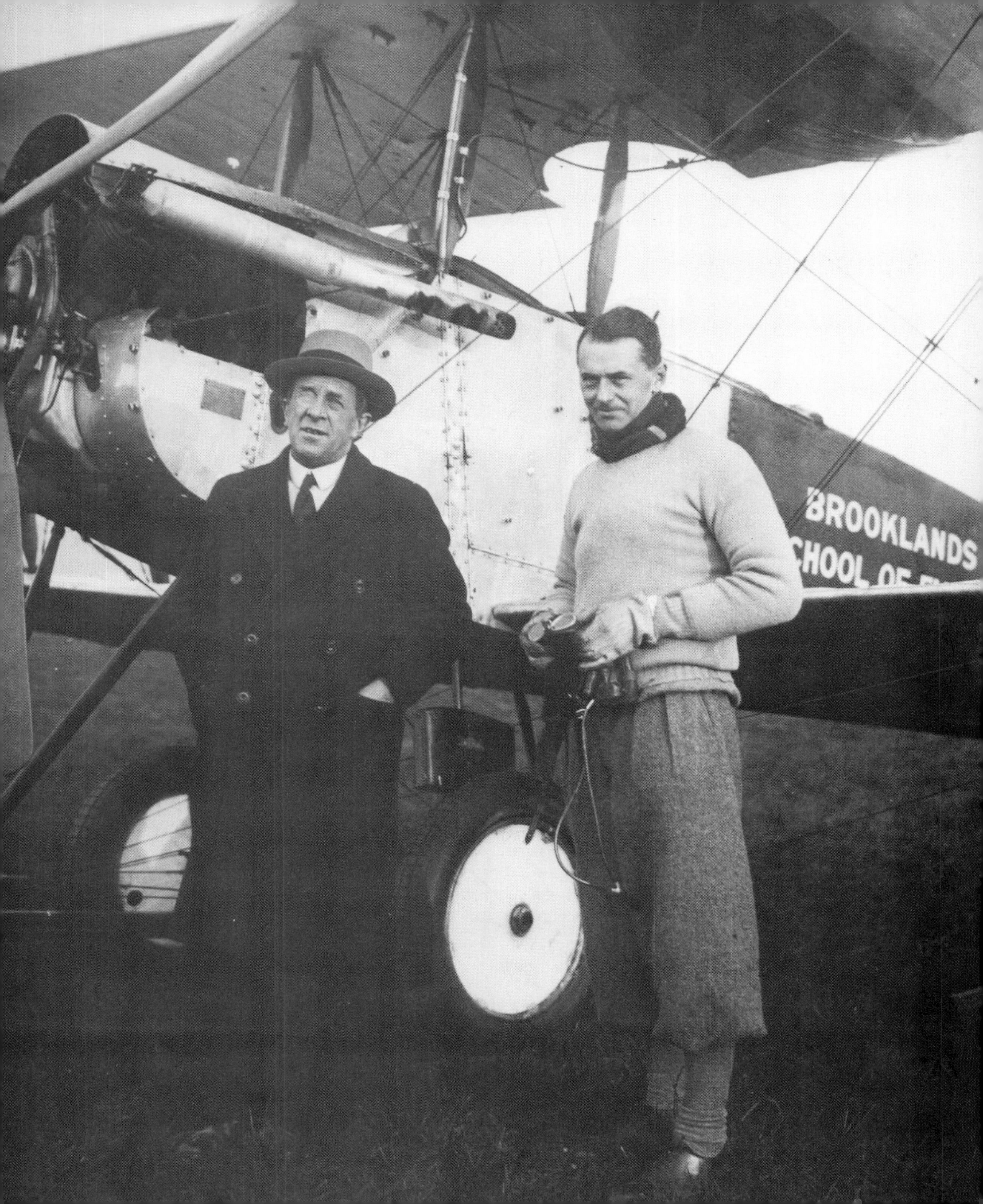
BROOKLANDS
CHOOL OF

ABOVE *Walter Hope is congratulated by Winifred Spooner after his King's Cup win. Spooner finished in third place in a DH60. (Brooklands Museum)*

aircraft, the Duiker, was tested at Brooklands but no order was forthcoming. A new fighter, the Woodcock, had a better reception. After test flying at Brooklands by Fred Raynham and some modifications a Mk 2 version was accepted, an order received, and 63 were supplied to the RAF. Sydney Camm's first design, the Cygnet, was Hawker's only venture in the private flying world. It appeared in 1924 and was produced for the Royal Aero Club and Air Ministry Light Aeroplane competition, where it performed most creditably.

Vickers had developed a commercial version of the Vimy and received an order for 40 from the Chinese Government. This was an impressively large order in the thin commercial climate of 1920 and a production line was laid down at Brooklands. Another buyer was S. Instone & Co, a shipping company which saw the future of commercial aviation. The Instone Vimy Commercial was used for short-haul flights to Europe including the London–Paris run. In 1924 the small commercial airlines, including Instone, were amalgamated into Imperial Airways and the new company became owners of the Vimy. While working on the large fuselage Vimy Commercial, Pierson designed the Vulcan, an eight-seat single-engined passenger aircraft. It was an ugly machine, but Instone ordered four straight off the drawing board and Imperial Airways subsequently bought two more. The Vulcans were used on the London–Paris and

London–Brussels runs. A Vulcan was entered in the first King's Cup Air Race in 1922, flown by Stan Cockerell, who had succeeded Alcock as Vickers's chief test pilot. It finished in seventh place. Another 1922 King's Cup entry was a Martinsyde F3 which had been rebuilt by Camm and Raynham at Brooklands and it gained a commendable second place.

The RAF ordered five Vimy Commercials, converted to serve as air ambulances at a price of £6,300 each. A modified design became the Vernon, a troop transport also described as a 'bomber-transport'. In all the RAF bought 55 Vernons. Other overseas orders were coming in, and Chile bought 19 Vixens, a single-engined light bomber.

The Vickers design office had moved to Pinewood House adjoining the factory in the early 1920s and here Pierson began the design of a new series of heavy bombers, intended to replace the Vimy. Vickers were invited to tender for the design by the Air Ministry in 1920 and the outcome was the Virginia, Victoria and Valentia series which would be the main heavy bombers and transports of the RAF until the mid-1930s. The prototype Virginia made its first flight at Brooklands on 24 November 1922. Between 1924 and 1932 126 Virginia bombers were built for the RAF at an initial cost of £13,250 each and 97 of the transport version, the Victoria, were produced. The RAF subsequently bought 28 Valentias, an improved version of the Victoria. Completed aircraft were taken out of the Vickers workshops at the Fork and were towed round the track to the Byfleet Banking and through the 'Village' to the airfield. When Vimy production began it was found that the tail skids were being damaged by the track surface, so the tail was mounted on a trolley which could be steered, usually by Percy Maxwell-Muller, who felt an especial responsibility to ensure that the aircraft made its first journey safely.

There was a growing interest in private and club flying, although, despite the stimulus given to aviation by the war, there was at first less private flying at Brooklands in the years immediately following the war than there had been up to 1914. The Brooklands Aero Club had died in 1914, but a resurgence of interest brought about its revival in 1923, when it operated from a small bungalow on the road inside the track leading to the Byfleet footbridge, behind the 'Village'. The many flying schools had also gone in 1914, but the Club began to offer tuition to enthusiastic newcomers. With the aim of encouraging an interest in flying and in training amateur pilots up to 'A' licence level, the Government-sponsored British flying club movement, administered by the Air Ministry, was begun in 1924, and the Brooklands Aero Club was one of those which received financial support. The introduction of the de Havilland 60 Moth in 1925 provided the relatively cheap machine which the club movement needed, and being the selected machine for the Government scheme many appeared at Brooklands.

Apart from the stimulus to membership provided by the scheme, Brooklands was ideally placed as the principal airfield in the south-western environs of London. A number of racing drivers kept aircraft and flew from the airfield, and a growing interest in learning to fly resulted in the establishment in May 1925 of a flying school by Lieutenant-Colonel G.L.P. Henderson based in three of the hangars adjoining the Byfleet Banking. This used three Avro 504s for instruction, which as a sideline provided a taxi service at a rate of £4 an hour and were also hired out for towing advertising banners.

The King's Cup race, from its inception, had become the main aerial competition in Britain and was supported by entries from Hawker and Vickers. A Vickers Vixen came fifth in the 1924 event flown by Major H.J. Payn, Pierson's technical assistant. In 1925 Payn flew the Vixen again but was unplaced, while a Hawker-entered Woodcock dropped out when it was damaged after making a forced landing at Luton in deteriorating weather. The Vixen was uprated for the 1926 race, with Flight Lieutenant 'Tiny' Scholefield as pilot. It started from scratch but came through to second place at the finish. Hawker was back in the race in 1927 with a Horsley light bomber flown by P.W.S. 'George' Bulman, the company's chief test pilot. The race was based on

Hucknall in Nottinghamshire and Bulman came sixth in a field of 26.

In 1928 Brooklands was chosen as the finishing point for the King's Cup race, which started at Hendon. The course of 1,096 miles ran to Renfrew in Scotland, then to Brooklands on the second day. There were 36 starters and 12 had dropped out by the end of the first day. There was no Vickers entry, although 'Mutt' Summers, the Vickers test pilot, was flying an Avro Avenger. Unfortunately a Hawker Heron, flown by Bulman, was a non-starter, as it collided with a spectator's car while taxiing to the start at Hendon. As the aircraft approached the finish it seemed possible that victory would go to Winifred Spooner, the only woman pilot in the race, flying a DH60 Cirrus Moth, but she was overtaken by the DH60 Gipsy Moth of Walter Hope, who, when he landed, did not cross the official finishing line so had to take off and land again in the correct place. This he managed to do before the second aircraft, a Bristol 101 flown by Captain Cyril Uwins, landed. Miss Spooner was third.

The Horsley was a profitable exercise for Hawker and 130 were erected at Brooklands for the RAF, as well as six ordered by Greece. In 1926 the Air Ministry issued a specification for a light bomber which was to have a much higher performance than the current machines. Sydney Camm produced a design, the Hart, which was first flown at Brooklands by Bulman in 1928. Flight trials continued at the track for six months before the Hart was announced to the world, but meanwhile it was being evaluated by the RAF. It was soon accepted and over the years about 360 Kingston-

BELOW *A Vickers Type 143 Scout which was ordered for the Bolivian air force in 1929. These aircraft saw action in the Bolivian-Paraguayan war of 1932–5. (BAE Systems per Brooklands Museum)*

built Harts were erected at Brooklands, while the company subcontracted construction to other manufacturers including Vickers, which built a batch of 114 in their Brooklands factory. A number of variants came from the Hart, including the Demon, Osprey, Audax, Hardy, Hind and Hector. The majority of these, including 527 Hinds, were built at Kingston for erection at Brooklands, but the number ordered meant that some batches were subcontracted.

In 1928/9 Camm designed what is considered by many to be the most beautiful aircraft ever built, the Hawker Fury. It emanated from an earlier design, the Hornet, which first flew at Brooklands in March 1929. The performance was impressive and when George Bulman landed after the first test flight he told Camm 'It's good.' An Air Ministry specification was written around the design and the outcome was an improved version, called the Fury by the Air Ministry and ordered in August 1930.

In November 1928 Lieutenant-Colonel Henderson decided to retire and the flying school was sold to his chief instructor Captain Duncan Davis for £3,000. Davis, who was 32, had run away from school to work with Cody at Farnborough, then after war service in the RFC had worked for A.V. Roe before joining Henderson. Renamed the Brooklands School of Flying it was formally opened

on 9 November. Among the pupils who 'went solo' in the first week was Jill Scott, who showed she was as competent in an aircraft as a racing car. The capital to fund the school came from pupils and former pupils.

The Government had meanwhile announced the formation of National Flying Services Ltd, which was to subsidise a network of flying schools throughout the country and enable a much wider public to learn to fly on standardised aircraft. This announcement caused great concern to some flying clubs, but Captain Davis did not join the scheme and carried on as an independent. Over 40 pupils gained their 'A' licences at the school in 1929. Sadly, Lieutenant-Colonel Henderson was killed in July 1930 when a Junkers F-13 he was piloting crashed at Meopham, in Kent, after breaking up in flight.

While Vickers was producing Virginias and Valentias in sufficient numbers to keep a modest production line going, it continued seeking orders for other aircraft. The Vixen series was sold in limited numbers to the Chilean air force and there were several designs which it was hoped would catch the eye of the RAF. A French manufacturer, Wibault, had produced a parasol monoplane fighter, the 7.C1, which was unusual as it was of all-metal construction using a corrugated skin reminiscent of the German

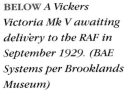

BELOW *A Vickers Victoria Mk V awaiting delivery to the RAF in September 1929. (BAE Systems per Brooklands Museum)*

Junkers aircraft. An example of the Wibault was purchased by Vickers in 1925 and was copied, with modifications, to become the Vickers Type 121 Wibault Scout. It did not appeal to the RAF, but an order was received from Chile for 26 aircraft. The first production Wibault built at Brooklands was tested by chief test pilot 'Tiny' Scholefield in June 1926. It went into an uncontrollable spin and he had to bale out at 1,500ft, the plane crashing into the Vickers sports ground at Byfleet. Despite this setback the order went ahead and Chile seemed pleased with its purchase.

The Wibault principles of construction were applied to a series of light transport aircraft, the Viastra, Vellore and Vellox, but these were built in the Supermarine works at Southampton which had been acquired by Vickers in 1928. There was a further attempt to build a Wibault-principle fighter, the Vireo, but this was turned down by the RAF and Admiralty for inadequate performance, as the Wibault corrugated surfaces caused too much drag. It is surprising that this was not discovered in the design stage, as there was a wind tunnel in the Brooklands factory which had been used when Pierson was asked to design the body for Malcolm Campbell's Napier-Campbell which took the Land Speed Record at Daytona in February 1928 at 206.95mph.

Vickers was striving to build a successful fighter and several prototypes came from the Brooklands factory in the late 1920s. The Type 143 biplane was first flown by 'Mutt' Summers at the track in June 1929. There were no British orders, but six were sold to Bolivia to back up the Vendace trainers and Vespa army co-operation aircraft which had already been bought. These aircraft saw action in the little-known and almost forgotten Bolivian-Paraguayan War of 1932–5. The Vespa achieved fame, as one aircraft was sold to rival manufacturer Bristol and, fitted with a Pegasus engine and flown by Cyril Uwins, captured the World Altitude Record in 1932 at 43,976ft.

In 1928 reorganisation and regrouping in the engineering industry led to a merger between Vickers and Armstrong-Whitworth and the formation of a new company, Vickers-Armstrong Ltd, a subsidiary of which was Vickers (Aviation) Ltd.

A civil version of the Victoria, the Vanguard, had been developed for Imperial Airways. One aircraft was built and after proving trials on the London–Paris route it was returned to Brooklands for modifications to the rudder. On 16 May 1929 'Tiny' Scholefield took it for a test flight, accompanied by Frank Sherratt as observer. It seems the tail broke away while turning and the aircraft crashed on the Middlesex side of the Thames at Shepperton. Scholefield and Sherratt were killed.

BELOW *A contrast in sizes: the Cygnet, the smallest aircraft made by Hawkers, beside a Vickers Virginia Mk X outside the Brooklands Flying Club clubhouse. (Brooklands Society)*

CHAPTER EIGHT

CAREFREE RACING

1931 The customary track repairs were made during the winter of 1930/1. Many thousands of square yards of concrete were laid and it was stated confidently that the major bumps had been eliminated. The most prominent improvement was the erection of a bridge across the track at the Fork which enabled spectators to enter through the entrance beside the Vickers factory and cross over the track to the Members' Hill. In addition an 'overseas' testing track was opened in the gravel pits beside the Aerodrome Road which enabled manufacturers to test vehicles in off-road conditions. The BARC published new racing rules which included confirmation that cars more than ten years old would be banned. The wearing of goggles was made compulsory and drivers were banned from smoking while racing or practising. The club also instituted the '120mph' badge, which was awarded to drivers who had lapped the track in excess of that speed. It was awarded retrospectively, though no award was made to Nazzaro for his 1908 lap. Early in the year the press made much of a proposed scheme to build a rival track on reclaimed ground at The Wash, but nothing came of it.

The opening meeting on 14 March drew a small crowd and also a small entry, despite good weather. Cobb won the Lincoln Lightning Short Handicap in the V12 Delage, lapping at a relatively slow 114.23mph, then got into his stride when taking

A picnic party stands beside an MG Magna at the JCC 1,000-Mile race on 3/4 June 1932. (LAT)

ABOVE *8 May, the first day of the 1931 Double-12, was wet. Victoria Worsley's Ulster Austin is passed by the Talbot 105 of Tim Rose-Richards and the 2-litre Lagonda of Mike Couper on the approach to the Finishing Straight. (LAT)*

second place in the Lincoln Long with a lap at 127.70mph, just failing to catch Bouts in the elderly 4.9-litre Sunbeam which had the 'ten-year' ban looming over it.

The Easter meeting was wet and the faster races were postponed. The very popular Sammy Davis suffered a broken femur when his Invicta

overturned during a Mountain handicap and Malcolm Campbell had a fortunate escape when the track rod of his Type 39A Bugatti broke as he braked for the Fork in another Mountain race. The meeting concluded with a demonstration in a BAC glider by C. Lowe-Wyld who, as one report commented, 'lived up to his name'. He concluded

RIGHT *The C-type MG of 'Goldie' Gardner is worked on in the pits during the 1931 Double-12. The work was in vain and the car retired with a broken piston. (LAT)*

ABOVE *A Brooklands Riley accelerates away from the start of a handicap at the Inter Club meeting on 20 June 1931. (Brooklands Society)*

his display by diving under the Finishing Straight Bridge, removing part of a wing en route. The postponed races were run the following Saturday and the main event, the Founders' Gold Cup, was won by Craig in a Type 37A Bugatti. He ignored the lines at the Fork and was fined £8 but kept ahead of Cobb, who was second in the Delage lapping at 130.72mph.

On 8 and 9 May the JCC ran the 'Double-12' again. The format was similar to previous years, but the course was reversed and the cars ran clockwise around the track. It was claimed by some drivers that this resulted in the cars hitting the sharper and less worn edges of the uneven bits of the track, causing additional chassis damage. The race was the debut for the 750cc C-type MG and marked a serious entry into international motor racing by this company, as 14 were entered among the total entry of 54, of which 48 started. One report commented that it was more of a high-speed trial than a race and was critical of the BARC 'red tape' imposed on the JCC, including insistence on the painted lines being obeyed at the only corner, the junction of the Members' Banking and the Finishing Straight.

The handicappers had misjudged the speed of the MGs and these dominated the field. Birkin, who had become Sir Henry Birkin Bart on the death of his father, drove a Speed Six Bentley entered by Jack Barclay, but this retired with a run

bearing after leading on the road for the first hour. A 2½-litre Maserati driven by Eyston and Ramponi was the fastest car in the race, lapping at over 100mph, but it kept stopping with minor troubles then retired with a broken back axle. With the Maserati out the fastest cars in the race were the three 105 Talbots, which, although impressive with their speed and silence, could make no impression on the MGs on handicap. The MG of Dan Higgin and Field was the leader, lapping much faster than the other MGs, and had pulled out a lead of nearly three laps when it retired with a broken piston at 5:00pm. This left the MG of the Earl of March and Chris Staniland in front for the rest of the first day. The Talbot challenge had been blunted when the Rose-Richards/Cobb car lost over an hour changing a cylinder head after a valve broke, and the other two cars were delayed by broken wing stays and collapsed dampers.

Thirty-six cars began the second day and there was silence as the flag fell for the start and teams began frenzied work. An Invicta had all six pistons changed and Archie Frazer-Nash changed a complete engine on his Ulster Austin. The March/Staniland MG set off in the lead again and stayed there throughout the 12 hours of the second day, coming home to win followed by MGs in the next four places. There was only one car with a greater capacity than 750cc in the first nine places. The Rose-Richards/Cobb Talbot was the

RIGHT *George Harvey-Noble grins as he throws his Salmson round the bend on the paddock approach road during the High Speed Trial at the JCC Members' Day on 4 July 1931. He is followed by the Ulster Austin of R.C. Mouatt. (Brooklands Society)*

BELOW *Bill Humphreys spins his C6 Amilcar in front of Philip Fotheringham-Parker's Alvis Silver Eagle at the Fork, during the First August Mountain Handicap. (LAT)*

fastest finisher in tenth place, as the other Talbots had long delays changing split radiators.

The race was not a success. The track had been too hard on the cars, there were too few fast cars to appeal to the spectators, and the handicapping error had taken any drama out of the race. Fortunately there had been no accidents, so the BARC probably felt the 'red tape' had been justified; it could not afford another fatal accident involving spectators.

For the BARC Whitsun meeting the entrance fee was cut to 2s 6d and the attendance surged, as there was a big attraction. Malcolm Campbell had broken the Land Speed Record at Daytona in February at 246.57mph. He had been knighted, and as Sir Malcolm he demonstrated the Napier-

ABOVE *Gwenda Stewart in her 2-litre Derby-Miller when she made an unsuccessful attempt at the lap record during the 1931 August meeting. (LAT)*

Campbell over two laps of the Outer Circuit. This car now had a strong Brooklands connection as it had been rebuilt as a virtually new car in the workshops of Thomson & Taylor in the 'Village'. This firm which used part of Parry Thomas's old premises had become the track's foremost preparer and tuner of racing cars. Another attraction was Birkin, who was driving the 'Blower' Bentley and was expected to break Don's lap record.

It was a windy day and conditions were unsuitable for an outright lap record, though Cobb set a new standing lap record of 115.55mph driving the V12 Delage into second place in the Sprint Handicap behind Munday's 30-98 Vauxhall. Unfortunately the Delage retired with a broken con

LEFT *Livesey, the winner of the 'Old Crocks' race at the 1931 August meeting in his 1903 Rover, receives congratulations. (LAT)*

ABOVE *Ted Baragwanath winning the Sidecar Handicap with his Brough Superior at the BMCRC meeting on 18 July 1931. During the race he set a new sidecar lap record at 102.48mph. (Brooklands Society)*

rod in the Gold Star Handicap, though the race was a Delage win, as Lord Howe was victorious in a 1½-litre GP car, lapping at 126.41mph; the Bentley was off-form in this race.

The Mountain races provided excitement: in the Whitsun Mountain Handicap there was a three-cornered Bugatti duel between Penn-Hughes in Type 35B, Campbell in a Type 39A and Staniland in a Type 37A, while Campbell drove his 38/250 Mercedes-Benz in the last Mountain Handicap of the day, over ten laps, and came through the field to third place, setting a new Mountain lap record on the way at 73.86mph.

The Light Car Club produced an innovation on 25 July with a handicap relay race over 100 laps for teams of three cars under 1,500cc. It drew 22 teams and was a great success despite heavy rain. The victors were three single-seater Austins, entered by Sir Herbert Austin and known as 'Dutch Clogs' because of their appearance.

At the end of July the Government announced that there would be a ten per cent cut in civil service and armed forces pay to meet a growing national economic crisis, but this news seemed to have little effect at Brooklands, where reduced entrance charges brought another big crowd to the BARC August Bank Holiday meeting. Lap record attempts were expected, not only from Birkin but also from Gwenda Stewart, who as Gwenda Janson had broken the motor cycle Double-12 Hour record in 1922. She had the 2-litre Derby-Miller, a bored-out 1,500cc front-wheel-drive Miller 91 which had been modified by Douglas Hawkes at

the Derby factory in Paris. With this she had taken the outright record at the Montlhéry track earlier in the year at 141.36mph. Unfortunately, however, the Derby-Miller had engine problems and her best lap was at only 112.17mph. The 'Blower' Bentley had been fitted with a Powerplus supercharger supplied by George Eyston to get more power. Though strong winds made high speeds difficult, Birkin did his best lap yet in the Lightning Long Handicap at 136.54mph to take third place. The winner was Purdy in one of the 1,500cc Thomas Specials.

The first of the Mountain races saw a fierce duel between Brian Lewis in the single-seat Talbot 90 and Raymond Mays in a 4½-litre Invicta. Mays spun and Lewis took second place behind Fothringham's Type 35 Bugatti. Birkin was on scratch in a 2½-ltre T26 GP Maserati, owned by Bernard Rubin and drove spectacularly, with wheelspin out of the corners. Although unplaced he set a new Mountain lap record at 75.21mph. He also made a timed attempt on the Outer Circuit lap record near the end of the meeting, but was slower than his earlier race lap. The meeting ended with a two-lap veterans' race around the Mountain which was won by Livesey's 1903 Rover.

The BRDC returned to Brooklands on 3 October for the 500-Mile race. This had 47 entries and 40 of these started. During practice on 30 September Birkin unofficially equalled Don's lap record, but the Bentley caught fire so there was no official attempt. As before, although a handicap the cars all had to cover the full distance, and the first unblown 750cc MG, away at 10:30am, had to run alone on the track for 24min 8sec before being joined by its supercharged brothers. It was expected to be another MG benefit, but the handicapper had made adjustments and after an hour a works Brooklands Riley driven by Cyril Whitcroft led on handicap, followed by the Speed Six Bentley 'Old No 1', driven by Jack Dunfee and Cyril Paul. Further back the 'Blower' Bentley driven by Benjafield retired with stretched valves, while Birkin in an 8C-2300 Alfa Romeo, which had been up into second place during the first hour, lapping at 122mph, was delayed by electrical bothers.

After two hours Whitcroft led the Bentley, which was being harried by the single-seater Talbot 105 of Brian Lewis, but at half-distance Whitcroft stopped with a defunct clutch and the Talbot passed the Bentley into the lead. The pair swapped places but with half an hour to go Lewis, who was leading, with enough fuel to go through non-stop, had to make a stop for tyres. This cost him the race and Dunfee and Paul took the Bentley into the lead and stayed there until the end, winning by six minutes from the Talbot at 118.39mph and making the '500' the fastest long-distance race in the world. An MG driven by Eddie Hall was third and the Riley of Miller and Eggar was fourth. There were only seven finishers and three cars were still running when flagged off.

The final BARC meeting, held on 17 October, had a new race, the 15-lap Mountain Championship which, rare for the club, was a scratch event. Birkin ran the 8C-2300 Alfa Romeo in the Cumberland Senior Short Handicap and won, beating Lewis's Talbot to the line. His best lap was at 124.51mph. Froy brought the Leyland-Thomas into third place. The Mountain Championship attracted the fastest road racing cars in the country and eight came to the line. Campbell led from the start in his 38/250 Mercedes followed by Aldington's Frazer Nash and Staniland's Bugatti, but Birkin, who had made a slow start in the T26 Maserati, came through and took the lead on lap three. He pulled away and went on to win, equalling his lap record. Campbell was pursued by Penn-Hughes's Type 35B Bugatti which went into second place coming onto the Members' Banking on the last lap, but the engine faltered slightly so Campbell repassed and stayed in second place to the flag.

Although in the wider world, women had achieved political equality with men, the BARC was still unwilling to accept women drivers on level terms, but compromised with a Ladies' Handicap which was won by Fay Taylour with a works Talbot 105, beating the scratch car, Elsie Wisdom's 4½-litre Invicta.

Birkin had a busy day and ran the 'Blower' Bentley in the Senior Long Handicap, coming third behind the GP OM of Swedish driver Henken Widengren and Cobb's Delage. In the gathering dusk he carried on for two more laps after the end of the race, hoping to take the lap record, but his best lap was at 136.82mph, so Don's record remained intact for another year.

In its report of the closing meeting *Motor Sport* commented: 'What a pity we cannot have some more scratch races so the winner really wins.' Sadly, this view reflected the opinion of many. From its pinnacle before the war and in the immediate post-war years Brooklands had slipped by the end of 1931, until it had become a backwater in the mainstream of international motor racing. In the eyes of the truly keen enthusiast proper motor racing was happening on mainland Europe, where handicap racing was almost unknown. The keener and more ambitious

BELOW *Bill Lacey, sitting on his 500cc Norton, receives a handshake from Tommy Atkins after winning the 25-mile Bacon Cup at the BMCRC meeting on 15 August 1931.* (Brooklands Society)

British drivers who wanted to make a mark in international racing were turning away from Brooklands and looking across the English Channel.

The 1931 BMCRC season began with a Clubman's meeting on 28 March, where the longest race was ten laps around the Mountain for three-wheelers and sidecars and the victor was Clive Lones in a Morgan, who pursued and caught Les Archer (New Imperial). The Champions' meeting on 18 April was spoiled by high winds and sleet. A match race between a motor cycle, a car and an aircraft was cancelled following an unspecified objection by the Air Ministry, but a match race between William Craig's Type 35B Bugatti and Bill Lacey's Norton 500 saw a motorcycle win when the Bugatti misfired. The three-lap Brooklands Championship was expected to be a win for Joe Wright on his lap-record-holding OEC-JAP, but he dropped out and the race went to Wal Phillips riding a Grindlay Peerless.

The meeting planned for 16 May was upset by the weather and postponed until 27 June. It drew a small crowd as the change of date clashed with the Hendon Air Pageant, which was probably a bigger pull for spectators. The main attraction at Brooklands was a match race between Tim Birkin in the 'Blower' Bentley and Oliver Baldwin on a Zenith-JAP. Birkin stayed away and Harold Purdy drove the Bentley for him, but the Zenith was sick and it was declared to be 'no race'.

A new sidecar lap record was established at the meeting on 18 July when E.C.E. 'Barry' Baragwanath, with a Brough Superior combination, romped away with the sidecar handicap and did a lap at 102.48mph, breaking the record set by Freddie Dixon in 1927. There was also a dead heat for third place in the over 350cc handicap between Ben Bickell (Bickell-JAP) and N. Anderson (Raleigh).

A big crowd came for the meeting on 15 August, perhaps drawn by the promise of a 175cc ladies' race, but there was disappointment as no lady entered, so consolation was offered with the 25-mile handicap for the Phillips and Bacon Cups. The Phillips went to the handicap winner, Ben Bickell riding his own Bickell-JAP, and the Bacon to the fastest finisher, Bill Lacey on a Norton 500, who averaged 105.52mph.

Bickell was on top form at the September meeting, winning a three-lap and five-lap handicap and taking second place in another three-lap race. Baragwanath was also on form, and with his Brough Superior raised his sidecar lap record to 102.48mph. The motor cycle season finished with the 'Hutchinson 100' on 10 October. It was a race of attrition: 23 machines started and only four finished. Perhaps some riders were disconcerted by a parachute descent during the race; fortunately the parachutist landed on the airfield. The winner was J.M. Muir riding a 350cc Velocette, who caught the limit machine, which had a 22-minute start.

BELOW *Tim Birkin looks at the rev counter of the 4½-litre 'Blower' Bentley as he starts an attempt on the lap record on 30 September 1931. He was unsuccessful, as the car caught fire. (Brooklands Society)*

1932

The usual repairs were made during the winter of 1931/2 and much of the Members' Banking was dug up and relaid. These repairs were necessary, as the breaking up of the track surface was a continuous problem and H.J. Aldington, competing in a minor JCC meeting during 1931, had been fortunate to escape serious injury when hit in the face by a piece of loose concrete. Among the cars rejected under the ten-year rule was the 200hp Benz, and the Leyland-Thomas was only admitted after Cobb reported to the club that he considered the car to be safe.

The BARC season opened with the Easter Monday meeting on 28 March, but there had been drama beforehand when Birkin, practising in the 'Blower' Bentley on the previous Thursday, had lapped at 137.96mph, thus breaking Kaye Don's record by 0.2sec. It had been hoped that Don would appear in a new acquisition, a 4.9-litre Type 54 Bugatti, but this was withdrawn after supercharger drive problems in practice. In the Norfolk Lightning Short Handicap, Cobb in the V12 Delage and Birkin in the Bentley, now painted red, came head-to-head as both started from scratch. Birkin made a slow start but then pulled back the gap and Cobb crossed the line only 0.2sec ahead. Between the races Sir Malcolm Campbell gave a demonstration of the Napier-Campbell 'Blue Bird', which had returned from the United States, where

Campbell had pushed the Land Speed Record up to 253.97mph in February. Birkin and Cobb met again in the Norfolk Long Handicap. Birkin gave Cobb a 3sec start and had a vicious skid on the Members' Banking but did not lift off, catching Cobb on the last lap to win by 3.4sec. In the last race of the day, a Mountain Handicap, there was a dead heat between the Type 35 Bugatti of Whitney Straight and the Type 43 of Faulkner. Straight was an Anglo-American, and the heir to the Whitney fortune. Nineteen years old and a Cambridge undergraduate, he had started racing with a Brooklands Riley in 1931 and in the next two years would become a leading driver, bringing a new and professional approach to British racing.

Perhaps heeding the need for scratch races, on 30 April the BRDC organised the British Empire Trophy. This was run in 50-mile heats with the intention that there would be separate heats for 750cc, 1,100cc, 1,500cc and unlimited capacity cars, with the first four from each heat running in the final. The three small capacity classes attracted poor entries so all the starters ran in one heat. The race was led all the way by Lord Howe in his GP Delage followed by Widengren's OM. The win gave Howe the Canada Trophy; Humphreys in his C6 Amilcar, which was third, won the India Trophy; and the 750cc class went to the Earl of March in an Austin, who gained the South Africa Trophy.

These four were the only finishers. There were

BELOW *Sir Malcolm Campbell demonstrating the Napier-Campbell 'Blue Bird' at the 1932 Easter meeting. He had set a new Land Speed Record of 253.97mph at Daytona in February. (LAT)*

ABOVE *Sir Malcolm Campbell's 38/250 SS Mercedes-Benz is prepared for the 1932 JCC 1,000-Mile race outside his workshop, which is now part of the Museum's car display. (Brooklands Society)*

ABOVE RIGHT *John Cobb's V12 Delage and George Eyston's Panhard lap Lord Howe's 1½-litre Delage during their fight for the lead in the 1932 British Empire Trophy on 30 April. Both cars are running along the 120mph line. (John Maitland Collection)*

RIGHT *A Wolseley Hornet in the pits during the JCC 1,000-Mile race. It was driven by 'H.H. Wanborough' and J.H.N. Justice. Justice was later to achieve fame as the film actor James Robertson Justice. (LAT)*

six starters in the big car heat, Cobb in the Delage, Birkin in the Bentley, Jack Dunfee in the Speed Six Bentley, the Talbots of Lewis and Hebeler, and an unusual runner, an 8-litre Panhard, which had been built to take records at Montlhéry and was being driven by Eyston. Cobb led at the start but was passed by Eyston, while Birkin moved up into second place. Then the Bentley threw a tyre tread and he dropped back, so Eyston won from Dunfee, followed by Cobb and Birkin. Between the heats and the final, Chris Staniland – who was now the chief test pilot for Fairey Aviation – gave a display of aerobatics in a Fairey Firefly IIIM.

The first four finishers in the big car heat came out for the 36-lap final accompanied by Howe and Widengren: the drivers of the smaller cars knew there was no purpose in racing again. Cobb led for three laps, followed by Eyston and then by Birkin. On lap four Birkin took the lead as the cars came off the Members' Banking and stayed in front until lap 18, when the Bentley came into the pits and retired, as the cylinder block had cracked. This left Eyston in front but on lap 26 Cobb took the lead. Eyston hung on and tried everything to get in front again, but the Panhard, although faster, did not have quite enough speed to make a decisive move and there was not enough room at the top of the bankings for both cars when flat out. Cobb came home the winner by 0.2sec and Howe was third, as Dunfee burst a tyre on the last lap and went into the pits. Eyston lodged a protest (he probably had

no choice, the Panhard being a works car), claiming that he had been baulked by Cobb. The stewards held a meeting for two-and-a-half hours and then announced that the result was reversed and Eyston was the victor. Cobb then lodged an appeal with the RAC, who after pondering on the matter concluded that Eyston had not been baulked and restored the original placings.

Cobb and Eyston were good friends, and when the RAC decision was announced Cobb stood Eyston a dinner. The press, however, were critical, emphasising that the problem was the limitations of the track, which made it impossible for cars which needed all the banking to pass each other. *Motor Sport* said: 'Brooklands is definitely unsuitable for such a contest.'

The Whit Monday BARC meeting was threatened with rain, and this fell during the meeting so that the main event, the Gold Star Race on the Outer Circuit, was held back until the end. Cobb in the Delage and Birkin in the repaired Bentley started from scratch in the Nottingham Senior Short Handicap. The Delage had better acceleration from the start and stayed in front to come third behind a Riley and 30-98 Vauxhall, but Birkin was only 2ft behind at the finish and could not find a way through, as the Delage was at the top of the banking. Lord Howe in a Type 51 Bugatti and Whitney Straight in the ex-Birkin T26 2½-litre Maserati were on scratch in the Nottingham Lightning Mountain Handicap and they came

through the field, with Howe taking the flag about two lengths in front of Straight. While the crowd waited for the track to dry for the main race Flight Lieutenant P.E.G. Sayer gave an aerobatic display in a Hawker Fury, which included inverted flying just above stalling speed.

In the seven-lap Gold Star Race Birkin was on scratch with Howe, who was in a Type 54 Bugatti, and Cobb had an 8sec start. Howe led initially, then Birkin went past, diving below the Bugatti coming off the Members' Banking, but retired on the fourth lap. The race went to Munday's 30-98 Vauxhall followed by Bouts in one of the GP Sunbeams, while Cobb was third. Ten days later, on Wednesday 26 May, Whitney Straight brought out the Maserati and made a successful attempt on the Mountain Circuit lap record, raising it to 78.00mph.

The JCC, appreciating the criticism of the Double-12, and especially its car-breaking nature, promoted a new event, the 1,000-Mile race, which took place on Friday 3 and Saturday 4 June. This was a class handicap for modified sports cars stripped of road equipment, run over the 2.61-mile Double-12 circuit in a clockwise direction with 200 laps (523 miles) covered on each day. There were 27 starters, who set off in class groups, so every car had to cover the full distance. By an extraordinary interpretation of the regulations the Earl of March was not permitted to start, being adjudged as 'inexperienced'! The 750cc MGs were the first away at 10:00am on the Friday morning and each group

ABOVE *Joan Richmond and Elsie Wisdom in their Riley after their victory in the JCC 1,000-Mile race. (LAT)*

was released in turn until the scratch 38/250 Mercedes driven by Campbell and Staniland was sent on its way at 11:46am. Sadly, at about 11:00am an MG driven by H. Leeson, an Eastbourne butcher, swerved as it was braking for the Finishing Straight

bend and hit the parapet of the bridge over the entrance road. The car crashed down onto the road and Leeson was killed instantly.

The handicapping did not favour the MGs, and by midday, although the race was led by the MG of Black and Gibson, the other MGs had been passed by the works Rileys, which held second, third and fourth places. The larger cars were unable to match the pace of the Rileys, although the three Talbot 105s were running silently and rapidly and the 8C-2300 Alfa Romeo driven by Birkin and Howe was lapping at 103mph. At the end of the first day, when the handicaps had been calculated, the Brooklands Riley of Sutton and Harvey led from the Talbots of Cobb/Lewis and Saunders-Davies, while the Riley of Elsie Wisdom and Joan Richmond was in fourth place. The first day's racing had attracted fewer spectators than the JCC members' meeting two week before.

On the Saturday morning the drivers were allowed to warm up their engines before the start and each group was released with the same time intervals as the first day. As soon as the starting signal was given work began on the cars, which trickled back onto the track as soon as the essential work was completed. It was clear that the Rileys

were uncatchable, although the Talbot team were challenging on handicap. The Harvey/Sutton Riley fell out with clutch troubles, but the Wisdom/Richmond team were well placed and when it seemed possible that the leading Talbot,

driven single-handed by Saunders-Davies, might move ahead the two women speeded up and increased their lead. Just before 5:00pm they were flagged off as the winners, having made a small piece of motor racing history.

Near the end the Talbot passed the Riley to get onto the same lap, but there was no time left to make up the deficit. The Black/Gibson MG was third and the Lewis/Cobb Talbot was fourth, the team prize going to Talbot. It is likely that the drive by Elsie Wisdom and Joan Richmond may have influenced the BARC concerning its attitude to women racing drivers, but the race was otherwise generally regarded as a failure. The crowd was very poor on the Saturday and even the reduction in distance did not prevent the track surface causing a massacre among the cars. *Motor Sport* was highly critical of the race and its correspondent said 'The entire race depressed me.' It went on to comment that Brooklands was probably unsuitable for a long-distance sports car race, and suggested that the BARC should concentrate on Mountain events with many more scratch races.

A successful Inter-club meeting where the Stanley Cup was won by the JCC team was followed by a Guy's Hospital Gala charity meeting on Saturday 2 July, which was attended by HRH the Duke and Duchess of York (later King George VI and Queen Elizabeth). There was an Hungarian orchestra playing on the lawn, a *concours d'élégance*, driving tests, and a race for London taxis. Some of the drivers were presented to the Duke and Duchess, who watched some good racing. Birkin in the 'Blower' Bentley won the Gala Long Handicap, then the Duchess of York's Trophy race for lady drivers

ABOVE *The Duke and Duchess of York (later King George VI and Queen Elizabeth) are accompanied by Percy Bradley at the Guys Hospital Gala meeting on 2 July 1932. (LAT)*

LEFT *The winner is flagged off in the London Taxi race at the Guys Gala meeting. (LAT)*

went to Eileen Ellison in a Type 37 Bugatti, beating Kay Petre's Wolseley Hornet by just over a length. The Duke of York's Trophy brought Birkin out again, who started from scratch, six seconds after Cobb in the Delage, and equalled his lap record but had to retire when the Bentley threw a tread on the Byfleet Banking. Cobb weaved his way through the traffic but could not catch Ashby in a much-modified Brooklands Riley, who averaged 102mph. During the meeting 'George' Bulman performed aerobatics in a Hawker Hart and as the day ended the *Graf Zeppelin* airship cruised over the track en route from Germany to Hanworth.

Two weeks later the LCC held the Relay Race, which drew 29 teams including works entries from Austin and Morgan. The race, which was attended by James Pybus, the Minister of Transport, was won by the underrated Wolseley Hornet team, followed by a team of Salmsons entered by Vic Derrington, who ran a 'tuning-goodies' shop in Kingston, possibly one of the first in its field.

A fierce storm swept across south-west London on August Bank Holiday Monday, but it almost missed Brooklands – the meeting was only slightly delayed and just one race was cancelled. The main attraction was a three-lap match race between Birkin in the 'Blower' Bentley and Cobb with the Delage. Cobb led from the start and had a 3.8sec lead at the end of the first lap. A high wind was making it difficult for both drivers, but Birkin was only 1.4sec behind at the end of the second lap, and on the last lap, as the cars came off the Members' Banking onto the Railway Straight approaching the finish, he just eased past Cobb to take the flag by 0.2sec. It was the last time Birkin would race at Brooklands.

There was more excitement in the August Senior Mountain Handicap when Tom Delaney driving a Lea Francis beat Raymond Mays's Invicta to the line by a length. Over 70 years later Delaney was still racing, and won a race at Silverstone in the same car. During the race Tim Fotheringham-Parker misjudged the turning onto the Members' Banking and went over the top of the banking in his Alvis Silver Eagle; he emerged shaken but unhurt. The meeting ended with a two-lap 'Old Crocks' race round the Mountain which was won by F.L. Wigginton in a 1902 Wolseley. It was noticed that some of the competitors had changed 'Old Crocks' to 'Veteran Cars' on their number cards.

The BARC closing meeting on 10 September drew a small crowd. It was a grey day and there was a shower before the main race, the Mountain Championship, so the start was delayed to give the

LEFT *The B and C cars of the teams await their turn at the LCC Relay race on 18 July 1932. (LAT)*

BELOW *Clive Dunfee in the Bentley 'Old No. 1' passes Brian Lewis's 105 Talbot on the Byfleet Banking in the 1932 BRDC 500, shortly before his fatal accident. (LAT)*

track time to dry. The crowd made noisy objections to this, but was entertained by an impromptu aerobatic display by three Aero Club members.

Favourite for the race was the V12 Sunbeam, which had been bought by Sir Malcolm Campbell and had been rebuilt, modified and updated by Thomson & Taylor. It was a small field of six and Campbell led all the way, being followed home by Mays's Invicta and Richard Shuttleworth's Type 35C Bugatti. A Ladies' handicap followed in which Elsie Wisdom was on scratch with the Leyland-Thomas, and her handling of the car was further proof of the BARC's short-sightedness regarding women drivers. She could not catch the leaders but lapped at 121.47mph, breaking Jill Scott's 1928 record. The race was won by Paddy Naismith in a Salmson, followed by Fay Taylour in a works 105 Talbot.

The season ended with the BRDC '500' on 24 September. It was a fine day, there was a good

crowd, and 34 cars started. There had been hopes that two works 8C-2300 Alfa Romeos driven by Nuvolari and Borzacchini would be present, but the entries did not materialise. The unblown 750s began, and were followed by the blown 750s 30 minutes later. The pace of this group was impressive and after an hour the two MGs of Ron Horton and George Eyston were leading, followed by the only foreign competitor, the Polish/French Count Stanislas Czaikowski in a 2-litre Type 51 Bugatti. Behind him was the scratch car, the Bentley 'Old No 1', now owned by Woolf Barnato and fitted with an 8-litre engine, with Jack and Clive Dunfee as the drivers. Czaikowski retired with a broken piston and the leading MGs swapped places, now pursued by the Brooklands Rileys of Campbell and Paul, all averaging over 100mph.

Clive Dunfee, who had stopped to change a wheel, was lapping at almost 130mph when he went up to the rim of the Members' Banking as he passed another car and put a wheel over the edge. The Bentley cut down some saplings and then hit a tree. Dunfee was thrown out and killed instantly and the car fell onto the entrance road outside the banking.

The race continued, and after four-and-a-half hours the single-seater Talbot 105, driven by Lewis and Cobb, caught the two MGs on handicap and led. Eyston's MG retired with a broken piston, but Horton, who was sharing his car with Jack Bartlett, speeded up, as did Cyril Paul, and the MG and Riley passed the Talbot on handicap. The result was in doubt until the end, but Horton and Bartlett were the winners, averaging 96.29mph. The Paul/'Phillip' Riley was second and the Talbot, which had been 300rpm down throughout the race, was third.

Clive Dunfee had been a popular driver and was missed by the racing community. Sadly, his fiancée Jane Baxter, a well-known actress and rising film star, had been present in the pits during the race. At the subsequent inquest the coroner made critical comments about safety measures at the track and during the following winter the entrance road was re-sited as a safety precaution.

Record attempts were few in 1932, so as an encouragement a 'records week' was announced at the end of October. George Eyston and Freddie Dixon broke Class F (1,500cc) and G (1,100cc) records with Rileys – Dixon's car being a specialised single-seater, 'Red Mongrel', based on Riley parts – and Eddie Hall set Class H (750cc) records with an MG. R.G.J. Nash started the week by breaking the car Test Hill record on 24 October in his Frazer Nash 'Terror'. His record of 7.45sec was never beaten and stands for all time.

The 1932 BMCRC season opened on 19 March with the *Motor Cycle*-sponsored Clubman's

meeting. To amuse the crowd there was a match race between Driscoll's Lea Francis and Archer's Velocette motor cycle, which was won by the car. Bad weather caused two postponements of the second meeting until 7 May, when in the three-lap All Comers' Handicap Baragwanath equalled his sidecar record, though he could only take third place, while in a five-lap Mountain handicap Fernihough, riding a 500cc Excelsior-JAP and starting from scratch, came through to win and set a new motor cycle lap record at 67.93mph.

A Ladies' Day was held on 11 June, with a 'Ladies' Trial' as the feature event and with the Mountain races started by Sir Malcolm Campbell. The Ladies' Trial was a proper race and was won by Teresa Wallach on a 350cc BSA, Miss J.R. Hole (500cc BSA) being second and Miss B. Painter (172cc Excelsior) third. *Motor Cycling* described the race as a flop! The magazine was more enthusiastic about the

LEFT *The field goes onto the Members' Banking during the High Speed Trial at the Motor Cycle Clubmans meeting on 19 March 1932. (Brooklands Society)*

BELOW *The field rounds the Finishing Straight turn in the 350cc race at the 1932 BMCRC Grand Prix meeting. H.J. Bacon (No 8 Velocette), who won the race, leads Claude Bickell (No 14 Ariel) and E.R. Merrill (No 4 Excelsior). (Brooklands Society)*

Sir Henry Birkin, Bt

'Tim' Birkin, as he was affectionately known, was born in 1896 to a lace-making family in Nottingham. He served in the RFC during World War One and first appeared at Brooklands in 1921 driving a DFP. He did not race again until 1927, when he drove a 3-litre Bentley in the Essex Six-Hour race. This began an association with Bentley for which he is always remembered. He drove a 4½-litre in the Essex race in 1928 and in the 1929 Double-12. His first major success was with a win at Le Mans in 1929. During the same year he began an association with the Hon Dorothy Paget, who sponsored a team of supercharged 4½-litre Bentleys which was instigated by Birkin. A single-seater 'Blower' Bentley was built, and Birkin took the Brooklands Lap Record with this at 135.33mph during the 1930 Easter meeting.

Perhaps his greatest drive came at the end of the 1930 season when he took second place with a sports-bodied 'Blower' car in the French GP, racing against pure GP racing cars. Dorothy Paget withdrew from racing in 1931 and only kept the single-seater which Birkin continued to race at the track, gaining several victories and taking the lap record again in March 1932 at 137.96mph. In 1931 Birkin won again at Le Mans sharing an 8C-Alfa Romeo with Lord Howe. He also drove a 2½-litre T26 GP Maserati, in which he won the 1931 Mountain Championship at Brooklands and took the Mountain Lap Record. He continued to race the Maserati and an 8C-Alfa Romeo in 1932 but had little success, as it seems he was very hard on his cars.

During the winter of 1932/3 he published his autobiography *Full Throttle*, in which he made a savage attack on Brooklands and the BARC organisation. For the 1933 season he had a new 8C-3000 Maserati, and while racing this in the Tripoli GP he had a recurrence of the malaria from which he had suffered during the war and died a few weeks later.

Birkin was the epitome of the dashing racing driver hero and had a large circle of admirers, though in reality he was an unhappy man in deep financial trouble when he died. With his death some of the excitement and glamour went out of Brooklands racing.

meeting on 25 June, saying that 'the real spice of the programme' was the many 100mph laps, though the best effort came on the Mountain where Ben Bickell won the ten-lap All Comers' scratch race on a Chater Lea-JAP and set a new lap record on the way, at 69.74mph. Bickell was on form again on 27 August when he won the three-lap Gold Star Handicap riding his Bickell-JAP and lapping at 110.68mph, while Les Archer also had a good day on the Mountain, winning the five-lap and ten-lap solo handicaps on his 350cc Velocette.

The 'Hutchinson 100' was held on 1 October. It was a wet day, but unlike the BARC the BMCRC did not flinch from racing on the Outer Circuit, though the supporting races around the Mountain were cancelled. Before the '100' there was a three-lap All Comers' Handicap and Baragwanath brought out his Brough Superior combination and came through to win, setting a new sidecar record at 103.11mph despite the conditions. There were 31 starters in the '100' and Bickell was on scratch with his Bickell-JAP. After 25 laps he had worked his way through the field up to sixth place and in the remaining 12 laps passed the rest to come home the winner at 99.61mph. The Mountain meeting was held the following week and in the Senior Mountain Championship for 500cc machines, over 25 laps, Williams (Douglas) led for 23 laps but then

had problems with his front brake, and Harold Daniell went into the lead on a Norton. Williams hung on but could not pass Daniell, who crossed the line 0.2sec ahead.

The BMCRC season had provided good racing, but it was a shadow of earlier years and apart from the '100' there had been no long-distance races. The absence of serious trade support had made a noticeable difference. There were some local short-distance record attempts during the season, but on 18 October an attempt was made which harked back to the golden days of the 1920s. The BSA Blue Star was a relatively humble road machine, but a 350cc model fitted with a sidecar set out to break the International Double-12 350cc sidecar record. Sponsored by the Ardarth tobacco company and ridden by Percy Brewster, Alan Dussek and Mike Couper, who also raced cars and was Birkin's partner in the firm which maintained the Paget Bentleys, the team rode from 8:00am to 8:00pm, the last hours being illuminated by Couper's Lagonda. The next morning the team set out again and despite repairing a broken gearbox and extracting Brewster and the combination from the sewage farm when the sidecar wheel spindle broke, the run was completed successfully and the record was taken at 42.88mph. This was one of the earliest tobacco company sponsorships of motor sport.

BELOW *The BSA Blue Star team puff contentedly at their Ardarth cigarettes after their sponsored Double-12 Hour sidecar record-breaking run on 19 October 1932. (Brooklands Society)*

1933

Brooklands suffered several setbacks during the winter of 1932/3. Early in March, soon after the usual winter repairs had been completed, the River Wey flooded. The supports for the bridge which carried the track across the river between the Byfleet Banking and the Fork were severely damaged and some were swept away. This caused the track surface to subside and extensive repairs were needed. The new public entrance, built as a consequence of Dunfee's accident, was sited further north along Brooklands Road and was called 'Shell Way', as the oil company had bought the advertising rights for the entrance.

Since 1907 Brooklands had been the only permanent motor racing venue in England, and the only circuit, but in March 1933 a new road circuit was opened at Donington Park, on the Leicestershire–Derbyshire border. At first it only staged minor club meetings, but it was a road circuit – a facility which, it was generally agreed, was essential for British motor racing – and within two seasons Donington would expand to the point where it would be challenging Brooklands as the country's premier circuit.

Meanwhile, in the autumn of 1932 Sir Henry Birkin published his autobiography *Full Throttle*;

although he employed a ghost writer, Michael Burn, the account was Birkin's story and it expressed his views. He made a fierce attack on Brooklands, describing it as 'the most out-of-date, inadequate and dangerous track in the world'. He went on: 'the surface is abominable … meetings can only be considered as a joke … the place has become a farce'. His attack was not only on the track itself, but also on the BARC's organisation and the preponderance of handicap races. The book caused a great furore and Brooklands Estates Ltd brought an action against Birkin and the publishers for alleged libel. The matter was settled by a formal published apology by Birkin, which was inserted in subsequent editions. There the matter rested, but many admitted that Birkin had a strong point and that his attacks, although perhaps too vehement, were justified. The BARC did nothing. It knew the track had the shortcomings which Birkin had criticised but could not make the changes and improvements that were needed. The money was not there.

The BARC season began on 11 March with an abbreviated programme, as the bridge repairs had not been completed. There were five Mountain races and two sprints running from the Fork to the Railway Straight. The major race was the five-lap Weybridge Lightning Mountain Handicap and Don

BELOW *A Wolseley Hornet about to start a test in unpleasant conditions at the JCC Rally on 25 February 1933. (LAT)*

ABOVE *E.W.J.H. Wright's C-type MG on fire during the Weybridge Senior Mountain Handicap at the opening meeting on 11 March 1933. The driver was unhurt but did not turn off the fuel pump, so the blaze was difficult to extinguish. (LAT)*

was on scratch with the Type 54 Bugatti, which had been modified during the winter. Don ran wide at the Fork and spun at the Members' Banking turn, but came third behind Aldington's Frazer Nash and Bowes's Type 35B Bugatti.

The track repairs were completed before the Easter meeting on 17 April. The star of the day was Whitney Straight, who ran his 2½-litre Maserati in the First Addlestone Mountain Handicap. He started from scratch with Tim Rose-Richards in a Type 51 Bugatti and came through to second place behind Roy Eccles's Frazer Nash, establishing a new lap record en route of 78.29mph. Rose-Richards was third. Sir Malcolm Campbell had established a new World Land Speed Record at Daytona on 22 February with 'Blue Bird', which had been rebuilt and fitted with a Rolls-Royce 'R' engine by Thomson & Taylor. He demonstrated the car on the Outer Circuit, though he explained to the spectators that the surface forced him to run at a very limited pace. After this demonstration Straight ran again in the Second Addlestone

Mountain Handicap, and this time he passed everyone to win.

The JCC, profiting from experience, did not run a long-distance sports car race again but produced a most imaginative innovation. Realising that spectators preferred to see racing cars at speed and found conventional handicapping confusing, and often boring, a handicap race was evolved which was effectively a scratch race. It used the Double-12 circuit running clockwise. In the Finishing Straight the entire entry went through a chicane, but beyond this, at the Fork, they divided according to engine size. The smallest cars had a clear run, the second group drove through a mildly severe barrel and sandbank turn, while the largest cars had to negotiate a virtual hairpin. For identification, the tails of the smallest cars were painted green, the intermediate group orange, and the largest white. The effect was a virtual scratch race over 100 laps, with the car in front leading. During practice the bends were adjusted to achieve parity and it was found that Campbell's V12 Sunbeam was setting virtually the same time over five laps as Horton's 750cc MG.

This race, the JCC International Trophy was held on Saturday 6 May and drew a very large crowd. It was the first major race at the track with a massed grid start since the 1928 200-Mile race and there were 28 starters. Campbell led at the end of the first lap followed by Brian Lewis (8C Monza Alfa

Romeo) and Straight (Maserati). Straight passed Campbell while Lewis battled with Rose-Richards (Type 51 Bugatti), and by lap 20 Straight had pulled out almost a lap lead. Then he retired with a broken back axle and Rose-Richards also fell out, so Campbell led Lewis and Don (Type 54 Bugatti), who was two laps down and slowed by failing brakes. Lewis closed up on Campbell, and when the pair made pit stops and Staniland took over the Sunbeam, the Alfa Romeo pit crew worked faster and Lewis took the lead. Staniland tried hard to close the gap, but the Sunbeam wilted and retired at 80 laps which left Lewis to cruise home to win. He was being followed by Don, but the Bugatti's transmission broke with eight laps to go, so second and third places went to Eddie Hall and Elsie Wisdom, both driving K3 MGs. The race was adjudged a great success. It had given the spectators the kind of racing they wanted and the winning Alfa Romeo was a current grand prix car, something rarely seen at the track.

Whit Monday was a very hot day, and although the entry for the BARC meeting was good the crowd was poor. *Motor Sport* commented that 'the accommodation for spectators is far from comfortable and the blistering heat of the ash dump at the Fork defied description'. History was made in a minor way, as the BARC had relented at last and permitted women drivers to compete on equal terms, though they were only admitted to Outer Circuit races; the Mountain was presumably too exacting. The Cobham Junior Handicap was the first race and had two women drivers, the Hon Joan Chetwynd and Eileen Ellison. The latter, in a Type 37 Bugatti, almost won, but was passed on the line by Aubrey Esson-Scott's Type 35 Bugatti. In the Cobham Senior Handicap Miss G. Hedges took second place in a Talbot 90. The main race of the day was the Gold Star Handicap over seven laps, with a prize of £100. This was won by Charles Brackenbury in a Type 37 Bugatti, by a substantial margin, from Oliver Bertram, who was racing the V12 Delage which he had bought from Cobb. In third place was the Leyland-Thomas, driven by journalist Tommy Wisdom.

The motor racing world was greatly upset by the death of Sir Henry Birkin in a London nursing home on 22 June. Birkin had driven an 8C-3000 Maserati in the Tripoli GP in May, where he had shown that his skill was equal to the top GP aces. He had burnt his arm during the race and it was certified that he died from septicaemia caused by the burn, though subsequent research seems to indicate that the true cause was a recurrence of malaria contracted during the war. Birkin was the epitome of the brave, debonair racing hero and

LEFT *The start of the JCC International Trophy on 6 May 1933. No 22 is Barnes (Austin), No 30 Elwes (MG J4), No 15 Howe (MG K3), and No 1 Campbell (V12 Sunbeam). (John Maitland Collection)*

ABOVE 'Ebby' flags away Robbins's MG Magna, Gaspar's Vale and Appleton's Riley at the LCC Relay Race on 22 July 1933. (LAT)

was adored by the Brooklands crowd for his skill and courage. But the real Birkin was an insecure, unhappy man who, at the time of his death, was beset with financial and personal problems.

The BRDC was back at the track on 1 July for the British Empire Trophy meeting. As in 1932 it was to be an all-out race but many of the expected track cars did not enter. There were two preliminary races, both over 18 laps (50 miles): the India Trophy for cars up to 1,100cc and the Canada Trophy for those over 1,100cc. Both were handicaps, with the fastest in each race going on to the 45-lap 125-mile British Empire Trophy to join the fastest cars in a scratch race. To give spectators who worked on Saturday mornings an opportunity of attending, the India Trophy began at 3:00pm. The two early starters, the J4 MG of Watson and the C-type MG of Kenneth Evans, could not be caught after Hector Dobbs's Riley fell back with a misfire, and they came first and second. The scratch K3 MG of Horton was third, followed by Dobbs and another K3 MG driven by Manby-Colegrave. The Canada Trophy had eight starters and was led for some time by the limit car, Baker's 6-litre Minerva. Frank Hallam was going well in a front-wheel-drive eight-cylinder Alvis and he took the lead and won, followed by Tom Delaney's Lea Francis and the Minerva.

Before the big race, 21 motor cycles came out for the 18-lap New Zealand Trophy which was won by Les Archer (350 Velocette) from Harry Lamacraft on another 350 Velocette, while Eric Fernihough was third on a 250cc Excelsior-JAP.

The favourite for the British Empire Trophy was Count Czaikowski in a Type 54 Bugatti. He had broken the World Hour Record with this car on the Avus track in May, and while it was ostensibly a private entry Meo Constantini, the Bugatti racing

manager, was supervising the car and it was rumoured that the wealthy Count was giving Ettore Bugatti financial support. Matched against the Count were Kaye Don with his Type 54 Bugatti and Oliver Bertram with the V12 Delage which had won the 1933 race. Don led at the start and was in front for ten laps. When the Bugattis came up to lap Bertram, Czaikowski dived inside Don and took the lead. He stayed there to the finish, winning from Don by 1min 10sec at an average of 123.58mph. Bertram had stopped when a bird had shattered his aero screen, so Manby-Colegrave took third place, just snatching it by 1.8sec from Horton, who had a slipping clutch.

A week later women drivers were prominent at the Inter-Club meeting. Mrs K.N. Roe won the Novices' Handicap in a Lea Francis, then Margaret Allan won the Junior Long Handicap in a 4½-litre Bentley and Charlotte Schwedler took the Lightning Short Handicap in a Speed-20 Alvis. The Stanley Cup went to the Frazer Nash Car Club team of Berry, Caswell and Dent.

Some of the club drivers were out again on 22 July for the Light Car Club (LCC) Relay Race. This had an entry of 29 teams, and as an indication of the race's prestige there were thinly disguised works teams from Austin, MG, Morgan, Singer and Vale. The Morgan three-wheeler team set the early pace lapping at 103mph, and the Austins were also fast, but the L-type MG Magnas came to the front with 20 laps to go and won, followed home by the Morgans.

John Cobb had sold the V12 Delage as he knew it was impossible to get any more speed from it. Hugh McConnell, the BARC scrutineer, had found creeping cracks in the crankcase in 1932, so had barred the car from races of more than 150 miles, and in 1933 there was also a possibility that it would fall foul of the ten-year rule. Cobb commissioned Reid Railton to design a new car which would be suitable for the Outer Circuit and would also be able to take World long-distance records up to 24 hours. It had a conventional chassis, was fitted with a 24-litre Napier Lion aero-engine and was called the Napier-Railton. It was built in the Thomson & Taylor workshops in the first half of 1933. It had been hoped that its debut would be at the Whitsun meeting but it was not ready. During July it was tested and run-in around the track, much of the driving being done by Dr Neville Whitehurst, the track medical officer.

The car made its appearance at the August Bank Holiday Meeting. It was a very hot day and there was mild dissatisfaction when the bars in the public enclosures ran dry by mid-afternoon. The Napier-Railton ran in the Byfleet Lightning Short Handicap, where it was on scratch behind the V12 Delage and Don's Type 54 Bugatti but came through the field to win. Cobb came up on the old Leyland-Thomas, driven by Bouts, at such a speed that the cars touched and an accident was only just avoided. Bertram was second and Don was third. Cobb set a new standing-lap record at 120.59mph. 'Ebby' re-handicapped Cobb by 13sec for the Byfleet Lightning Long Handicap and he could only rise as far as fifth place, despite a lap at 137.20mph. The last race of the day was a Mountain handicap for drivers who had raced at the track before the war. Nine took part, driving identical L-type MG Magnas loaned by the MG Car Co. The victor was Sidney Cummings, who led from the start, then spun, but regained the lead.

Since racing resumed after the war the Outer Circuit had usually been dominated by one car that was faster than the others, and this August Bank Holiday the spectators went home knowing that the Napier-Railton had taken the place of such outstanding machines as the Leyland-Thomas, the V12 Sunbeam and the 'Blower' Bentley.

It was stipulated in the regulations for the BRDC '500' on 16 September that every entry should be capable of lapping the track in excess of 90mph. Eyston proved that the 'Magic Midget' MG was wholly eligible by setting Class H records up 50 miles and 50 kilometres during practice two days before the race, at 106mph. There were 37 entries and 31 started. When the group of 15 blown 750s and unblown 1,100s were released at 11:39am the 'Magic Midget' driven by Eyston went into the lead and, lapping at 110mph, set a pace which put it well ahead on handicap. But it was being followed by Dixon with the 'Red Mongrel' Riley who, after an hour's running, was only 13sec behind. Eyston coasted to a halt on the Byfleet Banking when the

MG's distributor fell to bits, and walked across to the Aero Club for lunch.

At half-distance Dixon led from Charles Brackenbury, driving the 1932 race-winning MG, and the K3 MG of Eddie Hall. Kaye Don, who was on scratch with the Type 54 Bugatti, was fourth. Brackenbury dropped out, and then there was a most unhappy incident. Michael Watson, in the J4 MG with which he had won the India Trophy, came off the Byfleet Banking and lost control, the car overturned and caught fire. Watson was thrown clear, but received head injuries and died soon afterwards.

Dixon came on the scene as marshals ran across the track to help Watson, and when he lifted off a plug oiled up. In an attempt to clear the plug he weakened the mixture, the engine overheated, and the head gasket blew followed by a burnt piston. This let Hall into the lead followed by Don, but the rear axle of the Bugatti broke and Hall ran home the winner at an average of 106.53mph. An MG Magna driven by Charles Martin and Lewis Welch was second and the Brooklands Riley of Cyril Paul and Philip Turner was third. Eight cars finished the race.

The closing BARC meeting should have been held on 14 October, but heavy rain forced a postponement until the 21st. There was great excitement, as Tazio Nuvolari – at that time considered the top grand prix driver, and had awed the British motor racing world by his performance in winning the Ulster TT the previous month – was entered in the Mountain Championship driving Lord Howe's Type 51 Bugatti. He arrived at the track on the Thursday before the meeting and practised round the Mountain, but then departed. At the time he was deep in negotiations with Bugatti and Mercedes-Benz about a contract for the

BELOW *George Eyston finds that the distributor drive of the MG 'Magic Midget' has disintegrated while he was leading the 1933 BRDC 500. He abandoned the car and walked over to the Aero Club for lunch. (LAT)*

ABOVE *The start of the motor cycle handicap at the British Empire Trophy meeting. (LAT)*

1934 season and these probably had a higher priority than the Mountain Championship. Piero Taruffi, who drove for the Scuderia Ferrari and had a considerable reputation, took the wheel of the Bugatti in Nuvolari's place.

In the race, Taruffi led from the start. As the field reached the Members' Banking corner Rose-Richards spun his Type 51 Bugatti and it was struck by Campbell's V12 Sunbeam, which was left stranded in the middle of the track. At the end of the first lap, Taruffi was leading Lewis (Alfa Romeo) and Straight (Maserati) when he came up to the Sunbeam. An official waved him down and he almost stopped, but Lewis and Straight carried on and Taruffi set off in pursuit. He then encountered another hazard when Raymond Mays spun his Riley in front of the Bugatti at the Fork. Taruffi passed Lewis on lap five and chased after Straight, but was two seconds behind at the finish. If he had not been waved down it is likely he would have won.

Mays was driving the 'White' Riley, the forerunner of the ERA which would appear early in 1934, and with this he won the Oxford and Cambridge Mountain Handicap, coming through from scratch to lead Straight (MG K3) home. Among the runners in this race was Richard Seaman with a Type 35 Bugatti. Seaman had just begun his motor racing career, but within two years would become the leading British driver. The light was fading fast by the end of the meeting and the penultimate race was a Ladies' Mountain Handicap, which was won by Rita Don, Kaye Don's sister, who drove Dixon's Riley and led all the way, just beating Kay Petre (Type 35 Bugatti).

After its successful debut John Cobb had decided that the Napier-Railton would not race at the track again in 1933, but took it to Montlhéry for an attempt on the World 24-hour record. Although a clutch of records was captured, the 24-hour record did not fall, as the car developed a radiator leak. It was taken back to Thomson & Taylor's workshops and repaired, and on 31 October Cobb brought it out to make an attempt on the World standing-start kilometre and mile records. Unfortunately, Cobb did not know that the Swiss driver Hans Ruesch had taken the kilometre five days earlier with a Maserati, so his kilometre times, running in both directions on the Railway Straight, were too slow. But the mile was taken at 102.5mph. When he heard of Ruesch's record, Cobb came out again on 4 November and took the kilometre record at 88.52mph. Cobb also set a new local record, being timed over the flying kilometre at 143.67mph, the highest speed yet recorded at the track.

The BMCRC 1933 season was affected by the flood damage to the track in March and the opening meeting on 25 March was restricted to kilometre sprints, starting at the Fork and ending on the Finishing Straight, and some Mountain races. Then rain caused the postponement of the Brooklands Cup meeting on 27 May. There was a midweek meeting in June, but the first major race came at the BRDC British Empire Trophy meeting on 1 July. The New Zealand Trophy was a 50-mile Outer Circuit Handicap and had 21 starters. Les Archer came through to win on a 350cc Velocette, followed by Harry Lamacraft on another 350

Velocette and Eric Fernihough on a 250cc Excelsior.

The postponed Brooklands Cup meeting two weeks later had a programme of ten races and among the winners was Arthur Dobson on a 500cc Douglas. Dobson would subsequently become a leading car driver. The Grand Prix meeting, on 29 July, was held over the 2.6-mile course which used the Finishing Straight , Railway Straight and Byfleet Banking, with chicanes on the Finishing Straight. The Junior 350cc and Senior 500cc races were over 36 laps and in the Junior event Les Archer led on a supercharged Velocette known as 'Whiffling Clara', but had to stave off challenges from Ben Bickell on his Bickell-JAP. Bickell dropped out when a valve broke and Archer was followed home by White and

Norman, also on Velocettes. Norman had been leading the pair, but eased off too soon when approaching the flag, letting White through. In the Senior race there were 16 starters. Jock West, on an AJS, led in the opening laps and Archer, still on his 350cc Velocette, gave chase and was about to take the lead when he had a minor collision with Lamacraft (Velocette). Taking up the chase again he passed West in the closing laps to win.

Archer was at the midweek meeting on Wednesday 9 August, when he broke the 350cc lap record on his Velocette, lapping at 104.85mph. He gained a bigger success on the 350cc Velocette in the 'Hutchinson 100' on 26 August when he came through to win by over half a lap from Ben Bickell, who was on his 350cc Bickell-JAP. Charles Mortimer led on handicap for some time with his 350cc Chater Lea combination, but lost time after a plug oiled up when he stopped for fuel.

The 'Mountain' day on 30 September was given much publicity with the attraction of lady riders taking part, but there was some disappointment when only two entered. Jock Forbes had an easy win in the 350cc Mountain Championship riding Fernihough's Excelsior-JAP, while Harris (Norton) led all the way in the 500cc Championship, chased by Daniell (Norton), who fell off but remounted and regained his second place at the finish. Those who wanted to see lady riders in action were rewarded at the midweek meeting on 18 October, when Florence Blenkiron won a three-lap All Comers' handicap on a 500cc AJS.

Eighty miles in the hour on a 175cc machine had been a target for several riders, and just before the track closed for the winter Eric Fernihough brought out his Excelsior-JAP and took the record at 80.69mph.

BELOW *Two combinations battle on the Byfleet Banking during the 1933 'Hutchinson 100'. No 19 is Charles Mortimer (350cc Chater-Lea) and No 18 is E.G. Bishop (350cc Excelsior-JAP). (Brooklands Society)*

1934

The customary track repairs during the winter of 1933/4 were delayed by frost, but a new grandstand on the Byfleet side of the Fork was erected to give spectators a good view of the action at the Fork. The delays restricted the programme at the BARC opening meeting on 3 March to sprints from the Railway Straight to the Fork, and short runs along the Finishing Straight, together with some Mountain races. The full track was ready for the Easter Monday meeting, when the major attraction was an attempt on the lap record by John Cobb with the Napier-Railton. 17s 6d was charged to use the new stand, which upset some spectators as it was standing room only, with no seats.

Freddie Dixon had a good day in the 'Red Mongrel' Riley. He won the Ripley Lightning Short Handicap, then, despite a severe re-handicap, won the Ripley Senior Long Handicap and took second place in the Ripley Lightning Long Handicap. An Appearance Prize had been instituted for the best presented car and this was awarded to the Napier-Railton, which came out for its record attempt although conditions were not favourable, with a gusting wind. On the Byfleet Banking, Cobb held the car in a continuous slide with its tail higher than its nose. It slid at the Fork, raising a cloud of dust, and was exceeding 160mph on the Railway Straight. The outcome was a lap at 139.71mph. Such was the strain that after he returned to the paddock Cobb's fingers had to be eased from the wheel and his arms massaged.

Although the race had drawn some criticism the previous year, the JCC repeated the International Trophy on 28 April, running it to the same format as in 1933, over 100 laps with different handicap channels for the capacity classes. There were 37 starters and notable among them was a new 8CM Maserati, the latest type of grand prix car from the Italian factory which had been delivered to Whitney Straight in March. Another new car was a 2-litre Riley which had been much modified by Freddie Dixon.

At the start, Straight led Brian Lewis in a 8C-3000 Maserati and Walter Handley in an MG K3, but Dixon was gaining ground and at ten laps was in second place, battling with Lewis. Straight hit a marker barrel at the chicane in the Finishing Straight and stopped to replace a wheel, which put him down to tenth place and left Lewis and Dixon battling for the lead. At the 20-lap mark Lewis led,

BELOW *The spring sun casts the shadows of the Finishing Straight bridge as Kay Petre (Type 35 Bugatti) beats Joan Richmond (3-litre Ballot) off the line in the 4th Walton Scratch Sprint at the 1934 opening meeting. (LAT)*

but at 30 laps Dixon was in front and took a £10 bonus prize. Meanwhile, Straight had been working hard and was up into fourth place. Then Dixon stopped with fuel feed problems and Lewis stopped for fuel, so that at half-distance Straight was back in the lead.

At 70 laps Straight still led with a margin of 1min 49sec over Lewis, who was followed by Rose-Richards and Howe in Type 51 Bugattis. Straight came in for fuel and tyres and this enabled Lewis to reduce the gap to 23sec, but he was making no impression on the leader until a front tyre on Straight's Maserati began to break up. He could not afford to stop, but he had to ease up and the gap began to close. Lewis was pulling back over two seconds a lap and on the penultimate lap he was only 8.6sec behind and still closing. At the flag Straight won by four seconds, and just after he crossed the line the tyre tread flew off. Rose-Richards was third and Cyril Paul, driving another of Dixon's Rileys, was fourth. It was agreed to have been an excellent race and any criticisms of the previous year were forgotten.

The main race at the Whitsun meeting was the Gold Star Handicap and this was a victory for Lord Howe in his Type 51 Bugatti. He was up against stiff opposition, with Bertram in the V12 Delage and Don's Type 54 Bugatti. Don retired after a tyre tread hit his arm and Howe took the lead on lap

ABOVE *George Cholmondley-Tapper (Type 37 Bugatti) leads Fairfield's Riley and the Altas of Briault and Cormack on the first lap of the 1st Ripley Mountain Handicap at the 1934 Easter meeting. Cholmondley-Tapper was disqualified for jumping the start. (LAT)*

ABOVE *Richard Shuttleworth (Type 35 Bugatti) leads the C-type MG (No 28) of Charles Brackenbury at the start of the 1934 JCC International Trophy. (John Maitland Collection)*

RIGHT *Earl Howe unveils a memorial to Sir Henry Birkin on the Clubbouse wall before the British Empire Trophy on 23 June 1934. Sir Malcolm Campbell is on the left. (LAT)*

LEFT *Freddie Dixon stands beside his 2-litre Riley as a wheel is changed on his way to victory in the 1934 British Empire Trophy. (LAT)*

BELOW *A Triumph Gloria saloon is followed by a Singer Le Mans on the Byfleet Banking during the JCC High Speed Trial on 30 June 1934. (LAT)*

five and was not caught. He lapped at 129.70mph, the fastest lap of the track by a Bugatti at that time. Kaye Petre won another handicap in her Type 35 Bugatti, and in the Second Merrow Mountain Handicap, Campbell, in the V12 Sunbeam, started from scratch with Mays in the 'White' Riley and just beat him to second place.

The BRDC had realised that a flat-out Outer Circuit race for the British Empire Trophy was not popular with spectators so it was presented in a wholly new guise on 23 June, as a class handicap on the Outer Circuit but with straw bale chicanes on the Railway Straight, on the Members' Banking, at the top of the Finishing Straight and at the Fork, where the cars rounded the Fork then negotiated an artificial hairpin before returning to the Outer Circuit. The circuit distance was three miles and it was a 100-lap race. Before the start Sir Malcolm Campbell drove round the circuit in a Lagonda, with King Abdullah of Jordan as a passenger.

Unfortunately, much spectator appeal was lost as the field of 39 was released in handicap groups. After 30 minutes' racing an order on handicap had been established and the race was led by Whitney Straight in his 8CM Maserati, followed by Brian Lewis (8C-3000 Maserati), Freddie Dixon (1½-litre Riley) and Bill Everitt (Q-type MG). After an hour Dixon had moved into the lead with a 57sec margin over Straight, while Chris Staniland (Type

51 Bugatti) had passed Lewis into third place. The chicane at the top of the Finishing Straight was causing problems for some drivers, as a wide line took the cars onto the downhill slope which became an adverse camber. John Houldsworth slid too wide, and when he over corrected and hit the bales in his Type 35 Bugatti the car overturned and he was thrown out. He died of head injuries soon afterwards.

Dixon had increased his lead to 61sec over Straight, while Staniland had retired with a broken rear axle and George Eyston (K3 NG 'Magic' Magnette) came up into fourth place behind Lewis. Dixon began to fall back and was passed by Straight. Dixon then retired, while Lewis's Maserati broke a con rod. It seemed that Straight would win, but he made a long pit stop when a carburettor needle jammed in the jet. This let Eyston take the lead, and he went on to win, followed 1min 41sec later by Straight. Lindsay Eccles (Type 51 Bugatti) was third and John Cobb (Monza Alfa Romeo) was fourth. Eyston enquired why he had been flagged off and when told he had won said: 'Well I've been racing for about a hundred years, so it's quite time I won something!' The ERA made its racing debut during this event, driven by Humphrey Cook, who handed the wheel over to Raymond Mays during the race. It was still running when flagged off, but had made a good impression.

BELOW *The start of the Brooklands Championship at the 1934 August Bank Holiday meeting. No 2 is Dudley Froy (Type 54 Bugatti), No 3 Oliver Bertram (V12 Delage), No 4 John Cobb (Napier-Railton), and No 5 Tom Fothringham (Type 35B Bugatti). Cobb was the winner. (John Maitland Collection)*

The Junior Racing Drivers' Club, which was intended to give the impecunious a chance to race, won the Stanley Cup at the Inter-Club Meeting, the team members being Hodge (Singer), Perry and Potts (MGs) and Morgan (Austin). This was followed, on 21 July, by the LCC Relay race, called 'the big race for small cars'. Nineteen teams started and there were once again thinly disguised works entries from Austin, MG, Morgan and Singer. Heavy rain fell during the latter part of the race and there were some spectacular spins and slides, but a team of Austins driven by Thompson, Turner and Selby won. The works Morgans driven by Rhodes, Laird and Lones were second and a semi-official team of MG Magnettes, driven by Charlotte Schwedler, Margaret Allan and Doreen Evans, was third. The hand throttles on the Morgans were held open with rubber bands, leaving the drivers with both hands free to steer.

Racing car performance had surged at the beginning of 1934 with the entry of Mercedes-Benz and Auto-Union into the grand prix field, but there had also been a similar surge of performance in the minor classes and this was most evident at the BARC August Bank Holiday meeting. There was a new outright lap record and three Mountain class records. It was an overcast day, but there was a good attendance. The big race was the 1934 Brooklands Championship which, remarkably, was a scratch race over four laps. There were only four starters: the Napier-Railton, which had just been repaired after a serious crash while attempting the World 24-hour record at Montlhéry; Oliver Bertram with the V12 Delage; Dudley Froy with the Don Type 54 Bugatti; and the Type 35B Bugatti of Tom Fothringham, which had formerly belonged to Campbell. Off the line Bertram led, but within a short distance Cobb had forged ahead, leaving the rest behind. With a clear track, Cobb drove flat out and on the second lap established a new lap record at 140.93mph and came home to win easily at an average of 131.53mph, also setting a new record for the fastest race run on the track. The fight for second place went to Froy, who passed Bertram on the second lap.

On the Mountain, the Second Handicap saw a piece of history as Humphrey Cook was the winner in a 1,100cc ERA, the first win for the marque. He was pursued throughout by Pat Driscoll in the latest single-seater 750cc Austin, who broke the 750cc class record. In the Third Mountain Handicap, Raymond Mays came second in a 1½-litre ERA and also set a new class record. Earlier Mays had been awarded the Appearance Prize for the best-turned-out car and driver. Cook came out again in the final Mountain Handicap, and, starting from scratch, broke the 1,100cc class record with his ERA, though he failed to finish as he tried too

BELOW *The Napier-Railton outside the Dunlop depot in the paddock in 1934. John Cobb is in the cockpit, talking to Freddie Dixon, and second from the left is a very young Bill Boddy, to whom so much is owed for the preservation of Brooklands.* (Brooklands Society)

ABOVE *Before the rains came. Oliver Bertram's Type 54 Bugatti leads John Cobb's Napier-Railton and Donkin's K3 MG on the Byfleet Banking in the opening laps of the 1934 BRDC 500. (LAT)*

hard and spun into the bank at the top of the Finishing Straight.

Despite its handicap, the Napier-Railton was considered a strong favourite for the BRDC 500-Mile race on 22 September. The other entries were impressive: Straight had a Clemons-engined 4½-litre Duesenberg which had previously been owned by the Scuderia Ferrari; Froy was driving the Barnato-Hassan, a Bentley-based special using the

6½-litre engine from 'Old No 1'; while during practice Dixon had lapped at 125mph in his 2-litre Riley. Race day was dark and overcast, and the crowd had a disappointment as Straight was unwell and the Duesenberg was a non-starter. The small cars were flagged away at noon and the whole field of 30 cars was under way by 12:24pm. Eyston took the lead on handicap in the MG 'Magic' Magnette, followed by Cobb and Dixon, but then the whole race changed as torrential rain began to fall. Cobb had to ease off and was lapping at only 112mph, the same speed as the smallest cars, while Dixon had slowed to only 100mph.

Just after 2:00pm Cobb came into the pits and after a discussion with Reid Railton and Tim Rose-Richards, his co-driver, he withdrew from the race, as he realised that under these conditions it was foolhardy to continue. Eyston was still leading, but he stopped to hand over to Wal Handley and Dixon took the lead. Handley had a lurid skid on the Railway Straight and ended on the grass, but the MG was out of the race and Dixon's cars were now in first and second places, as he was being followed by his modified Brooklands Riley driven by Pat Fairfield. The Rileys, however, were coping well with the conditions and Fairfield was passed by the works 1½-litre car driven by Edgar Maclure and Von der Becke, which began to challenge Dixon and was only 30sec behind on handicap.

Fairfield dropped out when he spun at the Fork and then again on the Railway Straight, going backwards through the corrugated iron fence. At 4:00pm Maclure was only two seconds behind, then Dixon had to stop as a tyre had thrown a tread, and the stop cost him a lap. Even though he began closing the gap by seven seconds a lap it seemed impossible for him to catch Maclure until, with two laps to go, Maclure slowed and came into the pits with a blocked fuel line. It was cleared and he restarted, but Dixon had gone past and took the flag to win at 104.80mph. Maclure and Von der Becke were second and a K3 MG driven by 'Goldie'

Gardner and Dr Benjafield was third. Only seven cars finished the race.

Whitney Straight soon recovered from his illness and he booked the Mountain Circuit for a lap record attempt in the 8CM Maserati on Wednesday 3 October; he was successful, raising the record to 79.18mph. Ten days later, on 13 October, he was back at the track for the BARC closing meeting, where the main race was the Mountain Championship. This was a duel between Straight with his Maserati and Raymond Mays in a 2-litre ERA. Straight led all the way, but Mays fought hard, and in battling to keep ahead Straight set a new lap record at 81.00mph, while Mays established a new 2-litre class record. Lord Howe was a distant third in his Type 51 Bugatti.

ABOVE Whitney Straight drives out of the paddock in the 4½-litre Duesenberg to make a lap record attempt at the 1934 Autumn meeting. This car is now an important exhibit in the Museum. (John Maitland Collection)

BELOW The start of the 250cc race at the BMCRC Grand Prix meeting on 28 July 1934. (Brooklands Society)

The Women's Mountain Handicap was won by Doreen Evans in a Q-type MG from Fay Taylour in a Monza Alfa. Miss Taylour did not stop when the chequered flag was waved at her but carried on for several laps, and in doing so set a lap time only exceeded by Straight. The stewards barred her from racing for the rest of the day and fined her £3! The thin crowd was given more excitement when Straight made an attempt on Cobb's lap record, driving the 4½-litre Duesenberg. The drive was spectacular but the speed was only 138.15mph. Over 70 years later the Duesenberg, together with the Napier-Railton, now is a permanent exhibit in the Brooklands Museum.

Three days after the closing meeting Raymond Mays brought the 2-litre ERA to the track and set a world record for the standing-start kilometre. His speed was 89.73mph. He commented afterwards

that the ERA was difficult to hold going onto the Byfleet Banking at 140mph! This was the last world record to be established at the track and only stood for a few days, as it was broken by an Auto-Union at the Avus track.

A few days before the closing meeting Kay Petre had lapped the track at 124.41mph in Fothringham's Type 35B Bugatti and set a new ladies' record. This brought Elsie Wisdom out on Saturday 20 October in Dixon's 2-litre Riley, and she took back the record with a lap at 126.73mph. She was thrown around so much by the bumpy track that she had to use a lap strap to hold her in the seat. Kay Petre watched this drive and accepted the challenge. She borrowed the V12 Delage from Bertram and lapped at 129.58mph.

Although the track closed at the beginning of November, the Mountain Circuit was still available and Dudley Froy and J. Wren brought out a 995cc Fiat Balilla which had been an exhibit at the Motor Show at Olympia, and despite heavy rain, they covered 1,000 miles in two days. The average for the run, over 856 laps of the circuit, was 55mph.

In March an extraordinary machine had appeared at the track. This was the Vitesse, built by G.B. Gush, a diminutive cyclecar with a 350cc Blackburne engine. Aided by his sister and Clive Windsor-Richards, Gush set Class J (350cc) records at distances from 100 miles to 12 hours. The Vitesse was brought out again several times during the summer and broke its own records, bringing the owner and drivers some profitable bonuses.

Clubman's Day on 14 April opened the 1934 BMCRC season. It was a mixed card with kilometre sprints on the Finishing Straight which drew 114 entries. The first heat of the All Comers' three-lap handicap was won by Miss M. Mooret riding an Ariel, and during the race Florence Blenkiron lapped at 102.06mph on a Grindlay Peerless-JAP.

A dead heat was the surprise result at the meeting on 12 May, when T. Rhodes in a Morgan-JAP, who had lapped at 103.96mph, tied on the line with 'Spug' Muir on a 350cc Norton in the five-lap All Comers' Handicap. Rhodes had been a member of the works Morgan team in the LCC Relay race in 1932 and 1933. There was an 'Old Crocks' race over two laps on the Mountain Circuit, but it seems the motor cyclists were not as sensitive as the car drivers about the naming of their elderly machines. It was won by G.F. Billington on a 1905 Excelsior and George Reynolds came second on a 1909 Triumph.

The BMCRC continued to hold midweek meetings, though these were only for the enthusiasts, which was emphasised on 12 June when only 33 paying spectators arrived to watch.

Freddie Dixon

F.W. (Freddie) Dixon was born in 1892 in Middlesbrough, where he subsequently ran a motor cycle business. He began racing motor cycles in 1912, riding a Cleveland in the Senior TT, and resumed racing again at the end of World War One, during which he had served as a Staff Sergeant in the Army Service Corps. His first major event at Brooklands was the famous 1921 BMCRC 500-Mile race, in which he was second despite being thrown from his Harley-Davidson when a tyre burst.

Dixon continued to race Harleys at Brooklands in 1922 and 1923, gaining several successes, often with a sidecar. He won the 1923 Sidecar TT on a Douglas and was racing these at the track in 1924. He continued with Douglas in 1925 and 1926, winning the 1926 BMCRC Sidecar Grand Prix. In 1927 he abandoned Douglas and divided his attentions between Brough Superior and HRD. He won the Junior TT on an HRD and had several wins at the track, usually riding the Brough with a sidecar. He also made the first 100mph sidecar lap, becoming one of the first riders to receive a BMCRC Gold Star.

Dixon did little motor cycle racing after 1928, but he had established a considerable reputation as a tuner and in 1932 he turned to cars. He drove a Riley in the Ulster TT and led the race until he crashed, then appeared at Brooklands for the first time in the 1932 500-Mile race in a special single-seater Riley, which he raced with some success in 1933. Then in 1934 he produced his 2-litre six-cylinder Rileys and won the 500-Mile race with one of these. There was another win in the 1935 British Empire Trophy, while he also won the Ulster TT and followed this with another Ulster TT win in 1936, and also a second victory in the 500-Mile race.

Dixon was a tough, uncompromising man, and he had several disputes with the BARC, but his career virtually ended when he received a short prison sentence for drunk driving. Shortly before World War Two he had begun designing a revolutionary car intended for the World Land Speed Record, but this was not finished. After the war he worked with Harry Ferguson on his transmission developments. Dixon was perhaps the greatest all-rounder at Brooklands, combining riding and driving skills with a remarkable tuning expertise. He died in 1956.

Bad weather forced the postponement of the meeting scheduled for Wednesday 4 July for seven days, but those who attended on the 11th saw some good racing. Ben Bickell had a good day. He produced a new machine, the Bickell-Ariel, which had a supercharged Square-Four engine, and won the three-lap All Comers' Handicap with this at an impressive 111.42mph. He repeated the performance in a one-lap handicap. Then he rode a 500cc Excelsior-JAP to win the five-lap Mountain Scratch race and set a new Mountain lap record. In the three-lap non-trade handicap, Beatrice Shilling was the victor on a 500cc Norton. Miss Shilling tuned her own machines and achieved fame during World War Two while working at the Royal Aircraft Establishment at Farnborough, when she devised 'Miss Shilling's Orifice', an alteration to the carburettor which enabled Merlin-engined Spitfires and Hurricanes to perform violent aerobatics without the engine cutting-out momentarily.

The Grand Prix meeting on Saturday 28 July was restricted to riders who had international status. The three grand prix races were held on a course using the Finishing Straight, Byfleet Banking and Railway Straight, with a chicane at the Fork. This gave a 2.6-mile lap and each race was 39 laps, a distance of 100 miles. The 250cc race was dominated by Eric Fernihough, who led throughout on his Excelsior-JAP and was never challenged. The 350cc race was dominated by the Velocettes. Newman led initially but was passed by Les Archer, who went on to win. Archer came out again for the 500cc race with his larger engined Velocette and left the field behind, being followed home by 'Ginger' Wood (New Imperial).

The 'Hutchinson 100' was run on 28 August. Eric Fernihough was the limit man on his 175cc Excelsior-JAP and Ben Bickell was on scratch with the supercharged Bickell-Ariel. Bickell chased through the field in pursuit of Fernihough, but stopped with a defective magneto, so Fernihough was not caught and came home in front of Jock West on a 500cc Triumph. In a preliminary three-lap handicap, Beatrice Shilling took third place on her 500cc Norton, lapping at 101.85mph.

During September the Triumph company brought examples of all its current production models to the track, thirteen in all, and in a display of speed and stamina each did 60 miles in the hour. Half the Mountain Championship meeting was held on Saturday 6 October. It was a very wet day, so only the Outer Circuit races were run, and the Mountain races were postponed until Wednesday the 17th. On the Outer Circuit, Eric Fernihough won the main event, the five-lap scratch race, on his 350cc Excelsior-JAP. In the postponed Mountain races, Harold Daniell (Norton) fought throughout the 350cc race with Newman (Velocette) and won. It began to rain heavily before the 500cc race, but a further postponement was not possible so it went ahead and was led throughout by Jock Forbes (Norton).

ABOVE *Eric Fernihough, who led all the way, rounds the Fork chicane on his Excelsior-JAP in the 250cc race at the 1934 Grand Prix meeting. (Brooklands Society)*

CHAPTER NINE

CLOUDS GATHER

1935 At the beginning of 1935 the BARC announced some changes to the rules affecting racing at the track. Some were uncontroversial and intended to improve safety. Entries of cars which were considered too slow would be refused and unknown drivers of fast cars would also be turned away. More controversially, women drivers were still not permitted to race in Mountain events on level terms with the men, and there was anger when it was announced before the Easter meeting that outright and class lap records would not be recognised when made during a race. If a driver wanted a lap record to be accepted, either a fee of five guineas (£5 5s) had to be paid in advance so that the race laps could be specially timed, or the attempt had to be made on a closed track. *Motor Sport* commented: 'there is too much atmosphere of schoolmaster and schoolboy in the relations between the authorities and the drivers. Trivial offences are treated with a solemnity which would be amusing if it were not so irritating to the drivers.'

Although the BARC membership reached a peak during 1935 all was not well with the club, and *Motor Sport* again had some acerbic comments: 'Both the catering and the surroundings of the club leave much to be desired. Unfortunately, the host of untidy buildings which have grown up around

The Le Mans V12 Lagondas of Brackenbury and Lord Selsdon sandwich Seys's 4½-litre Bentley in the First August Outer Circuit Handicap at the very last Brooklands meeting on 7 August 1939. (LAT)

RIGHT *A Singer Le Mans in a 'downhill stop-and-restart' on the Test Hill during the JCC Rally on 2 March 1935. (LAT)*

BELOW *The start of the JCC International Trophy on 6 May 1935. (LAT)*

the Clubhouse prevents the authorities from preserving the Country Club atmosphere which one expects after entering along the new Shell Way … To be asked to pay 3/6d for a lunch consisting of Irish stew and complicated but cold puddings is quite excessive … Many people find it desirable to join the Aero Club … to enjoy well-cooked food in congenial surroundings.'

The opening meeting on 16 March saw the appearance of a new driver 'B. Bira', a pseudonym which disguised the 20-year-old Thai Prince Birabongse, who was making his racing debut in a stripped sports Riley Imp. By the end of the season he would be regarded as a leading driver. The Second New Haw Short Handicap was won by Doreen Evans in a Q-type MG, and Humphrey Cook with a 1½-litre ERA was the victor in the Third New Haw Mountain Handicap after a battle with Charles Martin in a Type 51 Bugatti. Martin cornered faster, but the ERA had better acceleration on the dash to the line. There was excitement as Richard Shuttleworth drove a Tipo B Alfa Romeo in the last race. Although by grand prix standards this was already obsolete, to the Brooklands crowd it was the height of motor racing fashion, but there was disappointment when it ran slowly and retired.

During April a remarkable and diminutive car appeared at the track. It was teardrop shaped with an enclosed cockpit, the driver sat at the front, and

it had a 500cc JAP engine prepared by Eric Fernihough. Its designer and builder, Myles Rothwell, intended to take class records, but it crashed while being tested and was not seen again.

At the Easter meeting there was a new contender for the claim to be the fastest car at Brooklands. The Barnato-Hassan had been fitted with an 8-litre Bentley engine and during practice Oliver Bertram was rumoured to have lapped at 140mph. Bertram ran in the Easter Senior Short Handicap and came through the field from scratch to win. Kay Petre was also in the race with the V12 Delage but was unplaced. The Delage was still permitted to race, but was closely examined by Hugh McConnell, the track scrutineer, before each meeting. Bertram drove it in the Easter Lightning Short Handicap and once again came through from scratch to win. The main event was the British Mountain Championship, run in three five-lap heats and a ten-lap final. After the heats, Sir Malcolm Campbell paraded 'Blue Bird', with which he had raised the Land Speed Record to 276.82mph in March. Kaye Petre, starting from scratch, won the Easter Junior Long handicap in a Type 51 Bugatti. In the final Freddie Dixon, who had been recovering from injuries received in a flying accident, was the winner, scoring an easy win over Lindsay Eccles, who drove an ex-works Type 59 Bugatti, another almost-current grand prix car.

The Silver Jubilee of King George V was celebrated in 1935 and Jubilee Day on Monday 6 May was a national holiday. Although London was thronged for the parades and celebrations a big crowd came to Brooklands for the JCC International Trophy, which was run to the same format as in previous years with class handicap chicanes. The chicane for the largest cars had been tightened to provide for the extra performance of the Tipo B Alfa Romeo and Type 59 Bugattis. There were 37 starters and at the end of the first lap Cyril Paul (Type 51 Bugatti) led Raymond Mays (2-litre ERA) and Chris Staniland (Type 51 Bugatti), while Brian Lewis, a favourite to win, was fourth in a Type 59 Bugatti.

Lewis soon retired with a broken con rod and Staniland took over the lead from Paul, who also retired, leaving Luis Fontes ('Monza' Alfa Romeo) in third place ahead of Mays, while Charlie Dodson was running in fourth place in a 750cc Austin and showing that the handicapping channels worked. Mays took the lead when Staniland stopped with a broken exhaust manifold, and was pulling out a good lead from Fontes when he stopped on the Byfleet Banking out of fuel, which had escaped from a leaking float chamber. At half-distance – 50 laps – Fontes led by over a minute from Arthur Dobson (Type 51 Bugatti). At the 70-lap mark Freddie Dixon (2-litre Riley) had moved ahead of Dobson, who

BELOW *Raymond Mays in his ERA in the JCC International Trophy. He retired with a loose carburettor float chamber while in the lead. (LAT)*

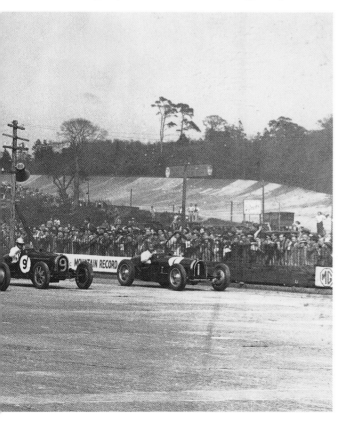

ABOVE *The winning Singer team, driven by Barnes, Langley and Bicknell, at the LCC Relay Race on 20 July 1935. (LAT)*

then stopped with a broken gearbox, but although Dixon tried hard Fontes was uncatchable and was flagged off as the winner, followed by Dixon and Eddie Hall (K3 MG). The press was full of praise for Fontes and his impressive driving style. Of Anglo-Brazilian parentage, he had won the race with very little racing experience. A month later he won the Le Mans 24-hour race with a Lagonda, but then in October 1935 he received a three-year prison sentence for manslaughter when he killed a pedestrian in a hit-and-run accident. Later he took up flying and was killed during World War Two while flying a Wellington with the Air Transport Auxiliary.

The inherent problems of Brooklands were emphasised at the BARC Whitsun meeting. In the Whitsun Short Handicap, Kay Petre was on scratch with the V12 Delage but found it impossible to get through the field and had to ease off. Bertram took over the Delage for the Lightning Short and found the top of the Members' Banking was blocked by a group of cars so had to dive below these to find a way through and almost lost control, though he went on to win. Matters came to a head in the Gold Star Handicap, the main event of the day. Most of the cars in the field could lap in excess of 120mph and there were several near misses. Charles Brackenbury came through to win in a Type 51 Bugatti, averaging 125.37mph, but Bertram, now in the Barnato-Hassan, could only manage third place, having been badly baulked.

The stewards decided that Freddie Dixon was the main culprit in failing to recognise the lines at the Fork and he was called before the stewards, who

subsequently issued a statement: 'The Stewards saw Mr Dixon regarding the baulking of a car in this race, severely reprimanded him, and told him if he cannot comply with the regulations, he had better not enter again for BARC races.' It is reputed that Dixon told the stewards that he realised he did not know much about motor racing, but the 2-litre Riley was still warm and if one of the stewards would like to show him how he should drive it they were welcome to try. The problem arose with the reverse curve at the Fork where there was only one line that could be taken by cars doing 130mph. It was expected that Oliver Bertram would make an attempt on the lap record after the last race, but he did not come out, perhaps upset by the day's events.

The BRDC returned to the track for the British Empire Trophy on 6 July. It drew a poor crowd, as it was an intensely hot day and there were rival attractions at Wimbledon, the Henley Regatta, and the RAF Silver Jubilee Review at Mildenhall. But as *Motor Sport* pointed out, it was 'ample proof – if any were needed – of the limited appeal of long-distance handicap racing'. The course used the Outer Circuit running clockwise, with chicanes at the Fork, on the Railway Straight, and at the top of the Finishing Straight. Perhaps mindful of Houldsworth's accident in 1934, this was entered through a long straw bale run-off, followed by a 180° hairpin. Thirty-three cars started and each capacity group was released in turn. After an hour the race order on handicap began to emerge and Cyril Paul (1,808cc Riley) led Freddie Dixon (2-litre Riley) and Adrian Thorpe (1,496cc Frazer Nash). Much had been expected of the ERA team, but it had been disappointing: Mays had retired, while Cook and Prinz von Leiningen, who had driven for Auto-Union in grand prix races, had made many stops. At 4:00pm, approximately half-distance, Dixon had passed Paul, and von Leiningen, despite his problems, was up into third place. Paul slowed,

ABOVE *Mays (No 1) takes a wider line than Bira (No 4) in their ERAs coming out of the Fork in the Siam Trophy at the 1935 August Bank Holiday meeting. (LAT)*

LEFT *The start of the MCC High Speed Trial on 14 September 1935. Construction of the Vickers extension has started. (LAT)*

Clouds gather **193**

as he had lost first and second gears, and the prince fell back, so Lindsay Eccles (Type 51 Bugatti) held second place for a while until he was passed by the works 2-litre Riley of Edgar Maclure. Dixon was flagged off as the winner, followed by Maclure and Paul. It was ironic that the first to give effusive congratulations to Dixon on his win was Sir Algernon Guinness, who had been one of the stewards at the Whitsun meeting!

The LCC Relay race, held two weeks later, was a success for a team of works Le Mans Singers. Thirteen of the 19 teams which started were finishers. Second place went to a mixed team of Frazer Nash, Lagonda and MG, while the third-placed team was comprised of an MG, a Singer and an Austin. Rain fell during the closing stages, but there were no incidents.

At the August Bank Holiday meeting there were

John Cobb

John Cobb was born in 1899 and after leaving Eton served in the Army in the closing days of World War One. After the war he joined the family fur-broking business and began motor racing in 1925, driving a 10-litre S61 Fiat at Brooklands and winning his first race at a West Kent CC meeting. In 1926 he drove Parry Thomas's ill-fated 'Babs' in its first race at the track and also drove a Ballot and a TT Vauxhall. In 1929 he bought the 10½-litre Delage which had held the Land Speed Record in 1924 and broke the outright lap record at the Whitsun meeting at 132.11mph. Between 1929 and 1932, Cobb in the Delage had many duels with Kaye Don in the V12 Sunbeam and Tim Birkin in the 'Blower' Bentley, and gained several victories. He also drove a Talbot 105 in the Double-12, 1,000-Mile race and the '500'.

In 1933 he commissioned Reid Railton to design the Napier-Railton, a dual-purpose car intended for the Outer Circuit and for long-distance world records. The new car, which was built in Thomson & Taylor's workshops at the track, made its debut at the 1933 August Bank Holiday meeting and was an immediate winner, also setting a new standing lap record. In November 1933 Cobb set a new World Standing Kilometre record at the track with the Napier-Railton, and at the 1934 Easter meeting a new outright lap record was gained at 139.71mph. Cobb raised the record again, to 140.93mph, driving in the Brooklands Championship race at the August Bank Holiday meeting.

The Napier-Railton was taken to the Bonneville Salt Flats in Utah in 1935, where Cobb and a team of drivers set a bunch of new world records from the Hour to 24-hours. The car was back in England in the autumn of 1935 and Cobb, sharing it with Tim Rose-Richards, won the BRDC '500' and then, in October, broke the lap record again, pushing it up to 143.44mph, a figure which would stand for all time.

Realising that the handicaps set for the Napier-Railton gave it no chance of further success in BARC meetings, Cobb raced the rebuilt 4-litre V12 Sunbeam in 1936 and the Napier-Railton went back to Utah to retake the World 24-Hour Record. In 1937, hoping the handicapper had relented, he brought the Napier-Railton back to the track and won the BBC Trophy at the Easter meeting. His final racing success at Brooklands was in September 1937 when, sharing the Napier-Railton with Oliver Bertram, he won the BRDC '500' again.

Cobb wanted to break the World Land Speed Record and Railton designed a car with two Napier Lion engines, which was again built by Thomson & Taylor. With this Cobb broke the record at Bonneville in September 1938 at 350.20mph, only to lose the record to George Eyston's 'Thunderbolt' the following day. Cobb returned to Bonneville in August 1939 and pushed the record up to 369.75mph. An experienced pilot, he served in the Air Transport Auxiliary throughout World War Two, ferrying aircraft from the manufacturers to operational units.

The Railton was taken back to Utah in 1947 and Cobb broke his own record with an average of 394.19mph, one run being done at 403.13mph. Cobb then turned his attention to the World Water Speed Record, but was killed while attempting the record in 'Crusader', a DH Goblin gas turbine-powered boat, when it broke up on Loch Ness on 29 September 1952 after exceeding 200mph on its first run.

A shy, modest, retiring man, Cobb achieved many great records including the Land Speed Record, and World Hour and 24-Hours records, and was also the first man to exceed 400mph on land and 200mph on water, but in Brooklands history he will always be remembered as the all-time lap record holder.

ABOVE *The Dunlop fitters hard at work during the 1935 BRDC 500. The wheel on the stand is from the Type 59 Bugatti of Howe and Lewis, which finished third. (LAT)*

some big attractions. A ladies' match race was announced between Kay Petre in the V12 Delage and Gwenda Stewart in the Derby-Miller, while Bertram was to make a lap record attempt. Early in the evening on the Saturday before the meeting Kay Petre had done a timed lap at 134.75mph, thus breaking her own lap record, so there was the prospect of an exciting race. The stewards decided, probably for safety reasons, that the match race would be against the clock, with each driver doing four laps. Mrs Petre came out first and did 134.24mph, just short of her lap record. Then Mrs Stewart ran, but only did one flying lap before the exhaust pipe broke. Her speed was 133.88mph, so the honours went to Kay Petre. It was a good day for the women drivers, as the first race, the August Short Handicap, was won by Margaret Allan in a 1½-litre single-seater Frazer Nash.

The main event on the Mountain was the Siam Trophy; this was given by Prince Chula, who was the manager and sponsor of Bira, and was a class handicap for cars up to 1,500cc. It was won by Pat Driscoll in a works 750cc Austin and the two scratch ERAs of Mays and Bira were second and third.

After the last race, the crowd waited and Oliver Bertram came out in the green Barnato-Hassan. On his second flying lap, holding the car notably low on the bankings, he was timed at 142.60mph, so he had taken the outright lap record from John Cobb. Bertram was the epitome of the amateur driver at Brooklands, as he was a practising barrister and his work in the courts was a world away from the dangers and drama at the track. The following day, Gwenda Stewart came out again in the Derby-Miller. With only a handful of spectators she did a lap in 135.95mph and established a ladies' lap record which would never be broken, as well as setting a 2-litre class record which would stand for all time.

Among the minor club meetings which had been held during the season, the MCC meeting on 14 September was significant, as several drivers aimed to cover 100 miles during the One-Hour High Speed Trial, a notable target for road-equipped sports cars. Mike Couper came within a whisker of it in his 105 Talbot, with 99.61 miles.

A week later, on 21 September, the BRDC ran the 500-Mile race and this drew an entry of the fastest cars, including the Barnato-Hassan, the Napier-Railton, the Derby-Miller and the Duesenberg, which had been sold by Straight, who had forsaken motor racing for flying. Earlier in the year *The Motor* had reported that Mercedes-Benz was considering entering a W25 grand prix car, but nothing came of it. There were 33 starters, and as the smallest capacity group was flagged away at noon there was a rain shower, but this soon stopped and the track was dry when Cobb started from scratch. It was an indication of the greatly improved performance of the smallest cars that these only had a 24-minute start over the Napier-Railton.

At 12:30 the race was led on handicap by Bertram with the Barnato-Hassan, but Cobb was only eight seconds behind and when Bertram stopped to change the front wheels he took the lead, averaging 125.90mph. Having built up a two minute lead over Bertram, at 1:30pm Cobb made his first pit stop, to pump in 50 gallons of fuel and change four wheels. This took ten minutes, as it was difficult to remove the rear wheels from the hubs. Bertram also stopped at this time and was at the pits for 11 minutes while there was an intense inspection of his fuel tank. He restarted only ten seconds behind Cobb, but stopped again and the Barnato-Hassan retired with a split fuel tank. Richard Seaman, who had been lapping in the Duesenberg almost as quickly as Cobb, also retired when his fuel tank broke loose.

Gwenda Stewart had been disappointing in the Derby-Miller and had been delayed with transmission problems, so it was Lord Howe who moved up into second place with a works Type 59 Bugatti running unblown, which he was sharing with Brian Lewis. Rose-Richards had meanwhile taken over the Napier-Railton from Cobb and at 2:30pm he had a three-minute lead over the

Bugatti. Cobb then took the wheel again and by 3:00pm the lead had increased to four-and-a-half minutes. The track surface was breaking up, particularly on the Members' Banking, and Cobb was hit in the face by a lump of concrete. At 3:30pm he made a final stop for 90sec and Rose-Richards took over for the last stint with a lead of six minutes. Freddie Dixon had come up into second place but then stopped with a broken con rod, and at 4:28pm the Napier-Railton crossed the line to win, having averaged 121.28mph. The 2-litre Riley of Edgar Maclure and von der Becke was second, just eight seconds in front of the Bugatti. Only six cars were classified as finishers though several were still running when flagged off.

Cobb had shown the superiority of the Napier-Railton but wanted to regain the lap record, so he booked the track for an attempt on Monday 7 October. There were no spectators, but most of the Brooklands community working in their sheds and in the small firms inside the track came out to watch as they realised the risks inherent in the attempt and the courage which it needed. The track was damp, but Cobb did two fast laps, sliding on the bankings and at the Fork. His speed was 143.44mph, a lap speed which would never be exceeded at the track and thus the all-time record. He was timed on the flying kilometre at 151.97mph, the fastest speed ever officially recorded at Brooklands. Afterwards he likened the attempt to 'seeing how far you could lean out of a ninth-storey window without falling'.

Some years later, in the BRDC Silver Jubilee Book, he made some observations about taking the record: 'The key to a fast lap at Brooklands consisted of a good entry onto the Home (Members') Banking. If it was taken too slowly time was lost; if taken too fast the resultant skid towards the top of the banking caused one to have to slow down – to say nothing of scaring one stiff. Down the Railway Straight I could reach 160mph and then ease a little to enter the Byfleet Banking. After that, full chat as far as the one-mile post and then about three-quarter throttle until reaching the Fork. This could be taken on full power provided there was no wind but could be very awkward if the car was not placed right.'

To the uninitiated it might have seemed that all that was needed to do a fast lap at Brooklands was to drive flat out, but a really fast lap needed all the skill required of a grand prix driver on the fastest road circuits.

The closing BARC meeting was postponed for a week until 19 October, to coincide with the Motor Show at Olympia. It was a cold day and darkness was falling as the last race was run. The main event was the ten-lap Mountain Championship. Raymond Mays led from the start in a 2-litre ERA, chased by Shuttleworth in his Tipo B Alfa Romeo. The pair exchanged the lead for three laps, then Mays dropped out with supercharger problems, which left Shuttleworth pulling away to win from Charles Martin in a Type 59 Bugatti and Bira in his ERA 'Romulus'. The Women's Mountain Handicap had Kay Petre in the 'White' Riley and Gwenda Stewart in the Derby-Maserati on scratch. The winner was Pat Oxenden in an Alta, with Mrs Petre in third place, while Mrs Stewart's car was off-form. Bertram drove the Barnato-Hassan in the First October Handicap but despite lapping at 142mph was unplaced, while Cobb ran in the Second October Handicap but was more circumspect, lapping at only 133mph. He too was unplaced.

The track was to have closed for the winter on 31 October, but as there had been a period of bad weather it was kept open for another week to permit record attempts. On Thursday 6 November Richard Shuttleworth, fresh from a victory in the Donington Grand Prix – now regarded by many as the premier British race – brought his Tipo B Alfa Romeo out and took the outright Mountain lap record , breaking Straight's record by a mere 0.01sec at a speed of 82.06mph.

The BMCRC 1935 season began on 6 April with the Clubman's meeting sponsored by *The Motor*

Cycle, for which an astonishing 598 entries were received. Many of these were competing in the flying kilometre events at the start of the programme. On the Outer Circuit, Jock West on a 500cc Triumph won the three-lap All Comers' Handicap by just a length from Eric Fernihough, who came through from scratch on his Brough. The BMCRC Members' Handicap on the Mountain went to Ben Bickell on his Excelsior-JAP 500, Daniell's Norton coming second.

Fernihough was out again at the midweek meeting on Wednesday 8 May, winning two three-lap handicaps and lapping at 115mph on the Brough. The Cup meeting on 25 May was dry and sunny. In the three-lap J.A. Prestwich Cup race Fernihough was on scratch and could not catch the leaders, the winner being Jock West on his Triumph 500. Noel Pope, riding the Brough formerly owned by Baragwanath, was second and Beatrice Shilling finished third on her Norton 500. The ten-lap Wakefield Cup went to Rhodes's Morgan, which had a 1min 10sec start. On the Mountain, the second Wakefield Trophy was run in two heats and a final. In the final Tony Rawlence (Norton 500) seemed to have victory in sight when he fell off at the Members' Bridge, and Charles Mortimer (Norton 500) took the flag.

Noel Pope wanted to take the outright lap record, so went to the midweek meeting on

BELOW *Les Archer (Velocette) is chased round the Fork by Jock Forbes (Norton) during the Junior Mountain Championship on 27 July 1935. (Brooklands Society)*

Wednesday 26 June for that purpose. He took third place in a three-lap All Comers' Handicap behind Shelly (Norton 500) and Bickell, then came out with the Brough Superior-JAP after the Outer Circuit races were concluded. In front of a small crowd he did a lap at 120.59mph and took the record, also receiving a BMCRC 'Super Award' for the feat.

Eric Fernihough

Eric Fernihough first appeared at Brooklands in March 1926, at the BMCRC opening meeting, while still an undergraduate at Cambridge. He drove a three-wheel Morgan with a JAP 500cc engine and at the end of March he took Class I records and came out to take records again several times during the year. In August, attempting more records, he shared the car with his fiancée, Dorrie Butler, and the Morgan overturned when a rear tyre burst, but neither was badly hurt.

He began racing motor cycles in 1927, when his first machine was a 175cc Montgomery, but he rode a 500cc HRD-JAP to third place in the 200-Mile solo race and ended the season taking more records with the Morgan. In 1928 he devoted his attentions to a 250cc Excelsior-JAP, taking second place in the 200-Mile solo race and coming third in the 'Hutchinson 100'. He continued with the Excelsior in 1929, also riding in some races with a 350cc engine, gaining several wins and places and coming third in the 200-Mile 250cc race. He was also establishing a reputation as a tuner and had a paddock shed at Brooklands as well as a business in Southampton. He specialised in tuning JAP engines and several manufacturers using these engaged his services.

Fernihough showed he was becoming a front-rank rider when he led Staniland for most of the 250cc GP race in 1930 until he fell off, and came third in the 'Hutchinson 100' with a 175cc Excelsior. Though his business gave him less time for racing he broke the Mountain lap record in 1932 on an Excelsior 500. At the beginning of 1934 he moved the business from Southampton to a garage beside the Byfleet Banking, and during the season he won the 250cc Grand Prix and the 'Hutchinson 100', both on an Excelsior.

Fernihough had his eye on larger prizes and in 1935 he built up a Brough with a 996cc JAP engine. With this he broke the outright lap record, despite a thrown tyre tread, setting it at 123.58mph, but he found the handicaps so tough that he raced the Brough only infrequently. In October 1936 he took it to Gyon in Hungary and broke the world motor cycle Land Speed Record at 163.82mph, breaking the record again in April 1937 at 168.58mph. He had a protracted duel with the German rider Ernst Henne, riding a BMW, as each broke the other's record, and when Henne set a new record in November 1937 Fernihough planned to take it again in the spring of 1938. As a preliminary he broke the Brooklands flying kilometre motor cycle record at the opening meeting in 1938 at 143.39mph, but was killed while attempting a new world record at Gyon on 23 April. He was just 35 years old.

In an era when motor cycle tuning was largely limited to good fitting, Fernihough brought a new and scientific approach which was ahead of its time, and his skill, combined with great courage, brought remarkable results. Percy Bradley described him as the Parry Thomas of motor cycle racing.

There was a sensation at the Mountain Championship meeting on 27 July, but it was on the Outer Circuit in the preliminary three-lap All Comers' Handicap. Eric Fernihough was on scratch with his Brough Superior-JAP and on his second lap he broke Pope's new outright lap record, going round the track at 123.58mph. The drama was not over, as the rear tyre threw a tread on the next lap and the flying rubber badly bruised his back and wrecked the saddle. Archer initially led the 25-lap Junior Mountain Championship with his Velocette but then dropped out, leaving Bickell (Bickell-JAP) in front until he was passed by Daniell (Norton), who went on to win, followed by Ron Harris on another Norton. Bickell led the Senior race on an Ariel but retired, as did Daniell and Harris, so Mortimer (Norton) won from Tony Rawlence (Norton). Fernihough and Pope both realised that considerable risks were taken in lap record attempts for little recompense, so they made a private agreement that neither would make any more attempts until the bonuses paid by the accessory and fuel companies had been improved.

The Motor Cycle sponsored the Clubman's Grand Prix meeting on 31 August. This used the Finishing Straight, Railway Straight and Byfleet Banking, with chicanes at the Fork and in the Finishing Straight. The 'Experts' had races over 38 laps of the 2.6-mile circuit and the clubmen did 19 laps. The 250s and 350s ran together: in the small class Ernie Nott had a runaway win on a Rudge, as did Les Archer on his Velocette in the 350 class. 'Ginger' Wood rode a new 500cc twin New Imperial in the Senior race and despite a misfire in the closing laps he led all the way, while Bickell was second on an Ariel.

Wood and Bickell were out again for the 'Hutchinson 100' on 28 September. Both were on scratch with 29 other riders starting ahead of them. Neil Christmas, who had an 8min 38sec start on his 350cc Velocette, was uncatchable, but in pursuit Wood set a new 500cc lap record at 115.82mph before falling off on the Byfleet Banking, without injury. Christmas finished two laps ahead of Jock West (Triumph 500).

There was a three-lap handicap at the BARC closing meeting where Christmas won again, on a 350cc Velocette. Then there was drama at the closing BMCRC meeting. The main race was a 50-mile Outer Circuit Handicap, won by Boulting on a 250cc Rex-Acme, but at the end of the meeting Ben Bickell came out to attempt the 350cc lap record. Dusk was falling and he had a bad slide on the Members' Banking. He fell off and the Excelsior-JAP went over the top of the banking into bushes below and caught fire. Fortunately Bickell was only slightly hurt.

1936

King George V died on 20 January 1936 and was succeeded by King Edward VIII, who, although not showing a great interest in the motor racing at Brooklands, as Prince of Wales had been the Patron of the BARC since 1930 and had owned aircraft which had been flown from the airfield. The patronage lapsed when he succeeded to the throne, but on 20 March the club was informed that the new King had consented to become Patron.

Perhaps of greater moment, early in 1936 Dame Ethel Locke-King began negotiations for the sale of the track and airfield. An announcement appeared in the press in April, revealing that buyers had been making approaches concerning the purchase for five years, but these had been rejected. Rumours circulated that the track was to be sold and become a housing estate and these were not wholly silenced by an ambiguous statement from Percy Bradley. As a preliminary, the track and airfield were transferred to a new company, Byfleet Estates Ltd. The negotiations were conducted by Electrical & General Trusts Ltd, and a new public company, Brooklands (Weybridge) Ltd, was formed on 20 June 1936, all the interests of Byfleet Estates Ltd being vested in Brooklands (Weybridge) Ltd in

August. The company paid £253,100 for the site and issued £160,000 in 4½ per cent debenture stock, 120,000 6 per cent preference shares, and 240,000 5s 0d ordinary shares, issued at 6s 0d. So, after 30 years, the track and airfield passed out of the hands of the Locke-King family and its associates. Brooklands House was included in the sale, so Dame Ethel moved into Caenshill, which adjoined Shell Way.

Sir Malcolm Campbell joined the board of directors of the new company and Percy Bradley was appointed managing director. Plans for a major expansion were announced. It was proposed that the airfield should be enlarged and improved to form a major airport for London, a grandstand would be erected on top of the Members' Banking, and there would be new pits, entrance roads and paddock, and an electric scoreboard. None of these proposals came to fruition and it emerged many years later that the concealed intention of the new owners was to develop the track site for housing and industrial development.

The usual repairs took place during the winter and there were some minor improvements. The biggest change came with an amendment to the BARC regulations, as the club decided that women drivers should henceforth compete on equal terms

BELOW Dorothy Summers is flagged away in her Marendaz on the way to winning the Second March Short Handicap at the 1936 opening meeting. She was the first woman victor after the BARC let women race in all events on equal terms with the men. (LAT)

ABOVE *Mrs Lace spins her Singer in front of Almack's Austin and Bowler's Bentley during the Second Short Mountain Handicap at the 1936 opening meeting. The extension to the Vickers erecting sheds, which was completed during the winter of 1935/6, can be seen in the background.* (LAT)

with the men. The axe fell on the V12 Delage, which was decreed to be too old to race. The '120mph' badge was supplemented by the '130mph' badge, which was much harder to gain. A total of 85 '120' badges and 17 '130' badges had been awarded by the outbreak of war in 1939.

The opening meeting on 14 March did not have the fastest Outer Circuit cars in its entry, though Charles Martin had a Tipo B Alfa Romeo and came second in the first Mountain Handicap. The first woman to win at the new 'unisex' Brooklands was Dorothy Summers, who was the victor in the Second Short March Handicap in a Marendaz entered by the fiery and notorious Captain Marendaz. Doreen Evans also showed she could race on equal terms by taking second place in the Second Mountain Handicap in her Q-type MG, ahead of Bira, whose new ERA 'Remus' was making its debut.

The crowds who came to the Easter Monday meeting were disappointed, as the stewards decided it was too wet to race, so the meeting was postponed until the following Saturday. John Cobb had realised that the Napier-Railton stood no chance of success in BARC meetings, as it was carrying too heavy a handicap, so he had bought one of the V12 Sunbeams from Sir Malcolm Campbell and he drove this in the First Easter Long

Handicap but was unplaced, and it was won by Mike Couper in his Talbot 105. The main event of the day was the British Mountain Handicap, run in three heats and a final. The final, over ten laps, was won by Birmingham stockbroker Denis Scribbans, a novice competing in his first race with a new ERA.

The BRDC had taken the British Empire Trophy to Donington, so apart from the '500' the JCC International Trophy on 2 May was the only long-distance race at the track during 1936. Run again with the usual handicap channels, making it a virtual scratch race, there were 42 starters, including ten ERAs. At the end of the first lap Mays led Bira in their ERAs followed by Dixon in third place in his 2-litre Riley and Paul (ERA). Mays fell back and at ten laps Bira led 'Ginger' Hamilton ('Monza' Alfa Romeo), Hector Dobbs (2-litre Riley) and Mays. The handicap channels were working well, and at 20 laps Dobbs led the field by one second, followed by Bira and Mays. There was additional excitement when Doreen Evans's R-type MG caught fire as she came off the Members' Banking. She jumped clear as the car hit the bank and only received slight burns.

Bira moved back into the lead at half-distance, while Mays had made a fuel stop and was almost a lap behind, but he was apparently in the quicker car and gradually cut back Bira's lead until at the

slightly too much for Mays's engine, and as the cars swung off the Members' Banking towards the finish it stammered slightly and Bira swept past to take the flag and win one of the most dramatic long-distance races at the track. Dobbs was third, three minutes behind, and there were 11 finishers.

The LCC ran the Relay Race on 16 May, earlier in the season than in previous years, and, hoping to boost the entries, opened the race to cars of unlimited engine capacity. This was not effective, as only 13 teams entered, though unlike previous years they raced in sunshine. Three Aston Martins comprised the winning team, driven by Campbell, Morris-Goodall and Anthony, and 12 teams finished the race, three of these being made up of Fiat Balillas.

The BARC Whitsun meeting had become regarded as the club's major meeting of the season and the main race was the Gold Star Handicap. In the second race on the card, the First Long Handicap, Lord Howe came up into third place from scratch in his Type 59 Bugatti and made the fastest lap ever recorded by a Bugatti at the track with 138.34mph. There were ten starters in the Gold Star race and Howe was on scratch, together with Bertram in the Barnato-Hassan, which had a new slim, polished aluminium body. Both retired with thrown tyre treads and the race went to the Pacey-Hassan, another Bentley-based special with a 4½-litre engine, driven by Bill Pacey. John Cobb was second in the V12 Sunbeam. Bertram's best lap was at 140.29mph and five of the runners lapped at over 130mph.

One of the starters was the old Leyland-Thomas, now with a sports body and driven by R.J. Munday. On the last lap, in sight of the line and challenging

60-lap mark the gap was only eight seconds. Bira stopped for fuel, which gave Mays a lead of nearly a minute, but he set off in pursuit of Mays and at 80 laps was only 29sec behind. On lap 90 Mays made a second unexpected fuel stop and restarted 18sec behind, but he cut into Bira's lead and in the final lap, by exceeding the rev limit, he passed Bira on the Byfleet Banking. The strain of the chase was

BELOW *A view of the field lining up for the 1936 JCC International Trophy. The handicap channels can be seen at the Fork and the new Vickers extension is evident. (LAT)*

ABOVE *John Cobb in the V12 Sunbeam and Oliver Bertram in the 6½-litre Bentley-Jackson 'Old Mother Gun' wait for the start of their match race at the 1936 August Bank Holiday meeting. (LAT)*

BELOW *The start of the Second August Mountain Handicap at the 1936 Bank Holiday meeting. Bert Hadley (750cc Austin) and R.F. Oats (T26 Maserati) wait to start from the 29sec mark. (LAT)*

for the lead, the engine exploded, much of it dropping onto the track, and the car crossed the line in flames – a sad end for a great car, as it never raced again and was destroyed during an air raid in World War Two. During the race it had lapped at 126.73mph so it went out in a blaze of glory. Unfortunately, during practice early on the morning of race day Kenneth Carr had been killed when he overturned his 'Monza' Alfa Romeo coming off the Members' Banking, proof of the fact that the Outer Circuit could be a dangerous place for the inexperienced driver of a fast car.

Motor Sport headed its report of the BARC August Bank Holiday meeting 'Brooklands Below Par'. The Barnato-Hassan had broken a con rod in practice so a proposed attempt on the lap record was abandoned, but a three-lap match race between Bertram and Cobb went ahead, as

Bertram was loaned the 6½-litre Bentley single-seater special built from the 1928 Le Mans winner 'Old Mother Gun', and now known as the Bentley-Jackson. Bertram had a nine second start but was caught by Cobb in the Sunbeam right on the line, pulling down the banking to give Cobb room to pass. The main event was the Locke-King Trophy, a handicap over five laps for cars up to 1,500cc running in capacity classes. It was won by Major A.T.G. 'Goldie' Gardner in a K3 MG, who was followed home by the two scratch cars, the Frazer Nash of Fane and the Alta of Bertram. In the First August Mountain Handicap there was a dead heat for first place between the J4 MG of Rex King-Clark, a young Army subaltern, and the Rapier special of Roy Eccles. After the last race, a Weir W-3 autogyro made a demonstration flight from the Fork.

The BRDC had only 18 starters for the '500' on

19 September. The smallest cars were flagged away at 1:00pm and the largest, Bertram's Barnato-Hassan, set off at 1:33pm. At 1:30pm the Rileys of Paul and Dixon were in first and second place, but Dixon took over the lead and was in front at 2:30pm, ahead of Paul and Bertram, who had brought the Barnato-Hassan up into third place. When Dixon stopped for fuel and tyres and handed the Riley over to Charles Martin, Bertram took the lead. He too stopped, taking four minutes for fuel and tyres, and Richard Marker took over. Soon afterwards the Barnato-Hassan stopped with a broken con rod. Dixon went back into the lead again and was unchallenged as he reeled off the laps, coming home to win at 116.86mph. The Pacey-Hassan driven by Pacey and Baker-Carr had gone steadily and came second, while a sports 4½-litre Lagonda shared by Lord Howe and Brian Lewis was third. Only one other car, Hamilton's Alfa Romeo, was classified as a finisher, though several cars were flagged off.

Saturday 17 October was a bitterly cold day for the BARC closing meeting. It seemed evident that interest in racing on the Outer Circuit was waning. There were three handicaps and one of these was for Bentleys driven by Bentley Drivers' Club members. The rest of the races were around the Mountain, and the Mountain Championship was the main event. It was led throughout by Mays in a 2-litre ERA, followed by Martin in a Tipo B Alfa Romeo. Behind him there was a fight between the Swiss driver Hans Ruesch in a 3.8-litre Alfa Romeo which had won the Donington GP the previous month, and Bira in the 8CM Maserati formerly owned by Straight. Ruesch caught Martin on the line. After the race there was a stewards' enquiry and Martin was penalised a minute, as he was found to have had his wheels over the line at the start, so Bira was awarded third place. The Siam Trophy was run for an all-ERA field and was another runaway win for Mays. Martin had some compensation, as starting from scratch in the Alfa Romeo he won the last race of the day in the gathering dusk.

The BMCRC season began on 1 April and Ben Bickell had two wins on the Outer Circuit and one on the Mountain with the Ariel Square Four 500, while E.G. Bishop also won twice with a 590cc Excelsior-JAP sidecar combination. The Clubman's day on 25 April had the usual huge entry and there was a fatal accident in the club team relay when J. Snowden, who had been riding a Vincent-HRD, was standing in a group after handing over the sash to his team-mate when he was knocked down by a skidding machine which did not stop in time. Bickell later scored again, winning the five-lap and ten-lap All Comers' Mountain Handicaps.

Charles Mortimer won the five-lap Wakefield Cup for machines over 245cc at the Cup Day on 23 May. He was riding a 350cc International Norton which he had bought for £25 the previous evening from Comerfords, a local motor cycle dealer, and had spent the night stripping and preparing it for the race. During the Mountain races, Whitworth, riding a 350cc Rex-Acme, came off and was struck by a following machine. Undaunted and heavily bandaged, he came out for the last race and was the acclaimed winner.

The midweek meetings started at 3:30pm. 'Early closing days' were almost universal and the later

BELOW *The Clubman 350s come through the Finishing Straight chicane at the BMCRC Grand Prix meeting on 18 July 1936. (Brooklands Society)*

start enabled workers to come to the track. At the meeting on Wednesday 24 June they had extra excitement, as R.C. Hogarth went over the top of the Byfleet Banking on his 350cc AJS, but walked away unhurt. Noel Pope won the five-lap All Comers' Handicap riding a 515cc Norton tuned by Francis Beart, but was out of luck in the ten-lap event when the Norton broke down, leaving another win to Mortimer.

Francis Beart broke the Test Hill record in June on a 500cc Grindlay Peerless-JAP with a time of 6.99sec, an outright record for cars and motor cycles. Uncertain if he would be able to stop safely, he had an ambulance waiting at the top of the hill! The Grand Prix meeting on 18 July was held on the usual 2.6-mile circuit with chicanes at the Fork and in the Finishing Straight. Harold Daniell had a runaway win in the 38-lap 'Experts' Senior race, Nortons taking the first five places after Ben Bickell fell off as a result of hitting a barrel. George Rowley won the Junior 'Experts' on a works AJS, while in the 19-lap Clubman's 350 race Johnny Lockett, who was later to become a leading rider, won on a Norton.

The Mountain Championships on 15 August attracted a very small crowd. Les Archer led all the way in the Junior (350cc) race and appeared to have scored an emphatic victory, but the stewards disqualified him as he had gone the wrong side of a barrel at the chicane in the Finishing Straight. He had been pursued by Ben Bickell on his Bickell-JAP, but he had retired through lack of fuel, so the surprise winner was M.D. Whitworth on a Rex-

Acme. Archer was so upset that he refused to ride in the Senior race, so it was an easy win for Noel Pope on a Norton. On the Outer Circuit, the main race was the Gold Star Holders' Handicap and Mortimer won again on a 500cc Norton. Fernihough was on scratch, giving a six-second start to Pope, both on their Broughs, but Fernihough passed Pope and came through to second place, lapping at 117.46mph.

Pope and Fernihough were facing the same problem as John Cobb. In his autobiography *Full Chat*, Pope commented: 'Brooklands was now fast becoming ludicrous to me – it made me like a dog trying to catch its tail! The faster I went, the faster I had to go to catch up with my handicap and the more my handicap went up, so the compression ratio of the engine went up too, and reliability became less each time. I had long given up any idea of winning a race with the Brough as I had no intention of trying to break the lap record each time I entered a race.'

The motor cycle racing world was greatly upset when Ben Bickell died of injuries after a practice accident at the Ulster Grand Prix, and at the meeting on Wednesday 23 September there was a five-minute pause in his honour before racing began. In the ten-lap All Comers' Mountain handicap, Ron Harris won, riding his Norton 500 with an arm in plaster, the result of an accident in the Manx GP earlier in the month.

The motor cycle season at the track finished with the 'Hutchinson 100' on 10 October. This had 44 starters and there was a diversion before the race when Chris Staniland flew low over the track in a Fairey Battle bomber. If riders needed to make a refuelling stop during the race, this had to be declared beforehand, and an allowance of one minute was given in their handicap, so an advantage might be gained through very quick pit work. The winner was Goddard riding a 246cc OK-Supreme, who had a start of 13min 34sec and won by a minute from Ron Harris, who worked his 500cc Norton through to second place.

The shareholders of Brooklands (Weybridge) Ltd must have been given some encouragement about their investment at the end of 1936. No dividend was paid to the Ordinary shareholders, but some of the company's activities had been profitable. The opening meeting made a profit of £162 and it was better at Easter with £1,998, though Whitsun, usually regarded as the major BARC meeting, only produced £1,837. The Aero Club made a loss of £631, though aerodrome rentals made £9,196. The hire of car badges to BARC members raised £70 and the bookmakers paid £123 for their permits.

1937

Although the new owners did not make the promised improvements to the track and airfield, during the autumn of 1936 work began on a project that was to make the biggest changes to the track since its 1907 opening. It was realised that the combinations offered by the Outer Circuit and Finishing Straight were inadequate; there was a need for a circuit which would keep up with the changes in the sport. An artificial road circuit was devised which was designed by Sir Malcolm Campbell and named after him. It began with a turning off the Railway Straight and doubled back on Solomon straight – named after a goat (with an evil reputation for smell and temper!) owned by the BARC, which had died in 1935 – to run parallel with the Railway Straight. It then turned right at Aerodrome Curve and ran on Sahara Straight, parallel with the Finishing Straight, and when approaching the Fork turned left over a bridge crossing the River Wey, crossed the Finishing Straight, then turned left again to run parallel with the Finishing Straight until, opposite the paddock, it took a sharp right climbing turn, the Test Hill Hairpin, and joined the foot of the Members' Banking. A row of concrete pits were built between the Finishing Straight and the Test Hill Hairpin.

The circuit was approximately 2.25 miles long, and the road, made of concrete, was 32ft wide with a width of 40ft at the corners. The River Wey crossing used a bridge which had been built in 1935 to enable Vickers aircraft to be towed direct from the factory to the airfield and the track owners charged Vickers a toll for each aircraft using it unless these wore RAF roundels.

The Campbell Circuit construction was carried out by the Demolition & Construction Co. It was a valiant attempt to bring the track up to date, though the design was circumscribed by the perimeters of the site and by the necessity of not encroaching on the airfield. It was also probably 15 years too late; if it had been built in the early 1920s the history of Brooklands might have been very different. There was an added pressure: a new road circuit was being opened at the Crystal Palace in the south London suburbs, which would offer genuine road racing in the Continental idiom and would probably draw spectators away from Brooklands.

The Campbell Circuit was not ready for the Easter meeting on 29 March, where the major race was a ten-lap Outer Circuit Handicap for the BBC Trophy and a cash prize of £100. The race was broadcast live on BBC radio and John Cobb entered the Napier-Railton, which came through the field of ten cars from scratch to win at an average of 136.03mph, the fastest race ever run at the track. Cobb did three laps at 139.90mph. A.P. 'Ginger' Hamilton was second in his 'Monza' Alfa Romeo.

BELOW An MG PA tackles a garaging test during the 1937 JCC Rally on 27 February 1937. (LAT)

RIGHT *Peter Walker (ERA) leads Lord Howe (ERA) and Bira (8CM Maserati) on the opening lap of the 1937 Campbell Trophy. This corner, the Banking Bend, is now part of the entrance to the Gallaher site. (LAT)*

BELOW *The ERAs of Dobson, Connell, Tongue and Cook in the new road circuit pits during the 1937 Campbell Trophy. (LAT)*

An exciting new car, the 'Bimotore' Alfa Romeo, which had attracted much interest, appeared at the track in the spring. It had two Tipo B engines and had been devised by Enzo Ferrari as an unsuccessful answer to the all-conquering German teams. The new owner was Austin Dobson, who hoped to take the outright lap record. At the end of the meeting Dobson brought it out and tried to take the Mountain lap record but was unsuccessful, though he did take the Class B record.

The Campbell Circuit was formally opened on Tuesday 20 April. The ceremony was performed by Dame Ethel Locke-King, who cut a tape across the track, and a parade of cars was then led around the circuit by S.F. Edge in a 1903 Gordon Bennett Napier. The first race, the Campbell Trophy, was held on Saturday 1 May and, remarkably for the BARC, it was a scratch race over 100 laps with a prize of £250 to the outright winner and another £250 going to the first 1½-litre car to finish. Despite the apparent attraction of the new circuit, only a modest crowd came to watch a field of 22 cars. Bira led from the start in his 8CM Maserati pursued by Lord Howe in an ERA. Howe stayed with Bira and took the lead on lap 19, but six laps later misjudged the turn over the river bridge and overturned, receiving severe

injuries. Bira carried on to win, followed for a while by the 'Bimotore', which then retired, and second place went to the 1½-litre 4CM Maserati driven by Eddie Rayson, which had led for a few laps when Bira refuelled. The 'Monza' Alfa Romeo of Anthony Powys-Lybbe was third and only four cars were classified as finishers, another five being flagged off. Bira took 3hr 16min 52.4sec for his drive at an average of 69.06mph, and it was agreed that the circuit was tough and not especially fast.

The BARC Whitsun meeting on 17 May was run to the traditional format and the main race was the Coronation Gold Trophy in honour of the Coronation of King George VI, which had taken place on 6 May, the new King having consented to become Patron of the BARC. It was a seven-lap Outer Circuit Handicap and Cobb was on scratch with the Napier-Railton. The handicap was too tough for him and he had to ease off when baulked by slower cars at the top of the banking and only came third, despite lapping at 141.89mph. The winner was Baker-Carr in a 4½-litre Bentley. The 'Bimotore' was entered and was expected to be a big attraction, but it did not run and notices were posted at the track entrances informing spectators that it would be a non-starter, possibly anticipating

grumbles from disappointed customers. On the Mountain, the Coronation Handicap had excitement in the first heat when Gordon Brettell went over the top of the Members' Banking in his monoposto Austin Seven and broke an arm. (Brettell would be one of the 50 RAF officers shot following the 'Great Escape' from Stalag Luft III prison camp during World War Two.) The final was won by Samuels in a Frazer Nash.

The LCC ran the Relay race again on 26 June but even the admission of the larger cars failed to boost the entry and only ten teams started. The works Austin team – which had two of the amazing twin-cam 750cc racers driven by Bert Hadley and Charlie Goodacre and the side-valve single-seater driven by Kay Petre – was on scratch but came through to win, Hadley lapping at 121.18mph. An MG team was second and a Frazer Nash team took third place.

The BARC held the first club meeting on the Campbell Circuit on 10 July. Despite good prize money the entry was disappointing, as was the crowd. There were five races, all handicaps, over three and six laps. The main event was the National Handicap, which was won by Bert Hadley in a twin-cam 750cc Austin. The paddock bookies realised he was a likely winner as he started at 6 to 4 on. He was followed into second place by Arthur Dobson

in an ERA, and Dobson won the last race of the day.

In a break with tradition, the BARC did not hold an August Bank Holiday meeting but the calendar date was taken up by the JCC for the International Trophy. A 3.37-mile circuit was devised for the 60-lap race; the start was in the Finishing Straight facing the Fork, the cars turned left onto the Mountain section of the Campbell Circuit, then turned right onto the Members' Banking and ran down to the Fork to the usual handicap channels, then round the Outer Circuit and back to the Finishing Straight. In practice one MG driver turned left onto the Members' Banking and found himself facing the traffic on the Railway Straight!

There was an innovation, as the race began with a rolling start. John Cobb in the V12 Sunbeam was the pacemaker and led the 20 starters round for a lap before the pack was flagged away. Mays went to the front immediately in a 2-litre ERA, followed by Bira in his 8CM Maserati. Mays stayed in the lead. Bira pushed past several times, but was overtaken immediately by Mays. The battle went on until lap 26, when the Maserati stopped in clouds of steam with a cracked cylinder block. Mays was now unchallenged and reeled off the laps to win easily by almost four minutes from the 1½-litre 6CM Maserati of Johnnie Wakefield. Billy Cotton, the bandleader,

BELOW *The start of the last BRDC 500 on 18 September 1937. No 29 is the Bimotore Alfa Romeo, No 11 the 1½-litre Riley of E.W.H. Dobson, and No 22 the Bowler-Hofman Bentley. (John Maitland Collection)*

was third in a K3 MG, and Arthur Dobson's ERA was the only remaining classified finisher.

The BRDC realised that the sport had changed and a full 500 miles around the Outer Circuit was lacking in appeal to drivers and spectators. The '500' on 18 September was therefore reduced to 500 kilometres (312 miles). Although a handicap race, the smaller cars would receive credit laps, so only the scratch car would go the full distance and the race would have a massed start. During practice there was an accident when Kay Petre's Austin and Reg Parnell's MG collided on the Byfleet Banking and Mrs Petre received serious head injuries. Subsequently Parnell was adjudged to have been at fault and was suspended from racing for a year.

The race had 20 starters and the Napier-Railton, which Cobb was sharing with Oliver Bertram, was on scratch, giving a lap start to the 'Bimotore'. The race began at 2:30pm and Cobb immediately surged away from the field and began lapping at 130mph. After 30 minutes the Rileys of Dobson and Paul were running in first and second places on handicap and Cobb was third. By 3:30pm the Napier-Railton was in the lead, averaging 129.40mph. Shortly afterwards it threw a tyre tread and Cobb stopped to change wheels, refuel, and hand over to Bertram, who kept up the pace and

the lead was maintained. At 4:15pm Cobb took the wheel again and pushed the lap speed up to 135mph as Charlie Dodson, in Dixon's 2-litre Riley, was challenging on handicap. The increase in speed was enough. Then, on the last lap, as the Napier-Railton came to the finish to take the flag, a rear tyre broke up, but the victory was secure. Cobb and Bertram had averaged 127.05mph and on the last lap of the race Cobb had lapped at 136.45mph. Dodson was second, Percy Maclure took third place in a works 1½-litre Riley, and the old V12 Sunbeam, which Cobb had lent to Charles Brackenbury and Anthony Powys-Lybbe, was fourth. There were nine finishers, Bira being seventh in a stripped sports 135 Delahaye, despite being burned by acid from a leaking battery. It was the last '500' and the last time the Napier-Railton would run at the track.

At the MCC Members' Day on 25 September there was a special prize for the drivers who covered 100 miles during the two One-Hour High Speed Trials. No one took the prize, though in the first trial Elgood's Bentley covered 98 miles and in the second Sir Lionel Phillips's Leyland-Thomas covered 97.85 miles.

The BARC had a mixed programme of Outer Circuit, Mountain and Campbell Circuit races at the

BELOW *John Cobb makes a pit stop during his winning drive in the 1937 BRDC 500. This was the last race for him and for the Napier-Railton at Brooklands. (LAT)*

closing meeting on 16 October. A new and legendary racing story began for a marque that would become world-renowned when Tommy Wisdom won the First October Long Handicap in a 3½-litre SS Jaguar 100, lapping at 118.02mph. Bertram won the Second October Long Handicap in the Barnato-Hassan, averaging 128.25mph, but the main action was around the Mountain. The Siam Trophy had reverted to a class handicap for cars up to 1,500cc and was won by Mays in an ERA. Another ERA driven by Peter Walker was second and Johnnie Wakefield was third in a 6CM Maserati. Mays's 2-litre ERA had been withdrawn from the Mountain Championship, which was an easy win for Hans Ruesch in his 3.8-litre Alfa Romeo, while Kenneth Evans was second in a Tipo B Alfa Romeo.

In September, Richard Seaman, who had joined the Mercedes-Benz team in 1937 and was becoming regarded as a leading grand prix driver, asked his great friend George Monkhouse to obtain details of the Brooklands silencer regulations, and it seems that Mercedes-Benz was considering an attempt on the Brooklands lap record, possibly at the closing meeting. The Mercedes team was in England to compete in the Donington Grand Prix on 2 October and consideration must have been given to the possibility of bringing a 5.6-litre W125 GP car to Brooklands, perhaps driven by Seaman, as it would surely have broken the lap record by a considerable margin. Unfortunately nothing more was heard of the project.

Although there were few record attempts at the track, manufacturers were using it continuously for testing and for publicity. On 15 April a 328 BMW

was brought along by the British importers AFN Ltd, and, driven by Sammy Davis, did 102.22 miles in the hour. The BMW run was seen as a challenge by Lagonda, and an LG45 4½-litre car which had run in the Tourist Trophy was taken round the track for an hour on 7 October in a grey drizzle, driven by motoring writer Alan Hess, and covered 104.44 miles. Almost every road test which was published in the press included performance figures taken at the track, and *The Autocar* did tests on up to 90 cars in a year. It was noticeable that many of the tests during the autumn and winter months commented on it being impossible to use the full track as it was under repair.

At the beginning of 1937 the BMCRC relinquished overall control of its activities to the BARC, the club's office was moved to the track, and a full-time secretary was appointed. The season began with the Clubman's meeting on 17 April and had an entry of 571 riders. It was a wet day and began with the usual kilometre sprints, the programme being delayed when T.B. Bruce fell off his Norton, which caught fire. With the prospect of racing on the Campbell Circuit, the Mountain Championship meeting was brought forward to Saturday 29 May. The Junior race was an easy win for Les Archer on his Velocette, but he did not come out for the Senior race, which was won by Jock Forbes, riding Mortimer's Norton.

At the midweek meeting on Wednesday 30 June, Wal Handley, who had done little racing since an accident in Dixon's Riley at Donington the previous year, rode a BSA 500 in the first three-lap All Comers' Outer Circuit Handicap and came home

BELOW *The start of the MCC High Speed Trial on 25 September 1937. (LAT)*

the winner, but in the next race he fell off and spent a week in Weybridge Hospital recovering from his injuries. The BMCRC had run a season in a minor key awaiting the first Campbell Circuit meeting and this took place on 17 July. There was a programme of handicaps and scratch races and the course was opened by Sir Malcolm Campbell, who did a lap of honour in a Type 57 Bugatti coupé. The distinction of winning the first race, the First Campbell Long Handicap, went to G.M. Hayden on a 350cc Velocette, followed by M.D. Whitworth on a 250cc Cotton. The main events were the Junior and Senior Brooklands Road Championships. In the 350 race Harold Daniell (Norton) led all the way, although chased hard by Les Archer (Velocette), and he repeated this in the 500 race, winning easily. Archer would probably have made the 500 win more difficult but had to work through the field from the back row at the start, although he was up to second place at the flag.

A Wednesday meeting on 25 August was cancelled through lack of entries, as many riders were in the Isle of Man for the Manx GP races, and bad weather had postponed the Grand Prix meeting, so the next meeting was the 'Hutchinson100' on 11 September. This had 33 starters, racing on a cold windy day. E.J. Tubb (Grindlay Peerless 500) was on scratch, giving a 14-minute start to the limit man. W.R. Lunn (350 Velocette) set the pace, but Ron Harris (Norton 500) came through the field and passed Lunn with three laps to go. Harris was flagged off as the winner having averaged 101.43mph but was then disqualified, as his silencer had split, so the race went to Lunn, with Jock West (350 AJS) in second place. As a small compensation Harris received a special award from the BARC for his frustrated efforts.

The postponed Grand Prix meeting was held on 9 October and, in a break from tradition, was on the Campbell Circuit. The 'Experts' had 28-lap races while the 'Clubmen' did only 14 laps. The 250 and 350 'Experts' ran together, and in the 250cc class 'Ginger' Wood (Excelsior-JAP) and Jock West (New Imperial) fought for the lead all the way. On the last lap both fell off at the Aerodrome Bend and Wood retired, but West remounted and went on to win. Harold Daniell (Norton) took the 350cc class from Les Archer (Velocette), though Archer gave him a hard race. Daniell showed his class again in the Senior 'Expert' race, and once more Archer gave chase before having to drop out with brake problems. Daniell then cruised home to an easy win, with the Nortons of J. Moore and Ron Harris in second and third places.

The BMCRC season closed with a Wednesday meeting on 20 October. J.B. Waters won two

Mountain races on a Norton 500, while in a three-lap All Comers' Outer Circuit handicap Ivan Wicksteed was the winner on a Triumph 500 Twin, lapping at 110.68mph, the fastest 500cc lap of the season. To overcome a problem with the Triumph's cylinder head lifting, a screw jack was wound between the head and the frame.

On 30 October, as the track was closing, Jack Surtees – father of the legendary John, then only three years old but later to be the only World Champion on both two wheels and on four – brought out a 600cc Norton combination and broke the Mountain sidecar record at 66.85mph.

ABOVE *Harold Daniel (Norton) leads the 350cc race at the Brooklands Road Championships on 17 July 1937. (Brooklands Society)*

BELOW *The start of the Senior Road Championship on 17 July 1937. (Brooklands Society)*

1938

At the beginning of 1938, anxieties were growing about the increasingly militaristic attitude of Germany. Hitler was making claims for the annexation of Austria, which were becoming increasingly strident when Brooklands reopened on 12 March. The BARC season began with a mixed car and motor cycle meeting, the first since 1914, and was rather low-key. There had been a change of policy by the BARC, which had decided that Mountain races were no longer a spectator draw, so this type of racing was abandoned for the season. The cars had four races, one on the Outer Circuit and three on the Campbell Circuit. In the second Campbell Circuit race the cars were lined up on the starting grid in incorrect order, so 'Ebby' started Fane in a 328 BMW instead of the limit cars. Fane won easily, so was given the equivalent of the first prize, but the race was awarded to George Harvey-Noble in a Q-type MG.

The highlight of the meeting was an attempt by Eric Fernihough to break the Brooklands flying kilometre record for motor cycles with his blown Brough Superior-JAP. Fernihough was planning to attempt the world motor cycle record, so the track run was a dress rehearsal. He started at the Fork

and kept low when he ran onto the Byfleet Banking, the result being 143.39mph, a new record. Two days after the meeting German troops marched into Austria and annexed it to the Third Reich. World War Two had moved appreciably closer.

The BARC Easter Monday meeting, which attracted a crowd of over 20,000, had one of the more spectacular Brooklands accidents. In the Second Easter Short Handicap, 'Tucker' Clayton, driving the C-type MG with which Horton had won the 1932 '500', was nudged in the tail by Hamilton's 'Monza' Alfa Romeo and the MG went over the top of the Members' Banking. The MG was completely destroyed and the crowd expected the worst, but Clayton escaped with a fractured shoulder. John Cobb's new Railton Land Speed Record contender, which had been built in the Thomson & Taylor workshops, was exhibited in the paddock. Later in the year it set a new record of 350.20mph at Bonneville Salt Flats. Apart from the serious racing, the crowd was entertained by a two-lap race on the Campbell Circuit for Fiat 500s. The main race was the Campbell Trophy, a ten-lap scratch event, which attracted foreign entries, the Maseratis of Villoresi and de Graffenried. There was a fierce battle between Bira and Arthur Dobson, both driving ERAs; Dobson led for five laps, then Bira went ahead to win by 1.6sec.

The JCC held the International Trophy on 7 May over 60 laps of the 3.37-mile circuit, using the Mountain section of the Campbell Circuit, with the handicap channels at the Fork. The 24 starters did a rolling lap behind John Cobb's 4¼-litre Bentley coupé, and were released when JCC secretary John Morgan, riding in the passenger's seat, dropped the flag. Mays (1,750cc ERA) led Bira (8CM Maserati) as the field rounded the hairpin to join the Mountain road section.

Back in the pack, French driver Joseph Paul swerved off the track as his works V12 4½-litre Delage caught fire, and the car ran through the trackside fence beyond the Campbell Circuit pits and into the spectators. One, Peggy Williams, was killed instantly, and Murray Jamieson, the designer of the twin-cam Austin and responsible for much of the ERA design, was severely injured and died shortly afterwards. Ten spectators were injured including Noel Pope and Kay Petre. The accident occurred in almost the same place as the Talbot crash in 1930.

The race nevertheless continued and for 40 laps Mays led Bira, with Percy Maclure (1,750cc Riley) in third place. Bira took the lead when Mays stopped for fuel and then stopped again to change a plug. Bira made a quick stop for fuel, but as he pulled away from the pits the back axle of the Maserati

broke, which left Maclure in the lead, being chased by Mays, whose engine was misfiring. Mays was closing the gap and eating into Maclure's lead, but at the flag the Riley was still about five lengths in front. The International Trophy had again given a dramatic finish. There was more drama as Norman Wilson, in third place in an ERA, ran out of fuel on his last lap as he came up to the finishing line. He coasted into the pits before the line, fuel was thrown in, and he restarted and crossed the line to keep his place.

In its report of the Whitsun meeting, *The Autocar* said: 'Something will have to be done about outer circuit racing at the track in the near future'. This was prompted by the lean entry for the three Outer Circuit races: the Locke King Trophy, formerly a major race, had only five entries and was an easy win for Elgood's Bentley, with the Duesenberg taking second place driven by R.L. Duller. The Gold Star handicap, which had moved to the Campbell Circuit and become a sports car race, brought out a good representative field and was won by Bennett's Alta from the Talbot 110 of Wooding. The real excitement came in the last race of the day, the Fourth Whitsun Road Handicap, with Bira and Dobson on scratch with their ERAs.

LEFT *Kay Petre congratulates Eric Fernihough on breaking the flying kilometre record on his Brough Superior at the 1938 opening meeting. (LAT)*

They duelled throughout and Bira just beat Dobson into third place, though the placings seemed unimportant to the crowd, which was thrilled by the battle.

Declining entries had forced the LCC to abandon the Relay Race and it was replaced by a three-hour production sports car event run over the Campbell Circuit on 16 July, though hardly any spectators came to watch the field of 14 cars. The

BELOW *Mays (ERA) leads Bira (Maserati) at the start of the 1938 JCC International Trophy. A few seconds later Joseph Paul (No 9 Delage) crashed into the crowd, killing two spectators. (LAT)*

race began with a Le Mans start and the drivers had to lower the hoods before setting off. In the early laps the 328 BMWs of Aldington and Fane led, but the Type 135 Delahaye of Jarvis came through after a slow start and took the lead after 16 laps. The Delahaye went on to win, covering 83 laps in the three hours, and was followed by Aldington, who had led again for a few laps when the Delahaye stopped to change a wheel and was 34sec behind at the finish. Fane was third and two more 328 BMWs were fourth and fifth, with an SS Jaguar 100 in sixth place.

The August Bank Holiday meeting was run on a very hot day, and unfortunately, as *The Light Car* put it, 'the racing failed to thrill'. The British Trophy handicap on the Campbell Circuit, with two heats and a final, was the main event, but the first race was the First August Long Handicap, in which Bertram brought the Barnato-Hassan into second place with a lap at 141.49mph. George Abecassis walked away with the ten-lap British Trophy final in his 1,500cc Alta and Dobson won a five-lap invitation ERA-only race. As a diversion there was a two-lap race for Talbot 10 saloons with a prize presented by the Rootes brothers.

Brooklands became a busy place at the end of August, as there were three major meetings in four weeks. The JCC had revived the '200' in 1936 but

BELOW *The timekeepers' box at the 1938 JCC International Trophy. The scoreboard shows Mays is leading Bira, Howe and Everitt. (LAT)*

had run it at Donington. However, it returned to Brooklands on 27 August, when it was run over 88 laps of the Campbell Circuit. In the 1920s it had been for 1½-litre cars, but it was now open to the larger machines. The crowd was small, although all schoolchildren were admitted free. There were 25 starters and in the early laps Bira in his 8CM Maserati led from the ERAs of Mays and Dobson. Both ERAs retired and second place was taken by Johnnie Wakefield, also in an ERA. When Bira stopped for fuel Wakefield took the lead and was never caught, winning by 34sec. Bira, slowed by weakening brakes, was second and Lord Howe (ERA) was third. In a break from tradition, but in keeping with Continental practice, all the cars were flagged off as soon as the winner had crossed the line.

The drivers were back again on Saturday 17 September. The BRDC, having realised that the '500' no longer had appeal, organised the 60-lap BRDC Road Race, a class handicap which used the Campbell Circuit but ran clockwise, so that when drivers joined the Members' Banking they turned right and ran past the Fork, round the Byfleet Banking, and then turned right from the Railway Straight onto the Campbell course on the Railway Straight. This gave a 3.2-mile lap course. The day began with an 18-lap Outer Circuit Handicap for the Brooklands Trophy, which was won by Geoffrey Wooding's Talbot 105. Bertram was on scratch but was badly baulked, despite lapping at 140mph in the Barnato-Hassan, and could only come through to third place. The Road Race was a duel between Mays with a 2-litre ERA and Bira with a 1½-litre ERA. Bira had a credit lap, but Mays pulled this back – helped by Bira losing time with a spin at the Test Hill hairpin – and took the lead on lap 55; but in the last two laps his engine began to misfire and Bira took the lead again, going on to win by 27sec. The Hon Peter Aitken was third in another ERA.

A week later, on 24 September, the Dunlop Rubber Company sponsored a meeting to celebrate its 50th anniversary. There was a prize fund of £1,200 and the entry fees for competitors were 3s 0d and 5s 0d. A total of 297 entries was received and the BARC had to erect temporary paddock stalls. Unfortunately, what should have been a happy, light-hearted meeting was wholly overshadowed by the worsening international situation. German demands to annexe the Sudeten province of Czechoslovakia had become brutally insistent, with the threat of war if these demands were not met. It was announced during the meeting that the French Army had mobilised and was already manning the Maginot Line. Gas masks had been issued to the British population and those with longer memories recalled the August Bank Holiday meeting in 1914. There were even visible signs of impending war at Brooklands, as the Vickers lettering on the factory doors facing the Fork had been painted over.

The meeting had attracted some Continental entries including two V12 GP Delahayes, but in the First Dunlop Outer Circuit Handicap these were no match for Chris Staniland's Multi-Union. This had been built by 'Woolly' Worters using the engine from the Tipo B Alfa Romeo which Staniland had raced in 1936, though the chassis was extensively modified and there was much use of light alloys. Worters had received support from companies using the car as a technical test-bed. In winning the race Staniland averaged 127.77mph. The main races were the two Dunlop Jubilee Trophy events, both over ten laps of the Campbell Circuit. The first, for cars up to 1,400cc – a limit designed to exclude the ERAs – was an easy win for Bert Hadley's twin-cam 750cc Austin, while the second, for unlimited capacity cars, was won by Raymond Mays in a 2-litre ERA followed by the 1½-litre cars of Wakefield and Dobson. The track was slippery from a shower before the race and on the opening lap Bira's 8CM Maserati was in collision with the 6CM Maserati of the German driver Berg and the Alta of Beadle.

The immediate threat of war had been lifted by the Munich Agreement, so at the BARC closing meeting on 15 October there was hope of 'peace for our time' as promised by Prime Minister Neville Chamberlain on his return from Germany. The sun shone and in its report *The Light Car* said 'the meeting was quite the best the club has held during 1938'. On the Outer Circuit, Staniland won the Second October Long Handicap in the Multi-Union, lapping at 141.49mph. The Siam Trophy on the Campbell Circuit was a scratch race for 1½-litre cars over ten laps and was a battle between the ERAs of Bira and Dobson, which Bira won by 1sec. The Mountain Championship, the only race on that circuit during the season, was an easy victory for Mays in his 2-litre ERA, winning by 12sec from the Multi-Union with Dobson's ERA in third place.

During the week after the meeting Staniland showed the potential of the Multi-Union on Thursday 20 October, when he broke the local Class D (3,000cc) lap record at 141.45mph and also established International Class D records for five and ten miles. Ten days later the track closed for the winter and the last full season ever held at Brooklands had ended.

The 1938 motor cycle season had begun with the mixed BARC meeting on 12 March, with Fernihough's kilometre run as its highlight. The

BELOW *J.D. Firth (3½-litre Jaguar SS100) leads Bira's 1½-litre HRG, Sidney Allard's 3,622cc Allard and Hugh Hunter's 328 BMW in the LCC Three-Hour race on 16 July 1938. This part of the Campbell Circuit was, for many years, the public entrance to the Museum site. (LAT)*

ABOVE *Charlie
Dodson's Delahaye
leads René Dreyfus's
V12 Delahaye and
Elgood's Bentley in the
Dunlop Jubilee
Handicap at the Dunlop
meeting on 24
September 1938. (LAT)*

RIGHT *Harry
Lamacraft leads Les
Archer, both on 350cc
Velocettes, at the BMCRC
Grand Prix meeting on
23 July 1938.
(Brooklands Society)*

BMCRC held the Clubman's meeting on 4 April
and there were 138 entries for the kilometre
trials. Pope was the winner in a three-lap
handicap for BMCRC members, lapping at
103.54mph in his Brough sidecar combination,
while Denis Minett set a new 500cc lap record
during the race riding Beart's Norton at
116.36mph, before going on to win the ten-lap
BMCRC Mountain Handicap. The Brooklands
motor cycle community was shattered when Eric
Fernihough was killed at Gyon, in Hungary, on 23
April while attempting to take the World Motor
Cycle record on the Brough Superior-JAP.
Fernihough, the lap record holder, who ran a
garage just beyond the Byfleet Banking, was
regarded as the leading figure among motor
cyclists at the track, being universally respected
for his courage, enthusiasm and technical ability.

The Brooklands Road Championships were held
on Saturday 14 May. There were 15 starters in the
ten-lap Junior race, which Jock Forbes (Norton) led
until he was passed by Les Archer (Velocette), who
went on to win. Forbes dropped back to third
behind Newman (Velocette). In the Senior race,

ABOVE *The field lines up at the Fork for an Outer Circuit Handicap at the BMCRC Mountain meeting on 3 September 1938. (Brooklands Society)*

with only eight starters, there was a battle between Pope and Croft on Nortons. Croft pulled away and Pope held off Minett (Rudge).

The BMCRC Cup Day on 25 June on the Outer Circuit and the Mountain clashed with a Crystal Palace meeting. The poor crowd saw Minett, riding Beart's Norton with a 515cc engine, take the 750cc lap record at 117.19mph, while Ron Harris on a Norton 500 won the ten-lap Mountain Handicap.

The Grand Prix meeting held on the Campbell Circuit on 23 July was better attended and there were five races. In the Lightweight event, Les Archer (New Imperial) led the field of 11 starters, though he was chased hard by Tyrell Smith (Excelsior-JAP), who fell off but remounted to hold his second place. Foster (AJS) had an easy win in the Junior race, then in the Senior event Ron Harris led the field on his Norton until he fell off on lap seven, which let Les Archer through to his second win of the day, this time on his 500cc Velocette. During the race he set a new motor cycle lap record for the Campbell Circuit at 70.11mph.

Sir Malcolm Campbell came to watch the Mountain Championships on 3 September, arriving on a 500cc Triumph Twin accompanied by his son Donald on a Coventry Eagle. They saw an exciting Junior Championship, as Les Archer (Velocette) led until a rocker broke and the lead was taken by Harry Lamacraft on another Velocette. Earle (Norton) chased him hard but ran out of fuel, so Lamacraft came home to win. There was less excitement in the Senior race, as Ron Harris led all the way on his Norton to win by a minute from Archer.

The 'Hutchinson 100' held on 8 October, with the apparent fear of war lifted, was run in very bad conditions with heavy rain. Before the racing began Sir Algernon Guinness unveiled a memorial plaque to Ben Bickell on the wall of the clubhouse. Noel Pope was on scratch with the 515cc Beart Norton and was giving a start of 14min 48sec to the 250cc New Imperial of J. Henry. Pope and Ron Harris stopped soon after the race began, saying the conditions were so bad and the visibility so poor that it was dangerous to continue. Maurice Cann was one of the riders who carried on and won on a 250cc Excelsior-JAP, being followed home by Jock West on a 350cc AJS.

1939

The British motor racing world was facing problems at the beginning of 1939. The long-distance races, apart from the Donington Grand Prix, were not attracting good attendances, and ERA, the country's only important manufacturer of racing cars, was in serious financial difficulty. The poor attendances were understandable. The public was tiring of seeing the same cars, most of which were at least three years old, being brought out for long-distance handicaps; and the scratch races, although sometimes more interesting, still had the same cars too. The JCC said the '200' had made a loss in 1938 and expressed doubts if the race would be run in 1939, so the International Trophy and the LCC sports car race were the only long-distance races confirmed in the Brooklands calendar. At the AGM of the BARC on 28 January it was announced that there would be a return to the Mountain in 1939, as it was realised that these races still appealed to the public.

The season opened on 11 March with a combined BARC/BMCRC meeting. There were two Outer Circuit and three Mountain handicaps for the cars, while the motor cycles raced once on the Outer Circuit and twice round the Mountain. The Easter Monday meeting had ten races on the card over the three circuits. It was a fine day which probably helped to boost the crowd, and the major race was the ten-lap Brooklands Road

BELOW Jack Lemon Burton (Type 51 Bugatti) takes the Fork in front of Ian Connell (4-litre Darracq) in the Second March Mountain Handicap at the 1939 opening meeting. (LAT)

Championship, which was a runaway win for Arthur Dobson in a works 2-litre ERA, the legendary R4D. During the race he set a new Campbell Circuit lap record at 75.57mph, while behind him there was a good fight which saw Billy Cotton (ERA) come second, with Kenneth Evans (Alfa Romeo) in third place.

LEFT *The drivers and cars line up, with Wellingtons and Hurricanes behind, before the start of the 1939 JCC International Trophy, to salute King George VI and Queen Elizabeth who were passing on the Royal Train en route to Southampton at the start of their state visit to the USA and Canada. (John Maitland Collection)*

Before the start of the JCC International Trophy on 6 May the drivers and spectators lined the Railway Straight to wave at the train carrying King George VI and Queen Elizabeth on their way to Southampton to begin a visit to the United States and Canada. The race should have been the debut of the new E-type ERA, but this wholly unsuccessful car was unready, though it was displayed in the paddock. The race had 20 starters, among which was a 1,500cc 4CL Maserati, a new model, surprisingly making its race debut at Brooklands. The race used the usual handicap channels and there was a rolling start, paced by John Cobb in a V12 Lagonda. Mays took the lead in his 2-litre ERA

BELOW *There was a cloudburst during the 1939 JCC International Trophy. Kenneth Evans splashes past the pits in his Tipo B Alfa Romeo. (LAT)*

ABOVE *Jill Thomas (328 BMW) gets away while J.O.C. Samuel (Q-type MG) looks at his instruments and waits his turn in the First Mountain Handicap at the 1939 Whitsun meeting. (LAT)*

ABOVE RIGHT *The cars line up for the Mountain heat of the Fastest Road Car race at the 1939 Whitsun meeting. Nearest the camera is the winning Delahaye of Arthur Dobson, while numbers are being painted on Aitken's Delage and No 3 is Count Dorndorff's 402 Peugeot. (LAT)*

RIGHT *A Ford V8 leaps an obstacle at the Ford Gymkhana on 17 June 1939. It was reported that this event attracted a crowd of 30,000, the biggest ever at Brooklands. (LAT)*

but soon dropped out. Bira then led the race in his 8CM Maserati until he made a fuel stop, which let Reggie Tongue in the 4CL Maserati into the lead. During a torrential rain storm, Bira resumed the lead followed by Leslie Brooke in the Riley-engined Brooke Special, while Tongue dropped back to third with fading brakes. The rain eased to a drizzle and Bira won by 1min 23sec from Brooke, with Tongue in third place. This was to be the last long-distance race run at the track.

The Whitsun meeting had glorious sunshine and an interesting innovation. There had been much speculation in the motoring press about claims to be the fastest road car in England, so a two-part race was held to decide the matter. The entry list lacked some contenders but still included many of the fastest sports cars in the country. The first leg was held over three laps of the Campbell Circuit and saw the 2900-B Alfa Romeo of Hugh Hunter, which had won the 1938 Mille Miglia, beat the ex-Bira Delahaye, driven by Arthur Dobson, by 0.8sec, with the T150C Darracq of Ian Connell, which had won the 1937 French GP and Tourist Trophy, in third place.

There was excitement before the start of the second leg, five Mountain laps, as the Delahaye caught fire, but this was extinguished and it had no effect on Dobson, who won the race by just 2sec from Connell. Hunter failed to leave the start, as the Alfa Romeo had a broken gear selector. The D6/70 Delage which had won the 1938 Tourist Trophy was third, driven by Peter Aitken. The Delahaye came out again, driven by its owner, Rob Walker – later to be Stirling Moss's entrant in Formula 1 races – and won the Second Whitsun Mountain Handicap. The main Outer Circuit race, the Locke King Trophy, was won by Geoffrey Wooding (Talbot 105), while Jock Horsfall was in third place driving the ex-Bira ERA 'Remus', the only ERA which was raced on the Outer Circuit.

The Ford Motor Company hired the track on 17 June for a gymkhana, where the entire range of Ford cars was demonstrated and owners took part in driving tests. It was reported that there was an attendance of 30,000, possibly the largest crowd ever to attend the track.

On 8 July the JCC held its Members' Day. Hugh Hunter put in the best performance of the day,

BELOW *Sammy Davis in his Léon Bollée follows a De Dion round Howe's Corner in the Veteran Car Handicap at the 1939 August Bank Holiday meeting. His energetic passenger is Head, who was his riding mechanic in many events. (LAT)*

setting the highest speed in the High Speed Trial, then winning three races in the 2900-B Alfa Romeo. There was a mildly bizarre incident during the High Speed Trial when Blackford, driving an Essex, was flagged off, as officials considered he was driving too fast! The Light Car Club cancelled the three-hour sports car race which should have been held on 22 July, as only four entries were received.

Germany had annexed the remainder of Czechoslovakia in March and had then pressed claims for the Danzig Corridor which gave Poland access to the Baltic. Throughout the summer of 1939 the claims once again became more strident and threatening. By the beginning of August war seemed almost inevitable, so it was an anxious crowd which came to the track for the August Bank Holiday meeting on 7 August. There was a programme of 12 races and there was to be an attempt on the Outer Circuit lap record by Chris Staniland in the Multi-Union. Much work had been done on the car by 'Woolly' Worters and it had new suspension and more power. Reg Tanner, the Esso manager at the track, frequently timed cars which were being tested and his timing was respected by the drivers for its accuracy. Tanner timed the Multi-Union during practice for the meeting and said in later years that it had broken Cobb's lap record.

The main race of the day was the ten-lap Campbell Trophy, a scratch event, and this was an easy win for Raymond Mays in his 2-litre ERA, leading Bira home in the 8CM Maserati by 13.4sec. The Multi-Union was to make the record attempt after the last race but it ran in the Second August Outer Circuit Handicap and a valve stretched; even so, despite running on only seven cylinders it lapped at 142.30mph. A record attempt was impracticable and remains one of the great Brooklands what-might-have-beens.

The last race of the day, and the last ever held on the track, was the Third August Outer Circuit Handicap. It was fitting that it was a close finish, as the 5.3-litre Graham Page of George Baker held off the Talbot 105 of B. Burton to win by 0.2sec, with R.C. Money's MG Magnette in third place. The following day Raymond Mays brought out the ERA R4D and took the Campbell Circuit lap record at 77.79mph. Having realised the imminence of war he wanted to hold the lap record before it was too late.

Before the first race meeting of the season, in the spring of 1939 Brooklands was the finishing point for two ACU-observed runs by manufacturers. Triumph ran a Twin and a Tiger 100 from John O'Groats to Land's End and on to Brooklands, while BSA did a round-England run. The first actual motor cycle meeting was the BARC combined programme on 11 March with an Outer Circuit and two Mountain handicaps. Noel Pope was expected to make an attempt on the Outer Circuit lap record with his supercharged Brough, but conditions were unsuitable.

The Clubman's meeting on 1 April had the usual sprints and Pope ran in the three-lap BMCRC

Chris Staniland

Christopher (Chris) Staniland was born in 1905, the son of a Lincolnshire landowner. On leaving school he went to the RAF College, Cranwell, and was commissioned into the RAF. He began racing motor cycles in 1923 and his first success was on a 250cc Velocette at a Kent & Surrey MC meeting. He had several wins in 1924 riding a 500cc Norton both as a solo and with a sidecar, then in 1925 he joined Nigel Spring, who had succeeded O'Donovan as the Norton representative at Brooklands, and scored his first major victory, winning the 600cc 200-Mile Sidecar Race.

In 1926 he bought a Type 35A Bugatti and won his first car race, a Bugatti handicap at the Whitsun meeting. The Bugatti was tuned by 'Woolly' Worters, beginning an association which lasted until World War Two. Riding Worters's Exelsior-JAP Staniland won the 350cc 200-Mile race, and also broke class records with a Norton. He rode for Worters and Nigel Spring in 1927 and with Spring's Norton won the 600cc sidecar championship and gained a BMCRC Gold badge for a 100mph lap. He won two races at the 1928 BARC Easter meeting with a Type 37A Bugatti tuned by Worters and rode an Excelsior-JAP to victory in the 250cc 200-Mile race. He repeated the 250cc 200-Mile victory in 1929, and also won the 250cc solo and 350cc sidecar Brooklands championships. His talents had been recognised in the car world and he was a member of the Riley team in the 1928 Ulster TT.

Staniland left the RAF in 1930 and became the chief test pilot of Fairey Aviation, but continued to race, scoring a third win in the 250cc 200-Mile race on an Excelsior, as well as gaining wins and breaking class records with the Type 37A Bugatti. His motor cycle career ended in 1930, as Worters abandoned the sport when the trade support at Brooklands was withdrawn.

In 1931 Staniland shared the winning MG with the Earl of March in the JCC Double-12 and also won the 1,100cc class of the Ulster TT with a Riley. He raced little in 1932 and 1933, but in 1934 he drove T.A.S.O. ('Taso') Mathieson's Type 51 Bugatti and gained several successes. He lapped the track at 133.16mph with this car. It was accepted that to lap at over 120mph in a Type 35 or Type 51 Bugatti needed skill and courage, but it was an exceptional feat to exceed 130mph.

The demands of his work at Faireys gave him less time for racing, though he was a frequent visitor to Brooklands, arriving with the latest aircraft. In 1936 he bought a Tipo B Alfa Romeo and after a season Worters began the development of the car into the Multi-Union, which by 1938 was one of the fastest cars in England. In 1939 it seemed likely that Staniland would take the Outer Circuit lap record with it, but a misfire prevented a successful attempt at the last meeting in August. Staniland continued test flying during World War Two and was killed in 1942 while testing a Fairey Firefly which apparently had a mechanical failure. In the latter half of the1920s he was the most successful rider at the track and brought equal skill to racing cars and flying aircraft.

handicap. Despite being third in an All Comers' handicap he was unable to reach record speeds, although one new record was established, as Freddie Clarke lapped at 105.97mph on his 350cc Triumph Twin. The Brooklands Road Championships on 13 May drew a poor entry, but spectators were encouraged to attend by the entry

charge being reduced to 1s 0d. Before the racing began Sir Algernon Guinness unveiled a memorial plaque to Eric Fernihough on the clubhouse wall. Newman (Velocette) ran away with the ten-lap Junior race with White (Norton) in second place. The field of five 500cc riders was startled when Newman led the Seniors on his 350cc Velocette in

ABOVE *'Goldie' Gardner demonstrates his record-breaking MG, the first 1,100cc car to exceed 200mph, at the 1939 August meeting. (LAT)*

LEFT *The great 'might-have-been'. Chris Staniland's Multi-Union, photographed on the Railway Straight before the 1939 August meeting. (LAT)*

the opening laps, but he fell out and the race went to Ron Harris (Norton), leading from Aitchison's Norton and Tisdall's supercharged BMW.

The Cup day on 24 June was described by *Motor Cycling* as 'dull racing', but conditions were good and eight riders won Gold Stars for 100mph laps. The conditions encouraged Pope to make another lap record attempt, but this ended in a cloud of smoke when a piston broke. Pope was determined to have the record, but the weather conditions were unsuitable. Despite wind gusts and wet patches on the track he brought the Brough Superior-JAP out again on Tuesday 4 July and in an unspectacular run in front of a handful of spectators and track regulars, much as for Cobb in the Napier-Railton, he broke the motor cycle outright lap record held by Eric Fernihough at a speed of 124.51mph and established a record which would stand for all time.

Although it was not appreciated at the time, the Mountain Championship Day on Saturday 15 July was the last motor cycle race meeting to be held at the track. It had a programme of six races on the Outer circuit and Mountain with the

Championship races as the main events. In the 25-lap Junior Championship, Les Archer (Velocette) led all the way. He was followed home by B.E. Keys (Norton), who was disqualified for going the wrong side of a barrel in the Finishing Straight chicane, so Harry Lamacraft (Velocette) was second and Johnnie Lockett (Norton) was third. In the 25-lap Senior race, the last race of the day, Lockett was a convincing winner on his Norton, while Tisdall's blown BMW was second and Lamacraft rode well to take third place on his 350cc Velocette. One last record was broken on 12 August, when Freddie Clarke brought out a 501cc Triumph Twin and broke the 750cc lap record with a speed of 118.60mph. The outbreak of war resulted in the cancellation of a BMCRC meeting in September and the 'Hutchinson 100' in October.

When war came in 1939 it ended a major chapter in the story of Brooklands, and for many the most important. For over 30 years it had been the centre of a unique community which worked, played, lived and died there, and for some it was even a home. It had seen every emotion, from joy

BELOW *G.L. Baker brings his Graham-Paige out of the paddock. In this car he was winner of the Third August Outer Circuit Handicap, the very last race at Brooklands. (Brooklands Society)*

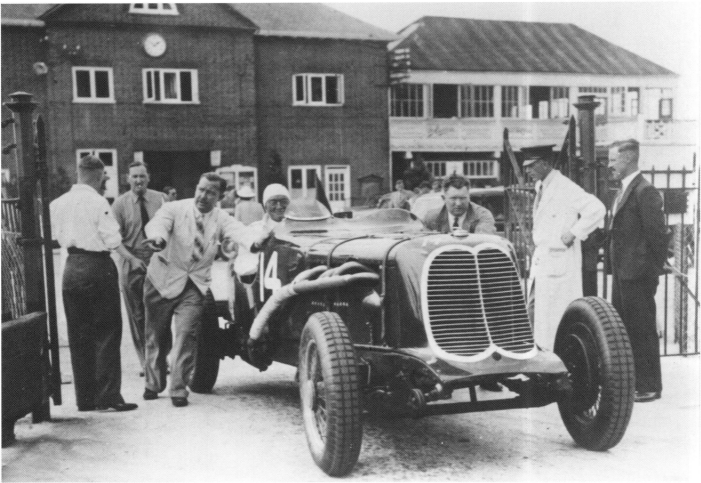

and elation to grief and anguish. As well as a sporting centre it had been an important business and industrial site, where many small businesses and industries had grown and flourished. It had also been a major testing ground for the motor industry. While its importance as an aviation centre was to burgeon in the future, its life as a motoring centre and a focus for motoring sport dwindled and died almost at once.

'Woolly' Worters, the motor cycle racer and tuner, probably summed up what those who were part of Brooklands felt about it in retrospect. In a comment he made in Charles Mortimer's book *Brooklands – Behind the Scenes*, he said: 'It was a marvellous experience. I flew from it and to it. I raced on it and I worked on it. I made most of my best friends there. It was very kind to me and I think it was the best period of my life'. There are very few left now who knew Brooklands before World War Two, but all those who did always spoke of it with an intense affection. It left an indelible mark on them and it seems that, like Worters, for them the years spent there were the best years of all.

LEFT *The Eric Fernihough memorial plaque which was unveiled on the wall of the BMCRC clubhouse at the Road Championship meeting on 13 May 1939. (Brooklands Society)*

BELOW *Noel Pope (right) and Francis Beart with the Brough Superior on which Pope broke the lap record on 4 July 1939. (Brooklands Society)*

CHAPTER TEN

AVIATION MATURES

During the 1920s the airship was considered to be the only practicable way to carry passengers by air over long distances, particularly over the Atlantic. In Britain it was also regarded as a means of rapid communication with the Empire. In 1924 the British Government launched the Empire communications scheme for an airship service to India and Canada. Vickers received a contract to build an airship, the R100, designed by Barnes Wallis, who had joined the company in 1913. The R100 was a successful design, but another airship, the R101, built to an official design from the Royal Airship Company, was a failure and crashed at Beauvais in France on its first overseas flight in October 1930, killing many passengers, including the Air Minister, Lord Thomson. Government support for airships ended immediately, and the R100 was scrapped. It was also realised that aircraft development had made immense advances in the 1920s and that the future of long-distance travel now lay with aircraft. Wallis had been working at Howden, in Yorkshire, but with the abandonment of airships he was moved to Brooklands, where he was appointed as Chief Designer (Structures), working under Rex Pierson.

In 1919 Lloyd George had formulated the 'Ten Year rule' which postulated that there would be ten years' warning of an impending war in Europe.

The Prince of Wales is greeted as he arrives at the GAPAN show on 20 May 1933. His personal pilot Flight Lieutenant Edward Fielden is alighting from the Prince's Vickers Viastra. (Brooklands Museum)

This rule was applied by successive governments in the 1920s, which kept the British services on little more than a care and maintenance basis, so aircraft manufacturers had few orders, and Sydney Camm said it was only the export market that kept Hawker alive. With surprising foresight, the rule was gradually set aside from 1930 onwards, though initially this provided little stimulus to the order books at Hawker and Vickers. Hawker continued with the production of the Hart and its variants, and a total of 1,430 were erected and test-flown at Brooklands. Almost as a sideline Hawker had produced the Tomtit, a Camm design, which was intended to be an elementary trainer for the RAF and a light aircraft for club flying. About 30 were built and some remained at Brooklands, but the need for space to build Harts soon ended Tomtit production.

The first production Fury was flown at Brooklands by Gerry Sayer on 25 March 1931 and the first batch of 27 had been test flown at the track within three weeks. Between 1931 and 1935 a further 213 Furies were built at Kingston, then erected and test flown at Brooklands. The RAF only equipped six squadrons with Mk 1 and Mk 2 Furies, but many overseas orders were received. A

separate design, the Nimrod, which had many similarities to the Fury, was developed for the Fleet Air Arm and Sayer flew the first production aircraft at the track on 14 October 1931. A total of 85 passed through Brooklands, including a handful for overseas customers. To assist development, a public company named Hawker Aircraft Ltd was formed in 1933 which acquired the assets of H.G. Hawker Engineering Co. The company expanded when the Gloster Aircraft Co was bought outright in February 1934, and there was further expansion when it amalgamated with Armstrong-Siddeley Development Co Ltd to form the Hawker Siddeley Group in July 1935.

Vickers was maintaining a small but steady production of Virginias for the RAF but, sadly, a Virginia crashed at the foot of the Byfleet Banking on 16 September 1933, the day of the BRDC '500', when it overshot while landing, killing the pilot, Flying Officer L.M. Few. There had been another fatal flying accident the previous day, when Lady Clayton, the pilot of a Spartan Arrow, was killed when she fell from the cockpit while taxiing.

The Air Ministry had issued a specification for a torpedo bomber in 1926 and Vickers produced a prototype, but with the government's lethargic

BELOW *A group of Hawker workers with a Fury Mk I of the first production batch, on the airfield in April 1931. (Brooklands Society)*

approach to defence contracts at that time an order for the aircraft, the Vildebeest, was not given until 1931, and the first production machine did not fly at the track until 5 September 1932. There were 220 Vildebeests ordered for the RAF and 12 went to the RNZAF. The aircraft was designed by Pierson, who also produced a development, the Vincent, as a general purpose aircraft and light bomber. Vickers received a contract in 1933 to build 197 Vincents.

During this period the company had also been working on the Vickers B.19/27, a biplane heavy bomber intended as a replacement for the Virginia. It became known as the Vanox and was a step forward, as it was of all-metal construction. Development of the Vanox continued from 1929 until 1933, with the prototype shuttling continuously between Brooklands and Martlesham Heath, the RAF evaluation and experimental unit. It was revised and rebuilt several times, but eventually the project was abandoned. In the meantime, in1932, there was a major reconstruction of the Vickers factory which provided more space within the existing walls.

In March 1930 the Air Ministry issued a new specification, M.1/30, for a biplane torpedo bomber, and Barnes Wallis began work on a design, utilising the experience of light alloy stressed members which he had gained while working on airships. The prototype was first flown at the track by 'Mutt' Summers on 11 January 1933. Test flying continued during the year and on 23 November the aircraft broke up while in a high-speed dive, Summers and his observer, John Radcliffe, escaping by parachute to land unhurt on the Members' Hill. The fuselage

and the dummy torpedo which was being carried landed in Weybridge cemetery, and the track was littered with pieces of the aircraft. Undaunted, Wallis returned to his drawing board, where he had been working on a design for a new general purpose biplane bomber to comply with specification G.4/31. In this he used a semi-geodetic construction, but both he and Pierson realised that, despite Air Ministry orthodoxy, the days of the biplane were numbered, and while working on the G.4/31 design they began parallel work on a geodetic monoplane bomber. When completed, the G.4/31 was first flown at the track on 16 August 1934, then taken to Martlesham for evaluation.

Adolf Hitler came to power as German Chancellor on 30 January 1933, and it became evident that the 'Ten Year rule' was obsolete when Germany withdrew from the Geneva Disarmament Conference in October. In May 1934 an expansion scheme was announced for the RAF, intended to increase the number of squadrons from 75 to 116 in five years. Already, in August 1933, Sydney Camm had been having discussions with the Air Ministry about a monoplane fighter which he had devised using the Rolls-Royce PV12 (later the Merlin) engine. The project complied loosely with the F.5/34 specification, but the Air Ministry soon issued a new specification F.36/34, intended for Camm's design, and Hawker received a contract for the building of a prototype in February 1935.

In the Vickers design office at Brooklands, Wallis had completed the design of the geodetic monoplane, and a prototype was built and flown for the first time on 19 June 1935. Summers took Wallis

ABOVE *The Vickers Vespa Mk VII in which Cyril Uwins set a World altitude record of 43,976ft (13,404m) on 16 September 1932. (BAE Systems per Brooklands Museum)*

as a passenger on its second flight. The Air Ministry had already placed an order with Vickers for 150 of the G.4/31 biplane, but it was realised that the new monoplane was a huge advance, so the G.4/31 order was cancelled and an order for 96 of the new aircraft, the Wellesley, was placed on 10 September 1935. A total of 177 Wellesleys was built, the last leaving the Brooklands factory on 30 May 1938.

Camm's monoplane fighter was finished at Kingston and taken by road to Brooklands, where it was first flown by George Bulman on 6 November 1935. He climbed away to the west, not retracting the undercarriage, and when he landed after a short flight Bulman said to Camm, who had jumped up onto the wing: 'Another winner, I think'. This historic flight, the first of one of the greatest aeroplanes of all, was wholly successful, and the aircraft was named the Hurricane.

Rex Pierson

Rex (Reginald) Pierson was born in 1891 and joined Vickers at the Crayford works just before World War One as a graduate engineering apprentice, after learning to fly with the Vickers School at Brooklands. He was appointed as chief designer in 1915 and given the task of redesigning the unsuccessful Bullet scout. In 1916 he moved with the design office to Imperial Court in Knightsbridge, London, and then after the war to Brooklands. His first major design was the Vimy, first flown late in 1917, and he allegedly carried out the design then supervised the building and testing of the prototype in four months. The success of the Vimy in making the first transatlantic flight moved him to the forefront of aircraft designers. Pierson followed the Vimy with the unattractive Vulcan and Viking amphibian, and then developed the Vimy into a civil aircraft, which led to the Virginia/Valentia series, providing the RAF with a heavy bomber and military transport into the early 1930s.

As a diversion from aircraft Pierson designed the body for Malcolm Campbell's Napier-Campbell 'Blue Bird', which took the Land Speed Record in 1928. The single-engined Vespa biplane gave another Pierson design a record when it took the World Altitude Record in 1932. It was also in 1932 that Pierson, with Barnes Wallis working on the structural engineering, began the design of an aircraft to Air Ministry specification B.9/32 which was to become the Wellington, one of the all-time greats of the RAF. Pierson developed the Wellington and also produced the Warwick design, but his proposals for four- and six-engined bombers were not accepted by the Air Ministry.

To prepare Vickers for post-war aviation, in the later years of World War Two Pierson designed the Viking, which used many Wellington components. In September 1945 he was appointed Chief Engineer of Vickers and began work on the Viscount design, but unfortunately he did not complete this, as he died in February 1948. To some extent Pierson is the forgotten man among the panoply of Vickers designers, although as Vickers' chief engineer for 28 years he was responsible for the greatest designs which came from the Brooklands factory, and was certainly the equal of such renowned designers as Mitchell, Camm and Chadwick.

Taking aircraft from Kingston to Brooklands was becoming an increasing problem for Hawker, and with the prospect of bigger orders there was a need for production lines to be set up at Brooklands. To provide these, the last of the pre-1914 sheds adjoining the Byfleet Banking was demolished at the end of 1933 and a new erection shop built by Boulton & Paul was completed in May 1935. In this, Hawker could build aircraft from scratch, though production still continued at Kingston.

In October 1932 the Air Ministry issued specification B.9/32 for a twin-engined medium bomber. Vickers submitted a design study, the joint work of Pierson and Wallis, Pierson having prepared the overall design while Wallis was responsible for the structure of the fuselage, using the geodetic method of construction. The original design was developed rapidly and at the suggestion of Vickers the weight limits imposed by the Air Ministry were soon abandoned. A prototype was built at Brooklands which was certainly the most advanced bomber design of its day, and this was flown for the first time on 15 June 1936 by 'Mutt' Summers, accompanied by Wallis and Trevor Westbrook, the production manager, as passengers. It was called the Wellington, and an initial order for 180 was placed in August 1936. At the end of that year Percy Maxwell-Muller resigned as works manager, having worked for Vickers since 1913, and was replaced by Trevor Westbrook, who, before moving to Brooklands, had been the manager of the Supermarine factory at Southampton.

The prototype Wellington was destroyed in a crash at Martlesham on 19 April 1937, but there had been extensive alterations to the design and the aircraft which went into production bore little similarity to the first machine. Speed of production was essential, and at the outset a target was set of making one Wellington a day.

During 1937 the factory was expanded to the south so frontage to the Fork was extended. The new frontage was similar to the existing one which bore the huge 'Vickers Ltd Brooklands' sign, and *Motor Cycling* commented that an unobservant motor cyclist might think he had reached the Fork sooner than he expected. As Wellesley production was tailed off more space became available and the erecting shop was reorganised, windows were let into the side facing the track, and the doors no longer opened onto the Fork but were placed at the southern end of the new shop. Two assembly lines were set up and the first production Wellington was wheeled across the Fork and over the River Wey for its test flight on 23 December 1937. Production gradually built up and 34 aircraft had been delivered to the RAF by the end of 1938,

but the imminence of war subsequently speeded production and 271 were delivered in 1939.

Another bomber design, the Warwick, had been developed in parallel with the Wellington and was superficially similar in appearance. It was intended to have Rolls-Royce Vulture or Napier Sabre engines but production problems with both held the Warwick back, so the first prototype was not flown at Brooklands until 13 August 1939.

Flight testing of the Hurricane prototype continued at Brooklands until March 1936, when it was taken to Martlesham, but the tests had been so successful that the directors of Hawker took a gamble. They assumed an order would be placed, so in April 1936 plans were made to start production of a batch of 1,000 aircraft. This galvanised the Air Ministry into action and an order for 600 machines was placed on 3 June. It has been estimated that the foresight of the Hawker directors provided the RAF with several hundred additional Hurricanes in the crucial summer months of 1940.

Production began at Kingston and Brooklands, though there was a delay as it was decided that an improved version of the Merlin would be fitted and some redesign was necessary. The first production aircraft – L1547, piloted by Philip Lucas – flew at the track on 12 October 1937 and by the end of the year five aircraft had been completed and four had been delivered to the RAF at Northolt. The wings, centre section and tail were made at Kingston, then taken to Brooklands where the engines, delivered from Rolls-Royce, were fitted, and the fully-equipped fuselage and centre section was covered

with fabric then doped at the end of the erection shop. After that the machine was wheeled across to the flight shed, where the wings were fitted in preparation for an engine run and ground and flight testing. By the end of October 1939 545 Hurricanes had been built at Brooklands.

King George VI visited Brooklands on 8 December 1937. He inspected the Wellington and Wellesley production lines and was then driven round the track to the Hawker sheds, where George Bulman showed him the assembling of the first Hurricanes.

On 6 September 1938 a production Hurricane was tested by John Hindmarsh, an active driver at the track who had won the Le Mans 24-Hour race in 1935 and had left the RAF to join Hawker as a production test pilot. For reasons that are unknown, Hindmarsh did not pull out of a dive and crashed fatally on St George's Hill, the estate adjoining the track. Hindmarsh was married to Violette Cordery, who had been awarded the Dewar Trophy for her Invicta record runs in 1929.

Vickers had built a fighter prototype, the Venom, to comply with specification F.5/34. It was a development of an earlier design, the Jockey, which had first flown in 1930 and had been abandoned in 1932. The Venom was first flown at Brooklands on 17 June 1936, but it had a Bristol Aquila radial engine and was underpowered. Development of the Venom nevertheless continued at Brooklands and Eastleigh until it was scrapped in 1939. It had a very high landing speed and Aero Club members would come out to watch it land in the expectation of a drama which was never fulfilled.

ABOVE A Virginia which overshot the airfield on landing on 16 September 1933, killing the pilot, Flying Officer Few. The cars in the background are competing in the BRDC 500-Mile race. (Brooklands Society)

ABOVE *A production line of Harts being built in the Vickers sheds adjoining the Fork in 1934. (BAE Systems per Brooklands Museum)*

While Hawker and Vickers built, tested and developed military aircraft at Brooklands, with increasing intensity throughout the 1930s, the sporting and club flying continued to flourish. By February 1930 the School of Flying was sufficiently busy that Captain Duncan Davis had three full-time assistant instructors. The School season that year opened with a meeting on 2 March which was attended by Lord Thomson, the Air Minister, and Sir Sefton Brancker, the director of Civil Aviation. John Tranum, a Danish professional parachutist, gave a demonstration jump, and to the delight of the crowd the wind carried him into the sewage farm!

In May 1930 the BARC introduced an associated flying club, the Brooklands Aero Club, which gave BARC members flying facilities at a reduced rate, cheap lessons, and the use of the BARC and aerodrome clubhouses. C.S. Burney was appointed as the secretary and 97 aircraft attended the formal opening on 17 May. HRH Prince George (later the Duke of Kent) consented to become an honorary member of the club, which had over 200 members by November 1930. In March 1931 the school moved into the smaller two-bay Belfast hangar, between those used by Hawker and Vickers. In spite of the economic depression the prospects for flying at Brooklands were sufficiently rosy that a new clubhouse was planned. It was designed by Graham Dawbarn and construction began in the summer of 1931, the contractor being F. & F.H. Higgs Ltd. It provided a restaurant, lounge, bars,

RIGHT *Hawker commenced production of Harts at Brooklands when the new sheds were completed beside the Byfleet Banking in 1935. (BAE Systems per Brooklands Museum)*

offices, an observation platform and a control tower. The cost was £7,439. The *Glasgow Herald* said: 'It will be the last word in ultra-modernity of design and construction. With its straight lines and solid masses of concrete, the main building typifies the latest thought in architecture.'

The clubhouse and its social activities were managed by the BARC and it became the venue for the club's dances, which had previously been held in the paddock clubhouse. Brooklands Aviation Ltd managed the airfield and was responsible for the Aero Club and the School of Flying. The clubhouse was formally opened on 28 May 1932 with a display organised by the Guild of Air Pilots and Navigators and was attended by some distinguished aviators, including Amy Johnson and Jim Mollison. It was a very wet day and the public attendance was small. A parade of aircraft was followed with displays by George Bulmer in a Fury and Chris Staniland in a Fairey Firefly. Four aircraft took part in a nine-lap race around pylons sited at each end of the track, then three RAF Furies did a formation aerobatic display. Among the aircraft demonstrated was a new de Havilland design, the DH82A Tiger Moth trainer, which was to become a flying legend.

The opening of the new clubhouse was timely, as the Royal Aero Club decided that the 1932 King's Cup Race should be based at Brooklands on Friday 8 and Saturday 9 July. On the first day the course was Brooklands–Portsmouth–Bristol–

Chester–Leicester–Ipswich–Northampton–Brooklands, a total of 747 miles, and on the second day it was Brooklands–Portsmouth–Bristol–Brooklands–Bristol–Northampton–Brooklands, totalling 493 miles. *Motor Sport* commented: 'The selection of Brooklands … is significant … This aerodrome may become principal centre of sporting flying once more. In the early days it vied with Hendon … but of recent years it has sunk rather into the background. I think this year will see its come-back.' There were 37 starters. The limit aircraft received 3hr 16min start from the

ABOVE *The first production Vickers Valentia on the airfield in May 1934. (BAE Systems per Brooklands Museum)*

ABOVE *The prototype Hurricane on the airfield when it first flew, on 6 November 1935. (BAE Systems per Brooklands Museum)*

scratch Avro Mailplane, and at the end of the first day the leader was W.H. Hope in a DH83 Fox Moth, while DH80A Puss Moths were in second and third places.

The starting order on the second day was decided by the handicap order, and at the finish

Hope was the winner, while in second place was a Comper Swift entered by the Prince of Wales and flown by his personal pilot, Flight Lieutenant Edward Fielden, who failed to cross the official finishing line when he arrived at Brooklands and had to take off again to cross it correctly. This he managed without

losing his place to Squadron Leader Walter Runciman, who was flying a Puss Moth.

There was another major race on 6 August 1932, the London–Newcastle, which should have been run when the clubhouse was opened on 28 May but was postponed because of the weather. This had a field of eight aircraft flying over a 264-mile course to Cramlington, outside Newcastle. The winner was the Hon Richard Westenra in a DH60 Gipsy Moth. Westenra repeated his victory in the 1933 race, held on 12 August. Earlier in 1933 Brooklands was honoured by a visit from the Prince of Wales, who was flown in to the second GAPAN display on 20 May in his Vickers Viastra, again piloted by his personal pilot 'Mouse' Fielden.

The College of Aeronautical & Automobile Engineering, which was based at Sydney Street in Chelsea, had opened a branch at the track in October 1931 to give the aviation students practical experience. The college leased a building in the 'Village' and the opportunity of working at Brooklands was a great incentive to students, though it seems that for many the other activities at the track had a greater attraction than attending the college courses.

Personal Flying Services Ltd, a charter company, moved from Croydon to Brooklands at the end of

1932 and became incorporated in Brooklands Airways Ltd, an associated company of the school, in 1933, operating a Junkers F-13 and a Puss Moth.

The King's Cup helped Brooklands to maintain its position as a centre of club flying, but there was strong opposition from Hanworth and Heston, both only a few miles away and offering equally good flying facilities, though Brooklands had the edge on the social side. The Brooklands Aero Club held many minor events and competitions; spot landings, navigational exercises and forced landing tests were organised to amuse and entertain members, the winners receiving a silver spoon surmounted with the club badge. A less-publicised benefit of these events was the extra revenue which they raised for the club. Despite government encouragement, National Flying Services went into receivership in 1933 and the chief instructor, Max Findlay, joined Duncan Davis at the Brooklands School.

The 'Dawn Patrol' was a regular feature of club flying in the 1930s. This was a pastime initiated at Brooklands in 1933. Members of a flying club had to land on the airfield of another club, having evaded a patrol of the 'raided' club's aircraft without their own aircraft registration letters being noted. The successful pilots received a free breakfast from the raided club. There was a club competition with a difference on 20 May 1933, a Vertical Interception Race in which pilots had to climb to 3,000ft to a 'finishing line' marked by a hovering Cierva autogyro. The winner was Laurence Lipton in a Gipsy Moth previously owned by Amy Johnson.

ABOVE *King George VI inspects a Wellesley cockpit during his visit to the Vickers factory on 8 December 1937. (BAE Systems per Brooklands Museum)*

LEFT *The engines of the prototype Wellington are run-up on the Fork in June 1936. (BAE Systems per Brooklands Museum)*

RIGHT *An early production Hurricane is displayed beside the Finishing Straight at a race meeting during 1938. (BAE Systems per Brooklands Museum)*

BELOW *A Vickers Virginia is in the foreground at the formal opening of the Brooklands Aero Club on 17 May 1930. (Flight)*

The 1934 London–Newcastle, with 14 competitors, was run on 11 August and Lipton was the winner in his DH Gipsy Moth, the third year this type of aircraft had won. An annual 'At Home', to which the Shoreham, Lympne and Northampton clubs were invited, was a popular event. There was an inter-club competition in which each club entered a team of three pilots, who had to fly a set programme of climbing turns, steep turns, a spin and a forced landing approach with engine off, to land as close as possible to the airfield centre circle. The London–Newcastle, now a regular fixture, with the finish moved to Woolsington, was run again on 27 July 1935. Flight Lieutenant J.B. Wilson, the chief test pilot of the British Aircraft Manufacturing Co, was the winner, heading the field of 11 in a prototype BA1 Eagle.

The last London–Newcastle was held on 8 August 1936. The first two aircraft to cross the finish line were disqualified as they had missed a turning point at Yeadon, and the winner was Bill Humble in a Miles Hawk Speed Six. He would subsequently become a Hawker test pilot.

To encourage the nation to become air-minded, annual Empire Air Days had been started in 1934 by the Air League. RAF airfields and selected civilian

BELOW *The Brooklands Aero Club building, opened on 28 May 1932. (Brooklands Society)*

airfields were open to the public, who could look at aircraft at close quarters and watch flying displays. Brooklands participated, and at the 1936 day, on 23 May, a 1915 Caudron G3 was demonstrated. This had been flown to Brooklands from Brussels three days earlier by Ken Waller, the chief instructor of the Brooklands School. It became part of the collection of R.G.J. 'Dick' Nash, the holder of the car record for the Test Hill. Nash had premises adjoining the 'Village' where he ran the International Horseless Carriage Co and preserved early aircraft and motor cars. Nash, together with Richard Shuttleworth, was one of the first to appreciate the importance of preserving early aircraft.

There was high drama on Saturday 24 October 1936 when the hangar of the Brooklands School of Flying burnt down. The fire began in the engine overhaul workshop on a mezzanine floor and soon spread to the roof. As it was a Saturday most of the school's aircraft were flying, but six machines which were being serviced or overhauled were destroyed. The fire had little impact on the school's activities and 15 hours' flying were recorded the following day. Sixty-three 'A' licences were gained by pupils during the year.

Until the hangar was rebuilt the Club's aircraft were housed in a Vickers hangar. The new hangar, constructed by Boulton & Paul, contained maintenance and engine shops, with offices, lecture rooms and stores in adjoining annexes. At the beginning of 1937 the club had 790 members and in

an aerobatic display with a production aircraft. At the 1938 'At Home' on 18 June there was great excitement when Jeffrey Quill arrived from Eastleigh and gave a display with the first production Spitfire. Quill was a Vickers test pilot and had made some of the early flights in the Wellesley. He had moved to Supermarine, a Vickers subsidiary, for the development of the Spitfire and the first prototype was often seen at Brooklands in 1936. It has been suggested, perhaps apocryphally, that Quill used it as transport when returning to his home at Weybridge.

By the spring of 1938 the possibility of war was beginning to make its mark. The growing numbers of new aircraft being test flown were camouflaged, with the upper surfaces painted in earth and dark green. In August the Civil Air Guard was established, but with the increasing number of Hawker and Vickers test flights it was decided that it was impracticable to have a branch at Brooklands. An Air Defence Cadet Corps section (later to become the Air Training Corps) was formed instead and by the end of November had 70 recruits. It was an indication of the importance that the Government attached to Brooklands that on 9 September 1938 the Air Minister, Sir Kingsley Wood, inspected the Vickers and Hawker factories.

In April 1939 Aero Club members flew along designated routes over Surrey to assist in the training of the Royal Observer Corps and a month later Vickers received a 'Secret' document from the Air Ministry giving details of how the factory, track and airfield should be camouflaged in the event of war. The last Aero Club event was held on 20 August, which, perhaps appropriately, was a 'bombing' competition.

LEFT A line-up of DH60 Moths in the Brooklands School of Flying hangar, which was destroyed by fire on 24 October 1936. (Brooklands Museum)

BELOW A Hart flies over the airfield in 1932/3. The Aero Club building is immediately beneath it. The School of Flying hangar is evident, and at the top right of the photograph are the original sheds which were demolished in 1934 to make way for the new Hawker assembly shops. (Brooklands Society)

the spring it re-equipped with Tiger Moths. These worked hard: after a year, the first had flown 850 hours and 60,000 miles and made 7,000 landings. Sixty students obtained 'A' licences in 1937 and seven obtained the 'B' commercial licence.

The 'At Home' days maintained their popularity, and a Hawker or Vickers test pilot would often give

1939–1945 WAR

T he outbreak of war on 3 September 1939 made little difference to Brooklands initially, although there was an immediate ban on private flying. The remaining BARC and BMCRC fixtures were cancelled, but club members could still go into the Clubhouse. Bill Boddy recalls visiting the track several times during September and October 1939, and early in September Charles Mortimer witnessed the BARC staff having a large bonfire behind the Clubhouse as the offices were cleared, and watched the tuning sheds being emptied while cars and motor cycles were taken away. Many of those who had worked at the track, tuning and preparing cars and motor cycles, were quickly recruited by aircraft manufacturers and aero engine companies, where their expertise was invaluable. At this time there was a great break with the past when 'Ebby' died on 11 December 1939.

This was the period of the 'phoney' war, when little happened after the fall of Poland. Vickers was producing Wellingtons and continuing work on the Warwick prototype and Hawker was increasing the production of Hurricanes. There were two fatal accidents in 1940: a Wellington crashed soon after take-off on 8 March, killing all the crew, and Flight Lieutenant E.G. Russell-Stacey, a Hawker test pilot,

The Wellington production line at Brooklands, late in 1939. The geodetic fuselages are being covered with fabric. (BAE Systems per Brooklands Museum)

was killed on 28 August when taking off from the airfield in a Hurricane.

A new Hawker factory had meanwhile been built at Langley in Middlesex in the late 1930s, and a Hurricane production line was laid down there which produced its first aircraft in October 1939. Brooklands was becoming crowded with the testing of production Wellingtons and Hurricanes, so the test flying of prototype and development Hawker aircraft, including the Typhoon – the next generation Hawker fighter – was moved to Langley as soon as the airfield became operational. Some of the small engineering companies at Brooklands took on war contracts, while Thomson & Taylor was enlisted to store parts and test engines for the Fairmile Marine Co at Cobham. This had been formed by Noel Macklin, using the small factory where he had formerly made Invicta and Railton cars, and had become engaged in building motor torpedo boats and light naval craft.

With the invasion of Norway in April 1940 the tempo of the war quickened. The Clubhouse had closed and the whole site was soon requisitioned for the use of Vickers. It is reputed that the last car to make a complete circuit of the track was the 1908 GP Itala driven by Sam Clutton, one of the founders of the Vintage Sports Car Club, who was alleged to have obtained access early in the summer of 1940.

With the fall of France and the basing of the Luftwaffe across the Channel, Brooklands was only 150 miles from the nearest German airfields in Northern France, so defence preparations were intensified. The track was covered with camouflage netting, the buildings were painted green and brown, a battery of Bofors 40mm anti-aircraft guns was mounted beside the Byfleet Banking, and about eight barrage balloons flew over the site to deter low level attacks. The Luftwaffe knew the value of Brooklands to the British war effort, since the air attaché at the German Embassy would have made regular visits to the track and reconnaissance photographs had been taken before the war began. There was a map of the track dated 26 June 1939 in the Luftwaffe atlas of targets, with the Vickers and Hawker sites delineated.

The first air raid on Brooklands occurred on 24 July 1940 when a Junkers Ju88 circled the track then lowered its undercarriage and followed several aircraft in 'the circuit' preparing to land. It levelled out and dropped 12 small bombs on the 'Village', but the aim was poor and they all missed their target. An aircraft which flew over on 2 September was possibly a reconnaissance flight, as no bombs were dropped.

The Battle of Britain was reaching its height and it was the aim of the Luftwaffe to destroy RAF

BELOW *Wellington geodetic fuselages under construction in the Vickers assembly shops at the Fork in the early days of World War Two. (BAE Systems per Brooklands Museum)*

Fighter Command so that air supremacy could be achieved as a precursor to invasion. Throughout August 1940 there had been continuous attacks on RAF airfields, but despite their intensity the RAF was still fighting as strongly as ever, so on 1 September the Luftwaffe had issued a directive for the destruction of factories building fighter aircraft. On Wednesday 4 September the Germans mounted a series of raids across southern England which seem to have been intended to mask a formation of about 20 Messerschmitt Bf110s of II and III KG/76 flying from Abbeville, which crossed the coast at Littlehampton at about 1:00pm and flew north across Sussex and Surrey. The Bf110 was a twin-engined fighter capable of carrying a bomb load and half the aircraft used carried bombs, the remainder serving as an escort. The formation, which was flying at about 6,000ft, was intercepted between Guildford and Brooklands by nine Hurricanes of 253 Squadron, which shot down six Bf110s. Unfortunately, however, the Hurricanes had attacked the escort and the bomb-laden aircraft carried on to Brooklands. Perhaps shaken by the Hurricane attack, the Bf110 pilots missed the Hawker site and directed their attack on the Vickers factory at the Fork.

It was about 1:20pm. The lunch break was soon to end and the workers were making their way back into the factory, where some were queuing to clock-on. At least six 500kg bombs were dropped, possibly more, and the factory was also strafed with machine-gun fire. Sadly 85 workers were killed and 419 injured, most of the dead being in the clocking-on queue. There was no warning of the raid, as the air raid sirens only sounded six minutes after it had ended. Although considerable damage was done inside the factory Wellington production restarted within 24 hours, though the rate of production was slowed for some time. To minimise disruption in the event of more raids, sub-assembly plants were set up in small workshops in the Weybridge area, and a dance hall in Addlestone was even used. The Ministry of Aircraft Production gave an immediate order that the two prototype Warwicks and all development and experimental Wellingtons were to be moved to the Vickers factory at Blackpool.

On the night of 6 September a single bomb was dropped on one of the Hawker assembly sheds. This hit a roof girder and bounced through the side wall without exploding or doing any significant damage. There was another attack on Saturday 21 September when a single Ju88 approached from the west and, dodging the barrage balloons and the fire from the Bofors battery, dropped three bombs on the Hawker assembly hangars beside the Byfleet

Banking. One fell on the boiler shed and did not explode; the second also failed to explode when it buried itself in the dope shop floor; and the third fell through the roof of the erecting shop and then bounced outside onto the concrete apron. A Canadian bomb disposal squad was called from Box Hill, and Lieutenant John Patton of the Royal Canadian Engineers found the bomb on the apron. Realising it would cause great damage if it exploded, he rolled it onto a sheet of corrugated iron and, using a truck, towed it to the edge of a bomb crater on the airfield and rolled it gently in, where it exploded the following day without causing any damage. For his bravery Lieutenant Patton was awarded the George Cross, while Captain Douglas Cunnington, the adjutant of the unit, who helped in the removal, received the George Medal. These were the first decorations awarded to the Canadian Army in World War Two. The other two bombs were defused and removed without exploding.

In addition to the Bofors battery, a detachment of 5th AA Division Royal Artillery was based at

ABOVE *Maurice 'Mutt' Summers, Vickers's Chief Test Pilot from 1929 until 1951, seen in 1941 after breaking the west to east Atlantic record in the first production Consolidated Liberator. (Brooklands Society)*

Brooklands with sixteen 3.7in AA guns, the troops manning these being billeted in the Clubhouse. When the Luftwaffe abandoned daylight raids and started its night Blitz in the autumn of 1940 these guns saw action almost every night as part of the ring of anti-aircraft defences surrounding London. They gained a success on the night of Saturday 20 April when a Ju88 of 1/KG76 was hit at about 10:30pm and crashed at Slinfold in Sussex, the crew of four being killed. There was a second success on 3 May, when a Ju88 of 9/KG77 was hit at about 1:00am and crashed on Fairmile Common, only a few miles from Brooklands. The crew of this aircraft baled out and became prisoners.

Throughout 1940 the Wellington was the main heavy bomber of the RAF, so the pressure on Vickers to produce more was intense. New factories had been built at Chester and Blackpool and production began at the former in 1940, with an output of 487 aircraft during the year. Production did not begin at Blackpool until 1941 and its output was initially slow, so the main burden fell on Brooklands. Despite the hold-ups caused by the raid in September, 506 Wellingtons were built at the track in 1940. At the beginning of 1941 the first four-engined Stirlings and Halifaxes reached Bomber Command, but the build-up of these types was slow and the Wellington continued to be its mainstay. During the year 721 left the Brooklands factory.

There was a great need for more production facilities and gradually the Vickers factory began encroaching onto the racing track. A gap was cut in the Byfleet Banking to make an entrance road to Hawker from the west and at the end of 1940 a huge excavation was made on the Members' Banking adjacent to the Members' Bridge, to recess a large workshop building into it. Wellington fuselages were built in this before being moved to a large Bellman hangar which was built on the Finishing Straight, just above the Clubhouse, where the fuselages went in at one end and completed aircraft came out at the other, ready to be taken across the River Wey for flight testing. Today this hangar – now known as the Wellington Hangar – houses the older aircraft of the Museum Collection.

Another hangar was erected adjacent to the Fork and two were built on the Railway Straight, one as a finishing shed to complete Warwicks and the other for aircraft repairs. Some dummy buildings were erected along the top of the Members' Banking, which was covered with camouflage netting held up by countless poles driven into the track surface. Holes were also made to plant saplings, intended to conceal the track. There was similar camouflage on the Byfleet Banking.

By the end of 1941 the Hurricane was being produced in large numbers at the Hawker factory at Langley, and also at Gloucester and by the Austin Motor Company at Birmingham. Late in October 1942 the Brooklands production line was closed down and all Hawker production at the track ceased. In all, 3,012 Hurricanes had been built at Brooklands and among these had been the majority of the machines which had fought in the Battle of Britain. With this closure the links with Brooklands begun by Tommy Sopwith and continued by Hawker were broken after 32 years. The workshops and buildings occupied by Hawker were taken over by Vickers, as Wellington production was still a high priority, and in 1942 679 Wellingtons were built. In addition more space was needed for a Warwick production line. Wellington production ended at Brooklands in 1943 and a total of 2,515 had been built at the track when the line was closed.

Barnes Wallis and his staff were moved to the adjacent Burhill Golf Club, and with the Warwick design established he directed his attentions to a new bomber design. In 1936 the Air Ministry had issued specification B.12/36 for a four-engined bomber and Wallis had worked with Rex Pierson to produce a design which was basically an enlarged Warwick. This design was not accepted, as the Short Stirling and Handley Page Halifax were preferred, principally because Wallis's design had a wingspan of over 100ft which was too big to enter standard-sized RAF hangars. When the hangar size stipulation was dropped an improved design was offered, but this too was rejected. Several other designs were considered, including two with six engines.

A new specification, B.5/41, was issued in 1941 calling for a four-engined high-altitude bomber, for which the Vickers design was accepted. This became known as the Windsor and used the geodetic method of construction. Three prototypes were built at Foxwarren, the development workshop near the track. The first was taken to Farnborough for erection and testing and first flew on 23 October 1943. The second was taken to Wisley for its first flight, Wisley being an airfield about three miles south of Brooklands, adjoining the A3 London–Portsmouth road. The site had been found when 'Mutt' Summers had made a forced landing there, and it was developed into an additional airfield for Vickers and opened in 1943. Many new aircraft were flown out of Brooklands to Wisley for additional flight testing. All in all 6,376 aircraft were manufactured at Brooklands during World War Two.

Since the beginning of the war, while working on his various aircraft designs, Wallis had been pondering upon the best method of damaging the

German economy and crippling Nazi war production. He concluded that if the dams which held the water supplying the hydro-electric schemes for the Ruhr industrial area could be breached, industrial output would be severely hampered if not halted. He suggested initially that giant bombs should be dropped on the dams, but there were no suitable aircraft to carry these. Persisting with his research, he calculated that if a bomb could be dropped into the water right up against the dam wall, and exploded at a fixed depth, the dam would be breached.

Wallis spent much time working out the size of the bomb, the height from which it would have to be dropped, and the speed of the aircraft, and concluded that a 6,000lb bomb would suffice if it was dropped against the dam wall. This led him to devise a bouncing bomb which would be released at a fixed distance from the dam and would bounce across the water until it hit the dam, then roll down the face of the wall until it exploded at a fixed depth, triggered by a hydrostatic pistol.

The importance of the Ruhr dams had been appreciated by the RAF before war began, but these were dismissed as targets as there was no suitable weapon to destroy them. When Wallis's bouncing bomb was suggested to Sir Arthur Harris,

the C-in-C of Bomber Command, he initially dismissed it as impracticable, but by the beginning of 1943 he was won over and Wallis's design was accepted. Trials of prototypes then began, to which George Edwards, the Experimental Works Manager at Brooklands, made important contributions. The outcome was the 'Dam Busters' Raid' on 16/17 May 1943, one of the greatest flying exploits of the war. A smaller version of the bouncing bomb was also designed to be carried by the DH98 Mosquito, and several Mosquitos came to Brooklands to be modified to carry it.

The development of the Avro Lancaster had meanwhile produced an aircraft which could carry the giant bombs conceived by Wallis at the beginning of the war, so he turned his attention to the design of these weapons. His first design was the 12,000lb 'Tallboy', which the RAF first dropped on 8 February 1944. These were used by Bomber Command until the end of the war, being deployed successfully against such targets as concrete U-boat pens and the battleship *Tirpitz*. Wallis next devised a development of 'Tallboy', the 22,000lb 'Grand Slam', which was designed on the same principles and had an even greater destructive effect. It was first dropped on 14 March 1945 but the war ended before many had been used.

BELOW *Camouflage on the Members' Banking during World War Two. (BAE Systems per Brooklands Museum)*

CHAPTER TWELVE

POST-WAR PROSPERITY

D uring the darkest and most depressing days of the war motor racing and motor cycle racing enthusiasts revived their spirits with the prospect of going back to Brooklands when racing resumed. The first indications that the future might be different came on 20 June 1945, when *The Motor* published a series of photographs showing the state of the track. It was evident that the needs of war and the pressures of aircraft production had inflicted massive damage on it. Repairs would be very costly and would take years to complete. In addition the track was still under the control of the MAP, the Ministry of Aircraft Production, and any casual visitors were turned away.

The Bentley Drivers' Club sought permission to visit the track and hold a members' rally in December 1945, but the correspondence was shuttled between the secretary of Brooklands (Weybridge) Ltd, the Air Ministry and the MAP, and the club was told that permission would not be granted. During a speech at the Bugatti Owners' Club dinner, Lord Howe expressed concern and pointed out that the price of the ordinary shares of Brooklands (Weybridge) Ltd had doubled in 12 months and stood higher than at any time since the company was formed in 1936. The directors of the company, including Sir Malcolm Campbell, refused to make any comment, though it subsequently transpired that

Brooklands in 1970. The Vickers assembly shops and workshops have been built over the Fork and Finishing Straight. (Brooklands Society)

Campbell had been an active buyer of the company shares.

Rumours circulated that a sale to Vickers was being proposed and on 2 January 1946 a protest meeting was held at the RAC, chaired by Lord Howe, but it was in vain. On 7 January a meeting of the shareholders of Brooklands (Weybridge) Ltd was told by the company chairman, Mr C.W. Hayward, that the 'Government consider it desirable that the present occupancy be continued', so the company was compelled 'either to accept the present position for an indefinite period with the possibility of the ultimate compulsory purchase by the Government department concerned (MAP) or to dispose of the property now.' No dividend had been paid by the company since its formation, and the shareholders, realising there was an opportunity of seeing a return on their investment, voted to sell the track to Vickers-Armstrong Ltd for £330,000. The undisclosed aim of the company at its foundation in 1936 – to develop Brooklands for housing and industry – had been realised.

BELOW *John Cobb is watched by his wife as he checks the Land Speed Record Railton cockpit outside Thomson & Taylor's workshops in 1947. (Brooklands Society)*

It was a huge blow to the British motor sporting world and there was much talk of 'betrayal', but the reality of the situation was overlooked. By 1939 the Outer Circuit was outdated and worn out, and the damage inflicted during the war would have made any repair uneconomic. The Labour Government elected in 1945 regarded motor racing, and even motoring, as pastimes for the rich, and with other economic problems confronting it no funds would have been provided for the restoration of the track. In addition the raw materials which would have been required were strictly controlled and were needed to replace or repair buildings destroyed or damaged during the war and to build new homes. Encouraging, or assisting in, the repair of Brooklands would have been anathema to the Government's supporters. Britain also had a huge foreign exchange debt. The aircraft which Vickers was planning to build would bring essential foreign currency into the country, and the Brooklands factories provided employment for thousands of workers. To help the country's post-war economic recovery, Vickers would need every encouragement. Even if Brooklands (Weybridge) Ltd had retained the track, and restoration had been possible, it is unlikely that work to repair it would have been started for several years and by then airfield circuits such as Goodwood and Silverstone would have been flourishing. The economics of a post-war Brooklands would therefore have been problematic.

Although the track had been sold there was still a small motor racing presence, as Thomson & Taylor continued to lease their workshops from Vickers and some racing cars were being prepared. Most importantly of all, John Cobb's Railton Land Speed Record holder was brought out of storage and work began on preparing it for a new record attempt. The car was taken to Bonneville Salt Flats in Utah, where on 14 September 1947 it set a new World Land Speed Record of 394.19mph; on one run Cobb was timed at 403.13mph, the first time the 400mph barrier had been broken. Cobb's record in his Brooklands-built car stood until 1963, though sadly he was killed while attempting to take the World Water Speed Record on Loch Ness in 1952. Other small companies also continued to work within the track for a while, including Brooklands Engineering which made the Martlet racing pistons, and Scale Models Ltd which had begun making cast metal model racing cars in the late 1930s and briefly continued production after the War.

The sale of the Brooklands site to Vickers was completed on 1 July 1946 and the first noticeable changes were made with the expansion of the factory at the Fork and the building of a huge stratospheric chamber beside the Clubhouse in 1947/8. This was designed by Barnes Wallis and his R&D Department to test components at low temperatures and pressures. It was realised at Vickers that civil aviation would grow enormously in the post-war world, so planning for this had begun in 1944 and was spurred on when all outstanding contracts for the Warwick and Windsor were cancelled as soon as the war ended.

Three design studies were produced, based on the Wellington, Warwick and Windsor. The Ministry of Aircraft Production had established the Brabazon Committee under the chairmanship of Lord Brabazon to advise on the post-war development of civil air transport and it was the Wellington derivative, the VC1 (Vickers Commercial 1), intended to rival the ubiquitous Douglas DC-3 Dakota, which was submitted to the Brabazon Committee in December 1944. To reduce development time this used Wellington wings, with metal covering replacing the fabric, and Warwick tail surfaces. The wide fuselage was of stressed-skin construction, the first time this had been used in a Vickers production aircraft, and provided accommodation for 21 passengers. The aircraft, called the Viking, was intended primarily for European routes. Much of the design was done by George Edwards, who had succeeded Rex Pierson as chief designer when Pierson was appointed the company's chief engineer in September 1945.

Three Viking prototypes were ordered by the Ministry of Aircraft Production and such was the pace of development that the first prototype made its maiden flight at Wisley on 22 June 1945. The three prototypes were subjected to an intensive flight test programme and a production order for 50 Vikings was placed by the Ministry on 5 April 1946. These were to be supplied to the newly formed British European Airways Corporation, and the first BEA Viking services began on 1 September 1946. To speed up manufacture of the production Mk 1A the first 19 aircraft had fabric-covered wings. A development, the Viking Mk 1B, had a longer fuselage, increasing the passenger capacity to 24 seats, and later 27. This appeared in April 1947.

BELOW *An impressive production line of Vikings circa 1950. (BAE Systems per Brooklands Museum)*

The Viking attracted overseas orders and aircraft were sold to Aer Lingus and also to India, Denmark, Iraq and South Africa. On 13 April 1950 a terrorist bomb exploded in the rear of a BEA Viking over the English Channel, but the pilot landed the aircraft safely and when it was returned to Brooklands for repair it became the first of the BEA Admiral class, with the seating capacity increased to

BELOW A Viscount flies over the assembly hangars which were built on the old sewage farm site. (BAE Systems per Brooklands Museum)

36. By the time the Viking production line was closed at Brooklands 163 aircraft had been built.

Early in 1946, for the first time since Vickers had begun building aircraft at Brooklands, the company had no orders for the RAF, and was relying wholly on civil airline orders to keep the Brooklands factory working. This soon changed. The RAF took over the three Viking prototypes and three production Mk 1As and, after giving them thorough trials, placed an order for eight Vikings, built to the RAF specification for Transport Command, which became the Mk 2. In addition four Mk 1As were supplied, specially equipped, for the revived King's Flight.

The success of the RAF Vikings resulted in the issue of specification C.9/46 for a military version which would replace the C-47 Dakota. This had a strengthened floor and a big cargo door and had to perform in a number of roles, as troop carrier, freighter, ambulance, glider tug, paratroop transport and for supply dropping. It was called the Valetta and could carry 34 soldiers with full equipment or 20 paratroops. A modified version, the T Mk 3, became a navigation trainer The prototype Valetta was first flown at Brooklands by 'Mutt' Summers on 30 June 1947 and production finished in 1952 after 252 had been built. The RAF needed a more specialised trainer than the T Mk3 and the Valetta was developed into the Varsity. This had a nose-wheel undercarriage and was larger than the Valetta. It was designed to fulfil all the multi-engined needs of RAF Flying Training Command. The prototype first flew at Wisley on 17 July 1949 and deliveries began at the end of 1951. A total of 163 Varsities was delivered to the RAF, 17 of which were built at Brooklands and the remainder at a new Vickers factory at Hurn near Bournemouth.

A civil version of the Varsity, the VC3, was planned but was dropped, as a much more radical aircraft was being developed. When Pierson and Edwards put forward the Viking design to the Brabazon Committee in 1944 it was realised that this would only be an interim project and a more advanced aircraft was discussed. Pierson and his design team concluded that the way ahead lay with a turbo-prop aircraft, which would be more practicable than a pure jet. The proposal was submitted to the Committee, which supported it and advised the Ministry of Civil Aviation that a prototype should be built. Pierson envisaged an aircraft powered by four Rolls-Royce Dart turbo-prop engines which would carry 24 passengers in a pressurised cabin. A development contract was issued to Vickers by the Ministry of Supply on 9 March 1946 for the building of three prototypes and work began in December 1946. The aircraft was to be called the Viceroy, but with the

ABOVE *The second 802 series Viscount G-AOJB on the production line in 1955. The Valiant production line can be seen in the background. (BAE Systems per Brooklands Museum)*

independence of India in August 1947 this was considered unsuitable and the name was changed to Viscount. Despite the enthusiasm of Vickers and the Ministry, BEA was not keen to pursue the Viscount, being concerned about operating costs, and it placed an order for the rival Airspeed Ambassador. Vickers, with a full order book for Vikings and Valettas, also began to lose interest in the Viscount project. Work continued on the first prototype at Brooklands, but that on the second slowed and the third was abandoned.

When the completed prototype Viscount, the Type 630, was taken to Wisley and flown on 16 July 1948 by 'Mutt' Summers it was evident that it was an exceptional design. Pierson, however, did not see his design come to fruition as he died early in 1948, perhaps receiving less recognition than he deserved. The Ambassador had meanwhile run into development problems and this fired Vickers's enthusiasm to continue. An enlarged Viscount was planned which would carry 43 passengers, and this became the Type 700. The Ministry of Supply placed an order for a prototype 700 on 24 February 1949. The components of the third original prototype were utilised in the 700 and this was completed and first flown at Brooklands on 28 August 1950 by 'Jock' Bryce, who succeeded Summers as chief test pilot in 1951.

The possibilities of the larger 700 renewed the interest of BEA, which used the prototype 630 on a proving flight to Paris on 29 July, then ran it for a week on a regular service to Edinburgh in August. On 3 August 1950 BEA signed a contract for 26 Type 701 (a modified 700) Viscounts. The first production 701 flew on 20 August 1952 and the aircraft went into service early in 1953. After the initial order from BEA Vickers waited for more business. Then in November 1951 Air France ordered 12 aircraft, followed by an order for four from Aer Lingus. Brooklands's grass airfield was no longer suitable for the latest generation of aircraft, and in 1951 the character of the original historic flying ground was lost when a concrete runway was constructed on the airfield's north-south axis.

Orders began to flow in, and to supplement the Brooklands production line a new line was set up at Hurn in December 1953. There was a major breakthrough when an order for 15 Viscounts came from Air Canada in November 1952. The largest individual order, for 60 aircraft, came in August 1954, from Capital Airlines in the USA, but these were built at Hurn. The Viscount was progressively enlarged through various types and the final version, the 810, would carry up to 65 passengers. Viscount production continued until 1959, and when it finished 445 aircraft had been built, 166 of them at

Brooklands. It was the most successful British civil aircraft of all time. In all 60 operators in 40 countries acquired Viscounts first-hand, and they were also bought by five governments. Some machines are believed to be still flying in South Africa.

Steady and increasing production needed more space, so the existing buildings which had fronted the Fork were expanded across the old track in 1951, utilising the existing concrete hard standing, and the outline of the track at the Fork disappeared for ever. This expansion was accompanied by the erection of many ancillary buildings including a new wind tunnel. When the demand for more manufacturing space arose again machine shops were built on the old 'Village' site, and, in a more radical move, the old sewage farm of legendary fame was filled in. A huge new shop was built on the site, using four redundant B1-Type T.2 hangars moved from disused wartime airfields, and it was extended in 1956 at the northern end by the addition of six T.2 hangars. A wide concrete apron led from this complex up to the Campbell Circuit junction with the Railway Straight.

The world entered the age of nuclear weapons at the end of World War Two, and this was followed almost immediately by the onset of the Cold War. These events resulted in a revolutionary reappraisal of the requirements of the RAF. By the end of 1945 the Air Ministry had issued Operational Requirement 230 for a high-speed, high-altitude, long-range bomber capable of carrying a nuclear weapon. This was incorporated in a draft Specification B.35/46 which appeared in January 1947. Several companies were invited to submit tenders, and the Vickers design, the Type 660/758 Valiant, was approved. An order was given for the building of two prototypes in February 1949. The aircraft had four Rolls-Royce Avon turbojet engines installed in the wing roots, swept-back wings, and a pressurised cabin for the crew of four. The bomb bay would hold a nuclear weapon.

To build the Valiant, Vickers introduced new manufacturing techniques at the Brooklands factory. Sculptured milling was used to produce the wing centre section spar web plates and powered stretch-forming tools were used for making the large skin panels. Glass fibre was used for some components and a special bonding shop was established. The design process continued through 1949 and the prototype was built at Brooklands and taken to Wisley for its first flight on 18 May 1951, piloted by 'Mutt' Summers, though an initial order for 25 aircraft had already been placed in April. Although the first prototype was lost in an accident in January 1952 production was not affected, though the complexity of the aircraft necessitated some subcontracting. Much of the responsibility for getting the Valiant into production rested upon Charlie Houghton, the manager responsible for prototypes. RAF instructors responsible for training the servicing crews attended long courses at Brooklands to learn the specialised skills needed for the aircraft. The first production Valiant was delivered to 138 Squadron at Gaydon in January 1955. Completed aircraft were flown from Brooklands to Wisley, and to ensure a safer take-off on the short runway a large section of the Byfleet Banking was removed. In all 104 Valiants were built at Brooklands and the aircraft went on to fill several other roles, including flight refuelling and photo reconnaissance.

An increasing defence emphasis on guided missiles resulted in much development work being done at Brooklands by a new Vickers Guided Weapons Department during the 1950s, on projects such as Blue Boar, Red Rapier and Red Dean, but each was cancelled, though orders were received from the Ministry of Supply for the production of the Vigilant anti-tank missile.

Another chapter in Brooklands history closed on 5 August 1956 when Dame Ethel Locke King died, aged 92. She had continued to live nearby, at Caenshill, until her death, and was buried in Weybridge Cemetery beside her husband. Despite the great changes which had taken place the work of the Locke Kings was not wholly forgotten and the 50th anniversary of the opening of the track

Sir George Edwards

George Edwards was born in 1908. He studied engineering at London University and joined the Vickers design office at Brooklands in 1935. He worked with Rex Pierson on the development of the Wellington and in 1939 was appointed as Experimental Works Manager. He did much development work on the 'bouncing bomb' design of Barnes Wallis, suggesting the reverse spin which made the bomb viable. Subsequently he advised the Ministry of Aircraft Production on the expedition of aircraft production, but in 1945 became Chief Designer and was responsible for the Valetta and Varsity, the developments of the Viking.

His greatest success was in completing the design begun by Rex Pierson for the Viscount, which became the most profitable civil aircraft made in Britain. From this he moved onto a much more ambitious project, the design of the Valiant and its commercial development the VC-10, the largest aircraft ever built entirely in Britain.

Edwards was appointed managing director of Vickers-Armstrong Aircraft Division in 1953, was knighted in 1957, and became the Executive Director (Aircraft) of the British Aircraft Corporation at its formation in 1960. He supervised the development and production of the BAC One-Eleven and was a major figure in the design and development of the Concorde. He retired as Chairman of BAC in 1975 and died in 2003.

ABOVE *A Valiant B1
nears the end of the
production line in 1955.
(BAE Systems per
Brooklands Museum)*

was recognised at a ceremony on 6 July 1957, when Lord Brabazon of Tara unveiled the Brooklands Memorial, sited near the Aerodrome Bend on the Campbell Circuit at the north end of the airfield.

At the end of the war Barnes Wallis was appointed as Head of Research and Development at Vickers, and working in his office in the Clubhouse he began to explore the possibilities of new frontiers for aircraft. He worked on variable geometry designs, with swing-wings which could be pivoted forward for take-off and landing, and swept back for supersonic flight. Large radio-controlled models were constructed to test his theories and the first, the Wild Goose, was ready for testing in 1951. Technical problems caused delays and the first trials were held at Predannack airfield in Cornwall in April 1952. The model hit a building and was wrecked, but a later version, the Swallow, made at least 31 flights, and the flight research programme continued until October 1954. Expense and commercial pressures prevented Wallis's experiments being developed,

but he continued to work on the project and envisaged a commercial passenger aircraft which would fly from Europe to Australia in five hours. Although long past retiring age, Wallis continued to work at Brooklands conducting research into advanced theories of flight until 1971. Vickers were unable to use the research he had done on swing-wing aircraft, but the principles were used by General Dynamics in the United States with the F-111, and Wallis saw the results of his research applied in the Panavia Tornado which began flying with the RAF in 1982.

In April 1953, soon after the Viscount had gone into service with BEA, Vickers was approached by the airline to discuss the possibility of building a successor. An aircraft larger, faster and more economical than the Viscount was stipulated, and with collaboration between BEA, Rolls-Royce and Vickers a design evolved from the Brooklands team, now led by chief designer Basil Stephenson under the guidance of Sir George Edwards. A contract for 20 of this aircraft, the Vanguard, was signed by BEA on 20 July 1956, followed by an order from Air Canada for 23 more in January 1957. In a return to tradition, the prototype was flown from Brooklands on 20 January 1959, piloted by 'Jock' Bryce. The four-engined turboprop Vanguard could carry up to 139 passengers and was economic to operate, but delivery was delayed by problems with the manufacture of its Rolls-Royce Tyne engines, and the first aircraft only went into service in the spring of 1961. Unfortunately, there had by then been a change in airline philosophy and a shift to operating pure jets, so BEA and Air Canada were the only customers and production was limited to 44 aircraft.

In 1951 Vickers was asked by the Ministry of Supply to prepare a design for a military transport based on the Valiant. This design became the Type 1000 (VC7) and an order was given for the construction of a prototype in October 1952 which was to have a passenger capacity of 120 or be able to carry large quantities of military freight. Vickers planned to build a civil prototype as a parallel venture, and after some reluctance the Air Ministry permitted detailed information to be given to BOAC, PanAm and TCA. The project was delayed by problems with the Rolls-Royce Conway engines and

in November 1955, in a Government cutback, the order was cancelled and Vickers were told to cut up the almost finished prototype.

Despite this major setback Vickers wanted to build an aircraft suitable for the transatlantic civil trade and work began on a development of the VC7, which led to the VC10. This carried 115 passengers and was an unusual design as the four Conway engines were mounted at the rear of the fuselage. BOAC were attracted to the venture and issued a specification in March 1957 from which the VC10 was developed. In May 1957 BOAC gave a provisional order for 35 aircraft, with an option for another 20, and the order for 35 was confirmed in January 1958. To build the VC10, a new building known informally as 'The Cathedral' was erected on part of the former sewage farm on the west side of the airfield. The completed prototype was rolled out at Brooklands on 15 April 1962 and made its first flight from the track on 29 June with 'Jock' Bryce at the controls. The flight was successful and it was flown to Wisley for trials.

Having watched Vickers develop the VC10, supported by BOAC, the RAF placed an order for 11 aircraft in 1962, and when an enlarged aircraft,

BELOW *Lord Brabazon of Tara unveils the Brooklands Memorial on 7 July 1957. (Brooklands Society)*

the Super VC10, was developed three were ordered for the RAF and 17 went to BOAC. The Super VC10 was built in a new building, 'The Vatican', which was erected adjacent to 'The Cathedral', and the first aircraft was flown on 7 May 1964. Unfortunately, BOAC was the only major airline purchaser and the production line was closed after 54 aircraft had been built, the last VC10 being flown out of Brooklands on 16 February 1970. It is perhaps ironic, in the light of the VC7 cancellation, that in later years the RAF bought a number of second-hand VC10s from BOAC and East African Airways for conversion to military use.

The VC10 was the last aircraft to be designed and built by Vickers, as in February 1960, orchestrated by the Government, the British Aircraft Corporation Ltd was formed, which incorporated Vickers, Bristol, English Electric and Hunting Percival into one company. The Brooklands factories and the whole site was owned by the new company.

BAC took over responsibility for a major project, the TSR2. This arose from an Operational Requirement issued by the Air Ministry in 1956 for the design of a general-purpose supersonic aircraft, capable of flying from small airfields and operating at high and very low altitudes and delivering a nuclear weapon. The major aircraft manufacturers were invited to submit designs and the Vickers design was chosen. This was of a complexity in advance of any aircraft produced in Britain and the need for subcontracting and close co-operation was a prime cause of the company amalgamation. An order for 20 development aircraft was given in January 1959 and this was followed in 1963 by an order for 30 production aircraft. The main structure of the first prototype was built at Brooklands, although some component parts were made at the English Electric factory at Warton in Lancashire. The prototype was finished in 1964 and was taken to the Aeroplane & Armaments Experimental Establishment at Boscombe Down for its first flight on 27 September 1964. However, before any development could be carried out the whole TSR2 project was cancelled in January 1965 and there was a Government directive that the aircraft under construction at Brooklands were to be broken up and the jigs and tooling destroyed.

When BAC was formed Hunting Percival brought with it a design for a twin-jet short haul airliner

BELOW *The prototype TSR2s under construction. (BAE Systems per Brooklands Museum)*

with a passenger capacity of 60. The Vickers design team had been working on a similar type of aircraft, a smaller version of the VC10, the VC11. Though this was dropped when the BAC board preferred the Hunting aircraft, which became the BAC One-Eleven, the Vickers team made some contribution to the later design stages.

The BAC One-Eleven was announced in March 1961 and most of the work on the prototype was carried out at Hurn, where the first aircraft flew in August 1963. Unfortunately, this crashed in October 1963, but buyers were not deterred and orders came in steadily. The principal buyer was BEA, but over half the subsequent production went to the United States, American Airlines and Braniff placing big orders. Initially, aircraft were only built at Hurn, although all the wings, tailplanes and moving surfaces were made at Brooklands, but to meet the demand for aircraft a production line was eventually established at

Brooklands and 13 of the total production of 235 BAC One-Elevens were built there. The last one to be completed at Brooklands was flown out on 19 December 1970, and was the last aircraft built at the track to be flown from it, bringing to an end more than 60 years of aviation history. It has been estimated that in that time 18,564 aircraft, comprising 258 types, were first flown, manufactured or erected at Brooklands, including prototypes.

The commercial success of the BAC One-Eleven came at an opportune time, as the cancellation of the TSR2 could otherwise have resulted in large redundancies at Brooklands. However, many disillusioned workers left the company as a result.

While BAC One-Eleven production was in full swing another famous Brooklands landmark disappeared. The Hennebique bridge carrying the Members' Banking over the River Wey was badly damaged by floods during the winter of 1968, the

BELOW *The prototype VC10 taxies out for take off on 29 June 1962. (Brooklands Society)*

supporting piles became dangerous, and the bridge was demolished in November 1969.

From the time that the jet engine became accepted as the recognised propulsion unit for military aircraft ambitious visionaries in the aircraft industry had looked ahead, first to the use of the jet to power airliners and then, when this became a reality, even further ahead to supersonic civil aircraft. In November 1956 the Supersonic Transport Aircraft Committee was established to consider the practicalities of a supersonic transport aircraft. The Committee reported in March 1959 and recommended that design studies should be initiated, but as these progressed it was realised that any project would be of such magnitude and expense that it could be beyond the capabilities of the British aircraft industry. However, the French company Sud Aviation had also been considering a supersonic transport, and in June 1961 discussions began between BAC and Sud Aviation at Brooklands and Paris about the possibilities of a joint project. Initially, the discussions centred on collaboration on engines, systems, electrics and hydraulics, but the British and French governments, with political aims, insisted on closer co-operation, and after protracted negotiations an Anglo-French specification for a Mach 2.2 airliner was issued in October 1962. This was followed a month later, on 29 November, by an agreement between the two governments for the joint design, development and manufacture of a supersonic civil aircraft.

There was an integrated organisation for the construction of the aircraft, which was itself based upon the marriage of two provisional designs, the Sud Aviation Super Caravelle and the BAC 223, though the final agreed version had strong similarities to a Bristol design, the Type 198, originated by Archibald Russell. BAC agreed to be responsible for the nose, flight deck, forward fuselage, rear fuselage, tail section and tail fin and also for the electrics, oxygen, fuel, engine instrumentation and controls, air conditioning and de-icing. There were two final assembly lines, at Filton near Bristol and at Toulouse in France, but the British-made components would be manufactured at Brooklands, including the fitting of the 90 miles of wiring for each aircraft. The allocation of these tasks to Brooklands was almost certainly prompted by the expertise gained there in the making of specialist components for the VC10 and TSR2, and particularly in the skills shown in milling large sections from solid metal. Much of the material used was a special alloy, RR58.

The aircraft was named the 'Concorde' early in 1963, and in June BOAC and Air France signed sales options. Design work continued throughout 1964

ABOVE *Sir George Edwards (left) and Tony Benn, the Minister for Technology, in conversation in 1967. (BAE Systems per Brooklands Museum)*

and it was settled that there would only be one version, a long-range aircraft. In the spring of 1965 the pre-production design was announced and in April the machining of the metal sections for the prototypes began at Brooklands. Two were to be built, one in each country, and the finished components were sent from Brooklands to Filton and Toulouse for assembly. In May 1967 it was announced that options had been taken for 74 aircraft by various airlines and in March 1969, the two governments gave approval for the construction of two test airframes, two pre-production aircraft, and three production machines. Approval for three more production aircraft was given in December 1969.

The first prototype flew in France on 2 March 1969, followed by the British machine on 9 April. The prototypes were followed by the two pre-production aircraft, and the first completed production aircraft for Air France and British Airways (which had succeeded BOAC) flew in December 1973 and February 1974 respectively. Unfortunately, the 74 options did not result in orders. The cost of the aircraft and the problems of flying over populated areas at supersonic speeds discouraged buyers, so BA and Air France were the only customers.

Concorde production continued after BAC and the Hawker Siddeley Aircraft Group were merged to form British Aerospace in 1977 and ended in April 1979, by then 16 production aircraft had been built. As Concorde production finished the lines at Brooklands were switched to building Hawk trainer fuselage sections and Airbus wings.

CHAPTER THIRTEEN

SITE STILL EVOLVING

I n the 1960s and 1970s, the value of land in the south-east of England, and particularly in suburban Surrey, soared. Land for development was scarce, and there were many restrictions preventing building on greenfield sites, so land which had already been developed had an enhanced value if it was no longer being used for its original purpose. Developers cast envious eyes on Brooklands, which had become an immensely valuable piece of real estate. When production of the VC10 ended and subsequent projects were abandoned the west side of the old track site, the old 'Flying Village' and the huge expansion on the old sewage farm became redundant to the needs of BAC. The continuing production work was moved to the original Vickers site at the Fork, east of the River Wey, where the buildings had expanded to cover the Fork and most of the Finishing Straight. The buildings on the west side were closed and kept on a maintenance basis.

In the early 1970s there came the greatest threat of all to Brooklands, when the route of the M25 motorway was provisionally planned to run across it, but fortunately the plans were changed and the road was moved to the west. In 1974 BAC, in collaboration with the company's majority shareholders, Vickers and GEC, formed a property company, Oyster Lane Properties Ltd, to develop

A view of 'Mercedes-Benz World at Brooklands' in the autumn of 2006. The preserved Sahara Straight of the Campbell Circuit can be seen to the right of the test-driving area, and on the right of the picture is the Museum site. (Brooklands Society)

the west side, which became known as the Brooklands Industrial Park. Initially, planning consent was given to use the existing buildings for warehousing or light industry and the whole site was given a provisional valuation of £15 million. In the spring of 1977 Surrey County Council, as the overall planning authority, decided that the Industrial Park should become permanent, but that the ground which had been the central part of the former airfield, west of the river, should remain an open space.

Meanwhile, in June 1967 the Godalming & District Round Table had organised a big rally at the old track for cars and motor cycles associated with Brooklands, to celebrate the 60th anniversary of its opening. This was so successful that, at the suggestion of Bill Boddy, the Brooklands Society was formed to keep alive the spirit of the track, and with the aim of preserving the fabric of the track wherever possible. The Society flourished, and in November 1977 Brooklands Track Ltd, a company formed by the Society, applied to the local planning authority for outline consent for the establishment of a museum on a 40-acre site comprising the remains of the Members' Banking, the Members' Hill, the Clubhouse and the Paddock, as British Aerospace indicated that this area was no longer required. Outline consent was granted, but the Society had no funds to buy the site from BAe, which, although sympathetic, had no alternative but to seek a full market price.

Although the Society was unable to proceed with its ambitious plans, dedicated members spent countless hours clearing the old track surface of trees, undergrowth and rubbish so that the parts of the track which remained began to assume their former appearance. This restoration work was probably decisive in getting the remaining sections of banking scheduled as an ancient monument and preventing destruction of these by developers. Much of the work in securing this legal protection was done by Kenneth Evans, who with his brother Denis and sister Doreen had raced at the track in the 1930s.

There had meanwhile been further moves to develop parts of the west site, and in July 1978 Oyster Lane Properties, in collaboration with the brewers Bass Charrington, applied for permission to develop the area containing part of the former 'Flying Village', including the old Thomson & Taylor workshops and the Hermitage. Sadly these buildings had no legal protection, and when permission was granted the site was cleared and the historic buildings were demolished. The 1932 Aero Clubhouse and the 1911 Ticket Office, however, were saved, having been scheduled as

ancient monuments, and the Ticket Office was subsequently moved to the Museum in 1989. The rest of the site was developed and the western side of the airfield has become an industrial and warehousing complex, while the south end is now a retail area with Marks & Spencer and Tesco as its main occupants.

The listed Aero Clubhouse having survived when the 'Village' was cleared, plans were made in 1980 to establish an aviation museum in the building, as a branch of the Weybridge Library and Museum. In 1977 the latter had staged a most successful temporary exhibition, 'Wings Over Brooklands', and this encouraged both British Aerospace and Elmbridge Borough Council to support the idea of a Brooklands museum.

In the meantime negotiations continued regarding the sale of the 40 acres which the Brooklands Society had wanted to obtain. When proposals for the purchase of the whole site by a pharmaceutical company fell through its future was

assured in the autumn of 1982 by its sale to Gallaher Ltd, the tobacco combine, which declared its intention to retain only part of the site for an office building while dedicating the greater part to be the home of a museum commemorating the track and its motoring and aviation history. Elmbridge Borough Council gave Gallaher planning consent for an office building on ten acres, sited at the beginning of the Members' Banking, adjoining the junction with the Campbell Circuit, and Gallaher leased the rest to the Council at a peppercorn rent so that the museum could be formed. As a preliminary, Gallaher completed the removal of the wartime dispersal hangar dug into the Members' Banking, which had been used as a workshop, and renewed that section of the banking following the original curvature. It also met the cost of restoring the Clubhouse and subsequently, in 1988, the replacement of the Members' Bridge, which had been demolished.

The Brooklands Museum Trust was formed in the spring of 1987 and was formally launched on 7 June, almost coinciding with the 80th anniversary of the track's opening. Its first chairman was Sir Peter Masefield, Sir George Edwards was the first Patron, and a message was received from Queen Elizabeth, the Queen Mother, wishing the Trust every success. Morag Barton, a curator at the Weybridge Museum, who had staged the 1977 'Wings over Brooklands' exhibition and had helped to get the Aero Clubhouse listed in 1979, was appointed as the first director of the Museum.

One of the first challenges was to start building a representative collection of Brooklands-related motor cars and aeroplanes. The new Museum already had a Wellington, which had flown on 'ops' with the RAF in the autumn of 1939 and had ditched in Loch Ness while on a training flight in 1940, where it lay until it was raised in 1985 in a remarkable state of preservation. A few days later it came back to Brooklands, where a painstaking restoration project, taking many years, was begun

BELOW Concorde G-BBDG is assembled and ready for opening to the public in June 2006. (Brooklands Museum)

by a dedicated team of Museum volunteers, staff and sponsors. Another early arrival was the last civilian-operated VC10, the gift of the Sultan of Oman, which was flown in on 6 July 1987, landing on the runway from which it had made its first flight on 17 October 1964.

Commercial flying returned to the track in 1973 when Air Hanson operated a helicopter service from one of the wartime hangars on the Railway Straight, using Bell 206 Jet Rangers and a Sikorsky S-76 for charter, load lifting and other applications. Limited car production also returned to Brooklands in 1980 when the Panther company began to manufacture cars with period-style bodies but modern components in a workshop adjoining the Railway Straight, continuing in production there until 1988. Then in 1986 Autokraft Ltd, successor to the AC company, which had closed down at its original factory in Thames Ditton, opened a workshop in a shed beside the Byfleet Banking before moving to a new building at the western end of the Railway Straight in 1988, where it made the updated AC Cobra. As a nostalgic link with the past, a Hawker Hurricane was restored in a corner of the Autokraft workshops and was flown from Blackbushe airfield when completed in the mid-1990s.

In the autumn of 1985 Oyster Lane Properties sold the whole Industrial Park site to Trafalgar House, a major property group, for £39.2 million, and in July 1986 BAe announced that it would be closing its operations at Brooklands and leaving the former Vickers site, so ending an association which had lasted for over 70 years. During the next two years the old aircraft factory was cleared away, and in the spring of 1990 BAe formed a partnership with Trafalgar House to develop the site. Plans were drawn up for mixed business space and housing in an area called 'The Heights' lying beside Brooklands Road, and, planning consent being given for housing on 25 acres, Ideal Homes began development.

HRH Prince Michael of Kent, who had become its Royal Patron, formally opened the new Brooklands Museum to the public in April 1991, and during its first summer there were 35,000 visitors. An application to the Heritage Lottery Fund subsequently led to the Museum receiving an enormous boost, as grants totalling £1.5 million were received in 1997–8. This met the cost of restoring many important buildings on the site and also enabled the Trust to buy John Cobb's Napier-Railton, the all-time lap record holder, for £800,000. An impressive collection of cars had been built up, but the Napier-Railton was an essential centrepiece. The aircraft collection had also grown impressively

and the Heritage Lottery Fund supported another important purchase, a Hawker Hurricane recovered from Russia.

However, the Museum received a severe setback in November 2000 when, after heavy rain, the River Wey broke its banks and the site was flooded to a depth of 2ft. There was no warning and staff and volunteers only had time to remove the archives and some smaller exhibits to safety. The damage was estimated at well over a million pounds and the Museum was closed for six months while repairs were made. It took at least a year for the Museum to return to normality, and during this time its founding Director, Morag Barton retired, on 31 March 2001.

In the spring of 2001 developers made a planning application for the erection of five multi-storey office buildings immediately beside the southern boundary of the Museum site. This application was opposed by everyone concerned for Brooklands and it was subsequently modified to reduce its impact on the historic site. The blocks were built as 'The Heights'.

The pressures of the housing market had resulted in planning consent being given for the development of many greenfield sites in the south-east of England and the open space forming the centre of the old track site was looked at covetously by many developers, who argued that little would be lost if planning consent was granted, as it was surrounded by business, industrial and housing developments and was bisected by Wellington Way, a road linking the east and west sites. Although used regularly for light aircraft fly-ins organised by the Museum since 1990, and later for Museum motoring events, the runway and its environs were eventually used for Sunday and Wednesday markets, a go-kart track, a lorry park, and as an illegal tip for litter and rubbish. It therefore seemed certain that the last open space of the original Brooklands would become a housing site.

In 2002 there was an unexpected development. DaimlerChrysler, the group formed by the amalgamation of Mercedes-Benz and Chrysler, made an offer to purchase the undeveloped central area and made a planning application to build a Heritage and Technology Centre, to be known as 'Mercedes-Benz World at Brooklands', at the north end of the site beside the Railway Straight. The Railway Straight would be cleared of buildings, the remains of the Campbell Circuit would be restored, a test track would be built in front of the Centre, and new entrance roads would be made. The southern part of the site would be cleared and given to the local authority as

ABOVE *The devastating floods in December 2000. (Brooklands Museum)*

a public park. Most importantly, for the Museum, a new public entrance and car park would be provided west of the River Wey, work would be done on the riverbanks, and a flood basin would be made to reduce the possibility of further flooding. As a longer term project the rebuilding of the Hennebique Bridge was mentioned as a desirable ambition for all concerned. DaimlerChrysler expressed their willingness to work with the Museum and acknowledged their appreciation of the responsibilities concerning such an historic site. On 26 June 2003, Elmbridge Council approved the DaimlerChrysler application and a new era in the history of Brooklands began.

In the summer of 2003 Allan Winn, as Director of the Museum, successfully applied to British Airways for a Concorde. By 5 June 2004 the Museum had acquired the dismantled Concorde 'Delta Golf', the first British production aircraft of the run of eight, which had been stored at Filton, first as a trials aircraft and then as a source of spares, but had never been used in passenger service. This was a most fitting exhibit for the Museum, as so much of the manufacture of all Concordes had been done at Brooklands. The

aircraft was brought to the Museum in five major sections and was reassembled by specialist contractors Air Salvage International, and restored in just over two years in a major project involving many Museum volunteers, sponsors, supporters and staff. The airliner was formally unveiled by Prince Michael of Kent at a ceremony on 26 July 2006 and opened to the public daily from 1 August.

'Mercedes-Benz World at Brooklands' was finished early in the autumn of 2006 and was formally opened on 26 October by the Chairman of the Board of Management of DaimlerChrysler, Dr Dieter Zetsche. In his speech at the opening ceremony, Dr Zetsche emphasised the historic importance of Brooklands and acknowledged the responsibilities of Mercedes-Benz in joining with the Brooklands Museum to preserve the track with its unforgettable associations. With the opening of 'Mercedes-Benz at Brooklands' and the revitalisation of the Brooklands Museum, Brooklands can look forward to its second century and a bright future. The vision of Hugh Locke King still lives on. The track he created 100 years ago has not died, as many feared it would; it has evolved, and will continue to do so.

CHAPTER FOURTEEN

ODDBALL SIDELIGHTS

Bookies

When racing began at Brooklands it was modelled in many respects on horse racing, and bookmakers were permitted at the BARC meetings from the earliest days and were given official licences. The most famous of them was Thomas Harris, generally known as 'Long Tom', who was present at almost every meeting until he died in 1926, and whose firm continued to run a book at the track until 1939.

The major bookies had pitches in the paddock, but they were also found on the Members' Hill and for a while a tote office was sited there. At some meetings in the 1930s a tote office was run from a converted London bus in the paddock. The sums of money wagered were relatively small and were paltry compared with the wads of notes which changed hands at horse racing events. The biggest bet taken by 'Long Tom' was £100 at evens on a Salmson in an early JCC 200-Mile race. The Brooklands bookies soon learnt about the vagaries of motor racing and there were few opportunities for punters to make a killing. *Sporting Life* sometimes published ante-post odds and even gave forecasting tips, while by the early 1930s the starting prices on cars which won or were placed in BARC races were given in the reports of meetings in *Motor Sport*.

In the horse racing world there is a strict rule that jockeys are not allowed to bet on races in

The World Road Race Championship Trial in June 1933. (Brooklands Society)

which they are riding, but this rule did not apply at Brooklands, and for members of the paddock community well-placed bets provided a chance to augment incomes. The leading paddock bookies, Jack Linton and George Cooper, soon realised that if a bet was placed by an insider he probably had secret knowledge about a tuning improvement which was unknown to the handicapper, so the price on the car came down sharply. Canny insiders would therefore get a friend who was unknown in the paddock to place their bets. Inevitably, those in the know would spread rumours in the paddock about the expected performance of cars, in the hope of affecting the odds, but it seems the bookies rarely fell for it. There was little betting at BMCRC meetings, as the bookmakers considered it was more difficult to predict the outcome, and the sums wagered were so small that there was little prospect of the book making any money.

Filming at the track

Cine cameras were at Brooklands from the beginning and the major races were being recorded by the 1920s. The more spectacular happenings were filmed for newsreels and the tragic accident to Clive Dunfee in the 1932 '500' was shown in detail. The British film industry was almost moribund until the passing of the Cinematograph Films Act 1927, which required cinemas to show at least one British-made film in every programme. This, together with the advent of the 'talkies', which came to England in 1930, stimulated action and studios appeared at Ealing, Elstree and Denham, churning out large numbers of 'B' movies, many of an execrable standard. Directors realised that excitement could be put into a plot with some motor racing scenes and a number of films had sequences with Brooklands as the background.

The first film with a track background was *The Love Race*, made in 1931 and featuring the Aldington brothers driving Frazer Nashes which had raced in the 1931 Double-12. This was followed in 1932 by a documentary, *The King's Cup*, which covered the race, starting and finishing at the track. C.G. Grey, editor of *The Aeroplane*, made some caustic comments about this film, suggesting that some of the shots of aircraft rounding pylons at the track were rigged. Students from the College of Aeronautical Engineering were recruited as

extras for a British remake of the German film *Spies at Work*, a flying melodrama made in 1934.

A motor racing drama was also made at Brooklands in 1934. This was *Death Drives Through* starring Miles Mander, who had raced at the track and later became a Hollywood second lead, and Chili Bouchier, who was a well-known West End leading lady. The film provided plenty of extra work for cars and drivers. An Alfa Romeo and Richard Marker's Bentley were disguised as 'The Lark', the car which was central to the plot, while an Invicta was used as a camera car, an Austin faked a crash, and the August Bank Holiday meeting provided background. It was reported that the Napier-Railton had appeared in one scene and had passed too close to a mock-up car with a cardboard body, which had disintegrated in the slipstream!

Comedian Will Hay, a big box office draw in the 1930s, starred in *Ask a Policeman*, released in 1938, which ended with Hay chasing a bus around the Brooklands track and meeting a race head-on. Robin Jackson, the tuner, provided a field of 12 cars for the mock race, and one driver made a slight error and there was a minor collision with the camera rig.

In 1938, with the threat of war growing, the Aero Club provided the flying scenes for *Q Planes*, a drama about spies stealing an experimental aircraft using a secret ray. This was the most prestigious film made at Brooklands, with Laurence Olivier and Ralph Richardson in the cast, and involved a mock dogfight between a Miles Magister defending the airfield from an attack by an Airspeed Consul masquerading as a bomber.

The war brought an end to the use of Brooklands as a filming venue, though in post-war years the work of Vickers and BAC featured in many documentaries and newsreels. More recently the Museum site has been the setting for several motoring TV programmes, and in 1990 the Paddock, Clubhouse and Members' Banking featured in an episode of the *Poirot* series, the dramatised version of Agatha Christie's famous detective novels, made by London Weekend Television. Paddock scenes were also filmed for the TV drama series *House of Elliott*, and for a docu-drama of the life of Tim Birkin which starred Rowan Atkinson.

Bicycles

The most popular competition activity at Brooklands, and the least known, was bicycle racing. The Museum holds records of over 8,000 competitors who took part in bicycle races at the track between 1907 and 1939. The first meeting

was held on 7 September 1907 and was a 100-mile event. It used the Finishing Straight, Railway Straight and Byfleet Banking, with a feeding station sited at the top end of the Finishing Straight. The winner was J.H. Bishop, who won by a margin of six miles and took 5hr 14min to cover the course. Another race was held in 1910.

After that there was no competitive cycling at the track until 1933, when members of the Charlotteville Cycle Club organised a preliminary 100km World Championship Trial in readiness for the World Road Race Championships to be held at Montlhéry. The course used the Outer Circuit running clockwise, with a loop into the Finishing Straight and round a barrel hairpin. The race length was 17 laps, and on every third lap there was a

BELOW *'Darling, I know where my duty lies.' Miles Mander and Chili Bouchier in a scene from "Death Drives Through", filmed at Brooklands in 1934. (Brooklands Museum)*

refinement as the Test Hill was climbed and the field returned to the course via the Members Bridge, Paddock Tunnel and Paddock entrance road. The event had full BARC approval and among the officials were S.F. Edge and Sir Malcolm Campbell. A demonstration by Oliver Bertram and a three-lap motor cycle handicap were in the programme, but it was a very wet day so Bertram toured round and the motor cycle race was cancelled. Ninety-one cyclists started, but the pace and the course were gruelling and there were only 14 finishers. J. Salt was the winner by a margin of three lengths over second-placed W. Burl, having taken 2hr 55min to cover the distance at an average of 21.4mph.

The race was repeated on 16 June 1934 when the NCU organised a trial to select riders for the World Championships, and was won by P.T. Stallard. Then there was another lull until the opening of the Campbell Circuit in 1937, which provided the cyclists with a course akin to the road courses on which Continental races were run. Three races were held in 1937, and the sport was fully accepted in 1938, when there were 23 races. The last pre-war season in 1939 saw 25 cycle race meetings and the BARC even promoted a race during the Easter Monday meeting. It was the cyclists who had the distinction of holding the very last meeting of all at the track before the start of World War Two, when on Saturday 27 August Jack Manning won a 100km race which was to wind the curtain down after 32 years.

Although racing at the track had ended for powered machinery the cyclists were not to be denied, and in July 1969 cycle racing was revived with a charity evening meeting organised by the Charlotteville CC, using the airfield roads. Such meetings continued into the 1980s, and in June 1993, to celebrate the Diamond Jubilee of the 1933 race, a 100km race was held using the airfield runway and the Sahara Straight of the Campbell Circuit.

The oddball, unusual and eerie

During its life as a racing track Brooklands was the scene of some odd and unusual happenings. In July 1926 the strangest race of all was staged. The competitors were Parry Thomas in the Leyland-Thomas, George Duller in a works racing Austin

Seven, Paul Dutoit in a works racing Alvis, and R.M. Hanlon driving a Greenbat railway platform electric truck. For the three-lap race the Greenbat was given a 1hr 25min 38sec start from Parry Thomas, who was on scratch, while Duller received 1min 24sec and Dutoit received 59sec. 'Ebby's' handicapping was nearly right, as the Greenbat won by 32.4sec from the Alvis, while Thomas and Duller retired with misfiring.

There was also an unusual race away from the track. In September 1923 bad weather caused the postponement of the Essex MC meeting, so BARC members persuaded some of the waiters in the Clubhouse to take part in a race up to the top of the Test Hill and back to the Clubhouse, with wagers being placed on the runners. The winner took 44sec to cover the course and it was suggested that those who backed him had inside knowledge, as it transpired that he was a successful cross-country runner.

In May 1923 the motor cycle riders challenged the car drivers to a cricket match, which was held on a wicket prepared in the public enclosure. Such eminent figures as Frazer-Nash, Duller and Eldridge turned out for the drivers while there was equal eminence among the motor cyclists, with Le Vack, Temple and Marchant in the team.

Barbara Cartland, the romantic novelist, often claimed that she had organised the first race for women at Brooklands. This so-called race took place late in 1931, when a party of young society women drove borrowed MGs round the track in a demonstration, filmed by newsreel cameramen. The stunt received much adverse publicity at the time, partly prompted by incidents of reckless and dangerous driving. Miss Cartland's claim overlooked the Ladies' 'Bracelet' event in 1908 and several subsequent women's races as well as the feats of such drivers as Jill Scott. Bill Boddy summed it up in the *Brooklands Society Gazette* in later years as 'a bit of unfortunate nonsense'!

Possibly the most bizarre vehicle to appear at Brooklands was the Dynasphere which was demonstrated at the 1932 autumn meeting. This was a vast single wheel about 10ft in diameter made of steel hoops. It was powered by a 600cc Douglas engine and the designer, Dr J.A. Purves, sat in the centre on a cradle. It was not a success as the driver oscillated violently when the machine accelerated and braked.

In 1929 an AEC Regent double-decker bus was tested on the track and made a continuous run of 12 hours without any problems, averaging 41.6mph, and finished its run by climbing the Test Hill. An AEC-engined Chrysler saloon driven by George Eyston set some unofficial diesel records in 1934, exceeding 100mph, and in 1935 an Austrian, Baron Coreth zu Coredo, appeared at the track to demonstrate a fuel he had devised made from vegetable oil and water. A GP Sunbeam fitted with a Rolls-Royce 20hp engine lapped the track using his fuel and the press showed great interest, but nothing more was heard of the baron and his concoction.

There was a much more sinister event in 1923 or 1924, when a man was murdered in a Brooklands cottage, one of the original farm buildings still standing on the edge of the airfield. Over the years there have also been many accounts of ghosts at Brooklands. People have spoken of odd and eerie sensations, particularly in the vicinity of the Members' Hill, while there have been several reports of the sound of car and motor cycle engines on the bankings. The only reputed 'sighting' has been of a figure in a leather helmet and goggles and wearing a leather coat, which has allegedly been seen on the Members' Banking and in the paddock tunnel which runs under it. He was also seen in the Vickers hangars which stood on the Railway Straight. It has been suggested that this could be Percy Lambert, who was killed nearby while attempting the World Hour Record in 1913. Another candidate who has been suggested is Lieutenant James Kennedy of the RFC who was killed in a flying accident in 1913. Ghosts or not, all those who raced or flew at the track have left it with an aura of nostalgia which many visitors will recognise and acknowledge.

Topography: then and now

A visitor to Brooklands 100 years after its inception will see much that has been changed but will also see many landmarks, obvious and less obvious, which have withstood the relentless passage of time. At least three-quarters of the bankings remain. Apart from the gaps made for the runway extension through which Sopwith Drive passes, leading to the retail centres, and a public road, Barnes Wallis Drive, cut through to Oyster Lane in the early 1990s, the Byfleet Banking is almost complete. The major development which forms 'The Heights' has removed all trace of the track and the adjacent buildings at the Fork, though the bridge across the River Wey which carried aircraft from the Vickers factory at the Fork to the airfield still exists, together with the Aerodrome Road bridge.

The line of the track from the bridge to the Fork is preserved as Staniland Drive, the central road through the housing estate. The entrance to the Members' Banking has disappeared under this development and also under the Gallaher's site, though some parts of the banking's profile still survive in this area and have been grassed over. From the western end of the Gallaher's site, the Members' Banking remains, still looking much as it did in the track's heyday and forming a major feature of the Museum.

The Members' Bridge has been replaced by a replica and the banking continues until broken by the gap over the River Wey where the Hennebique Bridge was sited. Just south of that gap is the bridge built by Vickers to move Wellingtons and Warwicks onto the airfield, and near this is the 1957 Memorial which was dismantled as part of the Mercedes-Benz development and re-erected on the Museum site, next to the resited 1911 ticket office. The western end of the Members' Banking, across the river, survives, as does the Railway Straight, now cleared of the hangars which were built during World War Two.

Outside the Museum site, the restored Aero Club building can be found alongside the retail park and three concrete pits from the Campbell Circuit are preserved in the car park of 'The Heights'. The line of the Finishing Straight through the car park is delineated by a double row of lighting poles. Solomon's Straight, Sahara Straight and Aerodrome curve, the sections of the Campbell Circuit which run across the 'Mercedes-Benz World' site, have been partly preserved, as has the bridge taking the circuit across the River Wey, which also carried aircraft from the Vickers factory at the Fork to the aerodrome. The car park for the Marks & Spencer superstore stands on the site of the Hawker erecting sheds where so many Hurricanes were built and BAe have kept a presence at Brooklands, still maintaining a small link with the aviation past, as a civil aircraft spare parts and accessories depot for BAe Systems stands on the site of the Thomson & Taylor workshops.

It is inside the Museum grounds that the most important preservation has taken place. A secondary entrance road from Brooklands Road is part of the Campbell Circuit and is lined with some of the original iron railings, though these have been repositioned. The Clubhouse has been restored and is now in much the same form as it was in the years immediately before World War Two. This has been done with great care, and even the colour of the interior paintwork has been faithfully reproduced. The railings surrounding the Clubhouse and between the paddock and the

remains of the Finishing Straight are those which were erected in 1907, although repositioned after World War Two, and the Shell pagoda in the paddock is preserved, as is the BP pagoda behind the Clubhouse, while the Pratts and Esso petrol pagodas are now also in the Museum grounds.

The paddock stalls are replicas of the originals but the Campbell shed, holding the Museum car display, is the original shed used by Sir Malcolm Campbell and subsequently by ERA. Adjoining this is the old Press Office. The bicycle collection is housed in the buildings which formed part of a row of paddock sheds used by well-known tuners, and at the end of this row is the former Dunlop tyre depot. Opposite these is the Grand Prix exhibition, which is in the buildings formerly known as 'The Robinery', the tuning shop of Robin Jackson in the 1930s.

Behind the Clubhouse are the stratosphere chamber, built in 1947–8, which now houses the aero engine collection and the Museum's Education Centre, and the wartime hangar in the middle of the Finishing Straight, which is the home of the older aircraft in the Museum collection. Adjacent to the hangar entrance is a wooden shed, a replica of the shed built by A.V. Roe in 1908.

The Test Hill survives and the posts and railings lining it have been carefully sited in the positions of the originals. At the top of the Test Hill is the old Members' luncheon room, and if the cinder and gravel track is followed round to the Members' Banking the tunnel through which spectators entered Brooklands to go to the Members' Hill is still there. Beside this are the remains of an anti-aircraft gun tower. At the foot of the Members' Banking near the Members' Bridge is a wartime air raid shelter, and there is another air raid shelter adjoining the Test Hill. At the top of the Finishing Straight, on the edge of the track, is a round concrete base, the remains of a wartime water tower.

If the surface of the banking is studied closely where it runs from the Finishing Straight and under the Members' Bridge fine ridges can be seen in the surface, made by generations of cars sweeping round the corner and up the banking while racing on the Mountain Circuit. Further along the Members' Banking, the tunnel which formed part of the competitors' entrance road to the paddock can still be seen. This was used for the early JCC members' high-speed trials and can be traced round to the Members' Bridge, outside the Banking. The tunnel is the scene of Leeson's fatal accident in the 1932 1,000-Mile race. Further along the banking, just before the gap where the track crosses the River Wey, is the paddock return road, used by cars returning to the paddock after a race.

APPENDIX ONE

OUTER CIRCUIT LAP RECORDS

Cars

Year	Driver	Car	Speed
1907	Nazzaro	(Fiat)	121.64mph [1]
1920	Guinness	(Sunbeam)	120.01mph [2]
1922	Guinness	(Sunbeam)	123.39mph
1923	Thomas	(Leyland-Thomas)	124.12mph [3]
	Eldridge	(Fiat)	124.33mph
1924	Thomas	(Leyland-Thomas)	125.14mph
	Thomas	(Leyland-Thomas)	128.36mph
1925	Thomas	(Leyland-Thomas)	129.36mph
	Thomas	(Leyland-Thomas)	129.70mph [3]
1928	Don	(Sunbeam)	131.76mph
1929	Cobb	(Delage)	132.11mph
	Don	(Sunbeam)	132.11mph
	Don	(Sunbeam)	134.24mph
1930	Birkin	(Bentley)	135.33mph
	Don	(Sunbeam)	137.58mph
1932	Birkin	(Bentley)	137.96mph
1934	Cobb	(Napier-Railton)	139.71mph
	Cobb	(Napier-Railton)	140.93mph
1935	Bertram	(Barnato-Hassan)	142.60mph
	Cobb	(Napier-Railton)	143.44mph

(1) The accuracy of this speed has always been doubted. It is perhaps significant that Nazzaro never appeared on the BARC list of 120mph badge holders.

(2) Although not recognised as a record, this was probably the fastest lap up to that time.

(3) These speeds were not timed by a BARC timekeeper, so were not recognised as official lap records.

Motor Cycles

Year	Rider	Machine	Speed
1921	Temple	(Harley-Davidson)	94.07mph [1]
1922	Le Vack	(Zenith-JAP)	100.27mph
1923	Temple	(British Anzani)	101.23mph
1924	Temple	(Montgomery-British Anzani)	109.94mph
1925	Wright	(Zenith-JAP)	110.43mph
1926	Wright	(Zenith-JAP)	113.45mph
1929	Wright	(Zenith-JAP)	113.71mph
	Wright	(Zenith-JAP)	117.19mph
	Wright	(Zenith-JAP)	118.86mph
1935	Pope	(Brough Superior-JAP)	120.59mph
	Fernihough	(Brough Superior-JAP)	123.58mph
1939	Pope	(Brough Superior-JAP)	124.51mph

(1) Before 1922 not all laps speeds were published, so it is difficult to ascertain the lap record holders. In October 1921 Temple set a 1,000cc class five-mile record at 96.54mph during a race, so must have broken his lap record.

WINNERS OF LONG-DISTANCE RACES

Cars

1911
RAC Production Cars	Cathie (Star)

1912
RAC Production Cars	Haywood (Singer)

1921
JCC 200-Miles	Segrave (Talbot-Darracq)

1922
JCC 200-Miles	Guinness (Talbot-Darracq)

1923
JCC 200-Miles	Harvey (Alvis)

1924
JCC 200-Miles	Guinness (Talbot-Darracq)

1925
JCC 200-Miles	Segrave (Talbot-Darracq)

1926
JCC Production Cars	Hazlehurst (Salmson)
RAC British Grand Prix	Senechal/Wagner (Delage)
JCC 200-Miles	Segrave (Talbot)

1927
Essex MC 6-Hours	Duller (Sunbeam)
JCC Sporting Cars	Harvey (Alvis)
RAC British Grand Prix	Benoist (Delage)
JCC 200-Miles	Campbell (Bugatti)

1928
Essex MC 6-Hours	Ramponi (Alfa Romeo)
JCC 200-Miles	Campbell (Delage)

1929
JCC Double-12	Ramponi (Alfa Romeo)
BARC 6-Hours	Barnato/Dunfee (Bentley)
BRDC 500-Miles	Barclay/Clement (Bentley)

1930
JCC Double-12	Barnato/Clement (Bentley)
BRDC 500-Miles	Davis/March (Austin)

1931
JCC Double-12	March/Staniland (MG)
BRDC 500-Miles	Dunfee/Paul (Bentley)

1932
JCC 1,000-Miles	Wisdom/Richmond (Riley)
BRDC 500-Miles	Horton/Bartlett (MG)

1933
JCC International Trophy	Lewis (Alfa Romeo)
BRDC 500-Miles	Hall (MG)

1934
JCC International Trophy	Straight (Maserati)
BRDC British Empire Trophy	Eyston (MG)
BRDC 500-Miles	Dixon (Riley)

1935
JCC International Trophy	Fontes (Alfa Romeo)
BRDC British Empire Trophy	Dixon (Riley)
BRDC 500-Miles	Cobb/Rose-Richards (Napier-Railton)

1936

JCC International Trophy	Bira (ERA)
BRDC 500-Miles	Dixon (Riley)

1937

BARC Campbell Trophy	Bira (Maserati)
JCC International Trophy	Mays (ERA)
BRDC 500 (km)	Cobb/Bertram (Napier-Railton)

1938

JCC International Trophy	Maclure (Riley)
LCC Production Sports Cars	Willing/Jarvis (Delahaye)
JCC 200-Miles	Wakefield (ERA)
BRDC Road Race	Bira (ERA)

1939

JCC International Trophy	Bira (Maserati)

Motor Cycles

1910

60-lap TT	Moorhouse (Indian)

1912

Junior Brooklands TT	Bailey (Douglas)
Senior Brooklands TT	Emerson (Norton)

1913

BMCRC 6-Hours	Haswell (Triumph)

1914

Brooklands Junior TT	Williams (AJS)
Brooklands Senior TT	Collier (Matchless-MAG)

1921

BMCRC 500-Miles	Le Vack (Indian)
Ealing DMCC Sidecar 200-Miles 350cc	Pullin (Douglas)
Ealing DMCC Sidecar 200-Miles 600cc	Bridgman (Indian)
Ealing DMCC Sidecar 200-Miles 1,000cc	Davidson (Indian)

1923

BMCRC 200-Mile solo 250cc	Johnstone (Cotton-Blackburne)
BMCRC 200-Mile solo 350cc	Le Vack (New Imperial-JAP)
BMCRC 200-Mile solo 500cc	Denly (Norton)
BMCRC 200-Mile solo 1,000cc	Le Vack (Brough Superior-JAP)
Ealing DMCC Sidecar 200-Miles 350cc	Marchant (Chater-Lea)
Ealing DMCC Sidecar 200-Miles 600cc	Bance (OEC-Blackburne)
Ealing DMCC Sidecar 200-Miles 1,000cc	Le Vack (Brough Superior-JAP)

1924

Ealing DMCC Sidecar 200-Miles 350cc	Marchant (Chater-Lea)
Ealing DMCC Sidecar 200-Miles 600cc	Tucker (Norton)
Ealing DMCC Sidecar 200-Miles 1,000cc	Humphreys (Harley-Davidson)
BMCRC 200-Mile solo 250cc	Walters (Zenith-JAP)
BMCRC 200-Mile solo 350cc	Le Vack (New Imperial-JAP)
BMCRC 200-Mile solo 500cc	Grogan (Norton)
BMCRC 200-Mile solo 750cc	Glover (Douglas)
BMCRC 200-Mile solo 1,000cc	Allchin (Zenith-JAP)

1925

Ealing DMCC Sidecar 200-Miles 350cc	Baxter (Rex-Acme-JAP)
Ealing DMCC Sidecar 200-Miles 600cc	Staniland (Norton)
Ealing DMCC Sidecar 200-Miles 1,000cc	Ashby (Zenith-JAP)
BMCRC 200-Mile solo 250cc	Worters (Cotton-Blackburne)
BMCRC 200-Mile solo 350cc	Handley (Rex-Acme-Blackburne)
BMCRC 200-Mile solo 500cc	Driscoll (Norton)
BMCRC 200-Mile solo 1,000cc	Longman (Harley-Davidson)

1926

Ealing DMCC Sidecar 200-Miles 350cc	Prestwich (Coventry Eagle-JAP)
Ealing DMCC Sidecar 200-Miles 600cc	Horsman (Triumph)
BMCRC 200-Mile solo 250cc	Worters (Excelsior-JAP)
BMCRC 200-Mile solo 350cc	Lacey (Grindlay Peerless-JAP)
BMCRC 200-Mile solo 500cc	Emerson (HRD-JAP)
BMCRC 200-Mile solo 1,000cc	Ashby (Zenith-JAP)

1927

Ealing DMCC Sidecar 200-Miles 350cc	Handley (Rex Acme-Blackburne)
Ealing DMCC Sidecar 200-Miles 600cc	Le Vack (New Hudson)
Ealing DMCC Sidecar 200-Miles 1,000cc	Baldwin (Zenith-JAP)
BMCRC 200-Mile solo 250cc	Worters (Excelsior-JAP)
BMCRC 200-Mile solo 350cc	Staniland (Excelsior-JAP)
BMCRC 200-Mile solo 500cc	Gibson (Sunbeam)
BMCRC 200-Mile solo 1,000cc	Longman (Harley-Davidson)

1928

Ealing DMCC Sidecar 200-Miles 350cc	Hicks (Velocette)
Ealing DMCC Sidecar 200-Miles 600cc	Denly (Norton)
Ealing DMCC Sidecar 200-Miles 1,000cc	Baragwanath (Brough Superior-JAP)
BMCRC 200-Mile solo 250cc	Staniland (Excelsior-JAP)
BMCRC 200-Mile solo 350cc	Phillips (Grindlay Peerless-JAP)
BMCRC 200-Mile solo 500cc	Le Vack (New Hudson)
BMCRC 200-Mile solo 1,000cc	Driscoll (Norton)

1929

Ealing DMCC Sidecar 200-Miles 350cc	Hicks (Velocette)
Ealing DMCC Sidecar 200-Miles 600cc	Tucker (Norton)
Ealing DMCC Sidecar 200-Miles 1,000cc	Driscoll (AJS)
BMCRC 200-Mile solo 250cc	Staniland (Excelsior-JAP)
BMCRC 200-Mile solo 350cc	Denly (AJS)
BMCRC 200-Mile solo 500cc	Nott (Rudge)
BMCRC 200-Mile solo 1,000cc	Barber (Matchless)

1930

Ealing DMCC Sidecar 200-Miles 350cc	Hicks (AJS)
Ealing DMCC Sidecar 200-Miles 600cc	Horsman (Triumph)
Ealing DMCC Sidecar 200-Miles 1,000cc	Waterman (Coventry Eagle-JAP)
BMCRC 200-Mile solo 175cc	Meetens (Francis Barnett)
BMCRC 200-Mile solo 250cc	Staniland (Excelsior-JAP)
BMCRC 200-Mile solo 350cc	Baker (AJS)
BMCRC 200-Mile solo 500cc	Denly (AJS)
BMCRC 200-Mile solo 1,000cc	Quinn (Triumph)

After 1930, no motor cycle races exceeding 150 miles were held.

AIRCRAFT BUILT AT BROOKLANDS

This appendix lists aircraft types manufactured at Brooklands (including those manufactured elsewhere and assembled or erected at Brooklands), with the approximate date at which production commenced. The manufacturers are listed in alphabetical order, and their aircraft in chronological order. Note that this list may not be complete and that some one-off types may not have been recorded.

Air Navigation & Engineering Co (Blériot)

Caudron	1911
Monoplane	1911
Parasol	1911
Avro 504	1913
Monoplane trainer	1913
Spad 7	1916
RAF SE5a	1917
Handasyde Ultralight	1923
ANEC 1	1923
ANEC 11	1924
ANEC II1	1925
ANEC Missel Thrush	1925

A.V. Roe and A.V. Roe & Co Ltd

No 1 Biplane	1908
No 2 Triplane	1909
Mercury Triplane	1910
No 3 Two-seat Triplane	1910
No 4 Triplane	1910
Type D	1910
E 500	1911
Type F	1912
Type G	1912
Hydro-Biplane	1912
Curtiss	1913
Duigan	1913
504	1913
Billing Biplane	1911

British Aircraft Corporation Ltd and British Aerospace Ltd

TSR2	1963
BAC One-Eleven	1966
Concorde	1968

British & Colonial Aeroplane Co Ltd

Zodiac	1909
Burga Monoplane	1912
Collyer Lang Monoplane	1910

Coventry Ordnance Works Ltd

Monoplane	1911
De Boltoff Triplane	1913
Edwards Rhomboidal	1911

Howard Flanders

F2	1911
F3	1912
F4	1912
B2	1912
Gaskell Blackburn Biplane	1914

Hammond

Biplane	1910
Triplane	1911
Monoplane	1913

Handasyde

Raynham Monoplane	1923

H.G. Hawker Engineering Co Ltd and Hawker Aircraft Ltd

Duiker	1923
Woodcock	1923

Danecock	1924	Transatlantic	1914
Cygnet	1924	Two-seater	1915
Hedgehog	1924	S1	1915
Heron	1926	RAF BE2c	1915
Horsley	1926	G100 Elephant	1915
Hornbill	1926	G102	1916
Hawkfinch	1927	RG	1916
Harrier	1927	F1	1917
Tomtit	1928	F2	1917
F20/27	1928	RAF SE5a	1917
Hoopoe	1928	F3	1917
Osprey	1930	F4 Buzzard	1917
Fury	1931	Raymor	1919
Nimrod	1931	F4a	1919
Audax	1931	F5	1919
Dantorp	1932	Type A	1919
Demon	1933	Type AS	1919
PV3	1934	F6	1920
Hardy	1934	Semiquaver	1920
Hind	1934		
PV4	1934		
Hartbees	1935		
Hurricane	1935		
Hector	1936		
Henley	1937		
Hotspur	1938		

Moore Brabazon

Biplane	1908

Henderson-Glenny

HSF II Gadfly I	1921
HSF II Gadfly II	1921
HSF II Gadfly III	1921

Neale

Pup	1909
6 Monoplane	1910
7 Biplane	1910
Parsons Biplane	1913
Perry Beadle Biplane	1913
Petre Monoplane	1913
Poynter Monoplane	1910

Hewlett & Blondeau Ltd

Farman	1913
Vickers Boxkite	1913
RAF BE2c	1915

Saunders-Roe Ltd

Supermarine Walrus	1942
Skinner Monoplane	1913

Lane

Biplane	1910
Single-seat Monoplane	1910
Two-seat Monoplane	1910

Sopwith Aviation Co Ltd

Wright Biplane	1912
Hybrid Biplane	1912
Three-Seater	1913
Tabloid	1913
Churchill Sociable	1914
Gordon Bennett	1914
Gunbus	1914
2-seater Scout	1915
Type 806 Gunbus	1915
S.L.T. BP	1915
1½-Strutter	1915
Pup	1915
Beardmore WB 111	1916
Triplane	1916
L.R.T. TR	1916

Martin & Handasyde (Martinsyde Ltd)

No 2 Monoplane	1910
No 3 Monoplane	1910
No 4B Dragonfly	1911
Monoplane	1911
Military Monoplane	1912
Military Trials	1912
Monoplane	1913
Waterbus	1913
Pusher Biplane	1914

Camel F1	1916		Virginia	1922
Ships Camel 2F	1917		Victoria	1922
Cuckoo T1	1917		Vigit	1922
B1 Bomber	1917		Valparaiso	1924
Bee	1917		Vulture	1924
B2	1917		Vagabond	1924
Dolphin	1917		Vanguard	1925
Hippo	1917		Vanellus	1925
Rhino	1917		Vixen	1925
Snipe	1917		Venture	1925
Bulldog	1917		Wibault Scout	1926
Camel TF1	1918		Valiant	1927
Dragon	1918		Vendace	1928
Snail	1918		Armstrong Whitworth Siskin	1928
Salamander	1918		Vespa	1929
Buffalo	1918		Jockey	1929
Snark	1918		Type 177	1929
Snapper	1918		Type 150	1929
Sparrow	1918		Type 143 Bolivian Scout	1929
Scooter	1918		Type 161	1931
Swallow	1918		PV Bomber	1931
Cobham	1919		Hawker Hart	1932
Atlantic	1919		Vanox	1932
Dove	1919		Valentia	1933
Gnu	1919		M1/30	1933
Wallaby	1919		G4/31PV	1934
Grasshopper	1919		Vincent	1934
Schneider Trophy	1919		Wellesley	1935
Antelope	1919		Vellox	1936
Rainbow	1919		Venom	1936
			Wellington	1936
			Warwick	1939

Spencer

Biplane	1910

Spencer-Stirling

Monoplane	1910
Biplane	1910

Universal Aviation Co Ltd

Birdling	1911

Vickers Ltd, Vickers (Aviation) Ltd, Vickers-Armstrongs Ltd

RAF BE2c	1915
RAF FE8	1915
RAF SE5a	1916
FB9	1916
FB14	1916
FB19	1916
Vimy	1918
Viking	1919
Vernon	1921
Vulcan	1921

F7/41	1942
Windsor	1943
Viking	1945
Valetta	1947
Viscount	1948
Varsity	1949
Valiant	1951
Vanguard	1958
VC-10	1966

Vintage Aeroplane & Flying Association

Vickers F5B replica	1965
Vickers Vimy replica	1969
Walton Edwards Collosoplane	1911
Weybridge Man-powered Aircraft	1971

Howard T. Wright

Wright Golden Plover	1909
Wright Co-Axial Monoplane	1909
Wright Avis	1910
Warwick Wright Monoplane	1910
Warwick Wright Biplane	1910

APPENDIX FOUR

MAPS

Re-drawn from originals by A. J. Hutchings

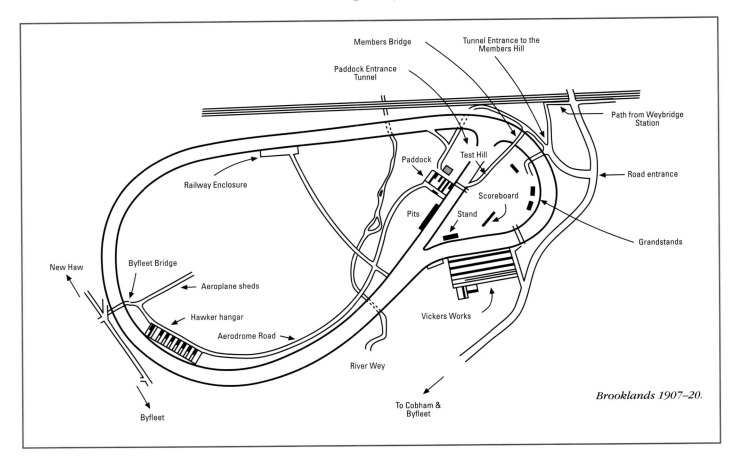

Brooklands 1907–20.

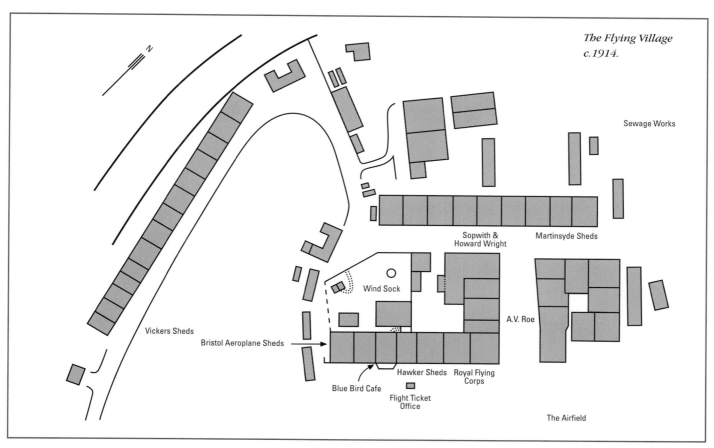

The Flying Village c.1914.

Sewage Works

Sopwith & Howard Wright

Martinsyde Sheds

A.V. Roe

Wind Sock

Vickers Sheds

Bristol Aeroplane Sheds

Hawker Sheds   Royal Flying Corps

Blue Bird Cafe

Flight Ticket Office

The Airfield

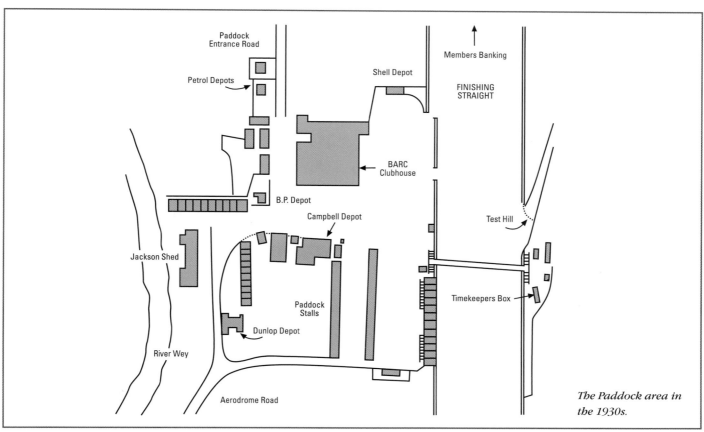

Paddock Entrance Road

Petrol Depots

Shell Depot

Members Banking

FINISHING STRAIGHT

BARC Clubhouse

Test Hill

B.P. Depot

Campbell Depot

Jackson Shed

Timekeepers Box

Paddock Stalls

Dunlop Depot

River Wey

Aerodrome Road

The Paddock area in the 1930s.

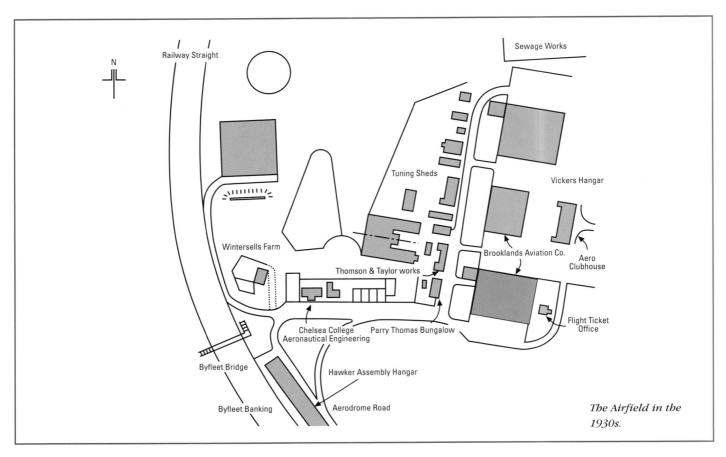

The Airfield in the 1930s.

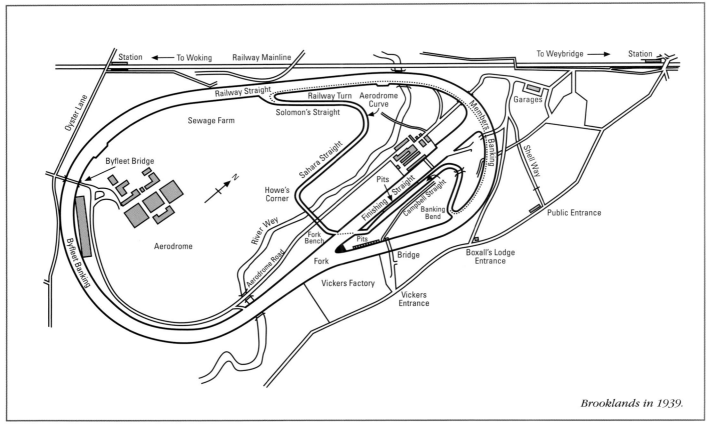

Brooklands in 1939.

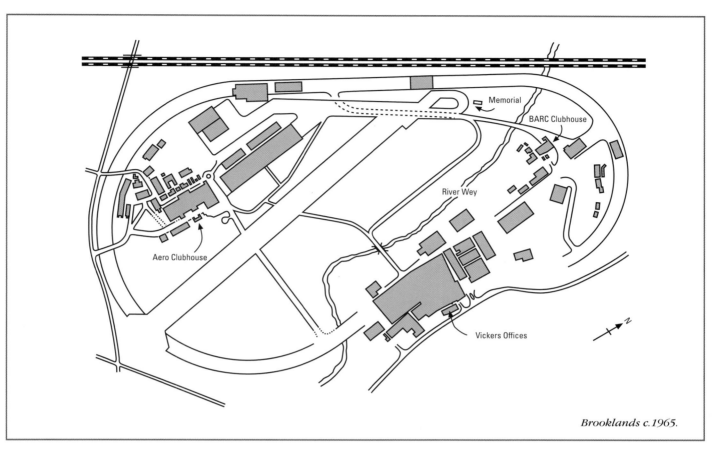

Brooklands c.1965.

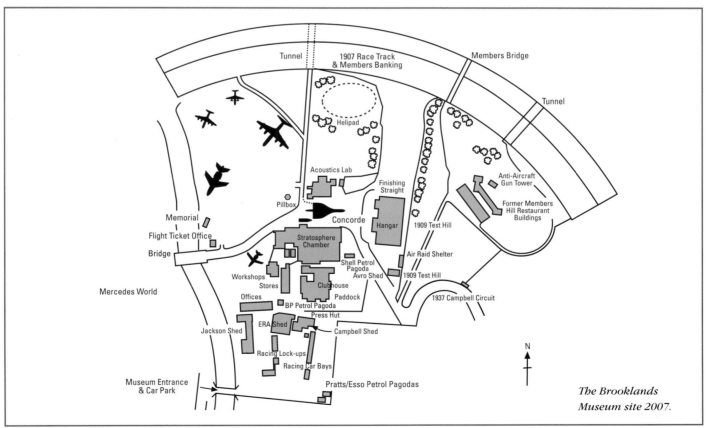

The Brooklands
Museum site 2007.

BIBLIOGRAPHY

Andrews, L.F., and Morgan, E.B. *Vickers Aircraft since 1908* (Putnam 1988).

Bacon, Roy, and Hallworth, Ken. *The British Motor Cycle Directory* (Crowood Press 2004).

Barrymore Halpenny, Bruce. *Action Stations 8: Military Airfields of Greater London* (Patrick Stephens 1984).

Berthon, Darell. *The Racing History of the Bentley* (Autobooks 1962).

Birkin, Sir Henry. *Full Throttle* (Foulis 1932).

Boddy, William. *Montlhéry* (Cassell 1961).

– *Brooklands: The Complete Motor Racing History* (MRP Publishing 2001).

British Racing Drivers' Club – Silver Jubilee Book (1952).

Brown, B. Canning. *Austin Competition History: The Cars and Those Who Drove Them 1922–1939* (Twincam 2006).

Chula Chakrabongse, Prince. *Dick Seaman* (Foulis 1946).

Gardner, Charles (editor). *Fifty Years of Brooklands* (Heinemann 1956).

Hartley, Peter. *Bikes at Brooklands* (Goose & Son 1973).

– *Brooklands Bikes in the Twenties* (Argus Books 1980).

Hay, Michael. *Blower Bentley* (Number One Press 2001).

Heal, Anthony S. *Sunbeam Racing Cars* (Haynes 1989).

Johnson, Howard. *Wings over Brooklands* (Whittet Books 1981).

Lewis, Peter. *British Racing and Record-Breaking Aircraft* (Putnam 1970).

Lloyd, F.H.M. *Hurricane* (Harborough Publishing 1945).

Ludvigsen, Karl. *The Mercedes-Benz Racing Cars* (Bond/Parkhurst Books 1971).

Mason, Francis K. *Hawker Aircraft since 1920* (Putnam 1961)

– *Battle over Britain* (Albion Books 1969).

– *The British Fighter since 1912* (Putnam 1992).

– *The British Bomber since 1914* (Putnam 1994).

McSwein, Donald R. *Brooklands Aircraft* (author).

Mortimer, Charles. *Brooklands and Beyond* (Goose Books 1974).

– *Brooklands behind the Scenes* (Haynes 1980).

Orlebar, Christopher. *The Concorde Story* (Hamlyn 1994).

Penrose, Harald, *British Aviation: The Pioneer Years* (Putnam 1967).

– *British Aviation: The Adventuring Years* (Putnam 1973).

– *British Aviation: Widening Horizons 1930-1934* (HMSO 1979).

– *British Aviation: Ominous Skies* (HMSO 1980).

Pope, Noel. *Full Chat* (MRP 1952).

Portway, Nic. *Vauxhall 30-98* (New Wensum Publishing 1995).

Posthumus, Cyril, and Tremayne, David. *Land Speed Record* (Osprey 1985).

Pulford, J.S.L. *The Locke Kings of Brooklands, Weybridge* (Walton & Weybridge Local History Society in association with Brooklands Museum 1996).

Ramsey, Winston (editor). *The Blitz: Then and Now, vols 1 & 2* (After the Battle 1987–8).

Thetford, Owen. *Aircraft of the Royal Air Force since 1918* (Putnam 1995).

Tours, Hugh. *Parry Thomas* (Batsford 1959).

Venables, David. *Napier: The First to Wear the Green* (Haynes 1998).

Newspapers and periodicals

The Aeroplane, Airfield Review, The Autocar, Brooklands Society Gazette, Flight, The Light Car, The Motor, Motor Sport, The Automotor Journal, Speed, The Times

INDEX

Abbeville 243
ABC (aero engine) 61
ABC (m/cycle) 48-50, 72-74
Abdullah, King, of Jordan, 182
Abecassis, George 214
Abercromby Sir George Bt 33
AC (car) 23, 75, 82, 83, 88, 92, 103, 262
AC Cars Ltd. 23, 262
ACU (Auto-Cycle Union) 34, 36, 106, 222
AEC (bus) 269
Aer Lingus 250, 251
Aerial Derby 63, 82, 143, 145
Aeroplane, The 266
Aeroplane Armaments Experimental Establishment 255
AFN Ltd. 210
AIACR (Alliance Internationale des Automobile Clubs Reconnus) 32, 49,112
Air Canada 251, 254
Air Defence Cadet Corps 239
Air France 251, 257
Air Hanson 262
Air League 237
Air Ministry 148-150, 160, 228, 231, 239, 247, 252
Air Ministry Specifications
   B9/32 230
   B12/36 244
   B5/41 244
   B35/46 252
   F5/34 229, 231
   G4/31 229, 230
   M1/30 229
Air Navigation & Engineering Co. 68
Air Salvage International 263
Air Training Corps 239
Air Transport Auxiliary 192, 194
Airbus (aircraft) 257
Airspeed (aircraft)
   Ambassador 251
   Consul 266
Aitchison 224
Aitken, Hon Max 135
Aitken, Hon Peter 214, 221
AJS (m/cycle) 49, 132, 139, 177, 204, 211, 217
Alcock, John (later Sir) 60, 61, 142, 143, 145, 148
Aldington, H.J. 136, 159, 161, 172, 214, 266
Aldington, W.H. 136, 266

Alecto (m/cycle) 75
Alexandra, HM Queen 49
Alfa Romeo (car) 120, 126, 127, 129, 130, 135, 158, 159, 164, 168, 169, 173, 176, 182, 186, 190, 191, 197, 200, 202, 203, 205, 207, 209, 210, 215, 218, 221, 222, 266
Allan, Margaret 174, 183, 195
Allery, F. 135
Alta (car) 197, 202, 213-215
Alvis (car) 92, 103, 112, 115, 118, 167, 174, 268, 269
America's Cup 56
Amilcar (car) 112, 113, 118, 123, 124, 161
Anderson, N. 160
André T.P. 144
Anglo American Motor Car Co. 24
Anthony, C.M. 201
Antoinette (aero engine) 54
Anzani (engine) 75
Anzani-Crouch (car) 90
Archer, Les 160, 169, 170, 174, 176, 177, 187, 198, 204, 210, 211, 216, 217, 224
Ardarth 170
Argyll (car) 45
Ariel (m/cycle) 186, 198, 203
Armstrong Siddeley Development Co. 228
Armstrong Whitworth Aircraft Ltd., Sir W.G. 151
Armstrong-Whitworth (car) 38
Army Service Corps 186
Ashby, Frank 134, 167
Ask a Policeman 266
Astley H.J.D. 32
Aston Martin (car) 85, 88, 92, 110, 134, 135, 201
Athlone, Earl of 83
Atkinson, Rowan 266
Austin Motor Co. 244
Austin (car) 27, 32, 33, 39, 92, 98, 99, 113-115, 120, 129-131, 137, 155, 158, 161, 174, 183, 194, 195, 208, 209, 212, 215, 266, 268
Austin, Sir Herbert (later Lord) 158
Austro-Daimler (car) 122
Autocar, The 40, 101, 114, 210, 213
Autocar, The Cup 114

Autokraft Ltd. 262
Auto Union (car) 183, 186, 193
Automobile Club of Great Britain & Ireland 10, 11, 15
Avis (aircraft) 57
Avon-Jappic (car) 112
Avro (aircraft)
   Avenger 149
   Biplane 56
   500 61
   504 61, 65, 66, 149
   Lancaster 245
   Mailplane 234
Avroplane 54
Avus 16, 186

BA 257, 263
BA1 Eagle (aircraft) 237
"Babs" (car) 95, 98, 108, 113, 122, 194
BAC 252, 255-257, 259, 266
BAC (aircraft) One-Eleven 252, 256
   TSR2 255, 256
BAe 257, 260, 262, 270
BAe (aircraft) Hawk 257
Bagshawe, Wilfred 108
Baker 139
Baker, D'Arcy 27,31
Baker, G.L.174, 222
Baker-Carr, C.T. 203, 207
Baldwin, Oliver 91, 106, 160
Ballot (car) 74, 95, 123, 124, 131, 194
Balls, Vernon 123, 131
Baragwanath, E.C.E "Barry" 160, 169, 170, 197
BARC (Brooklands Automobile Racing Club) 12, 13, 15, 21-23, 25, 28, 31, 36, 40, 41, 43, 48, 49, 53, 55-57, 59, 65, 71, 73-76, 85, 89, 93, 99, 106, 110, 112, 120, 122-124, 126, 129, 131, 133, 136, 137, 153, 155, 156, 160, 161, 165, 167, 169-171, 173, 174, 186, 189, 193, 196, 199, 202, 204, 205, 207-210, 212, 214, 218, 222, 232, 241, 265, 268, 269
BARC "120 mph" badge 153, 200
BARC "130 mph" badge 200
BARC major races
   3-litre Scratch 76
   BBC Trophy 194, 205
   Benzole Handicap 45
   British Mountain

Championship 191, 200
British Trophy 214
Brooklands Championship183, 194
Brooklands Road Championship 218
Campbell Trophy 207, 212, 222
Coronation Gold Trophy 207
Duchess of York Trophy 167
Duke of York Trophy 165
Dunlop Jubilee Trophy 215
Evening News 100 Mile Handicap109
Founders' Gold Cup 95, 99, 113, 126, 155
Gold Star 114, 115,122, 130, 136, 158, 162, 173, 179, 192, 201, 213
Gold Vase 129
Guy's Hospital Gala Charity 165
Inter-Club Meeting 165
Ladies' Bracelet 27, 264
Locke King Trophy 202, 213, 221
Marcel Renault Memorial Trophy 20
Montagu Cup 20, 32
Mountain Championship 159, 167, 169, 175, 176, 185, 197, 203, 210, 215
News of the World Handicap 101
O'Gorman Trophy 28, 32, 33, 41
President's Gold Plate 123
Siam Trophy 195, 203, 210, 215
Six Hour Race 129
Barclay, Jack 131, 155
Barnard, L.L.G. 67
Barnato Cup
Barnato, Woolf 73, 120, 122, 129, 130,134, 135, 169
Barnato-Hassan (car) 184, 191, 192, 195-197, 201, 203, 210, 214
Barnes 43
Barnes, J.D. 129
Barnes, S.F. 129
Barnwell, Harold 62, 63
Barrow, Cecil 108
Bartlett, Jack 169
Barton, Morag 261, 262
Bashall, Harry 32

Bass Charrington 260
BAT-JAP (m/cycle) 32, 34
Baxter, Jane 169
BEA 249-251, 253, 254, 256
Beadle, A.H. 215
Beadle, L 72
Beart, Francis 204, 216, 217
Beart, Harold 103
Beaufort, Duke of 13
Beaumont, Andre 60
Becke, A.W. von der 185, 196
Bedelia (car) 42
Bedford, George 72, 75
Bedford-Buick (car) 42, 51
Bell Jet Ranger (aircraft) 262
Bellamy 53
Benjafield, Dr Dudley 95, 114, 120, 122, 131, 137, 158, 185
Bennett, Charlie 34
Bennett, Fred 24
Bennett, James 146
Bennett, W.W.S. 213
Benoist, Robert 85, 92, 110, 115, 117
Bentley (car) 78, 88, 95, 113, 114, 120, 122, 124, 126-128, 131-133, 135-137, 157, 158, 161, 162, 165, 169, 174, 175, 194, 202, 207, 209, 212, 266
Bentley Drivers' Club 203, 247
Bentley, W.O. 31, 34, 45, 133
Bentley-Jackson (car) 202
Benz (car) 32, 36, 38-40, 48, 49, 78, 83, 85, 136
Berg, H. 215
Berliet (car) 33
Berry, N.A. 174
Bertelli, A.C. 134, 135
Bertram, Oliver 173, 174, 179, 183, 186, 191-197, 201-203, 209, 210, 214, 268
Bianchi (car) 32
Bianchi, Cecil 37
Bickell, Ben 160, 170, 177, 187, 197, 198, 203, 204, 217
Bickell-Ariel (m/cycle) 187
Bickell-JAP (m/cycle) 160, 170, 177, 198, 204
Bickford 222
Bickford, Oscar 24
Billing, Eardley, Mr & Mrs 57
Billington, G.F.186
Bira B, (Prince Birabongse Banubandh of Siam) 190, 195, 197, 200, 201, 203, 207-209, 212-214, 221, 222

Bird, Christopher 36, 41
Birkin, Charles 114
Birkin, Sir Henry "Tim" Bt 73,
    114, 120, 12, 127, 129-131, 133,
    134, 136, 133, 155, 157-165,
    167, 169-171, 173, 194, 266
Bishcoff, Rev. P.W. 34
Bishop, E.G. 203
Bishop, J.H. 268
Black, Norman 164,165
Blackbushe 262
Blackford 222
Blenkiron, Florence 177, 186
Bleriot (aircraft) 56, 57, 59,
    60, 62
Bleriot Aeronautics Ltd. 66, 68
Bleriot, Louis 55, 62
Blondeau, Gustav 34, 56, 57.
Blue Bird café 57, 65
Blue Bird (car) 40, 120, 151,
    156, 161, 172, 191, 230
BMCRC (British Motor Cycle
    Racing Club) 31, 32, 34, 36,
    39-41, 47, 48, 50, 65, 67, 71,
    73-76, 78, 79, 83, 85, 89, 91,
    93, 96, 103, 106, 112, 113,
    118, 120, 125, 126, 132, 133,
    137-139, 159, 169, 176, 186,
    197, 203, 210, 211, 215, 218
    222, 241, 267
BMRMC races
    Allcomers' Handicap 74
    Bacon Cup 160
    Brooklands Cup 176, 177
    Championship Meeting 160
    Clubmans' Grand Prix 198
    Cup Meeting 125, 203
    500-Mile 78, 186
    Gold Star 119, 204
    Grand Prix 112, 125, 132,
        138, 177, 187, 198, 204
    Hutchinson Hundred 103,
        108, 119, 132, 139, 160,
        170, 177, 198, 204, 211,
        217, 224
    J.A.Prestwich Cup 197
    Junior Mountain
        Championship 198
    Junior Brooklands TT 42, 49
    Junior TT 42
    Miller Cup 78
    Mountain Championship
        210, 224
    Olympic Passenger
        Machine 42
    Open Championship 42
    Phillips Cup 160
    Road Championship 216
    Senior Brooklands TT 49
    Senior Mountain
        Championship 170
    Senior TT 42
    Sir Charles Wakefield
        Cup 125
    Six Hours 47
    1000cc Solo
    350/1000cc Handicap
    200-Mile Solo 91, 118, 125,
        139, 198, 222
    Wakefield Trophy 197, 203
BMCRC Super Award 198
BMW (car) 210, 212, 214
BMW (m/cycle) 198, 224
BOAC 254, 255, 257
Boddy, William 241, 260, 269

Bofors 242, 243
Bolivian-Paraguayan War 151
Bone, Cyril 109
Borzacchini, Baconin 169
Bouchier, Chili 266
Boulting 198,
Boulton & Paul Ltd. 230, 238
Bourlier, Edmond 119
Bouts, E.L. 154, 163, 175
Bowes, R.L. 172
BP 270
Brabazon Committee 249, 250
Brabazon, Lord, of Tara 22, 54,
    249, 253
Brackenbury, Charles 173, 175,
    192, 209
Bradley, A. Percy 98, 133, 198,
    199
Brancker, Sir Sefton 232
Brand, Quintin (later Sir) 146
BRDC (British Racing Drivers
    Club) 67, 131, 137, 158, 161,
    174, 182, 193, 200, 202, 209,
    214
BRDC races
    British Empire Trophy 161,
        174, 176, 182, 186, 193, 200
    Brooklands Trophy 214
    Canada Trophy 161, 174
    500 Miles 131, 133, 137, 158,
        168, 175, 184, 186, 194,
        202, 209, 212, 266
    India Trophy 161, 174, 175
    New Zealand Trophy 174, 176
    Road Race 214
    South Africa Trophy 161
Brettell, Gordon 208
Brewster, Percy 170
Bridgman, E. 85
Brighton & Hove Motor
    Club 136
Bristol Aeroplane
    Co. Ltd. 59, 255
Bristol (aircraft)
    Biplane 60
    Boxkite 59, 60, 65
    Monoplane 63
    101 101
    198 257
    Scout 63
Bristol (aero engine) Aquila
    231
    Pegasus 151
Bristol Flying School 62, 65
British & Colonial Aeroplane Co.
    – see Bristol Aeroplane Co.
British Aerospace – see BAe
British Aircraft Corporation –
    see BAC
British Aircraft Manufacturing
    Co. 237
British Airways – see BA
British Anzani (m/cycle) 91
British Empire Michelin Cup
    57, 61
British European Airways
    Corporation – see BEA
British Motor Racing Cycle
    Club – see BMRMC
British Overseas Airways
    Corporation – see BOAC
British Petroleum – see BP
British Racing Drivers' Club –
    see BRDC
British Red Cross 49

Brooke, Leslie 221
Brooke Special (car) 221
Brooklands (Weybridge) Ltd.
    199, 204, 247, 248
Brooklands and Beyond 133
Brooklands Aero Club 148,
    149, 168, 175, 204, 231, 232,
    235, 239, 270
Brooklands Airways Ltd. 235
Brooklands Aviation Ltd. 232
Brooklands Automobile Racing
    Club – see BARC
Brooklands, Behind the
    Scenes 225
Brooklands Engineering Ltd. 248
Brooklands Estate Ltd. 105, 171
Brooklands House 9
Brooklands Museum 262,
    263,266, 270
Brooklands Museum Trust 261
Brooklands School of Flying 232
Brooklands Society 260
Brooklands Society Gazette 269
Brooklands to Brighton Race 59
Brooklands Track Ltd. 260
Brough Superior (m/cycle) 79,
    91, 96, 103, 109, 119, 160,
    170, 186, 197, 198, 212, 216,
    222, 224
Bruce, T.B. 210
Bryce, G.R. "Jock" 251, 254
BSA (m/cycle) 169, 170, 210, 222
Buchet (engine) 54
Buckley Cup 79
Bueno, Ramon 92
Bugatti (car) 81, 82, 89,92, 95,
    109, 110, 112, 113, 115, 117,
    118, 120, 122-124, 134, 136,
    137, 154, 155, 158-163, 167-
    169,172-176, 182, 183, 186,
    190-192, 194, 196, 201,
    211, 222
Bugatti Owners' Club 247
Bugatti, Ettore 174
Bulman, P.W.S. "George" 149,
    150, 167, 230, 232
Burgess-Wright (aircraft) 61
Burhill Golf Club 244
Burke 28
Burl, W. 268
Burman, Bob 49
Burn, Michael 171
Burney, C.S. 232
Burton, B. 222
Butler, Dorrie 198
Byfleet Estate Ltd. 199

Cadillac (car) 24
Caenshill 199, 252
Callingham, L.G. 130
Calthorpe (car) 47, 73
Cameron (car) 42
Camm Sidney (later Sir) 145,
    148-150, 228-230
Campbell, C. Lindsay 63
Campbell, D.M. 201
Campbell, Donald 217
Campbell, Malcolm (later Sir)
    36, 40, 51, 72, 81, 82, 92, 96,
    110, 112, 113, 115, 118, 120,
    123, 136, 137, 151, 154, 156,
    158, 159, 161, 164, 168, 169,
    172, 173, 176, 182, 191, 199,
    200, 205, 211, 217, 230, 247,
    248, 268, 270

Canadian Army 243
Cann, Maurice 217
Capital Airlines 251
Carbery, Lord 63
Carnegie, Lady Dora 10
Carr, Kenneth 202
Cartland, Barbara 269
Casse, Georges 127
Castrol 112
Caswell, Gordon 174
Cathie, C 37, 38
Caudron G-3 (aircraft) 238
Central Flying School 60
Chadwick, Roy 230
Challenger, Geoffrey 59
Chamberlain, Neville 215
Chassagne, Jean 46, 74, 85
Chater-Lea (m/cycle) 25, 125,
    142, 170, 177
Chetwynd, Hon Joan 173
Chiron, Louis 117
Chitty Bang Bang (car) 76, 78, 88
Chitty III (car) 131
Christie, Agatha 266
Christmas, Neil 198
Chrysler 262, 269
Chula, Prince, Chakrabongse of
    Siam 195
Cierva C-19 (aircraft) 235
Cinematograph Film Act 266
Cissac, Henri 32
Civil Air Guard 239
Clarke, F.J. 127
Clarke, Freddie 223, 224
Clayton, H.T.M.   212
Clayton, Lady 228
Clement Talbot 45, 46, 81
Clement, Frank 78, 88, 114,
    120, 122, 131, 135
Cleveland (m/cycle) 186
Clutton, Cecil "Sam" 242
Coatalen, Louis 33, 36, 39, 41, 46
Cobb, John 101, 115, 126, 129-
    131, 136, 153, 155, 157, 159,
    161-165, 169, 174, 176, 182,
    185, 194-197, 200-202, 204,
    205, 207-209, 212, 219, 222,
    224, 248, 262
Cocker, Jim 50
Cockerell, Stan 148
Cody, S.F. 57, 150
Coe, Major C.G. 99
Coes, Russell 103
College of Aeronautical &
    Automobile Engineering
    235, 266
Collier, Charles 24, 25, 28, 39,
    42, 49
Collier, H.M. 39
Colver, Bert 32
Comerfords 203
Comper Swift (aircraft) 234
Concorde 252, 257
Concorde "Delta Golf" 263
Connell, Ian 221
Cook, Humphrey 50, 96, 130,
    182, 183, 190, 193
Cook, Will 24, 32
Cooper Clerget (engine) 76
Cooper, George 266
Coppa Florio 10
Cordery, Violette 130, 231
Coreth zu Coredo, Baron 269
Costantini, Meo 174

Cotton (m/cycle) 119, 138, 211
Cotton, Billy 208, 218
Coupe de L'Auto 40
Couper, Mike 170, 195, 200
Coventry-Eagle-JAP (m/cycle)
    79, 108
Coventry-Victor (m/cycle)
    80, 217
Craig, William Y. 155,160
Cripps, S.T.B. 71
Croft 217
Crossman 43
Crouch (car) 90
Crusader (boat) 194
Crystal Palace 205, 217
Cummings, Ivy 84
Cummings, Sidney 40, 175
Cunnington, Capt. Douglas 243
Curzon, Lord (Viscount) –
    see Howe (Lord)
Cushman, Leon 92, 137
Cyclecar Club 133
Cyclecar Grand Prix 123
Czaikowski, Count Stanislas
    169, 174

Daily Mail 10, 59, 63, 142
Daily Telegraph 126
DaimlerChrysler 262, 263
Dambusters Raid 245
Daniell, Harold 170, 177, 187,
    197, 198, 204, 211
Darracq (car) 21, 23, 36, 40,
    81, 221
Davenport, Maurice 137
Davidson, Douglas 76, 78, 79, 85
Davis, Capt Duncan 150,
    232, 235
Davis, S.C.H. "Sammy" 114,
    127, 129, 131, 135, 137,
    154, 210
Davey, P 68
Dawbarn, Graham 232
Death Drives Through 266
de Dietrich (car) 20
de Haviland (aircraft)
    DH9 146
    DH60 Moth 149, 235, 237
    DH80a Puss Moth 234, 235
    DH82a Tiger Moth 232, 239
    DH83 Fox Moth 234
    DH 98 Mosquito 245
    DH Goblin (engine) 194
de Rosier, Jake 39
de Vizcaya, Pierre 82
Defries, Colin 25
Delage (car) 109, 110, 115,
    117,120, 123, 126, 129-131,
    134, 136, 137, 153, 155, 157-
    159, 161, 162, 167, 173, 174,
    179, 183, 186, 191, 192, 194,
    195, 199, 212, 221
Delahaye (car) 209, 214,
    215, 221
Delaney, Tom 167, 174
Demolition & Construction
    Co. 205
Denly, Bert 91, 118, 132
Dent, Dennis 174
Deperdussin (aircraft) 60
Derby-Miller (car) 158, 195, 196
Derby-Maserati (car) 197
Derrington, V.W.167
Desvaux, Lucien 85
Dewar Trophy 24, 130, 221

DFP (car) 45, 73, 169
Diamond (m/cycle) 67
Dicker, Bob 142
Dingle, J.P. 120, 122
Divo, Albert 110, 112, 117
Dixon, F.W. "Freddie" 78, 80, 91, 119, 160, 169, 175, 176, 178, 179, 182, 184-186, 191-194, 196, 200, 203, 209, 210
Dobbs, Hector 174, 200, 201
Dobson, Arthur 177, 191, 208, 209, 212-215, 218, 221
Dobson, Austin 207
Dodson, Charles 191, 209
Don, Kaye 78, 83, 90, 112, 113, 115, 122-124, 126, 127, 129-131, 134, 136, 157-159, 161, 171-176, 179, 183, 194
Don, Rita 176
Donaldson, Alexander 11
Donington Grand Prix 197, 203, 10, 218
Donington Park 171, 200, 210, 214
Dot-JAP (m/cycle) 79
Douglas (m/cycle) 40, 51, 74, 78, 83-85, 142, 170, 177, 186, 269
Douglas DC-3/C-47 Dakota (aircraft) 249, 250
Douglas, Jack 109
Dowding, Major Hugh (later Marshal of RAF, Lord) 69
Driscoll, L.P. 169, 183, 195
Dubonnet, Andre 110
Duesenberg (car) 184, 186, 195, 213
Duff, John 78, 85
Duller, George 96, 114, 268, 269
Duller, R.L. 213
Dunfee, Clive 131, 135, 137, 169, 266
Dunfee, Jack 123, 124, 127, 129-131, 134, 137, 158, 162, 169
Dunlop Rubber Co. 214
Dussek, Alan 170
Dutoit, Paul 268
Duzmo (m/cycle) 79
Dynasphere 269

Ealing & District MCC 84
200-Mile Sidecar races 84, 108, 138, 222
Earle 217
Earp, Clifford 23
East African Airways 255
Ebblewhite, A.V. "Ebby" 21, 22, 25, 27, 31, 42, 101, 106, 131, 175, 268
Eccles, Lindsay 182, 191, 194
Eccles, Roy 172, 202
Edgar, MacKay 63
Edge, S.F. 10, 16, 17, 20, 21, 23, 24, 27, 45, 82, 88, 207,268
Edward VII, HM King 33
Edward VIII, HM King 133, 199, 234, 235
Edward, HRH Prince of Wales – see Edward VIII
Edwards, George (later Sir) 245, 249, 250, 252, 253, 261
Edwards, H.F. 67
Eggar, K. 159
Eggleston, H.P. 32

Eldridge, Ernest 89, 90, 95, 100, 101, 269
Electrical & General Trust 199
Elgood, F.E. 209, 213
Elizabeth, HM Queen (later Queen Mother) 165, 219, 261
Elliott Bros 25
Ellison, Eileen 167, 173
Elmbridge Borough Council 260, 261, 263
Elphinstone, K. 25
Emerson, Jack 42, 48, 49, 72-74
Empire Air Day 237
English Electric 255
ERA (car) 50, 176, 182, 183, 185, 190, 191, 193, 197, 200, 203, 207-210, 212-215, 218, 219, 221, 270
Essex (car) 222
Essex Cup 122
Essex Motor Club 75, 78, 83, 110, 112, 114, 120, 124, 129, 269
Duke of York Long Handicap 84
Earl of Athlone Handicap 84
Six Hour Race 114, 120, 126, 169
Esso 222, 270
Esson-Scott, Aubrey 173
Eton College 194
Evans, Dennis 260
Evans, Doreen 183, 186, 190, 200, 260
Evans, Kenneth 174, 210, 218, 260
Everitt, W.G. 182
Excelsior-JAP (m/cycle) 118, 125, 132, 137-139,169, 174, 177, 186, 187, 197, 198, 203, 211, 217, 222
Eyston, Basil 123
Eyston, George 92, 110, 118, 120, 123, 131, 135, 155, 158, 162, 169, 175, 182, 184, 185, 194, 269

F.I.C.M. (Federation Internationale des Clubs Motocyclstes) 112, 119
Fairey (aircraft)
Battle 204
Firefly IIIM 162, 232
Firefly 222
Fairey Aviation 222
Fairfield, Pat 185
Fairmile Marine Co. 242
Faisal, King of Iraq 112
Fane, A.F.P. 202, 212, 214
Farman (aircraft) 34, 55, 57, 60, 62, 65
Faulkner, Tom 161
Ferdinand, Archduke of Austria-Hungary 49
Ferguson, Harry 186
Fernihough, Eric 112, 125, 139, 169, 174, 177, 187, 191, 197, 198, 204, 212, 215, 216, 223, 224
Ferrari, Enzo 207
Fiat (car) 20, 27, 31, 33, 76, 78, 83, 85, 89, 90, 92, 95, 100, 186, 194, 201, 212
Field 155
Fielden, Flt Lt Edward (later Air Cdre Sir) 234, 235

Filton 257, 263
Findlay, Max 235
Fisher 60
Flanders (aircraft) 60
Fleet Air Arm 228
Flight 59
Fontes, Luis 191, 192
Forbes, Jock 177, 187, 210, 216
Ford (car) 41
Ford Motor Co. 221
Ford, Henry 41
Foster, A.R. 217
Foster & Dicksee 12
Fotheringham-Parker, Tim 167
Fothringham, T.S. 158, 183, 186
Foxwarren 244
Francis Barnett (m/cycle) 139
Frascati's 39
Frazer Nash (car) 103, 108, 136, 159, 169, 172, 193-195, 202, 208, 266
Frazer-Nash, Archie 73, 82, 85, 92, 103, 155, 269
Frazer Nash Car Club 174
French Grand Prix (GP de l'ACF) 20, 22, 27, 42, 46, 48, 72, 81, 89, 169, 221
Froy, Dudley 101, 131, 136, 159, 183, 184, 186
Full Chat 204
Full Throttle 169, 171

Gallaher 261, 270
GAPAN (Guild of Air Pilots & Navigators) 232
Gardner, A.T. Goldie 185, 202
Garrett, Sydney 42
Gavin, Mrs 57
Gaydon 252
Geach 40
GEC 259
Geiger, Martin 31
General Dynamics F-111 (aircraft) 253
General Strike 108
Geneva Disarmament Conference 229
George V, HM King 24, 39, 60, 143, 191, 199
George VI, HM King 78, 83, 165, 207, 219, 231
George, Arthur 41
George Cross 243
George, HRH Prince – see Kent, Duke of
George Medal 243
George, HRH Prince of Wales – see George V
George, Sidney 48
Gibson, D.J. 85
Gibson, Gordon 28
Gibson, R.132
Gibson, Ron 164, 165
Gill, Stanley 75
Gladiator (car) 38, 40
Glasgow Herald 232
Gloster Aircraft Co. 228
GN (car) 73, 82, 85, 89
Gnome (engine) 61
Godalming & District Round Table 260
Goddard 204
Godfrey Cup 76,79
Godfrey, Oliver 42
Godfrey, Ron 85

Goodacre, Charles 208
Goodwood 248
Gordon Bennett Races 10, 23
Gordon England, E.C. 92, 98
Gore Browne, Ethel – see Ethel Locke-King
Gore Browne, Thomas 9
Goutte, Pierre 106
Goux, Jules 43
Graf Zeppelin (airship) 167
Graffenried, Baron E de 212
Graham-Paige (car) 222
Grand Slam 245
Graphic, The 55
Great Ormond Street Hospital 98
Green, W.H. 15
Greenbat (truck) 268
Gregoire (car) 51
Grey, C.G. 266
Grimley, Horace 125
Grindlay-Peerless-JAP (m/cycle) 110, 125, 160, 186, 204, 211
Grogan, Terry 96
Guinness, Kenelm Lee 46, 76, 81-83, 85, 96
Guinness, Sir Algernon Bt 23. 194, 217, 223
Gunter, Sir Roland Bt 127
Gush, G.B. 186
GWK (car) 42, 43

Hadley, Bert 208, 225
Halford, Frank 92
Halford Special (car) 110
Hall v. BARC 135
Hall, E.J. "Jimmy" 124
Hall, E.R. 137, 169, 173, 175, 192, 194, 217, 224
Hall, Jimmy 124
Hallam, Frank 115, 174
Hamel, Gustav 59, 63, 142
Hamilton, A.P. "Ginger" 118, 200, 203, 205, 212
Hamilton, Hugh. C. 135
Hancock, A.J. "Jock" 32, 33, 35
Handley, Wal 103, 178, 185, 210
Handley Page Halifax 244
Handley Page, Frederick (later Sir) 62, 63
Hands, G.W. 47
Hanlon, R.M. 268
Harbutt, Sydney 32
Harley Davidson (m/cycle) 72, 76, 78, 91,103, 186
Harris, Air Chief Marshal Sir Arthur 245
Harris, Ron 177, 198, 204, 211, 217, 224
Hartshorne-Cooper, Jack 75, 76
Harvey, Maurice 92, 103, 204, 211, 217, 224
Harvey-Noble, George 212
Harveyson, Reuben 75, 80
Haswell, Jack 47
Hawker Aircraft Ltd. 228
Hawker (aircraft)
Audax 150
Cygnet 148
Demon 150
Duiker 148
Fury 150, 163, 228, 232
Hardy 150
Hart 149, 167, 228
Hector 150

Heron 149
Hind 150
Hornet 150
Horsley 149
Hurricane 56, 187, 230, 231, 241, 242, 244, 262, 270
Nimrod 228
Osprey 150
Tomtit 228
Typhoon 242
Woodcock 148, 149
Hawker, H.G. Engineering Ltd. 56, 82, 144-146, 228, 232
Hawker Siddeley Group 56, 228, 230-232, 239, 241-244, 257
Hawker, Harry 61, 62, 68, 73, 82, 83, 142, 145
Hawkes, Douglas 158
Hawkins, G. 85
Hay, Will 266
Hawthorn, Leslie 138
Hawthorn, Michael 138
Hayden, G.M. 211
Hayward, C.W. 47, 248
Haywood 40
Hazelhurst, H. 108
Headlam, Leonard 130
Hebeler, R.S. 135, 162
Hedges, Miss G. 173
Hemery, Victor 32, 42
Henderson, Lt Col G.L.P. 149, 150
Hendon 59, 82, 145, 160, 233
Hendy, Gordon 134
Henley Regatta 193
Henlys 115
Hennebique 11, 28, 256, 263
Henry, J. 2117
Henry, Prince of Prussia 60
Heritage Lottery Fund 262
Herman, Vincent 22
Hess, Alan 210
Hewitt, Joe 132
Hewlett & Blondeau 57
Hewlett, Hilda 57
Hicks, Freddie 125, 132, 139
Hieatt, Bernard 138
Higgin, Dan 155
Higgs, F. & F.H. Ltd. 232
Hillman (car) 75
Hindenberg, Field Marshal Paul von 136
Hindmarsh, John 231
Hispano-Suiza (car) 51
Hitler, Adolf 212, 229
Hives, Ernest (later Lord) 39
Hodge, Sir John Bt 183
Hogarth, R.C. 204
Holden, Col Henry C.L. 11, 12, 16, 25
Holder, N.F. 135
Hole, Miss J.R. 169
Hollicks Farm 9
Holt Thomas, George 55
Hood, HMS 96
Hope, W.H. 234
Hope, Walter 149
Hornsted, Ligurd.G. "Cupid" 36, 38-40, 45, 48, 49, 78
Horsfall, St. J. "Jock" 221
Horsman, G.E. 139
Horsman, Victor 75, 80, 103, 108
Horton, R.T. 169, 173, 174, 212

Houghton, A.W.E. "Charlie" 252
Houldsworth, John 182, 193
House of Elliott 266
Howard Wright (aircraft) 56, 57
Howe, Lord (Earl) 120, 122, 134, 137, 158, 161-164, 169, 175, 179, 185, 196, 201, 203, 207, 214, 247, 248
Howey, J.E.B. 90, 95
HRD (m/cycle) 79, 186, 198
Humber 59
Humble, Bill 237
Humphreys, W.E. 161
Hunter, Hugh 221
Hunting Percival 255
Hurst Park 13
Hurworth 35
Hutton, J.E. 20, 22

Ideal Homes 262
Imperial Airways 148, 151
Indian (m/cycle) 32, 34, 39, 42, 48, 75, 76, 78-80, 85
Indianapolis 500-Mile race 73, 89, 131
Inland Revenue 144
Inns of Court Volunteers 9
Instone, S. & Co. 148
International Horseless Carriage Co. 238
Invicta (car) 130, 154, 155, 158, 159, 167, 168, 231, 242, 266
Irish Air Corps 143
Isotta Fraschini (car) 50
Isotta-Maybach (car) 95
Itala (car) 10, 13, 16, 48
Itala Automobiles 59, 66
Italian Grand Prix 98
Ivanowsky, Boris 127, 129
Ivy (m/cycle) 80

Jackson, Robin 266, 270
Jaguar (car) – see SS
Jamieson, Murray 212
Janson, Gwenda – see Stewart, Gwenda
Jarrott, Charles 10, 20
Jarvis Ron 214
Joerns, Carl 48, 51
Johnson, Amy 232, 235
Jowett (car) 124, 125
Joyce, John 88, 92
Judd, Rex 83, 91
Junior Car Club 74, 80, 92, 99, 117, 120, 123, 135, 155, 161, 163, 165, 173, 178, 212, 214, 218, 270
Junior Car Club races
  200-Mile race 80, 81, 85, 92, 96, 103, 112, 117, 123, 133, 173, 214, 21, 265
  1000-Mile race 163, 194, 270
  Double-12 Hour race 126, 129, 133, 134, 155, 163, 169, 173, 194, 222, 266
  Four Hour Sporting Car race 115
  High Speed Trial 99, 222
  International Trophy 173, 178, 191, 200, 208, 212, 213, 218, 219,
  Junior Grand Prix 120, 133
  Three Hours Production Car race 108
Junior Racing Drivers' Club 183

Junkers aircraft
  F-13 150, 235
  Ju 88 242, 244

Kedah, Sultan of 38
Kehoe, Edgar 136
Kendall, L.G. 67
Kennedy, Lt James 269
Kensington-Moir, H 85, 88
Kent, HRH Duke of 232
Kent & Surrey Motor Club 222
Kershaw, Ben 80
Keys, B.E. 224
Keyte, E 49
Kidner, Percy 31-33
King's Cup Race 123, 148, 149, 232, 235, 266
King-Clark, Rex 202
Kirkham, Eddie 24, 51
Knight, H.J. 110

Lacey, Bill 110, 125, 151, 160
Lacon 36
Lagonda (car) 119, 136, 170, 182, 192, 194, 203, 210, 219
Laird, Henry 183
Lamacraft, Harold "Harry" 174, 176, 177, 217, 224
Lambert, Percy 39, 41, 43, 45-47, 269
Lanchester (car) 23, 101
Lane, Charles 28, 57
Langley 242, 244
Langston, Beatrice 34
Le Champion, L.C.G.M. 95
Le Mans 24-Hour race 113, 126, 129, 136, 169, 192, 231
Le Vack, Bert 75, 76, 78, 79, 85, 88, 91, 96, 106, 118, 125, 269
Lea Francis (car) 115, 120, 123, 124, 129, 134, 174
Leader-Peugeot (m/cycle) 24
Lee Evans, Guy 32
Lees, E.H. 50
Leeson, H.164, 270
Leiningen, Prinz Hermann zu 193
Levitt, Dorothy 24
Lewis, Brian (later Lord Essendon) 137, 158, 159 162, 164, 165, 169, 173, 176, 178, 179, 182, 191, 196, 203
Leyland (car) 67, 71, 83, 90, 95, 98, 101
Leyland-Thomas (car) 95, 98-101, 108-110,112, 136, 159, 161, 168, 173, 175, 201, 209, 268
Le Zebre (car) 41
Liberty (engine) 95
Light Car Club 158, 167, 201, 208, 213, 222
  Relay Race 158, 167, 174, 183, 186, 194, 201, 208
  3-Hour Sports Car race 213, 218, 222
Light Car, The 214, 215
Lindsay, Lt. A. 67
Lindsay Lloyd, Major Frederick 29, 31, 55, 71, 93, 131, 133
Linton, Jack 266
Lipton, Lawrence 235, 237
Lisle 37, 38
Livesey 158
Lloyd George, David (later Earl) 227

Local Government Board 13
Locke King, Ethel (later Dame) 9, 12, 13, 16, 23, 55, 69, 105, 199, 207, 252
Locke King, Hugh 9, 10-13, 15, 16, 22, 23, 49, 53, 55, 65, 67, 99, 105, 263
Locke King, Peter 9
Lockett, Johnny 204, 224
Loder, Eric 29
Lombard, Andre 82
London & South Western Railway 12, 53
London Ladies' Motor Club 125
London-Newcastle race 235, 237
London University 252
London Weekend Television 266
"Long Tom" 265
Lones, Clive 123, 162, 183
Longden, Violet 74
Longman, F.A. 103
Lonsdale, Earl of 13, 15
Lorraine-Dietrich (car) 42, 72
Love Race, The 266
Lowe, Archibald 59
Lowe-Wyld, C. 154
Lucas, Philip 231
Luftwaffe 242 -244
  1/ KG 76 244
  2 & 3/ KG 76 243
  9/KG 77 244
Lunn, W.R. 211
Lurani, Count Giovanni 127
Lympne 237

Macklin, Noel 130, 242
Maclure, Edgar 185,194, 196
Maclure, Percy 209, 212, 213
Maconochie, Miss 123
Magdalen College, Oxford 24
Maginot Line 214
Manby-Colegrave, G.F.A 174
Mander, Lionel 56
Mander, Miles 266
Manning, Jack 268
Manz Grand Prix 211
March, Earl of (later Duke of Richmond & Gordon) 137, 155, 161, 163, 222
Marchant, Dougal 13, 43, 269
Marendaz (car) 200
Marendaz, Capt D.M.K 200
Marie Fedorovna, Dowager Czarina of Russia 49
Marinoni, Attilio 135
Marker, Richard 203, 266
Marks & Spencer 260, 270
Martin & Handasyde 59, 63, 66, 68
Martin, Charles (GB) 175, 190, 197, 200, 203
Martin, Charles (F) 112
Martin, Harry 40
Martin, Lionel 50
Martinsyde 63, 68, 142-145
Martinsyde (aircraft)
  Buzzard 69
  F3 148
  F6 142
  G100/102 68, 142
  Semiquaver 143
  S1 66
  Type A 142, 143
Martinsyde (m/cycle) 80, 144
Martlesham Heath 229- 231

Martlet piston
Mary, HM Queen 28
Mary, Princess of Wales – see Mary, Queen
Masefield, Sir Peter 261
Maserati (car) 155, 158, 159, 162, 163, 169, 172, 173, 178, 182, 185, 203, 207, 208, 210, 212, 214, 215, 219, 221, 222
Masetti, Giulio 103
Mason, Hugh 47
Materassi, Emilio 117
Mathieson, T.A.S.O. 222
Max-Muller, Percy 142, 145, 148, 230
May, Dennis 79
Maybach (engine) 76, 88
Mays, Raymond 158, 167, 168, 176, 182, 183, 185, 191, 195, 197, 200, 201, 203, 208, 210, 212, 214, 215, 219, 222
MCC 39, 75, 79, 136, 195, 209
McConnell, Hugh 174, 191
McCudden, Major James 132
McCudden, Maurice 132
McEvoy-Temple (m/cycle) 103, 106
McKenna, Reginald 49
McKenna, W.T. 49
McKenzie-Grieve, Lt. Cdr. K 142
McMinnies, Gordon 24
McNab, Arthur 34
Mechanical Transport Committee 29
Meeten, Tommy 139
Mena House 10
Mercedes (car) 20, 22, 24, 28, 31, 33, 36, 39, 42, 43, 74-76, 85, 95, 98
Mercedes (engine) 131
Mercedes-Benz (car) 136, 158, 164, 175, 183, 195, 210
Mercedes-Benz World at Brooklands 262, 263, 270
Mercury (aircraft) 55
Merriam, Warren 62
Messerschmitt Bf 110 (aircraft) 243
MG (car) 136, 155, 158, 163, 164, 169, 173-176, 178, 182-186, 190, 192, 194, 200, 202, 208, 209, 212, 222
Michael, HRH Prince, of Kent 262, 263
Middlesex Motor Club 123
Miles (aircraft)
  Hawk Speed Six 237
  Magister 266
Mille Miglia 221
Miller (car) 89, 158
Miller, Alastair G. 89, 159
Milner, Sgt A. 67
Minerva (car) 22, 174
Ministry of Aircraft Production 243, 247-249, 252
Ministry of Civil Aviation 250
Ministry of Supply 250, 251, 254
Minnett, Dennis 216, 217
Mitchell, Hurst 139
Mitchell, R.J. 230

Mollison, Jim 232
Money, R.C. 222
Monkhouse, George 210
Montgomery-British Anzani (m/cycle) 96
Montlhéry 103, 118, 158, 162, 176, 268
Moore, J 211
Moore-Brabazon, John – see Brabazon, Lord, of Tara
Mooret, Miss M 186
Moorhouse, Arthur 34, 42, 138
Morane-Borel (aircraft) 60
Morane-Saulnier (aircraft) 63
Morel, Andre 118
Morgan (car) 40, 42, 50, 82, 98, 100, 103, 123, 160, 167, 174, 183, 186, 197, 198
Morgan, Capt. C.W.F 142
Morgan, H.F.S. 42
Morgan, John 212
Morgan, R 183
Moriceau, Jules 112
Morris-Goodall, Mortimer 201
Mortimer, Charles 133, 177, 197, 198, 203, 204, 210, 225, 241
Moss, Alfred 90
Moss, Stirling (later Sir) 90, 221
Motor Cycle Club – see MCC
Motor, The 88, 195, 247
Motor Cycle, The 137, 169, 197, 198
Motor Cycle Cup 125
Motor Cycling 79, 138, 16, 224, 230
Motor Show, Olympia 196
Motor Sport 159, 162, 165, 173, 189, 193, 203, 233, 265
Motor Trade Benevolent Fund 88
Motosacoche (m/cycle) 79
Mouchel, L.G. & Partners 11
Muir, J.M. "Spug" 160, 186
Multi-Union (car) 215, 222
Munday, R.J. 82, 157, 163, 201

Naismith, Paddy 110
Napier (car) 10, 16, 20-24, 27, 28, 32, 36, 41, 109, 207
Napier Campbell "Blue Bird" – see "Blue Bird"
Napier (engines)
  Lion 175, 194
  Sabre 92, 231
Napier, Gerald 60
Napier, Montagu 23
Napier-Railton (car) 175, 176, 178, 183, 184, 186, 194, 195, 200, 207, 209, 224, 262, 266
Napier-Sunbeam (car) 108
Nash, R.G.J. 169, 238
National Flying Services 150, 235
National Rifle Association 9
Nazzaro, Felice 20, 27, 31, 76, 83, 153
NCU (National Cyclists' Union) 268
Neiber, General von 60
New Cyclecar Club 123
New Hudson (m/cycle) 39, 79, 106, 118, 125
New Imperial (m/cycle) 79, 80, 91, 96, 160, 187, 198, 211, 217

Newman, G 187, 216, 223
Newton, Frank 20, 22, 24, 27, 28
Nicholson 51
Nieuport Goshawk (aircraft) 145
NLG-JAP (m/cycle) 32
NLG-Peugeot (m/cycle) 24
No.10 Air Acceptance Park 69
Norman 177
Norris, N 80
Northcliffe, Lord 10
Northolt 231
Norton (m/cycle) 32, 42, 49, 50, 67, 75, 76, 80, 83, 91, 96, 118, 119, 142, 160, 170, 177, 187, 197, 198, 203, 204, 210, 216, 217, 222-224
Nott, Ernie 198
NSU (m/cycle) 31
NUT-JAP (m/cycle) 47
Nuvolari, Tazio 169, 175

O'Donovan, D.R. "Dan" 32, 50, 67, 71, 91, 118, 222
Oats, R.F. 122
OEC (m/cycle) 138, 160
OK-Supreme (m/cycle) 204
Olivier, Laurence 266
Olympic Games 1908 27
OM (car) 122, 123, 130, 159, 161
Oman, Sultan of 262
Opel (car) 48, 51, 73
Orde, Julian 10
Organisation for the Maintenance of Supplies108
Oxenden, Mrs Pat 197
Oyster Lane Properties 259, 260, 262

P&P (m/cycle) 103
Pacey, E.W.W. 201, 203
Pacey-Hassan (car) 201, 203
Paget, Hon Dorothy 133, 134, 137, 169
Painter, Miss B 169
PanAm 254
Panavia Tornado (aircraft) 253
Panhard (car) 163
Panhard (engine) 53
Panther (car) 262
Parham, E.W. 80
Paris Air Show 145
Parkes, G.L.109
Parnell, Reg 209
Patchett, George 106
Patton, Lt. John 243
Paul, Cyril 131, 136, 158, 169, 175, 179, 191, 193, 194, 203, 209
Paul, Joseph 212
Paulhan, Louis 55, 57
Payn, Major H.J. 149
Peacock, K.S. 115
Pegoud, Adolph 62
Pemberton-Billing, Noel 62, 63
Penn-Hughes, Clifton 137, 158, 159
Perak, Sultan of 38
Perry 183
Personal Flying Services 235
Petre, Kay 167, 176, 182, 186, 191, 192, 195, 197, 208, 209, 212
Peugeot (car) 43
"Philip" – see Turner, Philip
Phillips, Sir Lionel 209

Phillips, Wal 160
Pierson, Reginald (Rex) 141, 145, 148, 151, 227, 229, 230, 249- 252
Pinewood House 67, 148
Pixton, Harold 61
Pizey, Collyns 56, 60
Plaister, H.E. 131
Pope, Noel 197, 198, 204, 212, 216, 217, 222, 224
Portmore Estate 10
Potts 183
Powerplus 158
Powys-Lybbe, A. 207, 209
Pratts 270
Prestwich, E.S. 108
Prestwich, J.A. & Co. 79, 106
Price & Reeves 11, 13, 23
Progress (car) 137
Prowse, Keith 57
Pullin, Cyril 47, 83, 84
Purdy, Harold 112, 118, 123, 137, 158, 160
Purves, Dr. J.A. 269
Pybus, James 167

Q Planes 266
Queensborough, Lord 133
Quill, Jeffery 239

R 100 (airship) 227
R101 (airship) 227
Rabagliati, C.E.C. 135
Radcliffe, John 229
Raggio, Carlo 10
Railton (car) 194, 212, 242, 248
Railton, Reid 115, 175, 185, 194
Raleigh (m/cycle) 160
Ramponi, Giulio 120, 122, 127, 129, 155
Rapier (car) 202
Rapson 98
Rapson, Lionel 101
Rawlence, Tony 197, 198
Raynham, Fred 56, 142,143, 145, 149
Rayson, E.K. 207
Read, Harry 79
Red Cross 69
Regal-Green (m/cycle) 42
Remington, E.M. 41
Renault (car) 36, 39
REP (aircraft) 59
Resta, Dario 20, 22, 24, 28, 40, 42, 46, 51, 98
Rex-Acme (m/cycle) 31, 103, 138, 139, 198, 203, 204
Reynolds, George 31, 186
Reynolds, J.G. 28
Rhodes, T.A.183, 186, 197
Richards, T.H 39
Richardson, Ralph 266
Richmond, Joan 164, 165
Riley (car) 15, 123, 124, 130, 134, 135, 158, 159, 161, 162, 164, 165, 167, 169, 174-176, 178, 179, 182, 184-186, 190, 196,197, 200, 203, 209, 210, 212, 213, 222
Roberts, Field Marshal Lord 49
Rochet-Schneider (car) 13
Rodakowski, Ernst, Baron de 10, 12, 13, 17, 24, 29, 54
Roe, A.V. 54-56, 60, 61, 150, 270
Roe, A.V., Flying School 56

Roe, Mrs K.N. 174
Rollason 40
Rolls-Royce 39, 78, 253
Rolls-Royce (car) 39, 78, 269
Rolls-Royce (aero engines)
  Avon 252
  Conway 254
  Dart 250
  Eagle 142
  Merlin 229
  PV-12 229
  R 172
  Tyne 254
  Vulture 231
Rolls-Royce Campbell – see "Blue Bird"
Rootes Bros 214
Ropner, Leonard 95
Rose-Richards, T.E. 155, 172, 173, 176, 179, 185, 194, 196
Rothwell, Myles 191
Round Britain Air Race 59
Rover (car) 158
Rowley, George 139, 204
Royal Aero Club 56, 57, 60, 62, 68, 148, 232
Royal Air Force 61, 69, 71, 73, 126, 141, 142, 144, 146, 148, 205, 208, 225, 228-231, 243, 245, 250, 252-254, 261
  138 Sqn 252
  253 Sqn 243
  Bomber Command 245
  College, Cranwell 222
  Fighter Command 69, 243
  Flying Training Command 250
  King's Flight 250
  Silver Jubilee Review 193
  Transport Command 250
Royal Aircraft Factory 61, 66, 68
RAF (aircraft)
  BE2 66
  BE2c 66
  FE8 66
  SE5a 68, 69, 132, 141, 142
Royal Aircraft Establishment 187
Royal Airship Company 227
Royal Artillery, 5 A.A.Divn. 243
Royal Australian Air Force (RAAF) 145
Royal Automobile Club (RAC) 10, 23, 24, 27, 29, 36, 40, 117, 125, 130, 162, 248
  British Grand Prix 109, 112, 115, 117
  Standard Car Race 36, 40, 47
  2000-Mile Trial 27
  Tourist Trophy 123, 175, 186, 210, 221, 222
Royal Canadian Air Force (RCAF) 143
Royal Canadian Engineers 243
Royal Enfield (m/cycle) 49, 108
Royal Engineers 11, 29
Royal Flying Corps 49, 60, 61, 63, 65, 68, 69, 142, 150, 169, 269
  Airship Detachment 63
  No.1 Sqn 63, 65, 69
  8 Sqn 69
  9 Sqn 69
  10 Sqn 69
  46 Sqn 69
Royal Gun Factory 11
Royal Naval Air Service (RNAS) 63, 65, 66, 68, 69, 142

Royal New Zealand Air Force (RNZAF) 229
Royal Observer Corps 239
Royal West Surrey Regt. 66
Royal Westminster Opthalmic Hospital 120
RR58 257
Rubery Owen 95
Rubin, Bernard 122, 158
Rudge (m/cycle) 39, 142, 198, 217
Rudge-Multi (m/cycle) 47
Ruesch, Hans 176, 203, 210
Ruffell, May 125
Runciman, Sqn Ldr Walter (later Lord) 235
Russell, Archibald 257
Russell-Stracey, Flt. Lt. E.G. 241
RW Scout (m/cycle) 80

Sabella-JAP (car) 40, 42
Salamano, Carlo 92
Salmson (car) 82, 85, 92, 98, 106, 108, 123, 127, 129, 168, 265
Salt, J 268
Samuels, J.O.C. 208
Sanderson 78
Sandford 51
Sandow 17
Saunders-Davies, Owen 164, 165
Sayer, Flt. Lt. P.E. Gerry 163, 228
Scale Models 248
SCAR (car) 40
Schneider Trophy 56, 61, 132
Scholefield, Flt. Lt. E.R.C "Tiny"149, 151
Schwedler, Charlotte 174, 183
Science Museum 143
Scott, Jill 123-126, 150, 168, 269
Scott, W.B.123, 126, 136
Scott, W.G. 45
Scribbans, Dennis 200
Scuderia Ferrari 176, 184
Seaman, Richard 176, 196, 210
Segrave, Henry (later Sir) 73, 76, 81, 82, 85, 96, 103, 108, 110, 112, 114, 115, 122
Selby, T.V.G. 183
Selz, Rudolph 33
Senechal, Robert 110
Shanks, H. 25
Shell 270
Shelley 198
Sherratt, Frank 151
Shilling, Beatrice 187, 197
Shoreham 237
Short Bros. 54
  Stirling 244
Shuttleworth, Richard 168, 190, 197, 238
Sigrist, F.W. 61
Sikorsky S-76 (aircraft) 262
Silverstone 117, 248
Singer (car) 37, 40, 47, 50, 183, 194
Singer (m/cycle) 42
Sizaire-Naudin (car) 31
Smith, C.M. 36
Smith, Sidney 22
Smith, Sir Keith 145
Smith, Sir Ross 145, 146
Smith, Tyrell 217

Snowden, J 203
Society of Motor Manufacturers & Traders 126
Sopwith Aviation Co. 56, 66, 142-144
Sopwith (aircraft)
  Atlantic 142, 143
  B1 142
  Camel 56, 68, 141
  Cuckoo 69
  Dolphin 56, 141
  Olympia 61
  1½-Strutter 56, 68
  Pup 56, 68
  Snipe 56, 141, 144
  Tabloid 56, 61, 63, 66
  Three-Seater 62
  Triplane 68
Sopwith Flying School 56, 60, 65
Sopwith, Thomas (later Sir) 56, 57, 60, 61, 63
South African Air Force 146
Southern Railway 120
Spartan Arrow (aircraft) 228
Spies at Work 266
Spooner, Winifred 149
Sporting Life 265
Spring, Nigel 118
Spyker 23, 88, 222
SS Jaguar (car) 210, 214
Stalag Luft III 208
Stallard, P.T.268
Staniland, Christopher S. 118, 120, 124, 125, 132, 134, 138, 155, 158, 159, 162, 164, 173, 187, 191, 198, 204, 215, 222
Stanley (car) 32
Stanley Cup 135, 165, 174, 183
Stanley, G.E. 50
Star (car) 36-38, 40
Stead, G. 85
Stephenson, Basil 253
Stewart, Gwenda – see Hawkes, Gwenda
Straight, Whitney 161-163, 172, 173, 176, 178, 179, 182, 184-186, 195, 203
Sud Aviation 257
  Super Caravelle 257
Summers, Dorothy 200
Summers, Maurice "Mutt" 149, 151, 229, 230, 244, 250-252
Sunbeam (car) 33, 36, 39-43, 45, 51, 63, 73, 76, 81, 83-85, 95, 96, 98, 113-115, 122-126, 129-131, 134, 136, 137, 154, 163, 168, 173, 175, 176, 182, 194, 200-202, 208, 209, 269
Sunbeam (m/cycle) 67, 132
Sunbeam Talbot Darracq Combine 81, 109
Supermarine 63, 151, 230, 239
  Spitfire 187, 239
Supersonic Air Transport Committee 257
Surbiton Motor Club 115, 122
Surrey County Council 260
Surrey Herald 13
Surridge, Victor 39
Surtees, Jack 211
Surtees, John 211
Sutton Place 10
Sutton, R.M.V.164

Talbot (car) 43, 45, 47, 72, 109, 110, 112, 117, 134, 135, 137, 155, 158, 159, 162, 164, 165, 169, 173, 194, 195, 200, 212-214, 221, 222
Talbot Darracq (car) 81, 85, 92, 96, 98, 103
Tallboy (bomb) 245
Tanner, Reg 222
"Tarfaalt" 11
Tarrant Tabor (aircraft) 69
Tarrant, W.G. 69
Taruffi, Piero 176
Tate, Bobby 31, 43
Taylor, J. 122
Taylour, Fay 159, 158, 186
TCA (Trans Canada Airlines) 254
Teck, Prince Francis of 28, 34
Temple, Claude 76, 91, 96, 269
Territorial Army 9
Tesco 260
Thames (car) 23, 36
Thomas Special (car) 101, 103, 112, 117, 118, 123, 158
Thomas, E.M. 134
Thomas, Ernie 125
Thomas, J.G. Parry 79, 83-85, 89, 90, 95, 96, 98-100, 103, 105, 108-110, 112, 113, 115, 157, 194, 268, 269
Thomas, Jill – see Scott, Jill
Thompson, Muriel 27
Thompson, Oscar 32, 33
Thompson, W.L. 183
Thomson & Taylor 98, 157, 168, 1732, 174, 176,194, 212, 242, 248, 260, 270
Thomson, Ken 98
Thomson, Lord 227, 232
Thornycroft (lorry) 67, 71
Thorp, F.W. 59
Thorpe, Adrian 193
Thunderbolt (car) 194
Tikali, Maharajah of 39
Times, The 28
Tirpitz (battleship) 245
Tisdall 224
Tongue, R.E. 221
Toop, J.H. 45, 95
Tottey, George 91
Toulouse 257
Tourist Trophy – see RAC Tourist Trophy

Tourist Trophy, Isle of Man 39, 49, 106
Trafalgar House 262
Tranum, John 232
Trenchard, Major Hugh (later Marshal of RAF Lord) 60
Tripoli Grand Prix 169, 173
Triumph (m/cycle) 24, 28, 34, 47, 50, 103, 108, 186, 187, 197, 198, 211, 217, 222-224
Trump (m/cycle) 34, 84, 88
Tryon, Henry 20, 21, 28
Tubb, E.J. 211
Turcat-Mery (car) 41
Turnbull 122
Turner, Philip 169, 175
Turner, R.F. 183
Tysoe, G. 38

Ulster Grand Prix 204
Ulster Tourist Trophy – see Royal Automobile Club Ulster Tourist Trophy
Usmar, Gordon 38, 40
Uwins, Cyril 149, 151

Vale (car) 174
Valentine, James 60
Vandervell, G.A. 76, 78
Van Ryneveld, Sir Pierre 146
Vanwall (car) 76
Vauxhall (car) 31-33, 41, 45, 85, 95, 99,114, 115, 157, 162, 163, 194
Vedrines, Jules 60
Velocette (m/cycle) 118, 119, 125, 132, 139, 160, 169, 170, 174, 176, 177, 187, 198, 210, 211, 216, 217, 222-224
Ventura, Eddie 119
Vernon, Lord 33, 39
Vickers (Aviation) Ltd. 150, 151, 205, 227, 228, 232, 238, 239, 241, 242, 244, 249, 251, 253, 255, 256, 259, 266, 270
Vickers Ltd. 59, 66-69, 141, 142, 145, 148
Vickers (aircraft)
Blue Boar (missile) 252
B19/27 229
Boxkite 645
EFB3 63
FB5 66

FB9 66
FB14 69
FB19 69
No.1 59
Red Dean (missile) 252
Red Rapier (missile) 252
Swallow 253
Type 121 Wibault Scout 151
Type 143 151
Type 1000 VC7 254, 255
Valentia 148, 150, 230
Valetta 250
Valiant 252, 254
Vanguard 151
Vanguard Type 900/912 253, 254
Vanox 229
Varsity 250, 252
VC10 252, 254, 255, 257, 259, 262
VC11 256
Vellore 151
Velox 151
Vendace 151
Venom 231
Vespa 151, 230
Vernon 148
Viastra 151, 235
Viceroy 250
Victoria 148
Vigilant (missile) 252
Vildebeest 229
Viking 145, 146, 230
Viking VC1 230, 249, 250, 252
Vimy 141-143, 145, 146, 148, 230
Vincent 229
Vireo 151
Virginia 148, 150, 228-230
Viscount 230, 251-253
Vixen 148-150
Vulcan 148, 230
Warwick 230, 231, 241, 243, 244, 249, 270
Wellesley 230, 231
Wellington 192, 230, 231, 241-244, 249, 252, 261, 270
Wild Goose 253
Windsor 244, 249
Vickers-Armstrong Ltd. 151, 248, 252
Vickers Flying School 65, 230
Villoresi, Luigi 212

Vincent-HRD (m/cycle) 203
Vindec Special (m/cycle) 24
Vintage Sports Car Club 242
Viper (car) 90
Vitesse (car) 186
Voluntary Aid Detachment 49

Wagner, Louis; 20, 110
Wakefield, J.P. 208, 210, 214, 215
Walker, A.G. 125
Walker, Huntley 21
Walker, P.D.C. 210
Walker, R.R.C. 210
Wallace, Edgar 114
Wallach, Teresa 169
Waller, Ken 258
Wallis, Barnes (later Sir) 227, 229, 230, 244, 245, 249, 252, 253
Walters, P.M. 103
Walther, A.E.S. 136
War Department 71
War Office 40, 65
Ware, E.B. 50, 82, 98, 100
Waters, J.B. 211
Watson, Duncan 76
Watson, Michael 174, 175
Waverley (car) 72
Weatherell, Reg 80
Weir W-3 (aircraft) 202
Welch, Lewis 175
West Kent Motor Club 100, 194
West, Jock 177, 187, 197, 198, 211, 217
Westbrook, Trevor 230
Westenra, Hon Richard 235
Westminster, Duke of 13
Weybridge District Council
Weybridge Cottage Hospital 10, 211
Weybridge Library & Museum 260, 261
Weybridge Parish Hall 135
Whitcroft, C.R. 130, 135, 158
White 177, 223
Whitehurst, Dr. Neville 175
Whitten Brown, Arthur (later Sir) 142, 143, 145
Whitworth, M.D. 203, 204, 211
Wibault 7C.1 (aircraft) 150, 151
Wicksteed, Ivan 211
Widengren, Henken 159, 161, 162

Wigginton, F.L. 167
Wilhelm II, Kaiser 16, 23
Wilkinson, W.E. 36, 130
Williams 170
Williams, Cyri 49l
Williams, Peggy 212
Willis, Harold 119
Wilson, Flt. Lt. J.B 237.
Wilson, Norman 213
Wilson-Jones, Owen 92, 98
Wimbledon LTA Championships 193
Windsor-Richards, Clive 186
"Wings Over Brooklands" Exhibition 260, 261
Winn, Allan 263
Wintersells Farm 9
Wireless & Observer School 69
Wisdom, Elsie 159, 164, 165, 168, 173, 186
Wisdom, Tommy 173, 210
Wisley 244, 250-252, 254
Wolseley (car) 167
Wolseley-Hispano (car) 90, 141
Wood, "Ginger" 187, 198, 211
Wood, Bertie 62
Wood, Herbert 59
Wood, J.T. 42, 43
Wood, S.E.78, 84
Wood, Sir Kingsley 239
Woodhouse, Jack 72, 74
Wooding, Geoffrey 213, 221
World Championship Trial 268
World Road Race Championship 268
Worters, J.S. "Woolly" 118, 125, 132, 138, 139, 215, 222, 225
Wren, J 186
Wright, Joe 103, 106, 132, 138, 160

York, HRH Duchess of – see Elizabeth, Queen
York, HRH Duke of – see George VI, King

Zborowski, Count Louis 74-76, 78, 83, 85, 88, 90, 95, 98, 131
Zenith (m/cycle) 43, 67, 79, 85, 88, 89, 91, 93, 96, 103, 106, 110, 132, 138, 139, 160
Zetsche, Dr Dieter 263